VOLUME 49 JUNE 1987 PAGES 1–339

Melville's Confidence Men
and
American Politics in the 1850s

Helen P. Trimpi

TRANSACTIONS
The Connecticut Academy of Arts and Sciences

Published for The Academy by

ARCHON BOOKS   Hamden, Connecticut

© 1987 by The Connecticut Academy of Arts & Sciences
First published 1987 as Volume 49 of the
Transactions of The Connecticut Academy of
Arts & Sciences, New Haven, Connecticut
by The Shoe String Press, Inc. Hamden, Connecticut 06514.

Copies of the *Transactions* of
The Connecticut Academy of Arts & Sciences
may be obtained from Archon Books.

Set in Garamond No. 3 by Brevis Press, Bethany, Connecticut
Designed by Patricia Larsen

Library of Congress Cataloging-in-Publication Data
Trimpi, Helen P., 1927–
Melville's Confidence men and American politics in
the 1850s.
(Transactions / Connecticut Academy of Arts and
Sciences; v. 49, p. I–339)
Bibliography; p.
Includes index.
1. Melville, Herman, 1819–1891. Confidence-man.
2. Political satire, American—History and criticism.
3. Swindler and swindling in literature.   4. United
States—Politics and government—1849–1861.   I. Title.
II. Series: Transactions (Connecticut Academy of Arts and
Sciences); v. 49, p. I–339.
Q11.C9   081 s   [813'.5]   vol. 49, p. I–339   86–32158
[PS2384.C63]
ISBN 0–208–02130–2

Printed in the United States of America

The paper used in this publication meets the minimum requirements of American National
Standard for Information Sciences—Permanence of Paper for Printed Library Materials,
ANSI Z39.48–1984. ∞

THE CONNECTICUT ACADEMY OF ARTS AND SCIENCES

Officers for 1986–87

President
H. CATHERINE W. SKINNER

Vice-Presidents
LOUIS KUSLAN   RICHARD W. LINDQUIST
JAMES A. SLATER

Secretary
DOROTHEA RUDNICK

Treasurer
LEONARD V. WESOLOWSKI

Librarians
MILLICENT D. ABELL   RUTHERFORD D. ROGERS (Ret.)

Members at Large

ASGER AABOE	GEORGE KUBLER
RICHARD BUEL	EMILIANA NOETHER
FRED A. CAZEL	FRED C. ROBINSON
G. EVELYN HUTCHINSON	JOHN RODGERS
MARTIN J. KLEIN	FRANZ ROSENTHAL

Contents

Contents

List of Plates
Following Page 144

Preface

The last prose fiction that Herman Melville published in his lifetime, *The Confidence-Man: His Masquerade* (1857), is a pasquinade—a comic political satire. Although it has long been known that one of Melville's earliest published writings was a political satire on Zachary Taylor, and that portions of *Mardi* (1849) are directly related to American and European political events of the summer of 1848, and that Melville was concerned with the political problem of slavery, it has not been suggested by any scholar that *The Confidence-Man* refers directly to and is a satirical commentary on political and other public figures and events of the election year 1856 and of earlier years as far back as the middle 1840s. As far as can be determined, the book was written mainly during the months prior to Melville's departure for Europe on 11 October 1856, although certain portions of it, it has been suggested, may possibly date from the late 1840s. As long ago as 1956, Perry Miller, in *The Raven and the Whale,* called it a puzzling book, writing that "It cannot divest itself of problems which had fastened themselves on the writer while he was trying to accommodate his receptive intelligence to the nationalist propaganda" of the 1840s, and he suggested that Melville's "cattle-show" of characters was Clinton Place in New York, where his friends, the Duyckinck brothers, and the "Young America" circle gathered. It has become evident in recent years that although Miller was correct in his perception that certain problems had fastened themselves on Melville in the period during which he was connected with the Young America movement within the Democratic party and with the parallel literary movement that sought a great national literature, his deepest concern during the 1850s became his relationship to and perceptions of the antislavery movement—the single most important political movement of his time.

Many articles and books written since Miller made his observation take as their subjects Melville's reaction to the slavery controversy or his attitude toward the question of race, or both. The work of Adler, Arnaud-Marçais, Grejda, Franklin, Heimart, Kaplan, Karcher, Margolies, Parker, Rogin, Scorza, Sealts, Simpson, Widmer, Zirker, and others have opened up new perspectives and raised questions about Melville's political and social attitudes in his prose earlier and later than *The Confidence-Man* and in that book itself. For example, different scholars interpreting *Benito Cereno* have arrived at diametrically opposed conclusions about his attitude toward Babo and the blacks. And with regard to *The Confidence-Man,* taking a view that is opposite to the early view of Foster and of Shroeder that the Confidence Man is a demonic figure, Karcher has recently interpreted the work as dramatizing "an apocalyptic judgment" on the United States for permitting slavery, and she argues that the Confidence Man is a Christ-like figure who is conducting an "apocalyptic test" of the characters' fellow feeling for the slave. Different interpretive methods have, then, led to different scholarly views of Melville's attitudes on slavery and on the political problem of black Americans in American society. The recently issued Northwestern–Newberry edition of *The Confidence Man* (which regrettably was not available during the research and writing of this study) shows in the historical note the wide variety of interpretations of the work.

There seem to be at least two reasons for the failure to reach agreement about the meaning of those of Melville's works or passages in them in which most scholars would agree that the slavery controversy seems to be a subject or theme. First, frequently the literary form of the narrative discussed has been somewhat misunderstood, in part because grasping the exact nature of the traditional literary forms, such as "pasquinade," "satire," "romance," "sketch," "tale," or others, as the romantic and Victorian fictionists and poets themselves understood the forms, has not always been easy. This limitation may result in misinterpretations of some works, especially through the consequent imposition of modern misreadings. If the literary form as the author conceived it is not understood, the intended meaning will be obscured. Moreover, even when the form or genre has been recognized, as it has in part in the instance of *The Confidence-Man,* the more particularly conceived variations or specializations of the form in the period have proven difficult to discover. For example, in the case of *The Confidence-Man,* scholars have not often looked at other forms of satire preceding or current in the period for analogues to Melville's method in his satire; nor, if they have looked, have they demonstrated his reliance upon or his adaptation of other types of a given form, as I hope that I have demonstrated in my earlier article, in *Texas Studies in Literature and Language,* his adaptation of character-types and narrative structure from commedia dell'arte and Pantomime, and, in this book, his adaptation of graphic techniques of caricature.

A second reason that may account for the modern difficulty in interpreting, in particular, *The Confidence-Man* is that scholars—many of whom recognized early (especially Elizabeth Foster) that it was indeed a satire on contemporary attitudes and beliefs—did not probe deeply enough into contemporary exponents of those attitudes and beliefs (except in the notable instances of Emerson, Thoreau, Poe, and Abbott Lawrence) in order to see the particularity with which Melville was satirizing his contemporaries. This limitation (which I suffered in my earlier interpretation of the work), in turn, may be partly accounted for, I think, by the unfortunate circumstance that the political history of the antebellum period is not one that literary students are as familiar with as they should be. Important, also, is the fact that our present view of this period is indelibly colored by the historical facts that the Southern states seceded in 1860–61, that the Civil War occurred, that Emancipation took place in 1863, and that the North won the war. Most histories and biographies of the period that we read reflect these circumstances consciously or unconsciously by demonstrating a greater sympathy with and awareness of either the Northern or the Southern point of view.

For us, then, to minimize distortion in understanding the political background of *The Confidence-Man* it must constantly be remembered that Melville's satire was written more than four years before the war actually occurred—before the decades-old sectional conflict that forms the historical background of it had resulted in the breakup of the American Union and in actual military violence, although violence had emerged in verbal and in individual physical encounters in the streets and in Congress even while it was being written. Consequently, Melville's satire reflects, and is intended to contribute to, an American literary consciousness in a time of great crisis, which still, nevertheless, might entertain a variety of future possibilities besides the events which actually later took place—four years of armed conflict between the states, the scantly foreseen event of Emancipation, ending the moral nightmare of slavery, and the victory of the Northern side. Those scholars who have seen or suspected that Melville might be dealing with political questions in his works have too often approached him with a predisposition toward seeing him as taking a point of view more favorable to one side or the other in the sectional controversy.

It has always been sufficiently clear to most students of Melville that Melville was not ethically or morally uncertain about the evil of slavery, which he, speaking manifestly in his own person, called "man's foulest crime," in his poem, "Misgivings," and a "curse" in the "Supplement" to his Civil War poems, *Battle-Pieces* (1866). Nor was he by 1866 politically nonpartisan about the "Secessionist" party, whom he called the "conspirators" by whom "the people of the South were cajoled into revolution" and into a war "whose implied end was the erecting in our advanced century of an Anglo-American empire based upon the systematic degradation of man." But the consciousness which *The Confidence-Man* reflects in 1856, *before* secession and *before* the war, is one in which, although the various political choices are among greater and lesser evils, choice is still possible. The critical and reasoning process in which literature might greatly aid both the writer and the reader could still be of value in averting potentially greater or the greatest of evils. This book claims only to make a beginning in the effort to recover some understanding of this consciousness, first by defining in more particularity the literary form of Melville's satire; then by identifying, with varying degrees of probability, nearly all the persons who are the objects of his satire; and last by sketching his rhetorical and political analysis of the contemporary historical situation.

From the beginning in developing my interpretation I have tried first to see the literary form as Melville intended it to be understood, and second to let the evidence about the historical figures who emerged from the political context guide my interpretation, whether or not I was happy about the direction in which it led. The evidence has led to an interpretation that sees the form as a pasquinade—a political comedy—analogous to topical stage comedy and to graphic political prints of the period, and that shows Melville satirizing politicians, publicists, and preachers on both sides of the sectional controversy: the founders of the mainly Northern and Western Republican party as "confidence men" on the one side, and their Northern and Southern opponents in the Democratic and various other parties as gullible or skeptical self-seekers on the other. Confining itself to explicating the meaning of *The Confidence-Man* as satirical commentary on certain political exploitations of the issue of black slavery, my book makes no attempt to assess Melville's overall attitude toward the social issue of race.

Yet my investigation has led beyond only trying to demonstrate the nature of the literary form he is using and who the objects of his satirical commentary were to an attempt to sketch what I think is the deeper concern of the book. The interpretation presented in the following pages suggests that Melville in this particular work has probed through the specific issue of the slavery controversy in order to address the philosophical (or as his period termed it the "metaphysical") question of the trustworthiness of mankind—of any section, race, party, or color—to govern himself in a just manner. The larger background against which he has set his finely detailed gallery of caricatures is the historic American experiment in representative self-government, which was undergoing its greatest test since the Revolution, under the impact of the heightened realization that not all Americans agreed that Americans of African descent were entitled to be included in the experiment. My interpretation suggests that Melville saw the political split between North and South as manifesting a difference in philosophical assumptions about the nature of man, for upon one's view of the nature of man depends one's view of how well men might govern themselves. Melville saw the historic argument about how the United States Constitution was to be interpreted in terms of a disagreement between the optimistic view of human nature, associated generally with the antislavery movement and the emergence of the Republican party in the North, 1854–56, and the pessimistic one, associated with the Democratic party and certain other factions antagonistic to the Republicans. The question debated over and over by Melville's series of characters in their encounters is whether man (or the Nature or God who formed him) is trustworthy (naturally good or "benevolent"), for trustworthiness was considered to be the foundation of the American representational political system. One elected certain men to office because one had "confidence" in them and in their good intentions. Two different philosophical ("metaphysical") assumptions collide, as North and South did, when pairs of characters are juxtaposed, such as the Deaf-Mute to the Barber, or when they debate philanthropy versus misanthropy, as the Cosmopolitan and Charlie Noble do.

My reading of *The Confidence-Man* suggests that the implicit norm of Melville's satire is a politically nonpartisan (nonparty-affiliated) historical consciousness—Melville's—which is representative of the postulated political unity of the states as a nation. Against such a unity he has set up a multiplicity of fragmenting political and philosophical agents—satirizing each and all of them as betrayers, for various reasons, of the national "faith" in political unity and in the founders' "dream" of the trustworthiness of men to govern themselves. It is a consciousness which has been buried by subsequent history and that must be reconstructed imaginatively—and painfully—through historical research, with as objective an eye as possible, if *The Confidence-Man* (or any of Melville's works that take up political themes) is to be understood. As long ago as 1899 Thomas Wentworth Higginson in *Contemporaries* remarked, looking back to Charles Sumner's election to the Senate in 1851: "The whole situation was one which now seems as remote as if centuries had passed since then." If that period seemed remote to Higginson only some fifty years later, it is even more remote and irrecoverable to us 130 years later. But, even if Melville has relied upon ephemeral personalities and factions and events to bear the brunt of his sharp critical analysis of a major political crisis, still his analysis—like that of other great satirists from Aristophanes to Pope and Charles Churchill, has timeless application, if we understand his general critique and recognize his individuals as representative of enduring types of human character.

There are several questions that this book raises which it does not try to answer. The relationship of my interpretation of *The Confidence-Man* to political readings of Melville's earlier and later works—i.e., the place of this interpretation in the context of his political development as a whole—is beyond the scope of this book. I have not tried to deal with this large undertaking for several reasons. First, I believe that *The Confidence-Man* is so unusual and so innovative in its literary form and technique that a similar method of interpretation could not be applied to his other fiction or to his poems, for it would lead to a distortion of his intentions. Each book and each poem requires a careful study of its particular form and intention. It is evident that although political themes remained an abiding concern of his, Melville's literary intentions from his earliest narrative of adventure to his last poems and his last prose tale changed constantly as he developed as a writer and a thinker about men in society and about political questions. Nor has scholarly agreement been reached about the form and meaning of most of his works.

Most helpful thus far for comprehending his political concerns are historical studies such as Leyda's *Melville Log,* Parker's dissertation, "Melville and Politics," Hayford and Davis's study of his office seeking, and Sealts' *Melville as Lecturer* (and other such studies cited in my text), which confine themselves to facts not speculation and are the basic foundations for further work on this aspect of his oeuvre. Less satisfactory are studies which take the opinions expressed by Melville's fictional characters or by his narrative *personae* for his own personal opinions and construct therefrom a Melville who is an inconsistent blend of the early narrative *personae,* his more obviously fictional characters, and the scholar's own predispositions. Also unsatisfactory are studies that use speculative psychologizing about his feelings toward members of his family and his friends to construe his political attitudes. Both Marx and Freud are distinct parts of our present climate of opinion that I feel should be put aside lest we distort what should ideally be an objective philological view of his works. It seems to me that it is not the duty of a literary scholar to make over a writer of the past into his or her own image or the image of our age, even if we run the risk of ruining his reputation among most of our contemporaries by trying to remain loyal to the literary text.

Another question that I do not attempt to answer is why Melville wrote a book with the intention, as I claim he did, of satirizing contemporary political figures and factions, which was, as far as present historical evidence goes, quite obscure to nearly all his contemporary readers. For whom, we ask, did he write a pasquinade which criticizes both political sides in the controversy over slavery but which neither side apparently understood? All that I can do to answer this difficult question is to offer a few tentative hypotheses. He may have written for a small group of readers who, he believed, would understand his method—caricature similar to contemporary dramatic and graphic political caricature—and who might also themselves share his detached political stance, although leaning emotionally one way or the other—North or South. His "fit audience though few" might, on this hypothesis, include people such as his father-in-law Chief Justice Shaw, perhaps, or Hawthorne, who saw to its British publication, or some other readers unknown now to us, who were not yet committed by events to the Republican cause or to the Southern cause. Another possible explanation of the baffled response to *The Confidence-Man* might be that Melville wrote idealistically, as if he did hope through satire's caustic medicine to have some effect in moderating the drift toward polarized political opinions and fratricidal war (possibly even in response to the persuasiveness of Stowe's *Uncle Tom's Cabin*), but that he naïvely miscalculated the literary form and style that he should use to reach an audience of any scope. He chose a mode too elaborate and too new to be understood by the audience he hoped to reach. A third possible explanation—admittedly an extremely speculative one—is that the book *was* understood by some of the New York journalist-politicians, possibly all too well understood by several who were the objects of its satire, and that they (*e.g.* Bryant, Greeley, Raymond, Weed, or possibly Beecher) reacted by imposing a curtain of silence from their seats of power over public opinion. On this hypothesis, they might have reasoned that to appear to ignore an apparent attack on their characters and their political motives would be the best way to defend their reputations as noble-minded Republicans. They might also have reasoned that the overall complexity and detailed execution of Melville's comical-philosophical exposé of the political scene would, as it apparently did, put the understanding of it beyond the grasp of the average unsophisticated American reader and reviewer of novels, while its localization in the United States would put it beyond the understanding of even the more sophisticated British readers. The British might recognize the method, which bears some resemblance to Dickensian caricature, but would fail completely to recognize the persons and factions being satirized or even the political issues involved.

This last speculation, that Melville's quarry might have recognized their own faces in his caricatures and have deliberately responded with "no comment" or with hostile unpublished verbal attacks, is a more plausible one than the alternative speculation that Melville wrote a book whose meaning and referents were deliberately hidden by him—so hidden that apparently no one until this day has recognized them. No man likes to be called a "con man"—a fraud. Some of Melville's bitterness about and sensitivity to slander would be explained if it could be shown by research into letters and unpublished material of the 1850s that his criticism of the exploitation of the slavery issue in partisan politics triggered personal reprisals upon him and his fiction by the men and women who believed it best that the issue should become the focus of political action. However, for the time being, the reception of *The Confidence-Man* remains an historical problem, if, as I contend in the following pages, Melville is satirizing more than thirty of his prominent contemporaries and no reviewer admitted to recognizing his intention—with the single exception of Fitz-James O'Brien, who suggested in *Putnam's Monthly Magazine* (April 1857) that the Deaf-Mute might be the "portrait of a distinguished metropolitan editor" (Horace Greeley).

Acknowledgments

My debt to other scholars in Melville studies goes back to my student days at Stanford University, when I first read Melville under the inspiration of the late Yvor Winters, and to the year when I worked in Houghton Library, 1951–52, as assistant to the editor of the *Harvard Library Bulletin,* and among other duties read proof on the supplementary list to M. M. Sealts, Jr., "Melville's Reading," as it was appearing in that meticulously edited periodical. There, also, I first examined the manuscript of *Billy Budd, Sailor,* quietly reposing on the shelves awaiting the edition of Hayford and Sealts. Over the years of writing my dissertation at Harvard University on *Moby-Dick,* publishing articles out of it in the *Journal of the History of Ideas* and in the *Southern Review,* and teaching Melville at Stanford, the historical studies of the generation of Anderson, Davis, Foster, Gilman, Hayford, Howard, Levy, Leyda, Sealts, Vincent, and other distinguished scholars remained the standard of achievement that I recognized and from whom I learned the most.

When, ten years ago, I first hypothesized that all of the characters in *The Confidence-Man* might possibly be caricatures of individuals involved in the politics of the 1850s, I little imagined how much of my life would be given to finding the evidence to support the hypothesis. For early encouragement in this enterprise I wish to thank Barbara Glenn, Kenneth Fields, and Watson Branch, and for generous responses to letters, Merton M. Sealts, Jr. For help received in the years of research and writing I am grateful to Professor Don Fehrenbacher of the Stanford University History Department. Professor Michael Holt of the University of Virginia shared his knowledge of the Know-Nothing party generously with me. My dear friends Barbara Bundy and Janet Lewis Winters were supportive in more ways than can be counted. The friendship and encouragement of the late Eric Voegelin, political philosopher and penetrating analyst of political confidence men, meant much to me. I owe special thanks from beginning to end to Wesley Trimpi, and for patience, support, and love to Alison Trimpi and Erica Trimpi Light.

My debt to the many scholars of American history of the antebellum period can be only partially acknowledged in the notes and selected bibliography. I investigated through general and special studies, biographies, memoirs, autobiographies, and editions of contemporary writings and letters many more historical figures and factions than I record. My education in antebellum political history has been and remains exciting and rewarding, and it will, I hope, prove helpful toward future work on the relationship of that history to American literature.

For help in researching the many political prints necessary to this study my thanks go especially to William Allen of the Stanford University Library, to Georgia Bumgardner of the American Antiquarian Society Library, to Bernard Reilly of the Prints and Photographs Division of the Library of Congress, to James Davis of the University of California at Los Angeles Library, and to many other librarians and curators at the graphic print collections of the New York Historical Society, New York Public Library, Houghton Library at Harvard University, Boston Public Library, Massachusetts Historical Society, University of California, Bancroft Library, the Stanford Museum, and of the Huntington Library. For the privilege of presenting a lecture, incorporating the results of this book, at the University of Alberta, Edmonton, in 1982 I am grateful to C. Q. Drummond and Morton Ross.

Last, my deepest thanks go to Fred Robinson, past president of the Connecticut Academy of Arts and Sciences, and to the CAAS Committee on Publications for accepting the book and publishing it.

Woodside, California
20 September 1985

1

The Problem of
The Confidence-Man: His Masquerade

Before Herman Melville left New York City on 11 October 1856, for a seven-month tour of Europe and the Levant, he negotiated a contract delivering to his publishers Dix & Edwards the just completed manuscript of *The Confidence-Man: His Masquerade*, his tenth book in ten years of publication. When it appeared the following April in New York and London, it proved to be neither a literary nor a financial success. In the financial panic of 1857 the American publishers Dix & Edwards went bankrupt. The book was not well-distributed nor was it widely or especially well reviewed, although its reception in England (where it was published by Longman, Brown, Green, Longmans & Roberts) was slightly more favorable. It proved to be the last prose fiction that Melville published in his lifetime, whether deliberately intended so at the time we do not know. Since that time it has been something of a puzzle to its readers. The problem that it presents can be regarded on two different levels. First, the more general question: What is the book about? Second, the more specific interpretive question: If four of the characters in the book caricature four contemporaries of Melville (as scholars have demonstrated), is it possible that all or nearly all of the characters are similarly conceived? But first a description of the book is necessary.

The Confidence-Man is a prose narrative of forty-five chapters of varying lengths. In the course of the story more than forty different characters appear, most of them only once. Of these about twenty-four may be called major characters, in terms of the amount of space devoted to them, while ten or so are minor, though vigorously executed. The remaining six or seven appear only as "vignettes" or as "voices." The setting throughout is an American steamer called the *Fidèle* while it travels south on the Mississippi River from St. Louis towards New Orleans, a destination it does not reach. As it travels it veers between ports in the slave state of Missouri (*e.g.* Cape Girardeau in chapter 23) and the free state of Illinois (*e.g.* Alton in chapter 22 and Cairo in chapter 23). The time of the action is from dawn on 1 April (All Fools Day) until just after midnight, sometime in the 1850s. The narrative opens with the appearance on deck of a Deaf-Mute man who inscribes on a placard several quotations from the New Testament, all beginning with the word "charity," on the theme of "Charity thinketh no evil." His character and his message of trust are forcefully contrasted with the character of the ship's Barber and his message as posted on a sign displayed in his barbershop: "No trust"—meaning that no credit will be extended to customers. The Deaf-Mute, whose message is repulsed by most of the other passengers, goes to sleep and evidently leaves the scene. Next, the passengers and the ship generally are summarily described.

In the subsequent chapters the confidence of various passengers is solicited by seven major characters whom nearly all scholars agree are the successive appearances of the title-character, the Confidence Man, in seven different disguises. He appears in chapter 3 as a Negro cripple named Black Guinea, who entertains the other passengers and begs for pennies. When his honesty is questioned by a cynical passenger, called the Wooden-Legged Man, Black Guinea reels off a list of men on board who will speak for him. Subsequently six of these men do appear on the *Fidèle,* dressed just as Guinea has described them, and each of them is obviously a manifestation of the same single Confidence Man who is masquerading as Black Guinea himself and who is, less obviously, the same person who appeared as the Deaf-Mute in the opening of the narrative. Each manifestation solicits the trust of one or more of the other passengers, either in the form of money or of friendship.

Thus, the structure of the book may be described as a series of episodic chapters that enact over and over the same basic action of one character— presumably a knave or trickster—trying to win the trust of another man (or in two cases of a woman). There is very little physical action. There is only minimal description of the setting and almost no revelation of internal feeling or psychological analysis such as one finds ordinarily in a novel. The book consists mainly of capsule descriptions of the details of the physical appearance and clothing of each character, followed by the conversations held between the Confidence Man and his current interlocuter. Hence, although the structural elements of each scene are repetitive and the theme of the dialogues is always some aspect of trust or confidence in human nature, in the divine nature, or in nature itself, still the topics taken up by the conversationalists vary as determined by the personalities being depicted.

Parenthetically it should be noted that the last appearance of the Confidence Man himself is in the disguise of a character named Frank Goodman, the Cosmopolitan, who dominates the entire last half of the narrative in a long series of encounters and dialogues with seven different antagonists and who closes the story by putting out the lamp burning in the Gentlemen's Cabin, leaving all in darkness. Lastly, it may be observed that although the skeletal structure of the narrative as I have outlined it is relatively simple (revealing, in fact, a highly schematized organization devised by Melville), yet the texture of the book—the flesh of the text itself—is extremely variegated, consisting, as it does, of masses of fine descriptive detail of physical appearance, of gesture, or of personality, while the dialogues themselves are bewildering in the hair-splitting fineness of the arguments presented, the seeming deviousness of the points pursued, the rapid-fire repartee, and the variety of the rhetoric and speech styles displayed by the great number of characters. There are few narratives in English or American literature that resemble *The Confidence-Man*—a reason then and now for its readers to be puzzled by it.

What is the book about? Its earliest reviewers asked this about it, professing bewilderment as to the author's intentions. For example, a writer in the New York *Dispatch* found himself "wondering what on earth the author has been driving at," when he closed the book, while an English reviewer in *The Literary Gazette* spoke of laying it down "with an uncomfortable sensation of dizziness in the head" and called it "a book professing to inculcate philosophical truths through the medium of nonsensical people talking nonsense." Though not all were so severe on it, the English especially praising its crisp style, these comments were typical of the response it received.[1] In this century when Melville's work was revived beginning with his centenary in 1919, its readers tended to pass rather quickly over *The Confidence-Man,* either admitting dislike or simply saying that they did not quite understand what he was doing in it. However, critics in the last forty years have been more patient with it, and the work of such scholars as Egbert S. Oliver, John W. Shroeder, Edward Rosenberry, Harrison Hayford, Hershel Parker, and especially that of Elizabeth Foster, the editor of the Hendricks House edition in 1954, has illuminated it considerably.[2] Foster's long interpretive introduction and her voluminous notes summarize much necessary knowledge and add her own insights, giving thus a partial solution to the question of what the book is about in treating it as a "philosophical satire" generally on various forms of American optimism and progressive thought—a "modern *Candide*." Asserting more specifically—and questionably—that "religion itself [nineteenth-century American Protestant Christianity] is weighed and found wanting on every page of the book," and—more certainly—that Melville's "running satire on the difference between men's profession of Christianity and their practice is fairly obvious," Foster interprets "allegorically" the Confidence Man himself in each disguise as a "supernatural" embodiment of "an original or primal force in the universe," as, in short, an allegorization of the biblical Satan or Devil. Less persuasively, she claims that Melville has written a "religious allegory," using as his principle of order passages from the Sermon on the Mount and I Corinthians 13, and she treats several of the main characters as masquerades of faith, hope and charity while being in reality the opposite and revealing covertly to the reader the diabolical nature of each.

3

She sees Melville as offering to the reader a contrast between the pessimistic view that Christian ethics appears unsuited to human nature and the even more pessimistic view of the fanatical Indian-Hater Moredock, leaving the reader to choose.[3]

Despite the general justness of Foster's observations, her detection of a "religious allegory" based on New Testament texts as the principle of order by which Melville divides up his theme of American philosophical optimism has not satisfied all readers, nor has she conclusively demonstrated it. One still must ask why so many different appearances of the title character and so many different antagonists, each minutely distinguished from the others? And why so many diverse dialogues on the same question of trust, each minutely distinguished from the others by its stylistic, rhetorical, and philosophical aspects? Why is the question of the American trust in human nature worthy of such an extended and diversified treatment? The text seems to demand that one penetrate more deeply than Foster and the other scholars have to answer the general question of what the book is really about.

While considering the more general question, the reader is also confronted with a more specific interpretive problem raised by the discovery by scholars that Melville is caricaturing at least four contemporary American men in *The Confidence-Man*. Since, if four of the characters demonstrably allude to men in Melville's historical context, why may we not hypothesize that all of them possibly may? And if so, is there any principle of order in the historical context linking them together? As long ago as 1938 it was suggested by Yvor Winters and in 1946 demonstrated by Egbert Oliver that Mark Winsome, the Mystical Master in chapter 36, is a caricature of Ralph Waldo Emerson.[4] The evidence is indisputable, although there is debate about Melville's intention in so depicting Emerson. Likewise, Oliver's identification in the same article of another major character, Egbert the Practical Disciple, as a caricature of Henry David Thoreau has considerable evidence to substantiate it, although Foster finds fault with it, and there are still problems associated with it which will be discussed in Chapter 11.[5] However, Oliver's case for Thoreau is a powerful one. Yet a third identification of a caricature was published in 1959 by Harrison Hayford.[6] In a model demonstration of the correct method of correlating Melville's descriptive details with descriptive details of historical men, he showed that the character named the Crazy Beggar, who tries to sell Winsome a pamphlet in chapter 36, is a caricature of Edgar Allan Poe, the Southern poet. Lastly, a fourth, extremely good case has been made in an article in 1976 by William Norris that another major character, the Gentleman in Gold Sleeve-Buttons in chapter 7, is a caricature of the American millionaire manufacturer, philanthropist, and politician Abbott Lawrence of Boston.[7] If, then, these four characters have been identified with contemporary men, whose careers Melville surely was acquainted with, and if there is general—though not absolute—scholarly agreement on the matter, why may one not hypothesize that all the characters—or more cautiously most of them—have actual models in contemporary history? Is it possible that the entire gallery of characters may relate to a specific historical context? If so, where should one look for them? This, then, is the double-faceted problem that *The Confidence-Man* has presented for the last decade. What specifically is the book about and does it have an historical context that would illuminate both its themes in specific detail and the objects of its satire in their particularities?

The method that one uses to attack both these questions is one that is useful, if not essential, in trying to interpret any work of literature of any period. One examines the literary form of the work, tries to define it in its historical terms, and attempts to place it in a literary tradition known to its author by means of comparisons with its pertinent parallels and analogues. This approach should bring the reader or scholar—through both sympathy and understanding—as close to the author's own intentions as is possible.

What was recognized from the beginning about *The Confidence-Man* by its more sensitive readers was that it is a satire. That is, to use the Aristotelean definition of comedy as expressed in the *Poetics,* it is a comic presentation of man, or men, as worse than they really are, with—to add the Horatian moral intention—the aim of improving them. To place it more specifically within the tradition of literary satire requires an examination of the formal elements of the narrative—some of which have already been adumbrated in the description of it given above—and some comparisons of it to other examples of satire.

If we examine *The Confidence-Man* we find five formal elements in its composition: (1) the protagonist—the title-character (the Confidence Man)—is a shape-shifting trickster who assumes a series of personal disguises; (2) the narrative structure of the book is primarily episodic, in that it unfolds in a series of short repetitive scenes; (3) the main expository device is the use of dialogue; as in a stage comedy, the bulk of the book is dialogue; (4) the principal action—repeated over and over—is the action of a confidence man trying to trick a fool; and (5) the characters may all possibly be satirical caricatures of known public figures of the time.

In the body of literary satire that was available to Melville there are at least two traditions that might have offered models to him: the narrative and the dramatic traditions. Of these, the first, the narrative tradition, which offers such models as *Don Quixote* in prose, Pope's *Dunciad* in verse, and Swift's *Gulliver's Travels* in prose—to name only the most obvious—has proven less fruitful than the dramatic tradition of satire. Analogues much closer in structure and characterization to *The Confidence-Man* may be found in the various forms of stage comedy. For example, Aristophanes' comedies in antiquity display at least three of the formal elements of Melville's satire: dialogue as the main expository device, the principal action of knave duping fool, and caricature of contemporary men. Ancient comedy likewise displays considerable use of comic disguise. Similarly, the Latin comedies of Terence and Plautus use dialogue, exploit the dramatic potential of knave duping fool, and they satirize Roman types and perhaps individuals. In the English Renaissance, the comedies of Ben Jonson, written with classical models in mind, also display some of the same formal elements of structure and characterization.

However, closer than any of these stage models to Melville's book is the dramatic tradition of satire as it was currently available to him in English stage Pantomime and in its ancestor, the Continental commedia dell'arte (improvised comedy) as it might be known to him through literary essays and histories of the early nineteenth century. This kind of stage satire was a living theater—the most widely popular of his time—not only in America but in England, France, and Germany, where in fact he saw examples of it in his travels. Commedia dell'arte with its seven principal masks, as they were described by Isaac D'Israeli, the English essayist, and by other historians, offers model character types not only for the shape-shifting trickster but also for nearly all the characters in *The Confidence-Man*. The mask Harlequin, a clever, witty knave who customarily assumes a series of disguises, offers a model for Melville's main character, the Confidence Man, while the mask Pantalone, who was an elderly, foolish Venetian man of wealth, presents a model for Melville's series of property-owning antagonists to the Confidence Man, most of whom are deceived by him. Both these character-types were retained in English and American Pantomime, as Harlequin and Pantaloon. Moreover, this form of comedy offers models in its other masks (the pedantic Dottore, the blustering Capitano, the cynical Pulcinella and the innocent Pierrot) for most of the other principal characters in *The Confidence-Man*.[8]

Structurally considered, *The Confidence-Man* bears a striking resemblance to English stage Pantomime of the period. A Pantomime began, according to its historian David Mayer, *Harlequin in His Element,* with the silent enactment in a single scene of a serious tale, myth, or legend known to the audience. Similarly, *The Confidence-Man* opens with the mysterious appearance of the Deaf-Mute, his writing of his message, his rejection, and his disappearance from the scene. Pantomime, next, after the transformation of the hero of the "Opening" into the comic figure of Harlequin, proceeded in a series of short repetitive episodes to unfold the encounters of Harlequin with his antagonist Pantaloon—whose character had likewise been adumbrated in the opening scene as an antagonist to the main character. Likewise, *The Confidence-Man* unfolds in a series of episodes, in each of which the Confidence Man, like Harlequin, appears in a disguise and precipitates and guides the action of the narrative. In Pantomime, Harlequin consistently tricks his opponent Pantaloon. Likewise, in *The Confidence-Man,* Melville's protagonist in his various disguises, tries to obtain money, or trust, or both, from his antagonists, who are almost consistently characters who carry purses, as Pantalone characteristically did, are elderly, as Pantalone usually was, or otherwise resemble this traditional dramatic mask and his descendant Pantaloon. Again, like the Harlequin of both commedia dell'arte and of Pantomime, Melville's Confidence Man also tries to outwit other types of characters, who may be seen to be modelled on other masks. For example, Mark Winsome, the Mystical Master, is clearly based on the Dottore type, as are also the Episcopal Clergyman, the Methodist Minister, and, less obviously, the Collegian—all of whom are solicited by the Confidence Man. The Missouri Bachelor Pitch, who carries a rifle, and the Soldier of Fortune, Thomas Fry, are modelled on the blustering Capitano mask of commedia dell'arte and are similar to the military types that were represented in Pantomime of the period. Similar again to the characterization in this dramatic tradition, Melville's two most cynical characters, the Wooden-Legged Man and the Invalid Titan, who resist successfully the Confidence Man's solicitations, are modelled upon the cynical Pulcinella mask.[9]

Thus, in the three formal elements of a shape-shifting protagonist, of episodic structure, and in the pattern of knave duping or trying to dupe other type characters (who are regional or social variants of universal human types), Melville's satire has close analogues in a stage tradition that we know was available to him. Commedia dell'arte, although not alive in the forms in which it had existed all over Europe from the Renaissance until the end of the eighteenth century, was written about by Diderot in the *Encyclopédie,* where Melville may have read about it in his translation, by D'Israeli, whose literary works he owned, and by Thackeray and Lamb in popular essays. As noted earlier, its descendant, the Pantomime of English theater, was the most vital comic theater of his time. We have evidence of Melville's attending performances of Pantomime and of its competitors, the farces, "entertainments," or "comicalities" of the period, as they were called.[10]

For the fourth formal element discerned in *The Confidence-Man*—dialogue as the chief expository method—Pantomime does not offer a satisfactory model, since it relied only minimally on spoken dialogue and mainly on body action plus written placards. However, commedia dell'arte and other forms of stage comedy generally offer analogues to Melville's chosen method of exposition. Dialogue is, of course, the chief expository device of stage comedy generally.

For the fifth element of structure the stage tradition of comedia dell'arte and Pantomime offers an explicit and nearly unique model for satirical caricature of contemporary public figures through allusion, parody, and mimicry. One of its main characteristics and cause of its great popularity was that this kind of comedy did satirize contemporary well-known persons (domestic and foreign) and took its subject matter from contemporary customs, fads, topics of conversation, social and political events, fashions—in fact, anything in the contemporary world that might offer itself for humorous or critical comment. David Mayer's study of English Pantomime emphasizes the popularity of this kind of topical humor as the source of Pantomime's lasting success. Histories of the American stage, likewise, refer to American versions of Pantomime and of English farces as a kind of native commedia dell'arte, based on local and regional American variations of the generic or universal types that the masks represented.

Lastly, there existed on the New York stage while Melville was living in the city, a close theatrical analogue to his conception of the Confidence Man. As Johannes Bergmann discovered in 1969, John Brougham's farce "The Confidence Man," which derived its main character from a real thief, William Thompson (whose activities originated the term "confidence man"), was performed at William E. Burton's Chambers Street Theatre during the summer of 1849. This comedy was favorably reviewed in the *Literary World*, which Melville read and for which he did some reviewing in this period. We know of it only that it was probably based on Thompson's activities and on newspaper articles that applied the new term "confidence man" to other men engaged in politics, business, banking, and other fields.[11] We do not know whether Melville saw the farce, but the possibility remains that he knew of it and that it may have remained in his mind as the germ of a possible narrative satire on American types and individuals.

For the foregoing reasons it is possible, then, to place Melville's work in the dramatic tradition of satire—more specifically in that of the improvised comedy and of Pantomime—though it must always be kept in mind that it is not, in fact, written for stage performance. (It is probably most accurately termed, as it will be seen later, a "pasquinade"—a political satire). By locating the work in this literary tradition we are enabled to undertake the solution to the problems it still presents to its readers: what it is about and who are the objects of its satire. For if, like improvised comedy in the European tradition and like Pantomime and other comical "entertainments" in Melville's day, *The Confidence-Man* is about contemporary types and individuals and is satirizing contemporary public topics and events, it is to the contemporary scene that one must look to find its meaning and to interpret its satire.

Looking toward American public affairs of the 1850s and more narrowly to the period of the presumed composition of the book—roughly the first nine months of 1856—one becomes immediately aware that the all-absorbing topic of the times in newspapers, periodicals, public addresses, poems, sermons, pamphlets, letters, and books was domestic politics and, in particular, the political controversy over black slavery in the South and its possible extension into new territories—weighted as it was with potential disaster for the American union of states. This historical context both in its wider temporal dimensions, beginning in 1820 with the founding of Benjamin Lundy's early antislavery newspaper the *Genius of Universal Emancipation* and reaching up to Secession and the opening of the Civil War in 1861, as well as in its more narrow compass, focusing upon the presidential campaign of the summer of 1856, when the newly founded Republican party first presented a candidate, offers a wide range of well-known public figures of the time—most of whom are not very well known today. Most significantly one finds there the four men who have already been identified by scholars as being caricatured in *The Confidence-Man*: Emerson, Thoreau, Poe, and Abbott Lawrence. One finds that Emerson, who was well known as a literary essayist, poet, and lecturer also projected a public image in the political world of New England as a speaker against the Fugitive Slave Act and that Thoreau was as well known in Massachusetts—if not better known—as a militant anti-slavery political speaker than as the author of *Walden* or *A Week on the Concord and Merrimack Rivers*. And that Poe, although not a political speaker, was always publicly regarded in New York as a representative Southerner and therefore as being politically proslavery. Along with these men, who were primarily literary men, one finds that Abbott Lawrence was a very important Massachusetts politician of the late 1840s and the early 1850s, an ambitious Whig, who was puzzled as to how far to go along with the rising tide of antislavery-extension sentiment in the North and still not lose his Old-Line Whig support. Lawrence's political position in relationship to this sentiment—as it was becoming embodied in the new Republican party at the time of his death in 1855—correlates precisely with the stance that his caricature as the Gentleman in Gold Sleeve-Buttons takes in response to the solicitations of the charity agent (the Man in Gray Coat and White Tie), who is the disguised Confidence Man in chapter 7.[12] Lawrence and the three American literary men share, then, a common context in the political configurations of the period 1846 to

1856 as they may be seen in the public media of the period in the major cities—New York, Albany, Boston, Philadelphia, Washington, Richmond, Charleston, and New Orleans. This context in its detail of character and attitude may account for the complexity of detail and attitude in *The Confidence-Man,* if we hypothesize that it is a satire on the politics of the period.

2

Melville's Political World, 1819–1860, and His Early Satire on It

When Melville, a native New Yorker and a Massachusetts resident, left New York City in October 1856 for his seven-month tour, it was the last year of the presidency of Franklin Pierce. He left behind him both in his native and home states and in the nation the most complex and dangerous national political situation since the founding of the Republic—a political crisis which had been growing since his birth in 1819. Both Presidents George Washington and Andrew Jackson had warned in their Farewell Addresses of the dangers of party exploitation of the sectionally divisive issue of slavery in American politics.[1] Yet, in the presidential campaign of the early months and the summer of 1856 a Northern sectional party—the Republican—had been organized for the first time and presented as its candidate John C. Frémont of California, as well as contenders in the various state elections. Thus ended the decades-old attempt by thoughtful politicians of both the major parties of the 1830s and 1840s (Democratic and Whig) to keep the slavery question out of partisan politics. And although Frémont lost the election in November, while Melville was abroad, to the Democratic candidate James Buchanan of Pennsylvania, the Republican party entered American politics to stay. Subsequently, it elected Lincoln in 1860, precipitating a dramatic loss of confidence by the Southern states in the representational system of the Union, which led to the secession of South Carolina and other states during the winter of 1860–61, a period that Melville later called in *Clarel* (1876) "The dolorous winter ere the war; / True Bridge of Sighs . . . Sad arch between contrasted eras" (IV, v, 77–80). Before he left Melville had completed *The Confidence-Man,* and it was published in April, after the inauguration of Buchanan and after the reading of Chief Justice Roger B. Taney's opinion in the Dred Scott case, which further polarized North-South antagonisms.

Melville's birth occurred in the year of an earlier political crisis over slavery—the attempt in 1819 by the state of Missouri to join the Union—a crisis that was resolved by the Missouri Compromise of 1820, by which Missouri was admitted as a slave state, while Maine entered as a free state, preserving an equality in the numbers of free and slave states. During the 1830s, while Melville attended high school, joined a debating club in Albany, published some juvenile work, and held various jobs, the right to petition against slavery in the District of Columbia was bitterly argued in congressional debates led by John Quincy Adams of Massachusetts and Henry A. Wise of Virginia. The issue remained relatively quiescent during the years that he was a sailor in the Pacific, 1841 to 1843, and then in 1846, the year in which he published his first travel narrative, *Typee,* it erupted vigorously again in Congress with the debates over the Wilmot Proviso, an amendment to a war appropriations bill which would have forbidden the extension of slavery into any new territory acquired as a result of the war with Mexico. While the debates on the proviso were taking place Melville visited Washington, office-seeking, in February 1847, and he may have heard some of the speeches. Again, in 1849, the year of the publication of his third and fourth books, *Mardi* and *Redburn,* the admission of California as a free state exacerbated congressional and national debate about the political issue of slavery-extension, which resulted in the compromise proposals of Henry Clay of Kentucky and the momentous congressional debates of 1850 (while Melville was writing *Moby-Dick*), between Clay, Daniel Webster of Massachusetts (a good friend of his father-in-law, Chief Justice Lemuel Shaw of Massachusetts), and John C. Calhoun of South Carolina. The Compromises of 1850, which were arrived at through these debates, were intended to remove the slavery issue from partisan politics and lay it to rest. However, Northern resistance to the Fugitive Slave Bill (in the enforcement of which in two cases Shaw was actively involved) and Southern resentment of the admission of California as a free state continued agitation of the issue. More unexpectedly, in March of 1854, Stephen A. Douglas, Democratic senator from Illinois, introduced into the Senate the Kansas-Nebraska Bill intended to create two territories, one of which (Nebraska) would be free and the other (Kansas) open to slavery. Douglas's bill in effect repealed the Missouri Compromise, which had established that no slavery would be permitted in the territory of the Louisiana Purchase north of latitude 36 degrees, 30 minutes, where most of Kansas was located. It aroused an intense Northern reaction to the possibility of slavery and the black population being introduced into Kansas and to the breach of "faith" between North and South that this represented. The passage of the act and the ensuing reactions in both sections led to an extraordinarily complicated fragmentation and realignment of the political party system.

The two main parties throughout the 1830s and 1840s were the Democratic party (called the "Democracy") and the Whig party, which was formed in 1834 out of Anti-Masonic and old National Republican elements, as a coalition of the followers of Clay, Webster, and Calhoun in opposition to the policies of President Andrew Jackson of Tennessee. The Democrats won the presidency in 1832 with Jackson, in 1836 with Martin Van Buren of New York, in 1844 with James K. Polk of Tennessee, and in 1852 with Pierce.

In 1840 the Whigs won with Harrison, who died in office, leaving the presidency to John Tyler of Virginia, who failed to remain very Whiggish in his actions; and with General Zachary Taylor of Louisiana in 1848, who died in 1850 leaving his office to Millard Fillmore of New York, a solid Whig but one with enemies within his own party, including the powerful New York trio, former Governor William Henry Seward, Thurlow Weed of the *Albany Evening Journal,* and Horace Greeley of the New York *Tribune.* When Pierce succeeded Fillmore in 1853, the Whig party was considered to be extremely weak and many of its most prominent members, including Seward, Weed, and Greeley, were thought to be casting around for a new political organization. The Democrats, though numerous and strong, received weak direction from Pierce and were likewise suffering internal conflict, some but not all, occasioned by the slavery issue. Particularly in the state of New York the Democracy had split over the Wilmot Proviso as early as 1847 into the Barnburners and the Hunkers. The Barnburners, who were pro-Wilmot Proviso, included certain followers of Van Buren, as well as the editor William Cullen Bryant of the New York *Evening Post,* while the Hunkers were the party regulars, led by former Governor William L. Marcy. The Hunkers, in their turn, split in 1852 into the Softs, such as Marcy and John Adams Dix, who were willing to welcome back the Barnburners when they wished to return to the party, and the Hards, such as Daniel L. Dickinson, who refused reconcilement. In the South, disturbed likewise by the Wilmot Proviso, a faction appeared within the Democracy when at the 1848 convention the Alabama delegation, led by William Lowndes Yancey, presented the Alabama Platform demanding the right to hold slaves in any new territories or states. Thus, by the time of the Kansas-Nebraska Bill and the pressure it exerted toward sectionalization, the Whigs, who had come into being as an opposition party and had thriven only when led by a military hero of national stature, were on the verge of collapse, while the Democrats were internally polarized on the issue of slavery extension and were potentially threatened by a new alignment.

Besides the two traditional parties during the 1850s there were three others of significance: the Nativist or American party, the Temperance party, and—most important for the future—the Free-Soil party. The Americans were on record as opposed to electing any candidate to office who was of foreign birth or was a Roman Catholic. After the formation of a secret lodge (the Order of the Star Spangled Banner), opposed to immigrants and Catholics, whose password was "I don't know," this party was called the "Know-Nothings" in popular speech. The Know-Nothings reached a peak of success in the state elections of 1854, especially in Massachusetts, where they swept into nearly all offices, including the governorship. In early 1856 at their convention they passed over the New York millionaire George Law to nominate Fillmore, who was still a Whig, for president. They mounted a strong campaign, yet one that was injured by the defection of a group opposed to slavery-extension, who called themselves the "North Americans," and who, led by Law, endorsed Frémont after the new Republican party had nominated him. In the November election, they won only Maryland.

The temperance issue was a strong one in 1856, having influenced some successes in Maine, Vermont, and New Hampshire. Although as a party it did not present a presidential candidate, it did produce various state candidates and influenced nominations and voting patterns in the other parties—notably in the Republican and Democratic nominations in New York and Massachusetts. The governor of New York at the time of the writing of *The Confidence-Man*—presumably the early months and summer of 1856—was Myron H. Clark of the Temperance party, who was a concession to the "Dry's" by the Whig party boss, Thurlow Weed, who placed with him on the same winning ticket, as lieutenant-governor, the Whig editor of the New York *Daily Times*, Henry Jarvis Raymond.

The Free-Soil party had its origins in the rise of the antislavery movement and its entry into partisan politics: first through the Liberty party nominations in 1840 and again in 1844 of James G. Birney of Ohio; then through the Barnburner movement within the New York Democratic party, which took place concurrently with the Conscience Whig movement among the Massachusetts Whigs (both movements paralleled by similar patterns in other Northern states). The Free-Soil convention at Buffalo in 1848 nominated former President Van Buren, who was not particularly antislavery but was disgruntled with the regular Democratic party, and Charles Francis Adams of Massachusetts, a Conscience Whig. As a third party the Free-Soilers drew enough votes away from the Democrats to bring Zachary Taylor into office. When many of the defecting Democrats returned to party orthodoxy in 1852, the Free-Soilers' nomination of John P. Hale, an outspoken antislavery senator from New Hampshire, did not draw many votes in that year. In 1854 the passage of the Kansas-Nebraska Bill, approved by the Democratic President Pierce, which would extend "slave-soil," caused the disappearance of the Free-Soil party as such, because its members were able to merge into the more general anti-Nebraska movement, which resulted in the founding of the Republican party. Generally speaking, most historians agree that the passage of the Douglas-sponsored bill sharpened Northern sectional feeling on the issue of the extension of slavery and led to the coalescence of the new Republican party out of men from the Whigs, from the Democrats, from the Know-Nothings of the North American faction, from the Temperance movement, and from the earlier Liberty and Free-Soil parties—as well as from the Abolitionist movement and party itself. After several state Republican organizations had formed (the first at Ripon, Wisconsin in 1854), these disparate elements—mystifying to their opponents—came together first at Pittsburgh in February 1856 to organize and then on 17 June at Philadelphia to nominate in a great show of enthusiasm and high-minded politicking the Western explorer Frémont and William Dayton of New Jersey, on a platform of opposition to the extension of slavery into Kansas. In reaction to the new party many Old-Line Whigs, who feared its effects, such as the Bostonian lawyers, Rufus Choate and George Ticknor Curtis, turned dramatically to Pierce and the Democracy, while others chose the Know-Nothing party, who had nominated the former Whig President Fillmore (who received a second nomination from remnants of the Whigs at a convention late in the summer).

These five parties, dissimilar as they were, formed by 1856 a spectrum of opinion in the center between the two most extreme political movements. The abolitionists of the North wanted slavery abolished entirely, with the Constitution altered to forbid it everywhere, while in the South the "Fire-Eaters" wanted property rights in slavery recognized in all the states and to be extended with Constitutional protection into any new territories or states. Each extreme considered a separation of the states into two nations a viable solution, if their views did not prevail. The long-term abolitionists had mainly confined their activities to journalistic and oratorical propaganda, such as William Lloyd Garrison's *Liberator*, Wendell Phillips's oratory, innumerable pamphlets and sermons, and to the founding of antislavery societies. Meanwhile in the South for several decades until his death in 1850, Calhoun had led the defense of slavery either within the Democratic party or by abstention from endorsement of any candidate. A more extremist movement, however, was that represented by Yancey after 1848, in his oratory and his newspapers and by other fire-eating journalists and politicians, such as Robert Barnwell Rhett of the Charleston *Mercury* and Edmund Ruffin of Virginia.

So then, Melville's departure for Europe occurred at the point when a decades-long logomachy of massive proportions had culminated in the formation of a new multifaceted political coalition founded on the sectionally divisive issue of nonextension of slavery. In the eyes of its opponents, especially Democrats who recognized in its membership their ancient Whig enemies in a new dress, the new Republican party formed a threat not only to their own political hopes but in a more disinterested point of view to the continuance of the American Union because of the challenge that the party offered to Southern confidence in a federal government controlled by them.

In Melville's world, besides the men directly involved in politics there were others in the public life of the period who never, or rarely, ran for office or held it but who took active parts in influencing public opinion on political issues through their writing or public speaking—frequently with the unacknowledged hope of public office as reward. Until it resulted in the Civil War, the "crisis of the Union" was always present in the background of most discussions of social, political, or moral issues even when they did not bear directly on an election. Three principal professions that influenced public opinion significantly were the journalists, the orators or lecturers, and the preachers. Of a fourth profession, the writers, the most directly influential individual was probably Harriet Beecher Stowe, author of *Uncle Tom's Cabin; or Life Among the Lowly* (1852). Of the journalists probably the most influential in the North were the New York editors, of whom Greeley, an antislavery Whig and a founder of the Republican party, was the most powerful through his *Tribune* and its weekly and semiweekly editions, which were widely circulated throughout the North and West. Another Whig, Raymond, founder and editor of the New York *Times,* moved opportunely to the Republican party in 1856. Less widely circulated but prestigious were the strongly antislavery views of the New York *Evening Post,* edited by Bryant, who was a Barnburner Democrat, Free-Soiler, and in 1856 a Republican. Another powerful New York editor was Colonel James Watson Webb of the *Courier & Enquirer,* who abandoned the dying Whig party for the Republican at the founding convention. The Democratic editor Gerard Hallock of the *Journal of Commerce* spurned the new party. Most colorful and most widely circulated of all the New York papers was the usually Democratic but self-labelled "independent" *Herald,* founded and edited by the Scottish-born James Gordon Bennett, who was violently critical of the antislavery movement, even while professing also to despise the proslavery secessionists of the South. Mired in self-contradictory reasoning, surprisingly he endorsed Frémont in 1856, even while he disdained the "Black Republicans." In upper New York State the Whig party boss Weed edited the *Albany Evening Journal* while he transferred his well-organized statewide organization to the new party of which he was a founder. The Albany *Argus,* merged by 1856 with the Albany *Atlas,* edited by his long-time rival Edwin Croswell, represented Hunker Democratic views and accommodation with the South.

In western Massachusetts, where Melville had been living on his farm in Pittsfield since 1850, the two major newspapers—both of which he probably read—were the Pittsfield *Sun* (Democratic), whose editor Phinehas Allen he knew, and the *Berkshire County Eagle* (Whig and in 1856 Republican), whose editor J. E. A. Smith was Melville's friend and one of his first biographers. In Springfield, Samuel Bowles' *Republican* was an early force for antislavery views. In Washington, D.C., Gamaliel Bailey, one of the first men to promote Frémont as the Republican candidate, had also been for years editor of the *National Era,* an influential antislavery paper that published work by the antislavery poet and Democratic politician John Greenleaf Whittier, as well as Mrs. Stowe's *Uncle Tom's Cabin* in its early serialized version. In Virginia, Thomas Ritchie's *Richmond Enquirer,* Democratic and proslavery, was not as violently partisan and extreme as Rhett's Charleston *Mercury* nor as Yancey's paper in Alabama. In the West, the formation of antislavery opinion had begun in the 1820s with Benjamin Lundy's intermittently published *Genius of Universal Emancipation,* and Lundy's influence upon William Lloyd Garrison had resulted in the founding in 1831 of the most notorious of all antislavery papers, the Boston-based *Liberator.* Also, in the West, a Methodist minister, William Gannaway Brownlow, was famed for strident editorials, in his Whig and Know-Nothing journals, while Murat Halstead in the *Cincinnati Commercial* promoted the antislavery Democrat, Salmon P. Chase, and reported memorably and sympathetically the first Republican convention.

Another important journalist, whose political influence as a Democrat remained strong through the 1850s, even when he did not control a newspaper, was Francis Preston Blair, Sr., of Maryland whose editorship of the Washington *Globe* during the 1830s and 1840s had made him a major power and molder of public opinion for the administrations of Jackson and Van Buren. Blair and his sons F. P. Blair, Jr., and Montgomery Blair were influential as they entered the Republican party and remained so for decades. Journalists of lesser note who formed part of the world that Melville knew in New York City were Charles Anderson Dana, former Brook Farmer, editorial assistant to Greeley on the *Tribune* (later part-owner and editor of the New York *Sun*), and Parke Godwin, who wrote a series of essays on the political crisis for *Putnam's Magazine* at the time when Melville was publishing *Israel Potter* (1854) and several stories, including *Benito Cereno* (1855) in that journal.

It must be remembered that the wide diffusion of news reports and of editorial opinion was aided in this period by the journalistic practice of reprinting verbatim stories and editorials from paper to paper. Along with the reprinting went the custom of editorial comment directly on the reprinted material, either in rejoinder or in concurrence. That is, for example, the *Liberator* might reprint a particularly violent editorial from a Southern newspaper—the Charleston *Mercury* or Richmond *Enquirer,* typically—and print an equally violent rejoinder to it from the pen of Garrison. This, in turn, would provoke a third article in the Southern paper, to which the *Liberator* would again reply. Thus, in a single newspaper a reader might peruse an extended dialogue, usually evincing more heat than light, representing the diverse views on the slavery question. Such debate in the newspapers was even more common than debate on the public platform, although this also frequently took place and was strikingly influential on public opinion—most notably in the college debates on abolition at Lane Theological Seminary in

Ohio in 1832, which resulted in the defection of a group of faculty and students led by Theodore Weld and the founding of Oberlin College, as well as signaling the start of the long national debate on slavery.

On the public platform, mainly through the lyceum societies, the most successful speakers—those who commanded the highest fees—were usually men who also were important in other professions, such as Webster, Emerson, Theodore Parker, Oliver Wendell Holmes, Henry Ward Beecher, James Russell Lowell, George William Curtis, Charles Anderson Dana, Bayard Taylor, Edwin Whipple, and others. With the marked change in public opinion in the North beginning after the reaction to the Compromises of 1850 (especially to the Fugitive Slave Act and the ensuing legal cases) and increasing after the passage of the Kansas-Nebraska Bill, certain of these speakers were asked to speak on the slavery question, which had previously been the chief theme only of committed abolitionists such as Weld, Garrison, Frederick Douglass, Phillips, Lucy Stone, and Elizabeth Cady Stanton. Proslavery speakers did not often appear on the lecture platform in the North, yet as late as 1855 George Fitzhugh of Virginia appeared in New Haven speaking on "The Failure of a Free Society," and in 1856 Brownlow of Tennessee debated with an antislavery speaker in Philadelphia. After his return from Europe in 1857, Melville himself prepared a series of lyceum lectures on his travels, which he delivered in three tours from 1857 to 1859. He did not in these formally discuss political topics.

Even more pervasive in forming public opinion of the time than lyceum lectures was the influence of Christian ministers through their Sunday preaching, as well as through the publication of sermons in newspaper, pamphlet, and book form. As the tension over the slavery issue increased after 1830, certain Protestant churches split into Northern and Southern branches, while all felt the strain as their ministers felt obliged to speak out on the morality or immorality of the institution. When the issue of the extension of slavery entered into partisan politics in the 1850s certain ministers felt obliged to take partisan political positions. Even before then, however, Theodore Parker, Congregational minister, and Thomas Wentworth Higginson, Unitarian, had preached in New England and published against slavery, and when the Republican party formed, they became active in its cause. After 1850, the most popular and well-known Protestant minister in the country, Henry Ward Beecher, of Plymouth Church, Brooklyn, entered the political scene by lecturing and preaching directly on the North-South issue, and he was an active and formidable speaker for the Republicans throughout the North during the 1856 campaign for Frémont. A less famous commitment to the Republicans was that of a young Episcopal minister, Dudley Atkins Tyng, who attained some notoriety for a pro-Republican sermon in August of 1856, which cost him his position at a Philadelphia church. In the West, the Whig journalist Brownlow preached on political subjects, as well as Christian salvation, on the Methodist circuit, even while he dabbled in politics as a delegate to the Know-Nothing presidential convention. Most Southern ministers felt constrained to defend the slave institution, regardless of party affiliation.

Lastly, an important group but probably that with the least direct effect upon public opinion—except for Harriet Stowe—were the literati—poets, essayists, fiction writers, and dramatists. In the North they centered in New York City and certain parts of Massachusetts. In the South they were scattered but with some concentration of focus in Charleston. In the West they were mainly in Cincinnati. Of the New York City literati who constituted the world into which Melville entered in 1846 with the publication of *Typee* most were Democrats—for example, the editor, poet, and dramatist Cornelius Mathews, author of a novel, *The Career of Puffer Hopkins* (1841) on New York politics; the editors George and Evert Duyckinck, the novelist Charles F. Briggs, the poet Bryant, and the fictionist and essayist George William Curtis. A measure of one aspect of the change in the New York literary climate of opinion by 1856 is that the poet Nathaniel Parker Willis cast his "virgin vote"—as he called it—for Frémont in 1856, while Curtis became a Republican campaign speaker, attaining considerable fame for his address on "The Duty of the American Scholar to Politics of the Times" (1856). On the other hand, the Southerners Edgar Allan Poe and the romancer and playwright, William Gilmore Simms, were Democrats of the proslavery persuasion. Of the older generation but still influential as writers were the novelist, James Kirke Paulding, a New York Democrat, who published two works early in his career in defense of slavery, and the poet Fitz-Greene Halleck, who had published in the 1820s the *Croaker* satires on New York politics and was a Federalist to his end. James Fenimore Cooper, ardent Democrat and anti-philanthropist, was dead (as was Poe) by 1856, while Washington Irving, retired to Sunnyside on the Hudson, favored Frémont in 1856.

In Massachusetts well known nationally as a lecturer was the Transcendentalist poet and essayist, Emerson, and, less widely known, as poet and essayist, Henry David Thoreau. Both of these men spoke out against slavery, Emerson taking to the platform after the Kansas-Nebraska Bill with several regular lectures on the fugitive slave issue, while Thoreau was much less influential though more vehemently condemnatory. Neither spoke publicly for the Republican party, although Emerson favored it. The romancer, Nathaniel Hawthorne, living in England as consul at Liverpool by 1856—where he assisted Melville in the arrangements for the publication of *The Confidence-Man*—was an exception to most of his New England friends, adhering to the Hunker Democratic view of his old Bowdoin College friend, Franklin Pierce, that slavery was not an issue which ought to be allowed to disrupt the Union of the States. Living in eastern Massachusetts, the poet and Quaker, Whittier, was active against slavery both through his poetry and through Liberty party and Democratic party activity. Also in the Boston area, James Russell Lowell influenced opinion through his political satires on the proslavery aims of the Mexican War, *The Biglow Papers* (1848). Most influential of all, however, was probably *Uncle Tom's Cabin,* written by the New England-born Harriet Stowe, sister of Henry Ward Beecher, and in the antislavery spirit of many New Englanders. In the West the principal literary magazine for many years was the *Illinois Monthly Magazine* (later, *Western Monthly Magazine*) edited by Judge James Hall. Hall, a Whig, was author also of romantic and adventurous redactions of Western legends and history, among which were the several retellings of the story of Colonel John Moredock, the "Indian-Hater," of which Melville made extensive and important use in *The Confidence-Man.* Hall's views on slavery were those of an early "Colonizationist" who wrote vigorously against the Lane College abolitionist movement in the 1830s, and then in 1854 was swept into the anti-Nebraska movement aimed at keeping slavery and the black population in the South.

These, then, were some of the voices that Melville would have heard on the various levels of public life, either directly in public speaking or indirectly through publication. There were possibly others of equal or greater importance to him which the passage of time has obscured from our hearing. They formed a circumambient "man-show" of considerable publicity and interest going on around him in the late 1840s and the early and middle 1850s in New York, Albany, Boston, Washington, and the Berkshires, in all of which places he lived or visited. Of the farther reaches of this world he would be aware through secondhand accounts, such as written observations in periodicals, newspapers, and books. Nearer at hand, he had direct access to the observations, gossip, and opinions of his friends, such as Evert Duyckinck, who was at the center of New York literary life, and Hawthorne, as well as to those of his relatives, such as his brothers Allan, the lawyer (and, earlier, Gansevoort, the Democratic politician and orator), his uncle Peter Gansevoort, who was an intimate of the New York Democratic leaders, and his father-in-law, Chief Justice Shaw, who was an Old-Line Whig and friend of the Boston Curtises and of the eminent Whig lawyer Choate—to name only the most likely possibilities. Moreover, Melville unquestionably had access to descriptions of the appearances of public figures and to sketches or daguerreotypes of most of them, to accounts of their speeches, and some public evidence of their roles and attitudes toward the "all important question" (of slavery), as George W. Curtis termed it, through the reading rooms and libraries that he frequented throughout this period of his life. There is no evidence that, in this period, Melville isolated himself *intellectually* from the political life of his country or of his two home states—New York and Massachusetts—although he did not participate in that life as a party-member or even as a citizen who voted at the polls. It is more likely that he was a keen observer of it, though a disinterested observer of its main issues, and he was perfectly capable, as *Mardi,* it will be seen, in particular demonstrates, of arguing on the several sides of most philosophical and political questions.

Melville's own immediate family tradition was primarily Democratic (though Federalist in its remoter days), yet not exclusively so. His father Allan Melvill, who died when Herman was eleven, was Federalist and aristocratic in spirit, capable of writing skeptically to his friend Lemuel Shaw of the *"Demon* (I will not say spirit) of party,"* as an evil thing.[2] His political acquaintances included Webster, Van Buren, and DeWitt Clinton.[3] After Allan Melvill's death in 1832, through his brother-in-law Peter Gansevoort's activities the family was connected to the New York State Democratic organization—the Albany Regency—that served Jackson and was ruled by its senator, and later president, Van Buren, by Governor Marcy, Senator Dix, Benjamin F. Butler, Croswell of the Albany *Argus* and other long-standing Democrats such as Governor William C. Bouck and "Prince" John Van Buren. Hershel Parker writes in his study of Melville's political milieux:

> After Allan Melvill's death in 1832, Gansevoort Melville and later Allan Jr., looked to the Jacksonian-Van Burenite Peter Gansevoort for political guidance, and for political influence when they were seeking political office (or when Allan was seeking office for the diffident Herman). Because of Peter Gansevoort, Herman Melville became nominally at least a Democrat.[4]

Both Herman and his brothers, Gansevoort and Allan, grew up socially acquainted with the New York Democratic political leaders, as well as with many of their Anti-Masonic and, later, Whig and Republican opponents, such as Governor Seward and his political and close personal friend Weed. When Melville's older brother Gansevoort, who had trained as a lawyer, reached the age of twenty-seven he preferred the excitements of Tammany politics to law, and after giving several remarkably successful speeches on the democratically popular issue of Irish Repeal he launched himself in the presidential campaign of 1844 as a "stump-speaker" for the Democracy. He traveled through New York, Pennsylvania, Ohio and other states of the Border and the West, speaking to mammoth crowds for hours at a time for Polk and Dallas, whose platform insisted upon the acquisition of Texas—which, it was generally assumed, would be as a slave state. As a reward for his labor, after considerable waiting and application, Gansevoort Melville received from Polk, via Secretary of State James Buchanan, a post as secretary of legation in London—where after serving only ten months he died of a brain fever in May 1846. Allan Melville ran for the New York State Assembly as a Hunker Democrat (after the Barnburner-Hunker split) in 1848, lost, and did not pursue further office.

Melville himself made numerous attempts to secure an appointive government office (such as Paulding, George Bancroft, Irving and Hawthorne had held) for which the letters written by family members and friends alluded to his family's Democratic connections when the official applied to—whether Polk, Buchanan, Marcy, Dix, Caleb Cushing or some other—was a Democrat. Yet, in his other applications for office he sought help from Whigs and later even from Republicans, including Weed, who was the chief Whig and Republican dispenser of political patronage in New York, and from the Free-Soil, and later Republican, Senator Charles Sumner of Massachusetts, Melville's state of residence from 1850 to 1863. Nearly always a letter was sought for him from Chief Justice Shaw, who had always been a close friend and financial supporter of the Melville family (and who paid for Melville's trip to Europe and the Levant in 1856–57).[5] So, too much cannot be made of the family's attempt to exploit the Democratic connections for Melville's benefit, while it is most probable that he rested his hopes for appointive office principally on his stature as an American fictionist of distinction—similar to Irving and Hawthorne. The only civilian government appointment that he ever received was not, as far as is known, the result of partisan political connections. A deputy inspectorship in the New York Custom House, which he held from 1866 to 1885, was the result of a personal friendship that he had struck up in Switzerland in 1857 (and renewed in 1866) with Henry Augustus Smythe, a New York merchant and banker, who was appointed collector of customs by Andrew Johnson in order to "remove incompetent people and put in competent ones."[6] In one of the few direct statements that Melville ever made about his own views, in the prose "Supplement" to his Civil War poems, *Battle-Pieces and Aspects of the War* (1866), he refers to himself as "one who never was a blind adherent" in that conflict, and he asks why, the war being over, "serviceable truth should keep cloistered because not partisan."[7] His friend Richard Lathers, New York insurance executive, South Carolina slave owner, active Democratic "accommodationist" in the winter of 1860–61, and brother-in-law of Allan Melville, wrote in his posthumous *Reminiscences* (1907) of conversations with Melville during the 1850s and 1860s in which Lathers listened "with intense pleasure to [Melville's] highly individual views of society and politics."[8]

Melville's extant letters, of which there are not many, since both he and his family burned most of them, do not contain expressions of his attitudes on politics—after a brief flurry of comment on American-British tensions in 1846 in a letter to Gansevoort in London.[9] Leon Howard observes of him in the late 1840s that "he had the interest of a firsthand observer in the operations of international foreign policy and a disillusioned dislike for American politicians and their demagoguery."[10] There is a possible reason for Melville's apparent silence in his letters of the 1850s on political matters, which has not previously been suggested. If he was, as I believe him to have been, interested in them at a time when for nearly all American men politics was— for good reason—an absorbing and deeply emotional interest, it is possible that he refrained from expressing his views in letters because they could not be easily and informally stated. His views were, possibly, too complex to be summed up in a relatively simple commitment to one party or another, although the times—especially from 1850 on—seemed to demand such a commitment. It was during this period that Northern and Northwestern public opinion was influenced with increasing power and weight by antislavery arguments and anti-Southern feeling in the press, the pulpit, and on the platform. As a result it shifted away from a previous commitment to the Constitutional tolerance of slavery in states where it had been established and from indifference to the problem of extension to an attitude of open detestation of slavery and fear of its extension—and of the black population with it— into new territories and states. Public opinion in the North and especially in Massachusetts, where Melville was living from 1850 on, was decidedly against the extension of slavery and apparently became fanatically so during the agitation over Kansas—abetted by the widespread influence of Greeley's *Tribune* in its weekly editions—and after the spectacular caning on 22 May 1856 of Massachusetts's own Senator Sumner at his Senate desk by Representative Preston Brooks of South Carolina. It is of this atmosphere that Emory Washburne, Whig governor of Massachusetts, said that, "It is not enough that you agree with them . . . you must say your creed in their words with their intonation and just when they bid you or they hang or burn you as a heretic."[11]

As a literary man, Melville's mind was disposed to eschew easy partisanships. Moreover, his school training in public speaking and in the debating societies probably gave him skills in argument on the various sides of a question.[12] This talent for argument *in utramque partem* and possibly a temperamental skepticism may have led him to react to the rise of strong sectional feeling on the slavery-extension issue by silence in his social communications, even while he meditated the best way that he, as a literary man of genius (as he believed himself to be), should respond on a question of engrossing and potentially tragic national implications.

Melville's earlier narratives, *Typee* (1846), *Omoo* (1847), *Redburn* (1849), and *White-Jacket* (1850) contain some scattered expressions on political topics. However, as Hershel Parker and other scholars of Melville observe, these are not usually to be taken as expressions of his own views, but rather as rhetorical exercises or "set pieces" on given topics—in the manner of the debating exercises in which he and his contemporary schoolfellows and debating society friends were trained. As Parker notes, "None of the major political 'set pieces' in these books can safely be taken as a record of one of Melville's deeply-held convictions."[13] *Mardi* (1849), his philosophical romance, makes extensive use of the philosophical dialogue with its exploration of the different sides of various philosophical, religious and political questions. In particular, it uses this method to explore directly contemporary politics, both domestic and foreign, in the dialogues and transparent national and regional allegorizations of chapters 145–168. Of *Mardi* he wrote his publisher in 1849 that it expressed "the peculiar thoughts & fancies of a Yankee upon politics & other matters"—the thoughts and fancies being very diverse indeed.[14] These chapters in *Mardi* and his earlier essays in comic political satire published in *Yankee Doodle* in 1847 deserve special treatment.

Melville's "Authentic Anecdotes of Old Zack" published in *Yankee Doodle* in seven installments in 1847 are interesting for several reasons. First, they show him writing directly on a contemporary political topic—the rising star of the Mexican War hero, General Zachary Taylor, as a possible president—even before it had been determined which party (Whig or Democratic) would capture him as its candidate. Second, the techniques that he uses, which are typical of the literary satires by other authors in *Yankee Doodle* and in the other comic periodicals, are mainly those of caricature of salient personal traits, parody of various styles (such as those of newspaper dispatches, of public speaking and writing, of medical language, and of Barnumesque advertising), and allusive side-thrusts at current topics of public interest to be found in rival periodicals and newspapers.[15] The humor, that is, is of a peculiarly public sort, not private or self-referential, and is dependent to a large extent upon a contemporary frame of reference—much of which has to be reconstructed by research into the events of the time upon which it is based. And third, the satirical attitude (which is light) and many of the details of the satire of Taylor resemble those of the accompanying graphic prints of Taylor and public figures associated with him.

It is evident that the "squibs" on Taylor represent an early dip by Melville into a world where literary humor and graphic humor on political topics met. In the United States as in Europe the emergence of journals with graphic political prints that share ideas, topics, and techniques with literary pieces seems to have coincided with periods of intense political activity—on the Continent, with the various revolutions in France, Germany, and Italy in the

1830s and 1840s, and in Great Britain with the rise of the Reform movements.[16] In this country the six most important though short-lived comic periodicals appeared coincidentally with the rise in political activity at the times of the presidential campaigns of 1848, 1852, 1856, and 1860. They were *Yankee Doodle* (1846–47), where Melville's "Anecdotes" on Taylor were published; *John-Donkey* (1848); the New York *Lantern* (*Diogenes Hys Lanterne*) (1852–53); *The Old Soldier* (1852); *Young America* (1856), which was renamed *Yankee Doodle; or Young America* (1856); and *Vanity Fair* (1859–63).[17] In these, along with prints and literary pieces which are nonpolitical, the staple materials for critical humor are the potential candidates and other public figures, especially newspaper editors engaging in politics. The historian of American political art, Frank Weitenkampf, writes that "During the fifties New York newspaper editors through their development of an acrimonious personal journalism, dominating personalities and vigorous writing became equally subject with the political bigwigs to pictorial lampooning."[18] Melville's own comic pieces on Taylor parody newspaper styles and are keyed to the political maneuvering by politicians and publicists prior to the 1848 election and use the same caricaturable aspects of Taylor's personality, appearance, and career as do the accompanying cartoons of him. As far as we know now, he did not write again for any of these periodicals (though he may have undiscovered pieces in them) but turned instead to write a direct response to the revolutions in Europe in 1848 and to several American political questions of the late 1840s, in *Mardi*.

A series of chapters in *Mardi* (chapters 145 through 168) form a commentary on contemporary and historical events, using literary caricatures of national, and regional types and of certain well known individuals, most of whom have been identified by Merrell Davis or other scholars.[19] Beginning with chapter 145, the narrator-hero Taji travels through the archipelago of Mardi (the world), where he is given an education in political history by King Media of Odo (a conservative benevolent aristocrat). They are accompanied in the royal canoe by Babbalanja (the philosopher), Mohi (the historian), and Yoomy (the poet), each of whom expresses a different point of view in a continuing symposium, or debate, upon the problems of the islands (nations) that they visit. Through the caricature of Great Britain as King Bello of the Hump (a physical trait derived possibly from the title page caricature of *Punch*) Melville comments on the imperial ambitions of the British, while he names as rivals of Bello, in Porpheero (Europe), the "chiefs" of the various European nations—such as Franko (France), Ibeereea (Spain), Latianna (Italy), Vatikanna (the Papacy), Tutoni (Germany), Muzkovi (Russia), Hapzaboro (Austria) and the rest. Each leader is caricatured in nationalist terms. For example, "the king of Franko" is a "small-framed, poodle-haired, fine, fiery gallant; finical in his tattooing; much given to the dance and glory" (p. 467), while the thirty-eight kings of Tutoni are "an earnest race; deep thinkers, deep drinkers; long pipes, long heads; their wise ones given to mystic cogitations, and consultations with the devil" (p. 467). Melville voices through both King Media and the historian Mohi criticisms of American vaingloriousness in the Revolution and the War of 1812, under the caricature of Vivenza (pp. 472, 469). Several chapters of commentary on England and Ireland in the 1840s include an individual caricature of the Irish politician Daniel O'Connell, as "Konno." He is, on the one hand, termed "humane and peaceable" and "a great man" by Babbalanja, while on the other hand, Mohi thinks him "a knave," contrasting views which show Melville's interest in exploring through diverse points of view the question of the character of public men.

The same rhetorical technique of expressing diverse points of view is used to handle the question of slavery in chapters 157–162, when the travelers visit Vivenza, disembarking first at a midpoint (Washington) to attend a "convocation of chiefs" (Congress) and then visiting in turn the North and the South. Melville first makes a broad satirical point about American inconsistency when King Media directs Mohi to read *both* the inscriptions on the arch over the statue of Vivenza's tutelar deity—a helmeted female (Columbia). Beside the larger inscription, which reads ". . . all-men-are-born-free-and-equal," there is "a small hieroglyphic" one hidden in a corner, which reads "Except-the-tribe-of-Hamo" (except men of African descent). Slavery is again noticed ironically when a man with a collar around his neck and red marks of stripes on his back is seen hoisting up a flag—"correspondingly striped" (p. 515). Yet in chapter 162, where they visit "the extreme south of Vivenza," Melville uses multiple points of view to explore the political problem of slavery in the South. As a man of feeling, the poet Yoomy expresses sorrow at the sight of "collared men toiling in trenches," and he invokes divine justice upon the men standing over them "armed with long thongs," and even Media, questioning one of the slaves, admits that he "has Oro [God] in his eye" and Media swears "he is a man." Yet, through Nulli, a caricature of Calhoun as "a cadaverous, ghost-like man . . . [with] wondrous eyes," several proslavery arguments are presented. Though all the visitors are appalled by these and are sympathetic to the oppressed, yet their considered responses to Mohi's gloomy hint of war ("These South Savannahs may yet prove battle-fields") differ widely from one another. While Yoomy would fight for the slaves' freedom, Media and Mohi would let "Vivenza speak" (perhaps an allusion to the Democratic doctrine of "popular sovereignty"), while Babbalanja the philosopher would not fight over the slavery issue, saying "Better present woes for some, than future woes for all," *i.e.* suggesting that it would be better to retain slavery for now than bring on war, possibly through insurrection, through civil conflict, or possibly through conflict between the North and an independent Southern slave empire. In a long discursive paragraph Babbalanja reiterates many of the contemporary Northern arguments for not agitating the slavery question, such as the following: "Humanity cries out against this vast enormity;—not one man knows a prudent remedy"; wisely judge the South, for slavery was indigenous with the origin of the Southern states; it is easy to criticize evil in others; slavery seems natural to the Southerner born in the system; not all "serfs" are unhappy; those who abuse the system will suffer in their consciences and many will die "damned"; and last, that "Time—all healing Time—Time, great Philanthropist!— Time must befriend these thralls!" Though passionate in his denunciation of slavery, Babbalanja, the philosophic exponent, would still leave the solution to the "future"—though it is all "hieroglyphics" (pp. 531–35).

Melville shows an interest, then, even before the 1850s in exploring political problems through dialogue expressing a multiplicity of views and through literary caricature of both stereotypes and individuals. In caricaturing individuals he uses the techniques of selected physical details and of parody of speech style. For example, the Whig Senator Webster appears in chapter 158 as Saturnina, characterized by his extraordinary forehead, as Webster was in most contemporary descriptions and in graphic prints. His "one calm grand forehead among those of this mob of chieftains" (senators) is compared to the dome of St. Peter's, to an avalanche, and to Popocatepetl (p. 515). Another senator, Alanno of Hio-Hio, has been identified as William Allen of Ohio (1803–1879), a Jacksonian Democratic expansionist and later governor of Ohio, whom Melville satirizes for his "lunatic" oratory, minutely parodying Allen's speaking style—a bombastic compound of mixed metaphors, solecisms, and poor grammar. Allen is described as "a tall, gaunt warrior . . . with a beak like a buzzard; long dusty locks; and his hands full of headless arrows"—all traits that accord with descriptions of William Allen (pp. 516–18). [20] Likewise, the caricature of Calhoun in chapter 162 is based on descriptions of his appearance, personality, style and ideas. [21] The arguments Nulli offers in defense of "serfdom" in Southern Vivenza parody those of Calhoun. For example, Melville exaggerates Calhoun's opinion of the inferiority of the black man to an explicit denial of his humanity: "Their ancestors may have had [souls]; but their souls have been bred out of their descendants." Moreover, Nulli's bitter response to the criticisms of Media, Mohi, Yoomy and Babbalanja clearly reflects the typical Southern response to criticism as it became embodied in Calhoun as a symbolic figure of defense. The visitors are, he says, "Incendiaries! . . . firebrands, to light the flame of revolt" and they should "Go back to Odo [Media's land], and right her wrongs," for "these serfs are happier than thine" and happier than they would be if free (pp. 532–33)—all remarks demonstrating Melville's close attention to the long North-South argument in the 1840s.

Likewise, two other minor characters not previously identified by scholars of *Mardi* reveal Melville's technique of literary caricature by means of recognizable physical description and by allusion to roles or events in which a public figure is involved. A "white-headed old man with a tomahawk in his hand" who sits "perched high upon an elevated dais" and who oversees the oratorical tumult would appear to be the vice-president presiding over the Senate and holding in his hand the gavel (p. 517). At the time of writing *Mardi* this man would be George M. Dallas (1792–1864), who was distinctly white-haired in portraits and prints of the period.[22] Likewise, in chapter 160, which appears from its title—"A Scene in the Land of Warwicks, or King-makers"—to be referring to presidential politicking in the period 1844–48, there is a caricature of Znobbi, who boastfully claims to have made "our great chief" (President Polk) what he is, tweaks the chief's nose, and demands equality ("All kings here—all equal"). He is caught in the act of stealing a pouch, for which he is tied to a tree (pp. 521–22). This previously unidentified caricature fits in several respects (though not all) the personality and career of Gideon Pillow (1806–1878), law partner, close friend, and political supporter of Polk, who made Pillow a brigadier-general in the Mexican War. Just as Znobbi claims credit for "making" his chief "what he is" and tweaks his nose to show his familiarity with him, so Pillow exaggerated his own importance and boasted widely that he was the man who engineered Polk's dark-horse nomination at the Democratic convention in Baltimore in 1844 and presumed much upon his friendship with the president.[23]

Besides being interested in satirizing foreign nations, domestic politics, and Southern slavery, Melville displays in this sequence in *Mardi* a close interest in and knowledge of New York State political movements. In *Melville's "Mardi": A Chartless Voyage,* Merrell R. Davis shows that the visit of the travelers in the North of Vivenza, in chapter 161, to a "great valley," where they hear many speeches from "the stumps of trees," refers to events at the Buffalo Free-Soil convention in August 1848. Davis suggests that the "fiery youth mounted upon the bowed shoulders of an old man, his sire," who reads a speech from a written scroll, refers specifically to "Prince" John Van Buren, who managed that convention for the benefit of his father's ambitions (pp. 524–30). Davis does not, however, show that the speech reflects John Van Buren's own political views and it still remains somewhat of a puzzle.[24] Hershel Parker reaffirms Davis's general interpretation of the allusions in this chapter and while stressing the Burkean conservatism of the speech read from the scroll denies that this—or any of the political views expressed in the sequence of chapters on the geographical regions of the world—represent Melville's own views. Melville has, he writes, "in the political chapters of *Mardi* declared his independence of the political factions and parties to which his acquaintances, friends, and relatives were so vehemently allying themselves." It may be concluded, then, that in *Mardi,* although Melville focuses his critique upon contemporary political events and movements of the summer and fall of 1848, as Davis carefully demonstrates, the rationale of his critique does not ally him with any particular partisan point of view. As Parker concludes, he was more interested in developing "an original—personal—set of political opinions and values."[25]

3

Melville's "Graphic" Methods

The hypothesis that *The Confidence-Man* might be a satire specifically on the contemporary political situation and on certain of its principal public figures—including the literary figures of Emerson, Thoreau, and Poe, in their political roles—has led to an exploration of the political history of the period with the hope that it might prove fruitful in well-substantiated models for Melville's gallery of characters and in themes for his indictment of philosophical optimism about human nature and Nature itself. The cases made in the following chapters for individual identifications naturally vary in their strengths, depending upon the amount and quality of evidence that has been accumulated. Some are very strong indeed. About some there are hesitations and in some cases alternate, but similar, possibilities are offered. It seems likely that some of the very difficult cases and some of the minor figures may always remain problematic because of the scarcity of evidence. But for the major characters the evidence is frequently profuse and will probably be added to by future research. Materials for research have been the general histories of the period, studies of the political history of the antislavery movement, of the founding of the Republican party, of the secession movement, analyses of the "coming of the Civil War," and individual biographies of the men and women important in the various political movements—statesmen, politicians, clergymen, writers, jurists, and especially journalists of all parties. These secondary sources have been necessary in order to correlate the physical description Melville gives of each character and his or her action with the appearance and actions of an historical model. Likewise necessary have been the primary writings of the individuals themselves in order to discern their political ideas and attitudes as well as their stylistic mannerisms both of oral and written speech. These sources, which include the poetry of some of the claimed models, are necessary in order to demonstrate how Melville is parodying the style of the person.

Because Melville's method of caricature is uniform in nearly all instances, the same method of detection can be used consistently. First, he describes the physical appearance (face, height, complexion, or some other obvious physical traits), perhaps the age, the clothing, the manner of speech, the gestures each makes. Then he suggests the personality of the character through characterizing adjectives—usually repeated—and speech idiom.

Through the character's speeches he subtly parodies the rhetorical and stylistic habits of the person being caricatured. In some instances he parodies, mocks, or alludes to the man's ideas or the themes of his published or publicly presented speeches. Melville's method of literary caricature is so very clear and well established in Oliver's work on Emerson and in Hayford's on Poe that it is only a matter for wonder that someone has not sooner investigated its implications for all the other characters in *The Confidence-Man*.

Extremely helpful has been research into the graphic political prints of the period—an area not previously utilized by any scholar working on *The Confidence-Man*. Many of the most important figures on the public scene were depicted by artists working for the comic periodicals and for publishers of prints, such as Currier & Ives, at the same time as they were satirized in a few literary pieces. As was shown in chapter 2, Melville was already in his "Authentic Anecdotes of Old Zack" quite familiar with the techniques of comic emphasis upon readily identifiable physical traits, with parody of speech style and with ironic emphasis upon moral and mental faults, and the themes of his satires are precisely reflected in (or *they* reflect) the cartoons of Taylor in *Yankee Doodle* done by graphic artists. Both graphic and literary satire focused upon the same elements of personal appearance and character in the public figures that came under their scrutiny. Just as John Dixon Hunt has noted of Charles Dickens's early work, that his vision was "conditioned" by graphic art and that he extended into literary form "topics, treatment, and attitudes of popular engravings," so does Melville in certain specific ways adapt techniques of popular prints, as may be seen in the stereotypical and individual caricatures in the political chapters of *Mardi* and will be seen in the treatment of the characters in *The Confidence-Man*.[1] Some of the strongest cases for identification that will be presented in the following chapters utilize graphic prints from comic periodicals and separate lithographs.

There are three principal techniques used in the graphic political prints that I have examined for this study which have proven of value in the interpretation of Melville's satire in *The Confidence-Man*. They are (1) the use of a particularized setting or situation to make a satirical point; (2) the identification of a type or of an individual by some element or elements of his or her physical appearance or manner of speech; (3) the use of theatrical or mythical prototypes to make a satirical point.

The use of a certain setting or situation, usually merely sketched in, to represent a political situation as the printmaker (or his patron) wished it to be seen is an important technique of the political prints associated with American politics almost from the beginning of the electoral system. Typical examples are: depiction of a journey (by boat, horse, on foot, or by other modes) to represent a political party's effort to achieve its goal (plates 14, 15,

17, and 22); a solicitation scene—either begging or entertaining—to represent a political campaign of speechmaking and newspaper editorializing and reporting (plates 3, 7, 20, 23, and 24); a dining or drinking table as a setting for a political confrontation of opponents (plates 2 and 21); last, a competition in sports or games (a race, cockfight, prizefight, cardgame, hunt, or other) to represent a political competition (plates 2 and 4). For example, "The 'Mustang' Team" (1856) uses a journey by horse and cart to represent the Frémont campaign (plate 15), while another, "Col. Fremont's Last Grand Exploring Expedition in 1856" (1856), combines a foot journey with travel by horseback, showing the Republican leader Seward on foot leading Frémont, who rides the "Abolition Nag," toward "Salt River"—the usual symbol for defeat (plate 14). An anti-Republican campaign poster of 1856 is based on the idea of advertising a steamer named the "*Black Republican*" scheduled to depart 4 November 1856 for "Salt River." The widely circulated and reproduced lithograph of the Republican party leaders in 1860, " 'The Irrepressible Conflict' or the Republican Barge in Danger," in which Seward is being tossed from the boat (guided by Lincoln) to save it, is another of many examples of the use of this image (plate 22).[2]

Similarly, the *Fidèle*'s voyage, like that of a vessel in a graphic political print, may be interpreted with a political meaning. Its journey with its politically mixed group of passengers from St. Louis to Cairo, Illinois (the last port mentioned in *The Confidence-Man*) does not, however, it will be argued, represent the journey of only one party group as the graphic prints most often do, but rather of several of the opposing political contenders (and some of their forerunners) in a vessel that zigzags from bank to bank to take on or unload passengers and goods. If the reader recalls that the *Fidèle* in so doing touches alternately upon free-state land in Illinois and upon slave-state land in Missouri, he may perceive a "pictorial" representation of the political situation in 1856: a polity veering between one party that does not favor the expansion of slavery into new territories and states and another party that does favor slavery and its extension. I believe that Melville intended the reader to "read" the voyage of the *Fidèle* down the Mississippi with this general setting in mind, just as a print-viewer would "read" the image of a journey by boat, horseback, on foot, or in some vehicle as a political situation in a political print of this period. Furthermore, the author by placing his cast of characters on a vessel that alternately touches upon free soil and slave soil may be seen to retain an authorial party neutrality and is allowed to let his characters argue on the various sides of the questions at issue.

The use of a scene of solicitation—either begging or entertaining—is very common in prints throughout the period of our concern. For example, an early print, "Political Jugglers Losing Their Balance" (1840) portrays Van

Buren and his supporters, Francis P. Blair, Sr., editor of the *Globe*, and Amos Kendall, his postmaster-general, as a juggling act and another, "The Captain & Corporal's Guard" (1841?) shows Tyler on stilts (plate 3). Several prints use a scene of tightrope walking, as in a circus, to depict a political situation—for example, "Patent Balancing by an Amateur" (1848), on Greeley, and "Experiments on the Tight Rope" (1852), on the efforts of Seward and others to raise General Winfield Scott to the presidency. Another, "Presidential Trio," in *Young America* in 1856, shows all three presidential candidates in blackface performing as minstrels (plate 20).[3] This kind of "show" scene or situation, of which there are many examples during the 1860 campaign satirizing the Republicans (plates 23 and 24) forms the basis, it will be argued, for the important scene in chapter 3 of *The Confidence-Man* in which the "negro cripple," Black Guinea, first appears carrying a tambourine and "shuffling about" to make music to entertain the passengers. He raises "mirth" among them and collects "pennies" from them. He offers a further opportunity for "*diversion* and charity" when, "like an elephant," he offers to catch coppers in his mouth. Just as Black Guinea both entertains and begs, so in many prints politicians and editors are depicted as entertainers and beggars, and I believe that Melville intends his readers to "read" this scene in a way similar in its methods to those used in "reading" a graphic print. Other prints that aid in the interpretation of this scene will be described when the character of Black Guinea is treated in chapter 4.

The use of a dining table or a wine table—an eating or drinking scene—to represent the confrontation of political opponents has an important English model in James Gillray's famous print, "The Plumb-Pudding in Danger; or State Epicures Taking un Petit Souper" (1805), in which Prime Minister William Pitt and Napoleon Bonaparte carve up the world on a plate between them. Nearer in time to our period is John Leech's "The Old 'Un and the Young 'Un," in *Punch* during the Crimean War (1854–56), showing the Emperors of Austria and Russia genially dividing a bottle of port wine (punning on "port-Porte"—for Turkey) between them, just as Charlie Noble and Frank Goodman divide a bottle of port wine in chapters 29–35 of *The Confidence-Man*.[4] Such prints, it will be argued, lie as graphic models behind the several conversations that take place between Noble, whom I identify as a caricature of William Lowndes Yancey, representing the South, and Goodman, a caricature of Henry Ward Beecher, representing the North (see chapter 10). A political problem, the relationship between the slave states and the free states, is depicted as a problem of "boon companionship" between two very different men who meet and try to establish a friendship over drinks, just as in the prints two groups or two nations might be depicted as two men meeting over drinks or food.

Competition in a sport or a game, such as a race, a cockfight, a prizefight, a cardgame, or a hunt, as a representation of political competition, is the most common of all physical settings in the prints that I have seen.[5] "The Man Wot Drives the Constitution" (1844) shows a race among presidential candidates (plate 4). Amusingly, "The Great Presidential Race of 1856" shows a race among a goose, ridden by the Know-Nothing and Whig candidate Fillmore, Buchanan as a buck, and Frémont on horseback. Also during the 1856 campaign a print that puns upon "Buck = Buch-anan" depicts Buchanan as a buck being hunted by his opponents ("The Great American Buck Hunt of 1856").[6] Although none of these kinds of competition form any particular setting for major scenes in *The Confidence-Man,* still it may be observed that the narrative as a whole in its dialogue takes the form of a series of debates or contests between opposing speakers, who argue for and against a given proposition—that mankind or Nature is to be trusted—a kind of public competition that was very popular in the mid-nineteenth century both as entertainment and as serious effort. Melville's age was one of debating societies and clubs, membership in one of which formed an important part of his own education, as noted earlier. The famous series of debates between Lincoln and Stephen Douglas for the senatorship of Illinois in 1858 grew out of the background of great public interest in seeing and hearing two public men debate the major contemporary political issues. The series of disputations between Melville's Confidence Men and their antagonists mirrors, it will be seen, the ongoing national contest between opposing political candidates and opposing "creeds" for the "confidence" of different kinds of voters and supporters. The fact that competition in the form of argumentative debate is the primary form of structure *within* the scenes of *The Confidence-Man* reflects, I think, the graphic habit of the period of portraying political competition between party and party or between person and person within a party in terms of a race, a fight, a game, or a hunt. It may further be noted that Melville does evoke the image of hunting for a large portion of the *Fidèle's* passengers in the important introductory descriptive passage in chapter 2, when he writes of the presence of "farm-hunters and fame-hunters; heiress-hunters, gold-hunters, buffalo-hunters, bee-hunters, happiness-hunters, truth-hunters, and still keener hunters after these hunters."

A second major technique of graphic political prints which Melville shares with them is that of identifying a type or an individual by certain recognizable elements of appearance or occasionally of speech. This technique had been used by American printmakers from the beginning. Certain men, who were on the public scene for long periods of time, received in cartoons fixed identifying tags that alluded to some striking attribute or some well-known event in their careers. For example, the label "50 cents" on a rear trouser pocket always meant that the figure represented Governor Marcy, the New York Democratic leader (1786–1857), regardless of how well or badly drawn the figure might be, because he had been widely ridiculed for submitting a bill to the state government for fifty cents to mend his trousers (plate 12). Jackson's spectacles, top hat, and distinctive long coat were always recognizable, as well as his striking shock of hair. Likewise, a figure wearing a bedraggled coat, battered hat, disarrayed tie, and sloppy or mismatched boots always meant Greeley, although these details might be supplemented by a careful likeness of his rounded high forehead, his halo of fair hair, his stooping posture and his "baker's knee" (plates 6, 15, 22, and 23).[7] Other, less readily caricaturable public figures, even when drawn as likenesses based on sketches, daguerreotypes, or paintings, are sometimes difficult to identify today, although contemporary reproductions or descriptions can help to narrow down the field of possibilities. Less common, but occasionally used by artists is the imitation of speech mannerisms and style in the speeches printed in the "balloons" issuing from the mouths of the speakers or printed in the captions. An example is the parody of Webster's characteristically ornate style in "A Piercing Piece of Loco Foco Hocus Pocus" (1852).[8]

Besides using obviously caricaturable physical traits, American cartoons in the period 1835–60 frequently attempt to depict their subjects with faces that are intended to be realistic representations, while the bodies may be caricatured, sterotypical, realistic, or altogether unrealistic—as in the depiction of animal bodies. The realistic depiction of facial and in some cases of bodily traits for the purposes of political commentary was the innovation of the English artist, John Doyle (1797–1868), and was continued by his son, Richard Doyle, and by other artists. It owed its popularity as a method to the invention of the daguerreotype and the consequent increased possibility of general recognition of famous faces through that medium. John Doyle's technique of catching an actual likeness and using it without exaggeration apparently caught on with American graphic artists immediately, so that during the Jacksonian-Van Buren administrations and later they used it in many cartoons.[9] This artistic convention accounts for the curious (to our eyes) prints in which one sees a more or less realistic depiction of the face of an American politician, based on published daguerreotypes, attached to the body, for example, of a horse (plates 4, 14, 15), an ass, a bird, a fox (plates 4 and 8), a monkey (plate 7), a dog, a rat (plate 16), or even to a stickman made of rails, as in Frank Bellew's cartoon of Lincoln as "A 'Rail' Old Western Gentleman."[10] Melville does not, in *The Confidence-Man*, use the technique of animal bodies, although he does use, perhaps in a way related to the graphic technique, animal imagery frequently to characterize his figures. More importantly, he uses the technique which was John Doyle's innovation in the history of graphic art of selecting certain realistic details of his subject by which to indicate his or her identity. When Melville mentions a physical trait of a character, such as a "ruddy" or an "untanned" complexion, a "broad brow," "fair" hair, "blue" eyes, a "beaming eye," a "gimlet eye," a "sharp nose," a "shaved chin," a "waving hand," a "baker's knee," badly cut clothing, "tattered" clothing, a "cold" expression, or something similar, the particular trait can be linked directly to the appearance of his subject as he or she would be known to contemporaries, or to representations by daguerreotype, painting, or print, or to descriptions of the person written in the period. His descriptions of physical traits are, then, more in the style of the prints of John Doyle and his imitators than in that of the more typical caricaturist of earlier and later periods, who would seize upon some one or two physical traits and exaggerate them for the purpose of satire. Melville, like Doyle, usually relies upon several selected details of accurate physical description of his subjects for their depiction, while he occasionally uses exaggeration—more in the traditional manner of caricature—in depicting some of the speech habits and mannerisms of his subjects. Caricatural exaggeration of speech habits will be seen especially in his parodies of Theodore Parker's use of statistics, of Weed's rambling editorial style, of Francis P. Blair's countrified speech, of Sumner's latinate oratory, of Thomas Hart Benton's repeated senatorial "Sir," of Greeley's obsequious expressions, and of Beecher's anecdotal rhetoric.

The third technique of the graphic prints which has proven useful in reading Melville's meaning is the adaptation of theatrical and mythical characters to make a satirical point (plates 1, 4, 5, 6, 7, 9, 18, 20, 23, and 28). It seems most probable that Melville's inspiration to use the Harlequin theatrical stereotype as the basis for a new trickster type—the Confidence Man—came from his observation of theatrical performances and of their structure and characterization, yet the idea of using the theatrical type for satire on political figures was not, it may be surmised, uninfluenced by his observation of Harlequin's parallel uses in graphic prints (and in humorous satirical articles) almost as a cliché for the changeable politician or of the "party spirit" itself (plates 4 and 7).[11]

Another theatrical source for characterization and setting in the political graphic prints of the period are Shakespeare's plays, which were quite familiar to American audiences—if not always in their original forms. For example: "The Hurly-Burly Pot" (1850) showing Wilmot, Garrison, Calhoun, and Greeley as duncelike witches (plate 6) and "A Proslavery Incantation Scene, or Shakespeare Improved" (1856) showing Buchanan with other Democrats as the witches from *Macbeth* gathered around a cauldron of Free-Soil "trouble."[12] Melville does not, so far as I can presently see, use Shakespeare's plays in the formation of his scenes or in his characterizations, but Polonius from *Hamlet* and the merry rogue Autolycus from *The Winter's Tale* are the topics of an extended discussion in chapter 30 between Noble and Goodman, the possible political implications of which I discuss in that section.

From popular mythology the most consistently adapted figure in American political prints of this period is that of the Devil from the history of demonology and witchcraft—obviously because of the easily recognized connotations of evil—so usefully applied to one's political opponents (plates 1, 3, 6, and 28). The Devil appears early in American prints in the well-known "Mad Tom in a Rage" (1801?), in which he urges Jefferson to pull down the pillars of the federal government. During the 1830s in D. C. Johnston's "A Late Student," Duff Green, editor of the *United States Telegraph,* is portrayed teaching the Devil to lie better than Autolycus or Mercury, while in several pro-Jackson prints, the Devil is used to caricature "Nick" Biddle in Jackson's battles with the United States Bank. He appears to make the point that Locofocoism is worse than he is in "The Death of Locofocoism" (1840). Bennett has his cloven hooves in "The Captain & Corporal's Guard" (1841). He lies behind the witchcraft imagery of "The Hurly Burly Pot" (1850). (See plates 1, 3, and 6.) The Democrats worship the Devil (slavery) in "The Position of the Democratic Party in 1852." During the Civil War, in the work of Adalbert J. Volck, the German-born Southern artist, demonic imagery is used extensively for connotations of evil as in "The Worship of the North," where Republican leaders are caricatured worshipping a demonic figure, and in "Writing the Emancipation Proclamation," where Lincoln is surrounded by demonic symbols.[13] Melville's consistent implication that the Confidence Man—in each of his disguises—is a demonic agent—perhaps the Devil himself—is treated as the book's central theme by Elizabeth Foster and John Shroeder, while Hershel Parker regards it as the "standard line of interpretation."[14] This seems also to me to be the case. So then, if the Confidence Man himself and his actions are taken to be "allegorizations" or "symbols" of the Devil and his actions, and if, as I shall attempt to demonstrate, the Confidence Men and their antagonists allude to certain persons in Melville's historical context, then it may seem reasonable to suppose that Melville was adapting the habit of the graphic political prints of using the myth of the Devil to make a satirical commentary upon the political actors and actions of his period. The analogues in graphic political satire and this tradition of political commentary were certainly known to him and his audience.

Other less easily categorizable techniques of graphic art which are analogous to Melville's methods will appear in the course of the discussion of the individual characters in the following chapters. In particular, there is the figure of Black Guinea, who, as the stereotypical "Negro" of graphic prints, carries with him an allusion to the political issue of black slavery, as did the figure of a black person (whether man, woman, boy, or baby) or the quality of blackness in the graphic prints (plates 10, 13, 19, 20, 22, 23, and 24). Other stereotypes that will be taken up are those of the Southern "slave-driver" and the Eastern big city rough called the "B'Hoy" (plate 18), both of whom appear in prints and, likewise, on the stage. All of these graphic techniques, then, used in the depiction of individuals and of types, and the use of certain settings for political significance will contribute to the present interpretation of Melville's meaning.

Further study of these materials as well as of the theatrical materials and of earlier literary satire in American and English periodicals and books should further clarify our understanding of this difficult work. The relationship of *The Confidence-Man* to earlier American literary satire on political themes remains to be explored. It may be that Melville is carrying on a major theme of Federalist political satire in questioning the notion of the natural goodness of mankind. We do not know whether he owned or read any of the Federalist satirists such as John Quincy Adams, Josiah Quincy, Thomas Green Fessenden, Joseph Dennie, Timothy Dwight, or Oliver Wolcott. However this group share some of his attitudes.[15] During the period 1853–56, Melville's marginalia reveal that he was reading the great English satirists—Dryden and Pope—as well as Cervantes' *Don Quixote* and Irving's *Works* and Byron's—which would include their satirical pieces. He also read and annotated approvingly the satires of Charles Churchill in the Tooke edition of 1854.[16]

4

The First Two Confidence Men (the Deaf-Mute and Black Guinea) and Two Antagonists (the Barber and the Drover)

The Deaf-Mute

In the opening chapter of *The Confidence-Man* the Deaf-Mute appears on deck. As an American type he is the itinerant evangelical preacher or missionary. His "cream-colored" clothing and his message-bearing actions, besides linking him to the Pierrot mask of theatrical tradition (see Chapter 13) function also as specific allusions to two men associated with the origin of the antislavery movement in America. His "white fur hat" with a "long fleecy nap" and his suit of "cream-colors" (yellowish-white, the color of undyed wool) and traveling habits allude to the peculiar dress and "ascetic travel"—a Quaker means of self-discipline—of John Woolman (1720–1772), the eighteenth-century American Quaker preacher and antislavery advocate, while other details of appearance, his deafness, his nonresistance under persecution, and his itinerant apostleship in Missouri and other parts of the West allude to Benjamin Lundy (1789–1839), the Quaker founder of the very early antislavery periodical *The Genius of Universal Emancipation,* whose most famous disciple was William Lloyd Garrison. The *Journal* (1774) of John Woolman appeared in an English edition in 1840 and was at the time highly praised by Charles Lamb and by Carlyle, while the less positively disposed Governor Sterling Price of Missouri blamed Woolman for the origin of the antislavery movement. In his *Journal* Woolman relates how he decided to avoid using clothing that had been dyed, both because the source of dye was indigo produced by West Indian slave labor and because the dye itself and the process of dyeing seemed to him unclean. On conscientious scruples he wore a white, undyed beaver fur hat and undyed wool coat and breeches, and natural-colored stockings. His unusual clothing was noted and caused a disturbance in his church.[1] Whether Lundy wore undyed clothing in imitation of Woolman's scruples I have not been able to determine.

Descriptions of Lundy, of his career and his personality, and of how his career was regarded by the public strongly suggest that he is the historical person caricatured in Melville's Deaf-Mute. In Thomas Earle's biography, *The*

Life, Travels, and Opinions of Benjamin Lundy (1847), Lundy is described as "slightly under the middle size, of a slender form, light and rather sandy complexion and hair, a sanguine temperament," suggesting the Deaf-Mute's "fair" cheek and "flaxen" hair, while his portrait in Earle shows his beardlessness, which is reflected in the Deaf-Mute's "downy chin." Of his hearing, Earle writes, "He was afflicted with considerable difficulty of hearing," caused by overwork as a child. The Deaf-Mute displays his deafness when he fails to hear the two porters (p. 4). Of Lundy's personality, Earle writes that "His manners were gentle and very unassuming," and that his half-sister said that he had a "kind disposition and engaging manners," was "gentle and tender," and had "gentle and mild manners." His mental energy was "somewhat impeded in usefulness by a deficiency in hearing," yet "for many years [he] stood the buffeting of pro-slavery" attacks.[2] William Lloyd Garrison called him "weak and contemptible" in physique, like St. Paul.[3] William Goodell in *Slavery and Anti-Slavery* (1852), writing of Lundy's labors and travels, describes him as "small in stature, of feeble health, afflicted with deafness," and as "a feeble man, a quiet, unresisting Quaker."[4] These reported characteristics of Lundy seem to be reflected in Melville's descriptive terms: "mildly inoffensive," "quiet," "humble," "gentle and jaded," "unresisting," "simpleton," "deaf," and "not entirely ignorant of his place."

Lundy was a New Jerseyan who traveled extensively, even more than Woolman earlier, in his colonization and antislavery endeavors, propagating his views mainly through his writings. His first appearances in print were in Ohio, where he wrote for and coedited *The Philanthropist* at Mt. Pleasant in 1816, and in St. Louis, in 1819, at the time of the Missouri question and the formulation of the Missouri Compromise, where he published articles against slavery in newspapers and gained some reputation. He founded his own paper, *The Genius of Universal Emancipation,* in January 1821 at Mt. Pleasant and continued to publish it there and elsewhere, carrying his type with him on his travels, until his death in 1839. Earle's biography relates, on the basis of Lundy's own journals, that he traveled literally thousands of miles up and down the Mississippi and Ohio Rivers and on land, mainly on foot and alone—like the Deaf-Mute "unaccompanied by friends"—throughout the free and slave states, Haiti, Canada, the territories, Texas and Mexico, where in the extreme heat he traveled often by night. The Deaf-Mute's suit, "tossed . . . almost linty, as if, traveling night and day from some far country beyond the prairies, he had long been without the solace of a bed," may allude to Lundy's Texan and Mexican travels in particular.

Although partially and increasingly deaf, Lundy was not mute; he lectured on his travels. Yet he never enjoyed making speeches and thought of himself more as an itinerant editor than as an orator. He made his mark through the written word, as the Deaf-Mute does with the writing on his slate. He traveled sometimes under an assumed name and "in disguise in the Southern country as [his] life would otherwise have been endangered."[5] Whether placards similar to that posted on the *Fidèle* concerning "a mysterious imposter, . . . recently arrived from the East," were posted for Lundy (as they were for George Thompson, the English abolitionist) in the Southern states I have not determined, but it is possible they were. The detailed record of his travels, with a minimum of baggage and almost without friends, like the Deaf-Mute, up and down the Mississippi and Ohio Rivers, and his several journeys to Haiti, Canada, Texas, and Mexico in search of lands for African-American colonization, present the reader of Earle's biography with the picture of a man "persistent" and "persevering," indeed, like Melville's character, yet "gentle" in manner under very adverse, often exasperating, if not hostile conditions. Earle contrasts Lundy's gentleness and mildness with Garrison's acerbity, writing:

> Alone, often on foot, he encountered fatigue, hunger and exposure, the frost and snows of winter, the rains and scorching sun of summer, the contagion of pestilence, and the miasmatic effluvia of insalubrious regions—ever pressing onward toward the attainment of the great object to which he had dedicated his existence.[6]

Earle writes—not quite accurately—that Lundy was the first to publish an antislavery periodical and to lecture on slavery in the United States. More suggestive of Lundy's influence is Goodell's account of Lundy's influence upon John Quincy Adams's antislavery efforts in Congress: "It was chiefly to communications from Benjamin Lundy that John Quincy Adams was indebted for those astounding disclosures concerning the Texas plot with which he so suddenly electrified Congress and the nation, in 1836."[7] Lundy had met and corresponded with Adams as early as 1828 and furnished him in 1836 with information about American activity in Texas which was useful to Adams in his fight in Congress against the annexation of Texas.[8] Lundy's essays on Texas, published as the *Origin and True Causes of the Texas Revolution Commenced in the Year 1835* (1836) were widely circulated and influential in the battle against the extension of slavery.[9]

Throughout the opening scene the Deaf-Mute responds as a Quaker, or a "non-resistant"; even more specifically Melville shows him "thrust . . . aside . . . not without epithets and some buffets," carrying his message amid "stares" and "jeers" (pp. 3–4). Besides being typical of the usually violent public response to early antislavery advocates—Quakers and others—the public reaction on the *Fidèle* to Melville's "stranger" may possibly be a specific

41

allusion to the occasion in Baltimore in 1828 or 1829 when Lundy, unre-
sistingly, was "assaulted and nearly killed" by a slave-trader for commenting
on his conduct. [10]

I have not found that Lundy was particularly fond of quoting from I Corinthians 13 (the *Genius'* mottos were *Fiat justitia, Ruat coelum,* and the second
sentence of the Declaration of Independence, "We hold these truths . . ."),
but his doctrine generally seems to have been founded on the early Quaker
humanitarian ethic, emphasis upon unworldly values, and pacificism, which
were in turn founded on selected passages in the New Testament.

Lundy's death and disappearance from the antislavery agitation scene by
1839 seems to be alluded to in the "epitaphic comments"—some positive,
some negative—of the *Fidèle's* passengers upon the sleeping "lamb-like figure"
of the Deaf-Mute. Later abolitionists, who rejected Lundy's interest in colonization while praising his early efforts for emancipation, tended to minimize
his continuing relevance to their cause. Tributes to him at the founding of
the American Anti-Slavery Society in 1833 seemed "eulogies for a dead hero
rather than praise for an active comrade." [11] The various comments of the
Fidèle's passengers in chapter 2 may be interpreted as typical of the conflicting
opinions of Americans of the period upon the originators of the abolition
movement in America—including both Woolman and Lundy. For example,
a typical early newspaper critic in Providence, Sylvester Southworth, attacked
Lundy as "a visionary" and a "zealot" working for a quixotic cause, while on
the other hand he called him also "self-seeking," "fond of fame," and "intellectually incapable" of the work he was attempting. Southworth even
charged him with being a "secret agent for certain unspecified politicians." [12]
On the other hand, William Goodell wrote in 1852 of Lundy, "Thus does
Divine Providence raise up and direct the voluntary instruments of its high
designs," and saw him as "of indomitable purpose, perseverance, faith, courage, patience, self-denial, endurance," and as "a pioneer in the cause," concluding, "Such are the labors of men who commence moral revolutions, to
be completed by others after they have gone off the stage." [13] A man who
could be described in such terms might well be ambiguously viewed, as
Melville's persistent and then dreaming stranger is, as "Jacob dreaming at
Luz," and a forerunner to more active agents, and also as "Humbug," or
"Escaped convict, worn out with dodging" (p. 6).

Some verbal puns assume significance, if my general contention is correct
that the Deaf-Mute in his specific topical implications is a caricature of Lundy
as the originator of the journalistic agitation of the antislavery movement,
and, in his broader implications, of Woolman and other Quakers as founders
of the movement. These minute verbal allusions to Lundy may be noted: the
pun on "Lun-*lune*" in "lunacy of the stranger" (p. 3), the epithets "Moon-

calf" and "Kind of daylight Endymion" (p. 6), and possible puns alluding to Woolman, in the descriptive terminology involving "fleece" and "lamb." If the Deaf-Mute is, as I believe him to be, the first appearance of the "mysterious imposter" of the placard-notice, who is "quite an original genius," there may be an intended allusion to Lundy's periodical, the *Genius of Universal Emancipation,* in the word "genius." Last, there may also be an allusion in the sentence, "Where the wolves are killed off the foxes increase," to George Fox, one of the founders of the Society of Friends. [14]

The Barber William Cream

While the Deaf-Mute is presenting his chalked message of charity and confidence in human nature and is repulsed by most of the passengers, the *Fidèle*'s Barber William Cream opens his shop and hangs out his "No trust" sign. As the first of the antagonists to the Confidence Man (and one who appears again in chapters 42–43, where he is temporarily cheated), he is the forerunner here of a series of men, each of whom owns some kind of property (in the form of cash usually) or is commercial, and is in some way solicited by the Confidence Man. As an American type, the Barber does not differ greatly from the European Barber as he might appear, for example, in the comic theatrical or operatic representations of Figaro, whose skepticism, worldliness, and loquacity—like Melville's Barber—define him. To show that his character functions on the topical level as a caricature of Stephen A. Douglas, certain personal details from the later chapters must be anticipated here.

In the opening scene his face is briefly sketched as "rather crusty-looking for the moment, . . . from being newly out of bed." He shows "business-like dispatch" in rattling down his shutters, showing not "over-much tenderness for the elbows and toes of the crowd." Most importantly with regard to his physical appearance, he must "jump on a stool" to hang up his sign over his door. His costume is the informal "apron and slippers" of his profession. Both appearance and personality seem to be in harmony: the "No trust" meaning of his sign seems borne out by the "crustiness" of his face and the brusqueness of his manner in setting out his ornamental barber pole "at a palm-tree angle," and his "bidding people stand still more aside." His reception by the other passengers is clearly contrasted with that of the Deaf-Mute—the Barber's actions seeming "quite in the wonted and sensible order of things"—while his sign does not "provoke any . . . derision or surprise, much less indignation," nor does it gain for the Barber "the repute of being a simpleton." Melville's use of litotes here tells the reader that the Barber seems "wise" and sensible to the crowd.

Much later in the narrative, in chapter 42, his brusque, skeptical, down-to-earth personality emerges in more detail, as do his business-like attitude and his unadorned style of argument. He first reappears in chapter 42 cat-napping and dreaming in his barber's chair. A literary reference is made to Souter John and Tam O'Shanter in Robert Burns' poem *Tam O'Shanter*, an apt one if one recalls that Tam had a vision of "warlocks and witches" and of "Auld Nick in shape o' beast" (ll. 115, 120), for Cream awakens suddenly at the entrance of Goodman who, as the reader knows by this time, is Auld Nick in the shape of a Philanthropist. Startled by Goodman's "benediction" as he enters the shop, the Barber stands "all agape, eyes fixed, and one arm in the air." Melville goes on to depict him as "honest," "shrewd," "self-possessed" (after his momentary startle), "apprehensive," and "business-like," as he invites the Cosmopolitan to take his seat in the barber chair. Throughout his dealing with the Cosmopolitan, Cream manifests some "uneasiness" and occasional "disconcertment." He calls for plainer talk and repeatedly denies that Goodman's philanthropic conversation is "in his line." Even while con-versing he persists in carrying on the shaving of Goodman, yet at one point he loses "patience, and with it respect" (p. 258) and expresses "exasperation," saying, "All this sort of talk is, as I told you once before, not in my line." When Goodman tries a more cautious tack, the Barber is impressed and "conciliated" somewhat, yet when Goodman accuses him of misanthropy, he still persists "dryly" in mistrust: "Sir, you must excuse me. I have a family" (p. 260).

His mood alters in the following chapter (43) to a more "meditative" one. He is less business-like as he ponders his discovery that Goodman is that "strange creature," a philanthropist. While heating the water for shaving he becomes "almost as sociable as if the heating water were meant for whisky-punch; and almost as pleasantly garrulous as the pleasant barbers in ro-mances." He takes a seat and expounds with "some self-complacency" upon the insight into human nature which he has derived from his profession, where he sees and participates in deceptions, such as "hair dyes, cosmetics, false moustaches, wigs, and toupees": "Ah, sir, they may talk of the courage of truth, but my trade teaches me that truth sometimes is sheepish. Lies, lies, sir, brave lies are the lions." When he thinks he has answered Goodman well, he seems momentarily "well-pleased" with himself. Liquor appears again as a metaphor, when his shaving cup is compared to "a mug of new ale," as it foams up with white bubbles. Yet, after the shaving is done and after Goodman exerts his "power of persuasive fascination" in a "magical" manner, the Barber is "irresistably persuaded to agree to try, for the remainder of the trip, the experiment of trusting men." He becomes a victim of the Confidence Man. Saying it is "only for the novelty of the thing that he so agreed," and asking for "security to him against any loss that might ensue," still he engages "to trust men, a thing he had before said he would not do." Business-like to the last, he insists that the agreement be written down, dated "April 1, 18—," at "a quarter to twelve o'clock, P.M.," and he puts his "No trust" sign away in a drawer.

Despite this temporary capitulation, the Barber remains essentially the same personality. He asks for fifty dollars cash as a "money-pledge" to secure him against loss, when and if he trusts—which Goodman refuses—and then he quotes from *Ecclesiasticus* the caution of the Son of Sirach that: "An enemy speaketh sweetly with his lips" and that "I believed not his many words." The Barber seems, that is, to contradict his recent agreement, making it appear in retrospect all the more strange and magical, by remaining still the personality that mistrusts mankind. Then, when Goodman refuses even to pay for his shave and departs, the Barber is again left "in a maze, staring after," by Goodman's personal power. Once that power is removed, however, at the close of the scene, he is soon "restored to his self-possession and senses," puts back up the No-Trust sign, tears up the written agreement, and in after days, the narrator says, always spoke of Goodman, his "queer customer" as "the man-charmer—as certain East Indians are called snake-charmers" (p. 269).

In personality, several physical details, and in attitude and style, the Barber seems to be a caricature of Stephen A. Douglas (1813–1861), representative (1845–47) and senator (1847–61) from Illinois, Democratic party leader during the 1850s, and "the centre of the political history of the country" from 1854 to 1858.[15] The most suggestive physical detail pointing to Douglas is one, it should be noted, that is open to alternative interpretations. In the first scene, when Cream jumps on a stool to hang up his sign over his door, the reader is, as I interpret the action, meant to infer that the Barber is not tall enough to perform that operation without the stool, *i.e.* that he is short in stature. Douglas was five feet, four inches tall, and in nearly all graphic prints he is shown as extremely short.[16] John W. Forney, in an anecdote about Douglas, wrote that "he got up on a chair" in order to point out a spot on a wall map of the United States.[17] Because he had a large head and chest and a powerful personality, he was called "the Little Giant" from the early days of his public life. Another physical detail, the Barber's standing, in chapter 42, "with one arm in the air," may be derived from a characteristic oratorical gesture of Douglas, as displayed in a sketch of him speaking in 1860, and in cartoons of him as a gladiator in 1858 and as Zoyara, the bareback rider, in 1860, in both of which he has his right arm raised in a similar oratorical gesture.[18] Another detail of the opening scene that suggests Douglas, but which is debatable—for it may point to any of several politicians—is the comparison of his barber pole to a "palm tree."

The palm tree or the palmetto is a standard symbol in political cartoons for Southern origin, interests, or affiliation. The palmetto in conjunction with crossed sabres symbolizes South Carolina specifically. In this literary instance the palm tree, while clearly alluding to the South, is ambiguous in its specific reference. On the one hand, it may, if the Barber is meant to caricature Douglas (as I believe he is), allude to the fact that he was associated with Southern slavery interests through his first wife's ownership of a Mississippi plantation, of which he was the manager, or that he was regarded as a Southern sympathizer (a "dough-face," a Northern or Western man with "Southern principles"), because he tried to tread a middle path between North and South in his effort to save the Democratic party as a national party. On the other hand, it is possible that the palm tree comparison may mean that some Southerner is being caricatured. As in the political prints, the Southern figures in *The Confidence-Man* are more difficult to identify because their individual histories are more obscure to us today than the Northern and Western, and they were less frequently caricatured in the period.

In personality and attitude toward others there are several striking re-semblances between the Barber and Douglas, the most significant being the Barber's sociability—bordering on garrulity—his practicality, his energetic and business-like manner, and his down-to-earth quality. Douglas was emi-nently sociable, was praised for his amiability, his "familiar, friendly manner and his utter lack of pretentiousness." As a young man he was notable for his "quickness in conversation and his 'exuberant flow of animal spirits,'" and for his "bright, convivial nature." As a judge in Illinois he was noted for his "shirt-sleeve informality" and "democratic" habits. James Ford Rhodes, writing from personal memories, summarizes the impression Douglas made on his contemporaries: "He lacked refinement of manner; was careless of his personal appearance, and had none of the art and grace that go to make up the cultivated orator."[19] He was further characterized as "pragmatic" and "energetic" in manner.[20] President Polk called him "a sensible man."[21] When he was a judge in Illinois, even his opponents were impressed with "the dispatch with which he cleared the dockets." In manner he appeared plebeian, "democratic," "popular." He "never put on . . . airs of Senatorial dignity." He was a man "of sound practical sense" with a "shrewd and resolute coun-tenance." In manner of thrusting himself forward—a manner that put him into the front ranks of American politics in less than ten years—Johannsen describes him as "brash, aggressive, and frequently impudent." Attention was paid to him and he was valued in party counsels for his views. And he won elections. All this closely resembles the Barber's brusque but sensible manner, which does not, nevertheless, prevent his acceptance by the other passengers of the *Fidèle*. Johannsen writes that his defense of Manifest Destiny (hardly a "philanthropic" policy) in debates over Texas, Oregon, and the Mexican War "touched a responsive chord among Americans," while his Anglophobia "delighted those Americans who saw in the United States the great wave of the future," and "his frequent altercations with slave state Congressmen, and his denunciation of abolitionists brought him support from moderate and conservative men everywhere." And his "political acumen and shrewd ability as a manipulator of votes and bills won the respect of friends and enemies alike."[22] If Melville saw Douglas as the best exponent of the no-trust, self-interested policy, he evidently saw it as successful initially, at least, with the American people.

Two references to liquor of the more plebeian sort, in the later scene, where Cream shaves Goodman—to "whiskey-punch" and "new ale"—link the Barber's personality, again, to Douglas, who had a "taste for good American whiskey" and on the campaign trail was not above drinking "bad whiskey."[23] With such habits, he probably was not above drinking the even more "democratic" refreshment ale, though I have not found any mention of it. He also used profanity and coarse language, for which the Barber's "hity-tity" may be a euphemistic substitute. The politeness, which Douglas quickly learned in Washington society and his acquired courtesy may possibly be reflected in the Barber's consistent use of "sir" with his customer Goodman, though that may be simply part of his role as barber serving a customer.

With regard to Douglas's oratorical style, an early description by a political enemy calls it "plain, blunt, and logical, without much depth, and with no originality, and perfectly free from elegance of diction or eloquence of expression."[24] Other observers described it as "stark and realistic, with few rhetorical flourishes and seldom quotable," and as having "frontier informality."[25] It has been characterized as "staccato."[26] He was noted for seizing the great points of a subject and presenting these as they bore upon his argument and the conclusions he wished to establish with scant attention to the impression they would be likely to make on a listener. Edward Everett, a master of elegant eloquence, thought Douglas's speeches were "coarse and ungentlemanlike." In Congress his "pugnacious qualities" were almost legendary, and his language was always sharp, clear, strong, and knotty, never soft, and seldom beautiful. He did not use flights of fancy, splendid passages, prophetic appeals, or witty turns. All these stylistic characteristics—or rather lack of the more admired rhetorical graces and methods of political oratory of the period—are reflected in the blunt, down-to-earth manner and style of Melville's Barber. It is also possible that Douglas's lack of refinement, his ready conversational ability, his background as a cabinetmaker and the "democratic" role he played in politics—even after his two socially-advancing marriages—may have led Melville to caricature him as a pleasantly "garrulous" barber.

In the well-known print, "The Political Quadrille. Music by Dred Scott" (1860), he is portrayed dancing with a ragged man, symbolizing the votes of the poor.[27]

The principal sources for Douglas's ideas and attitudes were "observation and experience," according to a modern rhetorical analyst of his speeches. And he "received his major training in speech from the school of experience" in political campaigning and in congressional debate. Rhodes notes his lack of interest in speculative questions and in the history of other nations than his own.[28] In this regard, his character resembles Melville's portrait of the Barber who prides himself upon his observation of the facts and the realities of life, especially those revealed to him "behind the scenes."

Besides the implied symmetrical contrast of Douglas with Lundy in that both are Western opinion makers—one through oratory and the other through journalism—the Barber's function as the contrasting no-trust antagonist to the philanthropic protagonist Lundy is very appropriate to Douglas, for he had become by the middle 1850s the acknowledged leader in the West and North of the political response to the antislavery movement and the leader of the Democratic party in its attempt to meet the challenge of the new sectional feeling. His leadership of the Kansas-Nebraska Bill's passage in 1854 made him the natural opposite—in fact the obvious target—of the powerful response to that bill, which first appeared as the "Appeal of the Independent Democrats" in Gamaliel Bailey's abolitionist *National Era,* next emerged as the "Anti-Nebraska" party, and finally as the Republican party. Murat Halstead, writing of the Democratic convention in Cincinnati in May 1856, calls Douglas "the proper candidate," the one who more than any other embodied one side of the issue presented to the citizens for settlement in the 1856 election. After the convention had nominated Buchanan, Halstead wrote that, "We have been accustomed to look upon Mr. Douglas as the truest representative of the principles and policy of his party." Halstead regrets that Douglas was not chosen, because his nomination would have been "a tender to the other party of the true issue to be tried before the great popular tribunal"— of which Buchanan's nomination was an evasion.[29] In other words, in the polarization of popular feeling during the period of our concern, Douglas had come to represent outside of the South the response to the agitation of the slavery issue by the abolitionists and the rising tide of antislavery feeling stimulated by his sponsorship of the Kansas-Nebraska Bill, which contained the potential for extension of slavery. Moreover, if my identification of the Barber with Douglas is correct, Melville apparently wished to suggest, by casting him in the Barber's role, that he was symbolic of the underlying preference for and understanding of the principle of self-interest, as it was brought into the open under the impact of the agitations of philanthropy.

With regard to the relationship of Douglas to the main questions analyzed in the dialogue of the narrative—those of the trustworthiness of mankind and of the African-American in particular—Douglas, as representative of the no-trust position, is appropriate (see chapter 14). He did not believe that the Founding Fathers meant to include the African-American in the equality clause of the Declaration of Independence, denying explicitly that the signers ever "intended to place the Negro race on an equal footing with the white race." He accepted Chief Justice Roger B. Taney's notion that at the time of the writing of the Constitution African-Americans were "regarded as an inferior race." Still, he did not accept slavery of the African-American as a "natural condition" and he felt they should have rights consistent with the welfare of the community where they lived and which the people of a state or territory might determine.[30] Thus, again, Douglas must have seemed a suitable exponent of the negative side of the question of "trusting" man and specifically the African-American man in Melville's series of hypothetical illustrations of the question. In the context of the proslavery argument, the Barber's self-defensive remark, "I have a family," may be meant to allude to the frequent Southern evocation of their "hearths and altars"—the fear of a black insurrection.

There is probably an allusion to Douglas's relationship to New England preachers generally rather than specifically to one with Henry Ward Beecher (who, as will be seen in Chapter 10, is caricatured as the Cosmopolitan) in the Barber's repeated repulse of Goodman's philanthropic "talk" as "not in my line." Douglas, after he became the object of severe criticism especially by Congregational, Presbyterian, Methodist, and Baptist clergymen of New England as a result of the Kansas-Nebraska Bill, developed a lasting detestation of ministers. He felt, as George Fort Milton writes, that "the ministers had been led by an atrocious falsehood 'to desecrate the pulpit, and prostitute the sacred desk to the miserable and corrupting influence of party politics.'" It is barely possible, however, that there was a particular animus toward Henry Ward Beecher, since, as Milton notes, Harriet Beecher Stowe, his sister, had suggested and paid the expense of circulating the "monster" petition signed by three thousand clergymen and presented in Congress condemning Douglas and his bill.[31] The main relationship of Douglas and Beecher in the narrative would be as representatives of their respective and opposing factions, for Beecher, as I shall show later, by 1856 was a committed opponent of Douglas in the national battle for public opinion about potential slavery extension. The humor of their fictional encounter, in the course of which Cosmopolitan-Beecher "enchants" Barber-Douglas, resides in the reader's perception that even the most skeptical of men can be momentarily taken in, if enough pressure is applied. Douglas's expressed view that the preacher should keep to his religion would be sympathetic to Melville, who expresses a similar one in his poem "The Age of the Antonines"—calling that imperial Roman time a "halcyon Age," when "No demagogue beat the pulpit-drum."[32]

Black Guinea and the Drover

Appearing only once, in chapter 3, Black Guinea, the "grotesque negro cripple," who plays his tambourine to divert the crowd of passengers, is the second appearance of the Confidence Man—the Deaf-Mute being the first. He is central to Melville's narrative structure, for he names by descriptive epithets eight gentlemen who will "speak for" his case—six of whom correspond, in correct sequence, to the six following appearances of the Confidence Man. The remaining two on his list (a "ge'mman in a yaller west" and a "ge'mman as is a sodger") have no corresponding gentlemen anywhere in the narrative. These two descriptive epithets may be vestiges of some early unfulfilled intention of Melville with regard to the narrative, retained by oversight in Guinea's list in the final revision of the manuscript.[33] Since the few manuscript fragments available throw no light on this problem, no final conclusion can be reached about this crux in the text. The other six gentlemen appear later in the narrative as solicitors of confidence, although they do not all explicitly refer back to, or "speak for," Guinea by name. In the argument each of them is an exponent of the philosophy of benevolence and trust in the natural goodness of mankind, and hence they "speak for" Guinea's case.

In the dramatic structure as it will be interpreted in Chapter 13 Black Guinea is a "transformation" of Pierrot-Deaf-Mute into the second appearance of Harlequin in the disguise of a regional type, here the American stage stereotype of the "Negro," as he appeared in comedies (e.g. Anna Mowatt's *Fashion*) and in the minstrel shows of the 1840s and 1850s. Beyond this basic comic function, which I have discussed earlier, Guinea serves further to satirize contemporary politics, insofar as his image constitutes an allusion to the political issue of African-American slavery or, more accurately stated, to African-American slavery considered as an exploitable issue by politicians of the North and the South. This interpretation may be best understood by comparison of Black Guinea's image to the graphic images of the African-American in the political prints of the period and the uses that are made in graphic art of this image to make satirical statements about the political situations of the period. There are numerous political sketches and caricatures in which the figure of a black man or youth, or a woman, is used to represent the people of African descent, either within the slave system,[34] or the free men and women,[35] or to represent the issue of slavery itself.[36] Only occasionally does a dark-complexioned figure represent some particular African-American, such as Frederick Douglass, Henry B. Brown, a fugitive slave, or, later, Dred Scott.[37] In these political prints, single figures that represent groups—whether ethnic, political, social, or national—are frequently used in sketches with figures representing individuals. Similarly, some of Melville's literary figures allude to social or political factions or groups, while the greater number allude to individuals.

There is one particular physical detail that suggests strongly that Black Guinea's function is as a representation of American slavery as an exploitable political campaign issue: his deformity—his "stumps" for legs. It is fairly common in political cartoons of this period to represent a candidate for office as crippled in one or both legs—*i.e.,* having to "stump it." It is apparent that manifold puns, both graphic and literary, emerged from the verb "to stump," which had been derived from the Western custom of standing upon a tree stump in a forest clearing to deliver a speech. This imagery for speechmaking is well illustrated in a pro-Lincoln cartoon published by Currier & Ives in 1860: "'Taking the Stump' or Stephen in Search of his Mother" (plate 24).[38] Douglas, the Northern Democratic candidate, is depicted soliciting money (votes) and wearing a wooden leg. He complains that he "fell over a big lump of Breckenridge [sic]" and has been very "lame ever since." John C. Breckinridge, too, the Southern Democratic candidate, is shown as lame, while President James Buchanan, his supporter, offers him a wooden-leg apparatus, saying, "Here, Breck, as Dug has taken the stump you must stump it too." To this, Breckinridge replies, "I suppose I must but I know it will be of no use for I feel that I haven't got a leg to stand on." Lincoln comments, "Go it ye cripples! wooden legs are cheap, but stumping wont save you." In this print Douglas's wooden leg clearly represents both the act of speechmaking, in which he was one of the first presidential candidates to engage, and also the political liability under which he was forced to perform—the split in the Democratic party between his faction and the faction that nominated Breckinridge. Likewise, Breckinridge's injury represents both his liability on account of the party schism and his need to campaign actively by speechmaking for presidential office.[39] Thus, it is evident that "stump" in this period could mean to solicit political support—or the "confidence of the people"—while at the same time it denoted the existence of a political liability of some sort.[40] Both meanings blend in this print in a complex of puns that no doubt delighted its purchasers in 1860. For our purposes it serves to help interpret the meaning of Black Guinea's "crippled limbs" and his "leather stump," as well as the crippled condition of his wooden-legged challenger in chapter 3, and, later in chapter 19, the "interwoven paralysed legs . . . suspended between rude crutches" of the Soldier of Fortune, Thomas Fry. (See Chapter 9).

The meaning of Black Guinea's "leather stumps" has evidently two levels. As those of Melville's crippled "negro" they represent the African-American's common lack of political status or power in the North and West, where in most states he was denied the vote, as well as in the South, where, as a slave, he had no political rights at all and was counted as only three-fifths of a person in the count for representation. As the stumps of the *white* "operator," whom the challenging Wooden-Legged Man insists is disguised as Black Guinea, they represent the "Black Republican" party campaign oratory (possibly specifically that of Seward) exploiting the slavery and slavery-extension issues. Likewise, later in the chapter, the crippled condition of the Wooden-Legged Man, who will be treated as a caricature of James Gordon Bennett (see Chapter 5), is an allusion both to Bennett's political liability as a non-native—being of Scottish birth—and to his constant politically-motivated (usually Democratic) editorializing—a kind of "stumping"—which was by his enemies attributed to his desire for power or for ambassadorial or other office. Foreign birth during this period, 1854–56, when the Know-Nothing (Nativist or Native American) party reemerged to sweep many state elections and to present both a major presidential candidate (Millard Fillmore) and two minor ones (Nathaniel P. Banks and Robert F. Stockton), was a distinct political liability, which Bennett was not allowed to forget. Likewise, Thomas Fry's crippled condition, in chapter 19, will be treated as representing the brief presidential campaign efforts of the Northern Know-Nothing leader, George Law (see Chapter 9).

As a cripple, on the "stump," Black Guinea alludes most generally to the issue of the presence of the descendants—both free and slave—of African natives as that issue emerged finally in polarized political party confrontation in the years immediately prior to the presidential election of 1856. Although it remains possible that he may allude more specifically to an individual, it is important to recognize that, most generally, he represents the use of the issue of the African-American people and of their slavery as a manipulatable political theme by party politicians in both the North and the South. Black Guinea's relationships to the other characters may be seen, then, as representing the varying relationships of that issue to various individuals and factions of the period. This function can be illustrated well in his dialogue with the Drover, the first character to speak to him.

While Melville, at the opening of chapter 3, depicts Guinea as poor and humble, but mirthful and "good-natured"—functioning as the Negro stereotype that was offered to sentimental Northern eyes as an object of both charity and "diversion"—upon the other, more ominous, side, he is described in a metaphor as a "black steer"—*i.e.,* a valuable piece of agricultural property in his relationship to the "purple-faced drover." A "drover" is a cattle driver, and the Drover, who is described as purple-faced and purple-handed—most likely because of the effects of the hot Southern sun on fair complexions—is based on the Southern "slave-driver" of graphic and verbal caricature. An important example of the association of the slave with cattle in graphic art is the masthead of Garrison's *Liberator* (1831–1865), which, as it changes in each of three different periods, always features a sketch of a slave market, where slaves and cattle are offered for sale and a sign is displayed reading, "Slaves, Horses, & Other Cattle to be Sold," or a variation of that wording.[41] The Southern "slave-drivers'" attitude toward the African-American—as animal property—is clearly alluded to in the imagery of the following passage: "'What is your name, old boy?' said a purple-faced drover, putting his large purple hand on the cripple's bushy wool, as if it were the curled forehead of a black steer." Nor should a secondary meaning of Guinea's name be overlooked in enforcing the point that he represents property to the Drover. "Guinea," besides being a common nickname for blacks because of African origin, was the name for an English gold coin, in use until 1813, equal to twenty-one shillings. "Black Guinea" means, through a pun, "black wealth" or "black gold."

Beyond his stereotypical meaning, it is possible that a particular Southern leader is being caricatured in the Drover. The senator from Virginia, James M. Mason, received much criticism for his remarks about the price of slaves going up, if Kansas were made into a slave state, and Virginia was especially ridiculed by Charles Sumner for breeding slaves "as cattle for the shambles."[42] More relevant, however, to understanding the dialogue between the Drover and Black Guinea are the writings of the Virginian pamphleteer and author, George Fitzhugh (1808–1881), who wrote after 1854 for the Richmond *Examiner* and for *De Bow's Review,* engaged in widely published controversial correspondence with abolitionists, and published *Cannibals All! or, Slaves Without Masters* in 1857.[43] Fitzhugh termed both the Northern laborer under capitalism and the Irish under British rule "slaves without masters"—masters who would be obliged by law to provide for them in sickness and in old age, as were the Southern slaves—and he argued in his journalism and in his earlier book—part of the propaganda battle of the struggle over Kansas—*Sociology for the South; or, The Failure of Free Society* (1854), that the Southern slave was better off because he was treated better materially and was more secure in childhood, illness, and old age under that system.[44] Fitzhugh's attitude toward slaves and "slaves without masters," is clearly reflected in the Drover's response to Black Guinea's claim that he is a "dog widout massa": "'A free dog, eh? Well, on your account, I'm sorry for that, Guinea. Dogs without masters fare hard.'" And Guinea agrees: "'So dey do, sar; so dey do.'" Likewise, Fitzhugh's argument seems to lie

behind the Drover's subsequent response to Guinea's saying that he sleeps on
the pavements of the city at night: "'But that must be in the summer only,
old boy. How about winter, when the cold Cossacks come clattering and
jingling? How about winter, old boy?'" Guinea's "reminiscent shiver" and
his exclamation, "'Oh sar, oh! don't speak ob der winter,'" alludes to a view
of the unemployed and socially rejected African-American in the North that
is similar to Fitzhugh's and which can be seen represented pictorially in a
sketch in the New York *Lantern* in 1852, entitled "The Negro in the North—
and in the South." A two-part (diptych) sketch, it shows on the left a poorly-
clad black man walking on a snowy street past a cheerful grogshop from
which he is excluded, juxtaposed to a sketch on the right of a happy slave
fishing in a pleasant Southern stream beside his benevolent young master.[45]
The attitude expressed here is similar to the Drover's and to Fitzhugh's: that
the free African-American in the Northern cities suffered more from unem-
ployment and prejudice there than from slavery in the South.

Throughout chapter 3 the contrast of the Drover's skeptical attitude
toward sympathy with Guinea and with the attitudes of other members of
the crowd (especially that of the Country Merchant Henry Roberts), who
respond to his solicitation with trusting pity and with pennies and buttons,
carries on the opening contrast of chapter 1 where Southern and Western self-
interest (in the figure of the Barber, alluding to Douglas) is juxtaposed to
abolitionist benevolence (in the figure of the Deaf-Mute, alluding to Lundy).
After the verbal exchange between the Drover and Guinea, a "variety of
characters" appear whose responses to Black Guinea's appeal represent religious and political responses—both individual and typical—to the political
issue of African-American slavery and its extension. The first person to challenge Black Guinea, after the Drover, is the Wooden-Legged Man, who calls
him "sham," a "decoy," and him and all his friends "all humbugs" (pp. 11–
15). As will be seen later (see Chapter 5), in personality, relationship to
Guinea and to the two clerical characters, and in several striking physical
traits this figure caricatures James Gordon Bennett, founder and editor of the
New York *Herald,* an independent paper that most often held proslavery
opinions and supported Democratic candidates. His challenge to Guinea's
honesty reflects Bennett's constant vituperative criticism of the leaders in the
antislavery movement and of the political manipulation of the slavery issue
by politicians, especially by "Seward, Weed, Greeley & Co.," as that powerful
New York Whig (and later Republican) alliance was popularly called. Bennett
consistently used in his *Herald* editorials and news stories vulgar and deni-
grating language about blacks and about their sympathizers, regardless of
the sympathizers' motives. The relationships of the other characters to the
Wooden-Legged Man and to Guinea, as they sway back and forth between

sympathy and skepticism, allude to the shifting attitudes of certain individuals and of Northern and Western public opinion generally toward the slavery issue during the 1840s and 1850s, as they were affected alternately by militant antislavery propaganda and by the sarcastic and violent proslavery propaganda of editors such as Bennett and by the Bennett-incited violence of mob leaders such as Captain Isaiah Rynders, a New York City Tammany Hall Democratic leader, some of whose publicly-known traits—besides those of Bennett—may enter into the figure of the Wooden-Legged Man.

It should be recalled, here, that the kind of criticism of certain Northern attitudes which I claim Melville's satire is making—of sentimental philanthropy, of self-interested political and commercial motives, of hypocritical religion, and, especially, of dishonest politicking—is not unusual, and it is nearly identical to that made four years later by the African-American orator and journalist, Frederick Douglass, in a passage in his newspaper, *Douglass' Monthly,* in August 1860. The last sentence of the following passage could be a gloss on Melville's Black Guinea in particular:

> Our philanthropy melts itself away into maudlin tears at the story of his [the slave's] wrongs. Our sense of justice kicks the beam when his master's cotton bales are in the adverse scale. Our religion whines and snivels over his sufferings, but cannot leave its formal devotions long enough to bind up its [his] wounds. Our politics bellow in his behalf on the stump, but only employ his cause as a stalking horse for party effect, and to carry self-seekers into power.[46]

For widely differing reasons both Douglass and Bennett criticized the use of the slavery issue by self-seeking politicians as a "stalking horse" or "decoy." Likewise the ardent and early supporter of the antislavery movement, Lewis Tappan, said later specifically of the election of 1856 that, although he voted for Frémont, he regretted it, because "'it was a white man's party united for selfish purposes.'"[47] Melville is satirizing the same public situation when his Wooden-Legged critic attacks Black Guinea as a humbug, as a "painted decoy," and as "a white masquerading as a black." Many others, of course, both Democrats and ultra nonpolitical abolitionists throughout the period, attacked the Republicans, especially Seward, Weed, Chase, and Sumner for using the slavery issue for their own political advancement. Black Guinea should, I think, be read as a caricature of "the Negro," employed by Melville to represent the political *issue* of the role of the African-American in American society as it was tossed back and forth in public oratory and journalism throughout the period of antislavery agitation from 1830 to 1856. Even if there may possibly be an allusion to an actual person, the caricature seems to me to be one defined by journalism and by political intentions, more than by any one individual. More than any of the other seven appearances of the Confidence Man, Black Guinea is, I believe, an impersonal, almost abstract, caricature similar to the stereotypical figures in the graphic prints and stage representations.

For an interpretation of Black Guinea's begging and entertaining posture as satire on a presidential political campaign, founded in this case on use of the black slavery issue, the evidence from several graphic prints is strong. The satire of a political solicitation of trust by depiction of a beggar's or an entertainer's solicitation of attention and money may be seen in an early cartoon, "The Captain & Corporal's Guard" (1841), which shows Webster as a beggar, President Tyler performing on stilts, Bennett (with squint-eye and devil's hooves) playing the bagpipes, John Beauchamp Jones, the editor of the *Madisonian*, playing a drum, and James ("Jemmy") Barker as a woman playing the tambourine (plate 3). Another, closer in time to the period of our interest, depicts Martin and John Van Buren in the Free-Soil campaign of 1848, "The Blind Beggar & His Dog," which appeared in *John-Donkey*. The elder Van Buren is shown as a beggar with "Prince" John as his dog. Van Buren says, "Pity the sorrows of a poor old man, whose little dog John has brought him to the pass you see—a poor old blind man—led about by his dog—nothing more than a puppy as you see. Give him the presidency, or a kick, or a copper, or anything, or nothing—for he's a poor old blind man—very." Prince John, as a dog, holds the hat for coins in his mouth. This sketch satirized the retired president for reentering politics as the Free-Soil candidate in 1848, under the pressure of Prince John's ambition, and both of them for hypocrisy in espousing the antislavery issue.[48] Third, a famous poster of the campaign of 1856, reproduced in Allan Nevins, *Frémont: The West's Greatest Adventurer*, shows that the Republican party under Frémont was symbolized by its opponents by the image of a "Woolly Horse" placed on exhibition for public entertainment.[49] P. T. Barnum had in 1850 exhibited in his New York museum a "Nondescript or Woolly Horse" as a previously unknown animal which, Barnum claimed, Frémont had sent back from his explorations on the Gila River. This imposture was denounced by the skeptical Senator Benton, Frémont's father-in-law, who sued Barnum's agent for a quarter-dollar that he had paid to see the horse. For this reason—the association with Frémont—apparently the "Woolly Horse" became a graphic and verbal symbol of the Republican party, and, additionally, because of the earlier association of the horse's woolly coat with African "Woolly" hair, it became a symbol of their use of the slavery issue.[50] The poster associates two of Frémont's supporters with the "Horse": the "Philosopher" called "Free Love Greeley" and Henry Ward Beecher, "Commander of the 'Holy Rifles'" who was instrumental in the Woolly Horse's capture and "is now travelling through the New England States exhibiting the nondescript animal"—an allusion to Beecher's campaigning.

Finally, there is a graphic print that is especially helpful in interpreting the scene of Guinea's performance and the passengers' reactions, although it appeared later than 1856: "The Great Exhibition of 1860" (plate 23).[51] In this the political situation of the campaign of 1860 is depicted in terms of an entertaining performance. An anti-Republican campaign print, it shows in the background Seward dressed as a nursemaid holding up a black infant and saying, in reference to his "Irrepressible Conflict" speech of 1852: "It's no use, trying to keep me and the 'Irrepressible' infant in the background, for we are really the head and front of this party." In the foreground, on the right, James Watson Webb holds out a tambourine (such as Black Guinea carries and plays) labeled "Courier & Enquirer" (Webb's New York City newspaper), and says, "Please Gentlemen! help a Family in reduced circumstances, we are very hard up, and will even take three cents if we can't get more, just to keep the little [Negro] . . . alive." Raymond is depicted here as a boy in short pants, holding an axe and saying, "I'll stick fast to you General [Webb] for the present, because I have my own little axe to grind." Lincoln rides the fence rail, labeled "Republican Platform," with his mouth padlocked (because he did not campaign actively), while Greeley is pictured as a street organ-grinder offering to sing various songs. The purport of this print is that the Republicans are putting on their usual "show," begging for confidence in their party, which is still secretly engineered by Seward, though Lincoln is the nominee, and still exploiting the benevolent sympathy that the slavery issue can arouse. Images here with concepts behind them that are analogous to chapter 3 of *The Confidence-Man* are the African-American presented as an object for charity by a white man, the tambourine as part of the performance, and the general idea of a "diverting" performance soliciting money—pennies specifically. It will be recalled that Black Guinea's audience throws him pennies both as "charity" and as "*diversion*."

As suggested earlier in this Chapter it remains possible that Melville intended the caricature of Black Guinea to allude to a particular individual. There are several prints using the iconographic convention of a white political candidate who has the physical appearance of a blackface entertainer (based on the popular minstrel shows performed by white actors), which support this and suggest that the reader take seriously the Wooden-Legged Man's suspicions: "He's some white operator, betwisted and painted up for a decoy," and he is "a white masquerading as a black." Although the most likely candidate because of his political career obviously would be William Henry Seward, who was constantly accused of such machinations, I have not found any positive evidence yet to support his identification. Two political prints that use the theme of a white masquerading as a black are: "National Minstrels" (1844?), which shows Jackson, Van Buren, Tyler, John Tyler, Jr., Clay, Calhoun, Polk, Benton, Theodore Frelinghuysen, and Webster—all in blackface performing as minstrels and speaking, as Black Guinea does, in dialect; and "Presidential Trio," in *Young America* in 1856, showing Buchanan, Frémont, and Fillmore as the "National Minstrels" in blackface, Buchanan handling the tambourine, while Frémont and Fillmore manage the sticks (plate 20).[52] Last, too late to have influenced Melville, but strongly reinforcing the artistic tradition, there are two prints that use the image of a dark-skinned person to represent a white man allied with the antislavery cause included in Adalbert Volck's series of etchings, "The Comedians, Tragedians of the North" (1863)—the most interesting and by all odds the finest in artistic quality of the political prints of the period. Volck's "Broder Beechar" caricatures Henry Ward Beecher as a dark-skinned preacher, and "Under the Veil—Mokana" shows Lincoln as a dark-skinned oriental dancer removing his veils.[53]

5

Several Antagonists (the Wooden-Legged Man, the Episcopal Clergyman, the Methodist Minister, and the Country Merchant)

The Wooden-Legged Man

In chapter 3, Black Guinea is attacked and accused of shamming by the Wooden-Legged Man (pp. 11–15). In the physical traits of a gimlet-eye and sour face, in his abrasive personality and vituperative style, and in the roles of skeptic of humanitarian causes and of a moral outcast, the Wooden-Legged Man almost certainly caricatures James Gordon Bennett (1795–1872), the founder (1835) and editor of New York City's most successful daily, the *Herald,* in which he attacked nearly all reformist movements—antislavery in particular—for nearly thirty years. Melville describes his cynic as "a limping, gimlet-eyed, sour-faced person," who goes "on a wooden leg . . . halt," and when he reappears in chapter 6 speaks with "a horrible screw of his gimlet" eye. Since Bennett had no wooden leg, this deformity must be taken as a graphic metaphor for his political liability of foreign birth and his habit of "stumping" for political causes through editorializing. Bennett was famous for an eye defect that was termed a "squint eye" or a "cross-eye." The *Oxford English Dictionary* gives the meaning "squint eye" for "gimlet eye" in this period. Philip Hone in his diary in 1836 refers to Bennett thus: "There is an ill-looking squinting man called Bennett . . . who is now editor of the *Herald.*"[1] A contemporary engraving shows Bennett's right eye slightly turned in and a contemporary biographer asserts that his "squint eye" was the result of reading at night.[2] His modern biographer, Oliver Carlson, quotes a contemporary observation that he was "so terribly cross-eyed that when he looked at me with one eye, he looked out at the city hall with the other." Others described Bennett as a "scrawny, squint-eyed Scotsman."[3] Hone also mentions Bennett's showing "his ugly face in Wall Street"—a phrase parallel to Melville's adjective "sour-faced."[4] The many graphic prints of Bennett, both cartoons and sketches, nearly always show one or the other eye turned in.[5] Murat Halstead describes him gathering news at the Know-Nothing Northern bolters' convention in New York City, 13 June 1856, as a "tall, thin-faced, cross-eyed, . . . decidedly Scotch looking man, who walks slowly carrying a cane in his right hand."[6]

Melville's cynic's dress is not described, but his voice is characterized as "croaking" and in chapter 6 as a "long, gasping, rasping sort of taunting cry" and his laughter is "like a groan." Bennett was never a public speaker, and I have found no descriptions of his voice, but Pray mentions that by 1855 Bennett suffered from bronchitis, which may possibly have caused him to have a rough rasping voice like that of Melville's cripple.[7]

In personality Melville's character, one of the most markedly distrustful of the Confidence Man's antagonists, appears to be vengeful, hating, cynical, mistrusting, sarcastic, sneering, and splenetic. Like a "custom-house officer . . . stripped of convenient means of support," he

> Concluded to be avenged on government and humanity by making himself miserable for life, either by hating or suspecting everything and everybody—this shallow unfortunate, after sundry sorry observations of the negro, began to croak out something about his deformity being a sham, got up for financial purposes. (p. 11)

A careful perusal of the editorial pages of the *Herald* over a six-month period close to the probable writing of *The Confidence-Man*, January through June 1856, sufficiently demonstrates Bennett's abrasive, iconoclastic, personal style of journalism—the public personality for which he was famous. Hone called him a "scoundrel" and an "impudent disturber of the public peace, whose infamous paper the *Herald* is more scurrilous and of course more generally read than any other." Again, in connection with the naval court of inquiry in the *Somers* mutiny case, Hone mentions Bennett's reprinting of "offensive articles" and his "insulting remarks to the court." He calls him a liar and scandalmonger and a corrupter of the morals and degrader of the taste of the people of New York.[8] More sympathetically, Isaac Pray describes Bennett's habitual mistrust, characterizing his attitude toward reformers thus:

> Having no faith in any reform except as a wheel constructed for political purposes, [the *Herald*] does not treat any subject out of the considerations which attach to such a belief. It knows that all private sincerity of opinion is liable to be turned into public political hypocrisy, and it deals with the political rather than the moral aspects of those topics.[9]

Like Melville's cynic, whom he compares to a vengeful "discharged customhouse officer," Bennett had attributed to him a spirit of revenge because of an early disappointment in his relationship with the Democratic party. Pray refers to his being "injured by the persecuting spirit of politicians"— the Jacksonian Democrats—and this altering the course of his life. Pray records that he felt betrayed by Van Buren and his friends after ten years of party loyalty in the early 1830s. He was refused a loan and felt political prejudice against him in part for being "a foreigner." His pride felt "wounded," and he set out to create a powerful engine for influence upon public opinion in order to "humble" those who had injured him. Throughout his subsequent career in founding and building up the *Herald,* he exhibited a lack of trust of nearly all politicians and was concerned to use his great journalistic gift for invective and sarcasm upon them. [10] He wrote freely and truly about stock-jobbing, swindles, commercial frauds, and "bubble joint-stock companies" in his widely read reports on Wall Street. Again, exhibiting habitual mistrust, Bennett was the first American publisher to refuse any credit to either purchasers of, or advertisers in, the *Herald*—a business principle upon which he founded his fortune and set an example followed to this day by newspaper advertising departments. [11] He is an apt choice to represent the argument for "No Trust," generally.

One special aspect of Bennett's public personality that is clearly reflected in the Wooden-Legged Man's attack upon Black Guinea's humanitarian appeal, as well as in his contempt for the Episcopal Clergyman and in his quarrel with the Methodist Minister, is Bennett's constant habit of attacking ministers and other public persons who appealed to morality. Carlson relates his many attacks on all of the New York churches, including the Roman Catholic, in which he had been born and educated in Scotland. His constant theme in the 1830s was that "all public men were knaves—politicians, lawyers, brokers—with the clergy probably the greatest knaves of all." [12] One result of Bennett's attacks upon leaders in public life was a "Moral War" that was launched upon him in 1839, taking the form of a boycott of the *Herald* and social ostracism of him during 1840–41. Editors of the other New York City papers (Park Benjamin of the *Evening Signal,* Mordecai Noah of the *Star,* Webb of the *Courier & Enquirer,* Moses Yale Beach of the *Sun,* and others) joined with clergymen, teachers, brokers, bankers, merchants, and "men of distinction" in demanding a boycott of his paper and of his advertisers. He was treated as a pariah and called "this ink-smeared Satan of the press," and the *Herald,* the main "Satanic press." Some men responded to his abuse with libel suits, some with personal violence (Webb beat him with a stick), and once he received a postal package containing a bomb. This "Holy War"—as Bennett tauntingly called it—did not destroy him, for his sensational style and content still appealed to a mass audience, but it did change his style somewhat, according to Carlson, and he was never so venal again. Mott writes that it became the fashion to hold him up as a bogeyman and "never in his lifetime did he emerge from the cloud of obloquy the moral warriors of 1840 threw over him." [13] This concerted attack upon Bennett for criticizing the moral leaders of society forms part of the historical background of Melville's caricature of Bennett as the Wooden-Legged Man, who is the major skeptic of Black Guinea's honesty and that of his "worthy" sponsors, and who attempts to unmask his imputed fraud: "He [Guinea] is a white masquerading as a black." Bennett's career is the background especially of the remark in chapter 6 about him by the Man in Gray, a caricature of the clergyman, Theodore Parker: "A bad man, a dangerous man; a man to be put down in any Christian community."

I think that Melville perceived Bennett as temperamentally a Thersites-Pulcinella-Diogenes type, an outsider and an "Ishmaelite"—as Bennett was called—and cast him in the role of Black Guinea's challenger in order to allude to Bennett's constant challenging of antislavery orators, preachers, journalists, and politicians (ranging from Douglass to Seward, Weed, and Greeley—especially Greeley) as self-seeking knaves or fanatical fools, masquerading as humanitarians. Greeley, for his many "'ism's" and Seward and Weed for their hidden political "pipe-laying" in New York State came in for Bennett's invective week after week, year after year. Day after day during the period of the buildup toward the 1856 presidential conventions and elections (roughly December 1855 through early June 1856) Bennett editorializes in his inimitably sarcastic, self-assertive, frequently vulgar style on the political machinations of both the "[Negro-] worshippers" (the Republicans) and the "[Negro-] drivers" (the proslavery Democrats), with more hatred and suspicion expressed of the former than the latter. Bennett, who had lived in Charleston and worked on the *Courier* there during the 1820s, always believed in the rightness of slavery for African-Americans. He hated abolitionists, and though he opposed the extension of slavery into Kansas, it was because it would bring African-Americans into new territory and not because he opposed slavery for them. Time and again he claims that the slavery issue is a decoy or a stalkinghorse for the Republican leaders' personal ambitions, even while he claims that the extreme proslavery position is nearly as knavish on account of the danger of secession to the Union. Bennett's main editorial themes during the period of January through June 1856 are two: (1) a call for a new party that would neither be the Seward-dominated Black Republican "Abolitionist" one, nor the proslavery Southern-dominated Democratic one, but a new party in between that would be for the Constitution and the Union; (2) the reiterated accusation that the Kansas struggle between Northern and Southern settlers is being fomented by and misrepresented by the "Abolitionist" leaders, Seward, Weed, Greeley and Raymond. Typically, in one editorial, 14 May, he denies that there is a "war" in Kansas and writes that it is "a sham designed to delude simple people into voting the black republican ticket." Of Bennett's skeptical acumen and his journalistic gifts, Murat Halstead, who was no admirer of his politics, wrote of him at the Know-Nothing Northern bolters' convention in June 1856: "He watches (with a strange faculty for reading riddles in men and looking clearly through the mists of distance and time) not only the matters immediately around him, but the course of events throughout the world."[14]

Sufficient has been said to show with considerable probability that the Wooden-Legged Man caricatures Bennett's public personality as revealed mainly in the themes of his editorial writing, in his style, and in his relationship as journalistic satirist to his contemporaries. Yet one other element of his style also appears in Melville's satirical portrait of Bennett—anecdotalism. Pray notes Bennett's love for anecdotes, most often satirically humorous or biting stories illustrative of the less-savory aspects of human behavior.[15] This stylistic habit is exemplified in the Wooden-Legged Man's telling, "in his porcupine way, and with sarcastic details," the story of the unsuspicious old Frenchman of New Orleans, who finally "began to suspect" his "liberal" wife when "upon entering his apartment, a stranger burst from the alcove" (p. 34).

There are other minor reflections of certain aspects of Bennett's character and career. For example, his interest in horse races (which his newspaper was the first in this country to report on a regular basis) is reflected in the Wooden-Legged Man's use of an analogy between the "pitiless man" (himself) and the "jockey [who] loses his honesty" when he observes that "all horses aint virtuous, no more than all men kind," and his statement that "When you find me a virtuous jockey, I will find you a benevolent wise man" (p. 14). Bennett's custom of reporting personally on criminal trials seems reflected in the Wooden-Legged Man's distrust of such trials, as revealed in his ironic exclamation on perjury: "The charitable knave on the stand gives charitable testimony for his comrade in the box." Likewise Bennett's worldly ambiance (the sporting world, the world of crime and prostitution, Wall Street, and the political conclaves, upon all of which he reported personally during most of his career) is reflected generally in the portrait of the wooden-legged skeptic. Pray quotes Bennett as saying, "I have seen human depravity to the core. I proclaim each morning on 15,000 sheets of thought and intellect the deep guilt that is encrusting our society."[16]

Lastly, there may possibly be an allusion to Bennett's Scottish origin in the application twice of the epithet "Canada thistle" to the cynic, first by the Methodist Minister and then echoed by himself. The thistle was the national emblem of Scotland. Much was made of Bennett's Scots birth in the graphic prints of him. Contemporaneous with the writing of *The Confidence-Man*, a cartoon appeared in *Yankee Doodle, Or Young America*, 26 July 1856, entitled, "Don't Know Which Way to Go," which depicts Bennett looking at road signs leading toward the White House trying to decide which candidate to support: "Buchanan Turnpike," "Fremont Row," or "Fillmore Alley." He wears a Scots cap and argyle socks. The caption states that he is looking for the "nearest cut to the French Mission"—an allusion to Bennett's reputed longing for the French ambassadorship as reward for his editorial support. [17] Although Bennett actually came out in editorials of 17 June and 19 in support of Frémont, he in no way considered this an endorsement of the "Black Republican" party, but rather he construed and favored the Frémont "enthusiasm" as an expression of the "sentiment of the masses" and of the "independent"—such as he considered himself. [18] He continued to excoriate the new Republican party as consisting of deceptive scoundrels, even while he rather disingenuously regarded Frémont's nomination as actually representing the defeat of the political managers and "pipe-layers" such as Weed and Seward. Melville might have been less inclined to choose Bennett as a major critic of the Republican movement had he felt obliged to deal with Bennett's apparent last minute inconsistency and bandwagonism in endorsing Frémont.

As suggested earlier, certain public traits of Captain Isaiah Rynders (1804?–1884), sporting man, head of the New York City Empire Club of roughs, Tammany Hall Democratic leader for many years, and ex-custom-house weigher, after the Whigs came in, may enter into the caricature that is mainly one of James Gordon Bennett. In the public eye, Bennett and Rynders were closely associated in opposition to and ridicule of abolitionism, as the result of a notorious altercation at an antislavery meeting in May 1850. At an anniversary meeting of the American Anti-Slavery Society at the New York Tabernacle, 7 May 1850, at which Garrison, Douglass, and others spoke, Rynders and his group of Tammany toughs sat in as critics and challengers. Prior to this meeting for an entire week Bennett had announced it in the *Herald* and called in inflammatory language for a public demonstration of hostility—the "true opinion of the public." Garrison, while there to speak, wrote that "Our meeting will be a stormy one, . . .—perhaps brutal and riotous in the extreme—for Bennett . . . has been publishing the most atrocious and inflammatory articles . . . avowedly to have us put down by mobocratic violence." At the meeting, as Garrison reported it, "The pent-up feeling of the mobocrats broke out, and, with the notorious Capt. Rynders at their head they came rushing on to the platform, yelling, cheering, swearing, etc." After a verbal exchange with Garrison, who remained calm, Rynders remained on the platform and challenged another speaker, Douglass, of whom he is quoted as saying, "*You* are not a black man; you are only half" one, and of another African-American abolitionist, Samuel Ward, that he was the "original" Negro. At the following meeting Rynders and his followers exhibited "a fresh series of brutish demonstrations," of catcalling, hisses, and abusive interlocutions and took over and dominated through their numbers the final meeting of the antislavery group on 8 May.[19] This kind of verbal and threatened physical violence resembles the relation of the Wooden-Legged Man to Black Guinea, especially the attempted intimidation and the personal antipathy to Black Guinea.

Melville may well have had personal impressions of both Bennett and Captain Rynders, who was a campaigner for Polk and Dallas in the same presidential canvass in 1844 in which Gansevoort Melville was a prominent orator and campaigner and for which Gansevoort received his appointment as secretary of legation in London.

The Episcopal Clergyman

The charge of the Wooden-Legged Man that Black Guinea is a "sham" arouses suspicion in the previously trusting and charitable passengers, who ask whether he has any papers to prove the genuineness of his case. At this point there emerges from "another part of the boat" the Episcopal Clergyman, who responds favorably insofar as he not only asks for the names of Guinea's sponsors but volunteers to go find them. Later, in chapter 6, upon reassurance from the Man in Gray (a caricature of Theodore Parker; see Chapter 7) about Guinea, he claims to put his trust in him, despite doubts aroused by the Wooden-Legged Man. The Clergyman is described as "young," "small in stature," with a "clear face and blue eye," and he wears "a long, straight-bodied black coat"—as would a clergyman in this period. In personality, he is "manly" with "innocence, tenderness, and good sense triumvirate in his air," and he shows "kind haste" when he goes to find Black Guinea's sponsors. In chapter 6 he has a conversation with the Man in Gray, who persuades him to give a "mite" to him for Black Guinea and something, too, for the Seminole Widow and Orphan Asylum (pp. 32–38). There, his "conscience upbraids" him for his momentary mistrust, for which he blames the accusations of the Wooden-Legged Man. He is easily reconverted to trust when the Man in Gray calls the cynic, "A bad man, a dangerous man; a man to be put down in any Christian community" (p. 36). The young Clergyman affirms "full belief in his [Guinea's] honesty," saying that he is "sorry" for having mistrusted him. Although he is momentarily "irresolute" and uneasy about the Seminole Widow and Orphan Asylum, he gives something to it finally.

This brief, double appearance of the young, tender Episcopal Clergyman responding, after some hesitation, to the appeal of the slavery issue, as represented by Black Guinea, has a number of resemblances to a particular young Episcopal clergyman, who attained considerable notoriety during the summer of 1856 for his espousal of the Republican political cause. Dudley Atkins Tyng (1825–1858), the son of a more famous father, Stephen Higginson Tyng (1800–1885), would have been about thirty-one when, on 29 June 1856, as minister of the Church of the Epiphany in Philadelphia, he delivered what was termed a "political sermon," taking up the Republican cause.[20] For this he was forced by his parishioners' votes to leave his pastorate there and take up a new parish organized for him, called the Church of the Covenant. This sermon, published as a pamphlet in 1856, is a strong antislavery political statement, but one that does not say anything new, nor anything that had not been said already more vehemently, and with more power and eloquence by Theodore Parker, by whose lectures and thought it seems to me to be preeminently influenced.[21] Tyng calls for "right public sentiment" and active organizing for influencing opinion about Kansas. He gives practical advice, such as using the mails and sending out tracts, sending money to Kansas relief organizations, reinforcement of the Northern settlers, use of the vote for the Republican party, and, last but not least, prayer. I have not found any personal connections with Parker, but I suggest that the Clergyman's encounter with the Man in Gray alludes to the effects of Parker's antislavery lectures on Tyng.

Dudley Tyng's father, a renowned Low Church Episcopalian orator and editor, was rector of St. George's Church in New York City for thirty years, 1845–1875, where for a time the son was his assistant. Dudley Tyng took orders in 1846, and possibly was in New York City, whether well known or not, sometime between then and 1854, when he accepted the pastorate in Philadelphia. Melville lived in New York City from the fall of 1847 until September 1850, when he moved to western Massachusetts. Tyng published some lectures on religious and secular subjects, *Vital Truths* (1852), *Children of the Kingdom* (1854), and *Our Country's Troubles* (1856–57), which may have given him some notoriety before his "political" sermon. Proslavery Democratic newspapers, naturally, commended his parishioners for dismissing him. The *Democratic Review,* in October, referred disparagingly, in an article entitled "Right and Wrong," to "brother Tyng's conventicle," along with "brother Greeley's 'Kansas Aid Society.'"[22] The Philadelphia *Ledger,* on 4 November, reports Tyng's final dismissal from the Church of the Epiphany for his "political sermon preached in his church in the early part of the present political canvass," in which he felt it "incumbent on him to denounce slavery and to commend the candidates of the party opposing it." This journalist, like many other Democratic papers and speakers, deprecates "The pernicious practice of introducing politics into the pulpit."[23] However, Melville's local weekly newspaper, the *Berkshire County Eagle,* which switched during the period 3 August 1855 through 4 April 1856 from being Whig to being Republican (as the "white man's party" and as opposed to the "contamination" of free soil by "filthy negroes and lazy masters," 4 April 1856), notices on 15 August 1856 the Tyng episode and editorializes in defense of political preaching. In the context of noticing Northern scholars who have taken the "stump"—such as Emerson, Longfellow, Bryant, G. W. Curtis, Cornelius C. Felton, and Benjamin Silliman—this editorialist (J. E. A. Smith?) writes: "Just now there is a great fluttering because Mr. Tyng of Philadelphia, preached a withering sermon on the times." Responding to Democratic wrath, the *Eagle*'s writer defends the right of a preacher, as he phrases it, to "mention the decalogue and to preach against crime on Sunday, even if Atchison, Stringfellow, and Buford [proslavery settlers' leaders in Kansas] take it personally."[24]

If the Episcopal Clergyman is a caricature alluding to Dudley A. Tyng as a Republican political preacher, it would appear that this important and complex scene in chapter 3 (involving Black Guinea, as representative of the use of the slavery issue by the Republicans; the Drover, as representative of the proslavery view; and the characters alluding to Bennett, Parson Brownlow [see next section], and David Wilmot [see last section of this Chapter]), as well as the scene in chapter 6 involving the Man in Gray (a caricature of Theodore Parker), may possibly have been written after 29 June when Tyng attained his notoriety. If so, Melville must have written with great speed. Merrell Davis has shown that he was quite capable of doing this in his discussion of Melville's rapid composition after June 1848 of the satirical-political passages referring to the revolutions of 1848 in chapters 148 and 153 of *Mardi*.[25] On the other hand, it is possible that Melville was already familiar with Tyng's views on slavery through his earlier published writings, which I have not been able to consult.

The Methodist Minister

In the scene in chapter 3 in which the Wooden-Legged Man accuses Black Guinea of being a sham, one of the main characters who respond to his distrust is a Methodist Minister, who, stepping forth, asks, "Have you no charity, friend?"—appropriately picking up the "charity" theme introduced by the Deaf-Mute in chapter 1. Melville describes him as "tall, muscular, martial-looking"—this last trait illustrated by his career, in which he had been "in the Mexican war [as] volunteer chaplain to a volunteer rifle-regiment." He is "a Tennessean by birth." Though the quality of his voice is not described, one gesture is: he "raises his arms" while speaking, "as in the pulpit." In personality he is "soldier-like," finds it hard to remain "pacific" with the Wooden-Legged Man, loses his "patience," "waxes indignant," and finds it difficult to contain his emotion, although he tries "conscientiously" to hold back "the old Adam in him, as if it were a mastiff." "Indignation" boiling over, he calls the Wooden-Legged Man a "godless reprobate" and "seedy coward," and, seizing him by his coat collar, shakes him vigorously. His rhetoric generally is that of a haranguing pulpiteer and his language that of a rabble-rousing and name-calling sermon. For example, after he has given the Wooden-Legged Man a good shaking he calls him a "foiled wolf," adding:

> "Spleen, much spleen, which is the rickety child of his evil heart of unbelief: it has made him mad. I suspect him for one naturally reprobate. Oh, friends," raising his arms as in the pulpit, "oh beloved, how are we admonished by the melancholy spectacle of this raver. Let us profit by the lesson; and is it not this: that if, next to mistrusting Providence, there be aught that man should pray against, it is against mistrusting his fellow-man."

Yet, after all this indignation and his abuse of the man who distrusts Black Guinea, the Methodist Minister changes suddenly, becomes "irresolute and troubled," and his own "distrusts first set on foot" revive with "added severity" (pp. 13–17). His role is an ambivalent one.

In appearance, home state, profession, style, and rhetoric, Melville's Methodist Minister seems, with some striking evidence (though with an unsolved problem), to allude to William Gannaway Brownlow (1805–1877), who was called the "Fighting Parson" of Tennessee, was a Methodist circuit-riding preacher, faithful Whig and, later, Know-Nothing politician, newspaper editor, famed orator and debater on political topics, self-publicist, and author of numerous books. Later in his career he was a pro-Union Southerner and a Northern hero and public speaker during the Civil War, and a much-reviled Reconstruction governor and senator from Tennessee.[26] Brownlow's appearance, according to a contemporary, Alexander McClure, was that of a "tall, lank, hatched-faced" man, who never smiled and whose personality was "ungraceful in manner, never gentle in speech." He was only himself "when indulging in some tirade against real or imaginary foes that gave him an opportunity to open the sluices of the blackguard." His only virtue was courage; he was "fiendish in his vindictiveness," as he well exhibited in his Reconstruction policies in Tennessee.[27] Brownlow made his name as a master of vituperative rhetoric and a manipulator of the emotions of his audiences not only through the written word—as did Bennett—but also from the pulpit and platform. Brownlow, it is true, apparently, did not go to the Mexican War, yet, although he was a Whig and should have been against the war, he called upon the people of Tennessee to enlist, and he himself joined a company called the "Protestant Invincibles."[28] Here, I think, Melville is using the caricatural technique of exaggeration in calling his Methodist Minister a "volunteer chaplain to a volunteer rifle-regiment." He is also using Brownlow in this instance as an example of his point: the contradiction of the profession of Christian principle with the practice of a Christian minister.

Colonel Alexander McClure, in an extended portrait of Brownlow, writes in *Recollections of Half a Century* (1902) that Brownlow was a unique character, a sturdy mountaineer of eastern Tennessee, where he learned early to be hostile to the "aristocratic slaveholder"—though never sympathetic to the slave. Though he was an itinerant minister for ten years, "he mingled his piety very freely with politics and was often heard on the stump in the political conflicts of those days." His editorials in his newspapers, the *Jonesboro Whig* and others, were "always caustic and forceful, and many . . . [were] vulgar." He gained the title of "the Fighting Parson" because he was always in a "serious broil of some kind" and "was always armed for the fray." By the early 1850s Brownlow had earned that public name, while McClure himself had already crossed swords with him journalistically because of Brownlow's "always aggressive and generally violent, abusive editorials." Famous enough before the war even in the North for his journalistic and platform performances, Parson Brownlow gained even greater fame when his temperamental bellicosity carried over into anti-Rebellion attitudes in 1860–61, in which his criticism of Secession "exhausted the vocabulary of Billingsgate." Brownlow became a hero throughout the North when he was imprisoned in Tennessee for his rejection of Secession, and after his release he toured the North making speeches that were, according to McClure, the "most original and pungent ever heard." Concerning his typical style, McClure writes that his "vivid imagery and ribald arraignment of all the Southern leaders, divesting them of every virtue and charging them with every attribute of fiendishness, made his vulgarisms household words." He became an active politician and adopted and enforced "the most violent reconstruction policy by which he became Governor and U.S. Senator from Tennessee." This sketch that McClure draws from personal and contemporary sources is very suggestive of the vignette that Melville gives the reader of his "martial" Methodist preacher, engaged in violent conflict with the Wooden-Legged Cynic Bennett—another master of vituperative rhetoric and of sarcastic invective. [29]

Parson Brownlow was an early and intense anti-Catholic and became a rabid Know-Nothing when he had to give up the Whig party. He participated in the first Know-Nothing (American) convention in Philadelphia in February 1856 as a delegate from Tennessee. Murat Halstead wrote of him that the motion to nominate candidates for president and vice-president "was made by the famous Parson Brownlow, of Tennessee," and was carried. After the split in this convention over the Kansas issue and the withdrawal of the Northern antislavery-extension delegates, Brownlow moved that the governor of Florida and Percy Walker of Alabama, who had previously retired, "be invited to come back into the church now," amid laughter.[30] It appears that at this time Brownlow was still proslavery, for he participated actively in the Southern, proslavery portion of the Know-Nothing convention, after the antislavery-extension group had withdrawn to hold their own convention later in New York. Yet, in a curiously turnabout career later on Brownlow became a violent anti-Southern speaker and publicist, and by the 1870s he was identified with the most extreme Republican group, as appears by his inclusion in a graphic print showing seven "Liberal Republicans"—antislavery heroes—that includes Greeley, Wendell Phillips, Henry Ward Beecher, Garrison, Gerrit Smith, and Theodore Tilton.[31]

However, the striking similarities of the Methodist Minister to Brownlow's public image raise a serious problem of interpretation, for I have been unable to find evidence that Brownlow before 1860–61 and Secession, when he turned anti-Southern, ever publicly responded favorably to any aspect of the antislavery movement either in its early abolitionist agitation in the West or in its political phases of the Liberty, Free-Soil, Barnburner, and Republican parties. As late as 1858 he joined in a series of public debates with a Northern minister in which he defended slavery. There seems presently to be no parallel in his *early* career to the Methodist Minister's initial call for "charity" toward Black Guinea, while there is ample evidence of his distrust of the antislavery cause, a position to which the Minister ambivalently shifts (p. 17) under the influence of the Wooden-Legged Man's skepticism. Since Brownlow published constantly and evidently many times took a position merely for its shock effect or its rhetorical flair, with little concern for consistency, it is remotely possible that in some editorial or article or in an altercation with another editor (possibly Bennett), reprinted in papers that have not been available to me or to his modern biographer, George Coulter, Brownlow may have taken a position that might have been construed by Melville as momentarily favoring the antislavery cause and to which he may be alluding in the Methodist Minister's initially positive response to Black Guinea. Until more work may be done, I cannot reconcile entirely a caricature that seems in so many ways to point to Brownlow with the initial action that the Methodist Minister takes in wishing to place as "charitable a construction as one can" upon Black Guinea.

The Country Merchant Henry Roberts

The Country Merchant Henry Roberts, who is the Confidence Man's next victim (chapters 3, 4, and 10), has three important encounters with him.

First, in chapter 3, responding to Black Guinea's appeal, Roberts shows, in contrast to most of the crowd, his "confidence" by giving Guinea a half-dollar. Next, in chapter 4, when John Ringman, the Man with a Weed, claims to be a fellow-Mason, he successfully solicits Roberts' trust. Last, in chapter 10, inside the cabin Roberts falls into conversation with John Truman, the President of the Black Rapids Coal Company, and purchases, with "confidence," some stock in the company. Although Roberts shows "trust" in all three instances, his motive in the first two is charity, while in the third it is self-interest.

There is considerable evidence that Roberts is a caricature of David Wilmot (1814–1868), United States representative and senator from Pennsylvania, who attained notoriety when he introduced on the House floor 8 August 1846 the famed Wilmot Proviso. During the Mexican War President Polk had asked for a congressional bill appropriating two million dollars for negotiations with Mexico about territorial adjustments. To this bill Wilmot, concerned about slavery extension, presented an amendment which would forbid the extension of slavery into any of the territories involved in the negotiations.[32] The proviso never passed both houses of Congress, but it became an issue in the 1848 campaign, formed the basis of the Free-Soil party platform, and was widely viewed as responsible for reintroducing the slavery issue into congressional debate, leading to the polarization of North and South. Principal traits that link Roberts to Wilmot include: some physical similarities, Pennsylvania origin, middle age, benign temperament, good-natured personality, membership in the Masonic Order, and the similarity of Roberts' relationships with the three guises of the Confidence Man—Black Guinea, Ringman, and Truman—to Wilmot's relationships to the antislavery movement as it emerged in partisan politics.

Roberts appears as "a middle-aged person, a country merchant" with an "expressive face," that can "flush,"—presumably to a reddish or rubicund color—an eye that can "moistly beam," and lips that can "tremble with an imaginative and feminine sensibility" when he drinks champagne. As to his profession, he is a "forwarding merchant" from "Wheeling, Penna."[33] He admits to Ringman that he is a Mason. His clothing is not described, but he carries an umbrella (frequently associated in graphic prints with benevolent, sometimes Quaker, types), and has a purse and a business card. His voice is usually "benign" in tone. His personality is clearly intended to be seen as benevolent for he is consistently called "the good merchant." He shows both "natural good-feeling" and caution; he is humane, his donation of a half-dollar being larger than most of the passengers', who give only pennies or buttons. He is "honest," reluctantly candid, commiserative, modest about alms-giving, and he suffers some self-reproach for his suspicions. His emotions are not entirely benevolent or consistent, however, for he shows suspicion of the two "grave" doctors of civil law, whom he watches playing cards in the cabin; and after drinking with Truman and thinking about Guinea's deformity, about Ringman's troubles, and about the miserable Miser, he admits reluctantly a momentary loss of confidence in "Providence." This lapse sobers, shames, and mortifies him. Yet, he is scrupulously honorable, "sensible," and "religious." The only stylistic mannerism that Roberts shows is a slight habit of repetition, as in "really, really . . . stay, stay" (p. 19), and that recurs in "Ringman? Ringman? Ring? Ring?" (p. 20), "But still . . . still" (p. 20), "Yes, yes" (p. 22), and "A—a person" (p. 61). Otherwise his style is very direct, plain, unmannered, and unrhetorical.

David Wilmot would have been middle-aged (forty-two) in 1856. According to his modern biographer, Charles B. Going, he was a "rural Pennsylvanian" and came from and represented in Congress a "principally agricultural" section of the state, which may have suggested to Melville his suitability to be caricatured as a country merchant.[34] In physical appearance, he was remembered in Congress in the 1840s by his colleague George W. Julian as "short and corpulent in person." A comic poem about him as "Childe Wilmot," in *John-Donkey,* mentions his "fair, fat red face." His political enemies' accusation in 1855 of "drunkenness and profanity" probably reveals no more than that he was not above raising a cheerful glass of champagne, as Roberts does with Truman, nor above occasional use of a mild expletive, as Roberts does in saying "in my conscience" and "bless my soul" (p. 19). Murat Halstead describes him thus at the Republican convention in June 1856: "He is a short, portly gentleman, his face rotund and rubicund with good living, and wearing an expression of the most obstinate good humor. A smile shines over his broad face whenever he rises to speak."[35] Other observers mentioned his "smooth face and florid complexion." In 1857 a reporter described him thus: "A noble and commanding exterior, with a dignified bearing, are well harmonized with a good-humored portliness which bears testimony to generous cheer and a good conscience." Another reporter in 1857 described Wilmot as a "handsome, portly looking man, with an intellectual head and face."[36] In sum, these traits are not inconsistent with the adjectives Melville uses to depict his Country Merchant, though none are entirely conclusive. With regard to Roberts' admitted affiliation with the Masonic Order: Wilmot's biographer notes that he was a man of some independent courage in joining the Masonic Order and openly espousing Masonry in 1841—a time when the anti-Masonic political hysteria was at its height in Pennsylvania and nationally.[37]

As to his public personality, although Wilmot was a lawyer-politician associated early with the Jacksonian-Van Buren Democracy, he was, according to Going, never at any time a practical politician; he had a "vision of politics as a struggle of ideas rather than a conflict between candidates," a trait of idealism that seems consonant with Roberts's apparent simplicity about human nature in his first two encounters with the Confidence Man.[38] Although not a single-minded abolitionist and although a firm believer in granting Southern constitutional rights, he favored Van Buren over Polk in the 1844 nomination contest and campaigned in his state for Van Buren and Charles Francis Adams on the Free-Soil ticket in 1848.[39] He never got on well with the practical politicians of his state, yet was clever enough to lead the Free-Soil Democrats of Pennsylvania in a split similar to that in New York between the Barnburners and Hunkers. Moreover, he thwarted his political enemy James Buchanan's efforts to win the presidential nomination until 1856, when Wilmot and his Pennsylvania Free-Soilers left the Democracy to join the Republican party.[40] As chairman of the first Republican State Committee in Pennsylvania, he signed the announcement of a call to Republican sympathizers in August 1855 and was active in organizing the new party as a fusion of Democrats, Whigs, and Americans opposed to slavery-extension. Likewise, on the national level, he signed the invitation to the first national organizational meeting in Philadelphia on 22 February 1856, and he was named to the National Executive Committee—the only member from Pennsylvania. Along with Edwin D. Morgan of New York and Francis P. Blair, Sr., he signed the "Address to the People" of the National Republican Committee on 29 March 1856, inviting delegates to Philadelphia in June.[41] The name of David Wilmot was valuable to the Republicans, as Halstead reported: "The connection of his name with the famous proviso . . . makes him, especially in Republican Conventions a highly distinguished man."[42] More actively, he was chairman of the platform committee at the convention, helped write the platform, and he read it to the convention. In the vice-presidential balloting he received forty-three votes, more than Sumner, although fewer than Lincoln or Dayton, the winner. Going writes of him that he was regarded as the "man who had possessed foresight to foresee the designs of the South upon the territories and to set the ball in motion to defeat them."[43] In 1860, after Wilmot served as temporary president of the Republican convention at Chicago and had been instrumental in Lincoln's nomination, the New York *Herald* called him the "real founder of the Republican platform of 'no more slave territory, no more slave states,' and his patent is dated back as far as 1846."[44]

Wilmot's political career up to 1856 is, it may be seen, reflected in the actions of the Country Merchant. The three encounters that Roberts has with three of the disguises of the Confidence Man—as Black Guinea (the slavery issue), as Ringman (Bryant and the New York Barnburner faction [see Chapter 6]), and as Truman (Weed and the New York Whig-Republican politicians [see Chapter 7])—to each of which he gives his trust, should, I believe, be construed as allusions to the three main events in Wilmot's political career in relation to the antislavery movement as it developed between 1846 and 1856 into the formation of the Republican party. First, his encounter with Black Guinea, who represents the political issue of slavery and slavery-extension, may be read as an allusion to Wilmot's willingness to reintroduce the antislavery issue in Congress, when in 1846 he proposed the proviso to the "Two-Million Dollar Bill," forbidding slavery in any new territories to be acquired from Mexico—an event which immediately became *the* symbolic gesture of the antislavery movement in the North and West.[45] Second, Roberts' sympathetic encounter with and belief in the sad story of Ringman (who is, as interpreted in Chapter 6, a caricature of the New York journalist and Democratic spokesman Bryant) may be read as an allusion to Wilmot's sympathy with the Free-Soil–Barnburner movement in New York State in 1847–48, in which Bryant was one of the principal figures through the New York *Evening Post* and in which Wilmot participated through his attendance at the nominating convention at Utica in June 1848, which nominated Van Buren and C. F. Adams.[46] Third, Roberts' self-interested purchase of stock in the Black Rapids Coal Company from Truman, the company president and "Transfer Agent" (who is interpreted in Chapter 7 as a caricature of Thurlow Weed, New York Whig party boss and Republican party leader in 1855–56) may be read as an allusion to Wilmot's joining the new "Black Republican" National Executive Committee in 1855–56, behind which Weed was the real power, although his personal and political friend Edwin D. Morgan was the chairman. It is important to remember that Pennsylvania was agreed by all parties to be, with the possible exception of New York, the most important state in the election of 1856 to be won.[47] Therefore, it may be an additional reason for the importance that is given in Melville's pasquinade on the politics of the period to a politician from Pennsylvania, who was, besides, a symbol from 1846 on in both North and South of the intrusion of antislavery agitation into national politics.

As for the self-interest that Roberts-Wilmot displays by buying stock in the Black Rapids Coal Company, I have not yet found any specific commercial or monetary motive in Wilmot's history, beyond the natural opportunistic self-interest of a politician anxious to get ahead in government through a political party possibly viewed by him as on the rise and "a rare chance for investment," as Ringman had assured Roberts (p. 24). One source of the irony of the situation may be that Wilmot, a longtime, diehard Free Trade Democrat, is represented joining an organization with the fictional title of an industrial company—a coal company—at the solicitation of a party leader who represents the conservative Northern industrial and commercial interests of the Whig party and their commitment to high tariffs. Politics make strange bedfellows is an old observation and one that Melville invokes often, as here, and that provoked, I suggest, his authorial digression in chapter 14 on inconsistencies in human character.

As for traits of spoken or written style, Wilmot's style is not inconsistent with that of Roberts' speech, although I have not found any evidence of Roberts' slight habit of repeating a word or two. Alexander McClure describes Wilmot's speaking style as "guiltless of all the arts of the demagogue," "consistent and earnest," as not that of a "graceful orator," as "exhaustive, straightforward and manly." Others, such as the Philadelphia *Sun,* noted his "simplicity of manners . . . his frank, outspoken ways with the people." Another reporter called his style in 1857 "plain and cogent—his facts and arguments presented with clearness and occasional playfulness."[48] These observations of contemporaries are borne out by the selections from his addresses in Going's biography and are reflected in Roberts' straightforward, unmannered, unassuming speech style.

6

The Third Confidence Man (John Ringman the Man with the Weed) and His Antagonist (the Collegian)

John Ringman the Man with the Weed

After the complex interchanges of chapter 3, of which Black Guinea is the center, and in which he reads his list of "good, kind, honest ge'mmen," who will speak for him, he disappears from the scene and does not reappear. Chapter 4 introduces the first man on his list—the "werry nice, good ge'mman wid a weed"—whose name we learn is John Ringman and who is the third disguise of the Confidence Man.[1] As "a man in mourning, clean and respectable," Ringman first accosts successfully his fellow-Mason, Henry Roberts, the Country Merchant, by making devious use of the business card that Black Guinea intercepted when Roberts accidentally dropped it near his stumps (p. 17) and by relating the story of his "unfortunate" marriage to Goneril. In chapter 5, Ringman unsuccessfully solicits sympathy and support from the young Collegian while giving him a lecture on the beauty of melancholy. A cluster of personal traits, his attitude toward nature, and his relationships to the other characters, who are identifiable with Wilmot and with Henry J. Raymond (see next section) make Ringman almost certainly a caricature of William Cullen Bryant.

The theatrical stereotype on which Ringman is based is that of the sentimental, melancholy poet or lover of poetry, a type that the romantic movement in literature created and made popular and recognizable. In his personal traits Ringman is clearly associated with melancholy, the "weed" being the streamer of black mourning crepe on his hat, and he is described as having a "subdued air of softness . . . toned with melancholy, melancholy unreserved"—a melancholy which he hopes "is not catching" (chapter 5). A second trait—coldness—is mentioned three times. In chapter 4 his decorum seems "almost coldness," while in chapter 5 he is one of those "whom a ruling sense of propriety makes appear cold, if not thankless, under a favor," although he is capable of "throwing off in private the cold garb of decorum" and giving "loose to his genuine heart." A third trait appears when, seeking a loan from the Country Merchant, Ringman finds it extremely "painful" and difficult to ask a favor and struggles mightily with his feelings in order to do so (chapter 4). A fourth personal item appears when, in citing the unreliability of memory, he relates that he temporarily lost his memory when as a boy he was kicked by a horse. Fifth, he has an air of "self-respect" and of a "gentleman," further characterized as an air of superior "mild gravity" and of "painful conscientiousness." Sixth, he is a man of "earnest" emotions. In chapter 5 he appears "softened" from his earlier apparent "pride" which made him "appear cold, if not thankless, under a favor," and in private he reveals a "genuine heart." In his approach to the Collegian he uses a manner "strangely mixed of familiarity and pathos," and he claims a kinship of "melancholy" feeling with him (chapter 5). With him he shows both "earnestness" and "melancholy."

Ringman's method of persuasion varies with his object. With the Country Merchant he appeals to trust in mankind and to feelings of fraternity through the Masonic order. He claims to be a fellow-Mason and tells his hard-luck story about his errant wife Goneril. With the Collegian, although he claims some kinship of melancholy, the thrust of his appeal is a consistent attack upon the "ugly" melancholy view of the world exemplified by the Roman historian Tacitus. Ringman's distinction between the *ugly* melancholy view and the *beautiful* melancholy view—the latter of which he favors as being "true"—is a direct link with Bryant's main poetical themes, as I shall show below. Human nature, which Tacitus "libels" can be better studied, he says, in the "cemeteries of Auburn and Greenwood." Better reading than Tacitus is Mark Akenside's poem *The Pleasures of Imagination* (1757)—a popular restatement of the aesthetic sentimentalism of Addison and Shaftesbury. He contrasts Akenside's "serene and cheery book . . . fitted to inspire love and trust" with the "immorality" of Ovid, Horace, Anacreon, the "dangerous theology" of Aeschylus and others, and the "views so injurious to human nature as in Thucydides, Juvenal, Lucian, . . . Tacitus." In sum, Ringman argues consistently against the clear-sighted, historically founded classical appraisal of the wickedness of human nature that was associated in this period with the pessimistic philosophical view of Hobbes and Mandeville and in politics with the views of both the Old-Line Whigs and the Hunker Democrats—the conservatives of their respective parties.

William Cullen Bryant (1794–1878) was, with Halleck, Irving, Cooper, Longfellow, and Emerson, one of the most celebrated literary men of his time.[2] Although he made his reputation as a poet with "Thanatopsis" (1817) and thereafter collected his best poems into various editions, throughout his life he was equally if not more well known in New York as a journalist, a political writer and editor, who supported causes with his editorials (and occasional political speeches) from the intellectually prestigious and, in later years, very profitable position as editor of *The Evening Post*—for nearly fifty years—from 1829 to 1878. Politically, Bryant was early in his career a

Jacksonian Democrat and ardent foe of the Whigs; in 1847 he became a Barnburner (the antislavery-extension faction of the New York Democrats, which grew out of the faction opposed to borrowing money for expansion, such as canals), and in 1848 he supported the Free Soil party. In 1852 he returned temporarily to the Democracy to back Franklin Pierce. After the Kansas-Nebraska Act and the founding of the Republican party in 1854–56, he moved to that group, editorializing and speaking publicly for the Frémont-Dayton ticket in 1856.[3] On his death in 1879 the New York *Herald* obituary treated him mainly as a political editor, noting that "his influence was always actively felt in the politics of the country."[4]

There are many personal traits of Bryant that strongly suggest that he is being caricatured as Ringman. Concerning his physical appearance, many of his contemporaries agreed that he had a melancholy and cold expression, though some questioned whether he actually was so temperamentally. Parke Godwin, his son-in-law, upon meeting him for the first time noted his "wearied, severe, almost saturnine expression," "the exceeding gentleness of his manner, and a rare sweetness in the tone of his voice," and a "certain air of abstractedness." Godwin thought his greeting of strangers "cold and formal."[5] James Lawson wrote of Bryant in the *Southern Literary Messenger* in 1840 that he was "retiring," "modest," and "unostentatious," shunning "the public gaze," as Ringman appears to do. With strangers Bryant seemed "reserved and taciturn," even "cold and unsocial." Emerson expressed the fairly common view of Bryant, when he wrote to his wife in 1842:

> The cold man gets warm in telling his stories of his [homeopathic] cures. He is always to me a pleasing person so clean and unexceptionable in his manners, full of facts, and quiet as a good child, but Miss Sedgwick complained of his coldness, she had known him always and never saw him warm.[6]

Dickens in 1842 had found Bryant "a little sad and very reserved."[7] Godwin, writing a letter in 1845, three years after he had married Bryant's daughter, said of him that he lacked "human every day sympathies" and was "a little malignant" and that he was "a cold, irritable and selfish man."[8] Poe described his face in his fifties, in *Godey's Lady's Book* (1846), as "sallow, nearly bloodless" and the expression of his smile as "hard, cold—even sardonic." Yet Poe, according to Bryant's modern biographer Charles H. Brown,

> Like many who knew Bryant intimately, . . . thought his reputation for frigidity to be false: "The peculiarly melancholy expression of his countenance has caused him to be accused of harshness, or coldness of

heart. Never was there a greater mistake. His soul is charity itself, in all respects generous and noble."

Whitman noted his "rather bloodless complexion," and Hawthorne, writing of him in *French and Italian Notebooks*, when Bryant was older, said: "A very pleasant man to associate with, but rather cold, I should imagine, if one should seek to touch his heart with one's own." Meeting again in Italy, Hawthorne renewed his impression that Bryant had "an old-fashioned dignity," seemed "cool," and that "he is not eminently an affectionate man."[9] Lowell's caricature in *A Fable for Critics* (1848) emphasizes repeatedly Bryant's coldness of temperament as well as his love of natural beauty, noting also his devotion to Locofocoism, the radical branch of the Democratic party:

> There is Bryant, as quiet, as cool, and as dignified,
> As a smooth, silent iceberg, that never is ignified,
> Save when by reflection 't is kindled o' nights
> With a semblance of flame by the chill Northern Lights. . . .
> But he lacks the one merit of kindling enthusiasm; . . .
> Take him up in the depth of July, my advice is,
> When you feel an Egyptian devotion to ices. . . .
> He has a true soul for field, river, and wood in him;
> And his heart, in the midst of brick walls, or where'er it is,
> Glows, softens, and thrills with the tenderest charities—
> To you mortals that delve in this trade-ridden planet?
> No, to old Berkshire's hills, with their limestone and granite.
> If you're one who in *loco* (add *foco* here) *desipis,*
> You will get of his outermost heart (as I guess) a piece;
> But you'd get deeper down if you came as a precipice,
> And would break the last seal of its inwardest fountain,
> If you only could palm yourself off for a mountain.[10]

Besides his apparent temperamental coldness, Bryant was associated with "melancholy" partly because of the melancholy matter and tone of his best poetry, which was associated then as now with the English "Graveyard School" of Parnell, Young, Blair, and Gray, and partly because of what his biographer Charles Brown calls his "mortuary interest"—his peculiar habit of visiting the cemeteries in whatever city he happened to be visiting.[11] Having made his reputation with "Thanatopsis," Bryant took death as the theme of many of his poems—death in association with images of great natural beauty. Philip Hone was reflecting contemporary opinion of his poetry when he wrote in his *Diary* in 1832 that "A vein of sadness pervades all his writings, which is occasionally lighted up by soft and beautiful images. It is sad and melancholy, but never harsh or gloomy." However, despite the "beautiful melancholy" impression, Hone, who was a Whig, sees Bryant as an ambiguous character for his "virulent and malignant" editorial attacks upon Nicholas Biddle, when the banker opponent of Jackson died: "How such a blackhearted misanthrope as Bryant should possess an imagination teeming with beautiful poetical images astonishes me; one would as soon expect to extract drops of honey from the fangs of a rattlesnake."[12] Similar inconsistencies perceived in human character, the reader will remember, provoked Melville's digression on the character of the Country Merchant in chapter 14.

There are other personal characteristics of Bryant that confirm that Ringman caricatures him. Apparently because of his pride Bryant found it very difficult to ask favors. He wrote, for example, to Richard Henry Dana, Sr., in 1848: "The three things most irksome to me in my transactions with the world are, to owe money, to ask a favor, and to seek an acquaintance." The dislike of owing money might also allude to the early Barnburners' suspicion of borrowing money to finance canals and other developments favored by the Hunker Democrats and the Whigs. An incident from his childhood that Bryant relates of himself in the autobiographical sketch that forms part of Godwin's biography of him is that at the age of five he was kicked in the head by a horse, the scar from which he bore all his life.[13] Additionally, Bryant by several accounts already cited had the air of a gentleman and was, like Ringman, "clean and respectable." Last, as noted by Poe and others, those who knew him felt that he was capable of strong emotion though not appearing so.

Bryant's political views were founded upon the same general concepts of the goodness of man, nature, and God that Melville satirizes in the character of John Ringman. Brown notes that in his early Phi Beta Kappa poem, "The Ages," Bryant sought "from a survey of the past ages of the world, and of the successive advances of mankind in knowledge, virtue, and happiness, to justify and confirm the hopes of the philanthropist for the future destinies of the human race." Godwin wrote that his principles "were the results of his feelings rather than of his thoughts or of any deliberate process of reflection. His profound love and respect for his fellow-man; . . . his yearning for progress in all the noblest arts of life; and his deep, religious reverence for . . . humanity . . . were the sources of his abstract political convictions."[14]

Melville's highly critical analysis of Bryant's view of natural landscape and its effect on the human consciousness underlies Ringman's dialogue with the Collegian. Most importantly, "Thanatopsis" itself is a near-perfect exemplum in statement and style of the "beautiful melancholy" view that Ringman so insistently presses upon the Collegian as the correct attitude to

Nature. Among Bryant's poems that were included in the *Cyclopedia of American Literature,* coedited by Melville's old friends the Duyckinck brothers in 1856, were the universally admired "Thanatopsis," "June" (about his desire to die in June when nature is fair and when a friend might enjoy visiting his tomb), and "The Death of the Flowers," as well as portions of "Hymn to Death" and of "To the Past" (about his dead father and sister). The editors wrote that Bryant "fastened upon the genial influences of nature about him."[15] A close look at "Thanatopsis" reveals that Bryant is saying essentially this: Nature's "teachings" to man, when thoughts of death come to him, bring him a "mild and healing sympathy." The voice of Nature first tells him that the sun will no more see him, that his image will not exist, and that earth will reclaim him ("surrendering up / Thine individual being shalt thou go / To mix forever with the elements, / To be a brother to the insensible rock"). Yet what makes this potentially *ugly* and disturbing teaching of Nature possible to accept is Bryant's reminder that Nature sees to it that man does not go alone and that he goes to a *beautiful* tomb ("Yet not to thine eternal resting-place / Shalt thou retire alone, nor couldst thou wish / Couch more magnificent"). In memorable and beautiful language Bryant depicts the *beauty* of the tomb of all of previous humanity ("All in one mighty sepulchre"):

> . . . The hills
> Rock-ribbed and ancient as the sun; the vales
> Stretching in pensive quietness between;
> The venerable woods, rivers that move
> In majesty, and the complaining brooks
> That make the meadows green; and, poured round all,
> Old Ocean's gray and melancholy waste,—
> Are but the solemn decorations all
> Of the great tomb of man. . . .

Viewed, however, with a satirical eye, the poem can be read as an exercise in making the truly ugly and repugnant thought of death *seem* beautiful through considering it in association with beautiful images from nature: "the hills rock-ribbed and ancient as the sun," "rivers that move in majesty," "the golden sun," "All the infinite host of heaven," "the continuous woods / Where rolls the Oregon," and so forth. Even more relevant to Bryant as a Confidence Man, the poem concludes with a solemn and vague injunction to "trust" (Nature? God?) that places Bryant's most celebrated poem on the side of "trust" and "confidence" in Melville's satirical dialogue between "trust" and "no trust":

> So live that when thy summons comes to join
> The innumerable caravan . . .
> Thou go not, like the quarry-slave at night,
> Scourged to his dungeon, but, *sustained and soothed*
> *By an unfaltering trust,* approach thy grave
> Like one who wraps the drapery of his couch
> About him and lies down to pleasant dreams. (My italics)

In its rhetoric, which diverts the reader from the perception of the ugliness of physical decay in men and animals and from the pain of loss, this poem exploits the notion that the "good melancholy" view of Nature, unlike the "ugly melancholy" view, "may show the world still beautiful" and "may be compatible with benevolence," as John Ringman urges the Collegian to think. Likewise, in "The Death of the Flowers" Bryant expresses a melancholy view that shows the world as still beautiful, when, recalling his sister's death, he concludes: "Yet not unmeet it was that one, like that young friend of ours, / So gentle and so beautiful, should perish with the flowers." Associate death with beauty in Nature, and it will not seem so bad, Bryant is saying. Melville takes this notion and Bryant's well-known interest in visiting cemeteries to an absurd caricatural extreme in Ringman's belief that naturally beautiful cemeteries, such as Mt. Auburn in Cambridge and Greenwood in Brooklyn, should inspire cheery and serene views of Nature and of human nature.

In characterizing Ringman as an exponent of sentimental aesthetic melancholy, who counsels studying the human condition in aesthetically pleasing cemeteries, Melville is caricaturing the public image of Bryant, the poet of beauty in Nature, as well as Bryant's personal interest in cemeteries. He is satirizing the weakness in Bryant's thinking insofar as it reveals the weakness of the Shaftesburyan aesthetic morality—the association of the good with beauty and of evil with ugliness.[16] He is also apparently aware that Akenside's *Pleasures of Imagination* was a prime source for Shaftesburyan moral aestheticism. He has selected a serious intellectual weakness of Bryant's poetry (its foundation in sentimental aestheticism), exaggerated it in Ringman's doctrine ("Learn from me that though the sorrows of the world are great, its wickedness—that is, its ugliness—is small"), and thus brought into the open for understanding and correction the limitations of Bryant's thought properly understood. Melville took poetry and what poetry said very seriously.

It is likely, additionally, that Ringman's special bias against Tacitus may be an allusion to Bryant's customarily fairly radical Democratic politics, as opposed to the Whig views of Henry J. Raymond, whom the Collegian caricatures (see next section), for the Tacitean view of human nature was associated in this period with conservative political opinions. Bryant's liberal, often radical, positions allied him with the "Locofoco politico-literary system" that was represented by "Young America" and the *Democratic Review* in the 1840s—a group with whom Melville was intimate in his first years as a writer in New York.[17] Bryant supported most of the progressive views of his time as they developed from the revolutionary movements of the Enlightenment, according to Parke Godwin (himself a Fourierist).[18] That, on the other hand, Melville in the 1850s admired Tacitus is established by the comments of a newspaper reviewer of his lecture, "Roman Statuary," given in the fall and winter of 1857–58. Melville takes

> The robes from the printed pages of Tacitus and [puts] them upon the lifeless marbles of the Vatican. . . . His affection for heathenism is profound and sincere. He speaks of the heathenism of Rome as if the world were little indebted to Christianity; indeed, as if it had introduced in the place of the old Roman heroism, a sort of trusting pusillanimity.[19]

The encounters of Ringman-Bryant with both Roberts-Wilmot and with Collegian-Raymond should, I think, be read as allusions to Bryant's political relations with David Wilmot, as a fellow antislavery Democrat and with Henry J. Raymond, as a rival Whig editor. Insofar as Roberts caricatures Wilmot, his sympathetic trust in Ringman may be read as alluding to the sympathetic coming together of the author of the antislavery-extension proviso with the Barnburner Democrat—possibly to the occasion when both appeared on the same platform in the Free-Soil convention of 1848 or to some later occasion. Similarly, Roberts' trusting belief in Ringman's sad tale of his wicked wife, Goneril, and of her divorce from him may be read possibly as an allusion to Wilmot's ready sympathy with Bryant's political position in New York State after his quarrel with the Albany-based Democratic Hunkers (conservative Democrats) and his split with them, because Wilmot himself had experienced a similar schism within his own party in Pennsylvania. It is possible, however, that Ringman-Bryant's successful solicitation of Roberts-Wilmot does not refer to any specific action between 1846 and 1856, but rather should be read as alluding generally to the sympathy that existed between the two state movements during this time. After the passage of the Kansas-Nebraska Bill in 1854, they joined together in moving into the new Republican party. The ethical basis of Ringman-Bryant's encounter with Roberts-Wilmot is one of "charity" and "humanity," not, on the surface, a self-interested motive, just as the Free-Soil movement presented itself as noble in its motives, although those motives were questioned rigorously by opponents, especially when they nominated the "wily fox," Martin Van Buren.

Altogether different from Roberts-Wilmot's response in character and in motives is that of the Collegian to the sentimental ideas and the request for "confidence" of Ringman. This encounter alludes, as I interpret it, to the relationship of Bryant, as editor of the Democratic *Evening Post,* with Raymond, ambitious young founder and editor of the New York *Daily Times*—later the *Times*—a strong Whig up until 1855. The Collegian's repulse of Ringman parallels Raymond's general distrust of Bryant as an old-line Jacksonian Democrat and of the Free-Soil movement with which he became associated. As discussed in the following sections, Raymond stayed a true Whig at least through his election as lieutenant governor of New York in 1854, which was maneuvered by Weed; and only then, when Weed himself was ready to move, Raymond transferred himself to the rising new party—an event caricatured, it will be seen, by Collegian-Raymond's eager purchase of stock from Truman-Weed, president of the Black Rapids Coal Company.

Bryant, then, performs as a Confidence Man in pretending to believe in the natural goodness of mankind, which he only half really believes. He is only occasionally successful, however, for, while he can inveigle a fellow-humanitarian like Wilmot into trusting him, he is not successful at all with men such as Raymond, who like good hard reasons for changing their political allegiances—reasons like those that Truman-Weed can adduce: profit. The multiple faces of the new Republican party as Melville saw them include, then, both the cool, mournful one of William Cullen Bryant and the rosy, bustling one of Thurlow Weed—to the latter of which the prudent, young, educated journalist Raymond is most attracted, since it is, after all, that of his former fellow-Whig.

The Collegian

A number of important and conspicuous personal traits and aspects of the career of the New York journalist and politician Henry Jarvis Raymond make him an excellent candidate for the caricature that Melville intends in the Collegian, who is unsuccessfully accosted by John Ringman, the third guise of the Confidence Man (chapter 5) and yet, in another part of the *Fidèle* (chapter 9), is successfully approached by John Truman, the fourth guise, who sells him some stock in the Black Rapids Coal Company. As a theatrical type, the Collegian is modeled on the typical American college man of the period, with literary inclinations. His clothing is poetically careless: a "ladylike open shirt collar, thrown back, and tied with a black ribbon." He wears also what seems to be a fraternity pin, "a square, tableted broach, curiously engraved with Greek characters." He carries "a small book bound in Roman vellum," which turns out to be Arthur Murphy's translation of Tacitus' *Annals.*

In personality in this first scene the Collegian is "pensive," "apparently of a retiring nature," "diffident," and "embarrassed" by Ringman's emotional solicitation of his trust. He abruptly retires from the attack upon Tacitus and from Ringman's lecture on the subject of "beautiful melancholy." However, in the later scene with Truman, who displays to him a "genial jauntiness," he is markedly more forthcoming. He claims twice to be "naturally inquisitive." He drops his diffidence and embarrassment, seems "cool" and "self-collected," and, when it is a question of a business proposition with Truman, he considers it "sagely," and then claims to be "circumspect" about the company's books. Vigorously, he challenges Truman's account of the stock, yet when Truman asserts his great financial optimism and his scorn of "gloomy philosophers," the Collegian knowingly drawls, "I fancy these gloomy souls as little as the next one. Sitting on my sofa after a champagne dinner, smoking my plantation cigar, if a gloomy fellow come to me—what a bore!" He scorns the melancholy sentimentalism of Ringman, when Truman brings up his name, for he likes "prosperous fellows, comfortable fellows," like Truman. He says that he wants to invest in the company right then. His worldliness is fully evident despite the appearance of a scholar. When questioned about this discrepancy by Truman, he defends the nature of "the modern scholar," who is, in his opinion, a believer in experience as the only teacher and, "chiefly governed by the maxim of Lord Bacon," he is not a speculator in any philosophy except those "which come home to [his] business and bosom," *i.e.*, "good stocks." Truman calls him "prudent," when he is reluctant to purchase stock in the "New Jerusalem" land speculation in Minnesota. Melville is evidently satirizing here a man who has the looks of a young college intellectual, but who is really a cautious man of the world, who prefers the company of apparently prosperous business-like men such as Truman to that of melancholy "literary" types such as Ringman. Much of the humor here emerges only when the reader realizes that the supposedly "intellectual" or "literary" type such as Raymond pretended to be is repulsing vigorously the poet Bryant.

The target of Melville's satire here, the evidence strongly indicates, is again a man prominent in the literary, journalistic, and political life of New York in the 1850s: Henry Jarvis Raymond (1820–1869), founder in 1851 of the New York *Daily Times* and, during the period Melville was writing his satire, lieutenant governor of New York. Raymond was an early journalistic associate of Greeley on his literary and news periodical, the *New-Yorker*, and later on the *Tribune* (1840–43). He also worked for Webb's *Courier & Enquirer* (1843–51), and was managing editor of *Harper's Monthly Magazine* (1850–56), during the period when Melville contributed sketches and articles. He was elected to the New York State Assembly as a Whig in 1849 and 1850, and he was Speaker of the assembly in 1850. He was a powerful public opinion maker as editor, pamphleteer, and public speaker, and became an intimate political associate of Seward and Weed, one result of which was his nomination and election as lieutenant governor (1855–57).[20] Bennett always spoke of Raymond as the editor of "the Junior Organ" of the "Holy Alliance" of Seward, Weed, and Greeley—the *Tribune* being the "Senior Organ."

Several personal qualities link Raymond with the Collegian. His age would be thirty-six in 1856, but in physical appearance he was described as "of rather small stature" (five feet six inches), and as having an almost boyish appearance even in adulthood. His youthful appearance was frequently commented upon, and it led to his being caricatured as a schoolboy in short pants, who is markedly short and young-looking despite a long moustache and whiskers (plates 9, 15, and 23).[21] Raymond's appearance, however, like the Collegian's, was contradicted by his personality, which was described as "self-possessed," "urbane," "cool," "calm," and prudent. Bennett called him "cool" and "calculating" and writes of the "littleness of the stature of the inquisitive modern Zaccheus" (*Herald,* 8 June, 1 July 1856). Henry Adams, seeking a "teacher" in Washington in 1860, "took most kindly to Henry J. Raymond, . . . who was a man of the world,"—like Melville's Collegian as revealed in his second scene. Henry B. Stanton called him "a lively companion" and a good storyteller, as the Collegian appears to be with the convivial Truman.[22] As a journalistic genius, he may readily be assumed to have been "naturally inquisitive."

Certain aspects of Raymond's career, apart from his editorial and political interests, especially make him apt for caricature as a "collegian." He was a graduate of the University of Vermont (1840), where he had intended to pursue a career as a literary man, a scholar, or a teacher, and had belonged to Phi Sigma Nu, a literary society—to which the Collegian's Greek broach probably alludes. Throughout his life he kept unusually close ties with his college—returning each year for commencement, frequently as speaker, and serving on the board of trustees. He "always enjoyed the atmosphere of any university." Bennett called him a "blue-stocking."[23]

Evidently Raymond was a man who had literary and scholarly pretensions, although he became a journalist. As a student in his teens he was a close friend and correspondent of Rufus Griswold, the literary historian and scholar, and he sent literary work to Greeley's *New-Yorker.* During the years that he worked with Greeley on the *Tribune* his specialty was the literary department including general reviewing. While on Webb's *Courier & Enquirer* the literary articles were attributed to him. The Collegian's copy of Tacitus's *Annals* may, besides its conservative political symbolism, be an allusion to Raymond's short stint as Latin teacher in a private girls' school in New York City in his lean early years. His work for *Harper's Monthly Magazine,* which was mainly literary, and as a reader of manuscripts for the publishing house of Harpers Brothers undoubtedly gave him prestige as being more than a journalist in the new York literary-publishing world. Evert Duyckinck knew him both as a subscriber to the *Literary World* and as editor of the *Times,* for which Duyckinck wrote articles during 1857.[24] Melville may have known him personally.

One of Raymond's best known addresses, given to the alumni of the University of Vermont, August 1850, had the topic, "The Relation of the American Scholar to His Country and His Times." Frequently citing Francis Bacon, it is permeated by Raymond's version of the Baconian philosophy of the requirement of the scholar to pursue the active life. I believe that Melville is presenting a caricatural exaggeration of Raymond's Baconian views in the Collegian's emphasis upon "philosophies which come home to [his] business and bosom" such as those of "Lord Bacon."

Raymond defines the scholar as one who has acquired "mental and . . . moral power" through his studies, and says that it is his duty, "when he goes forth into active life, to use it, . . . to improve the condition and advance the well-being of his fellow men." He deprecates strongly scholars who would "isolate themselves [and] withdraw from the struggling activities of life, and become solitary worshippers of the studies which have enlisted their love." Calling such scholars, who pursue knowledge for its own sake, "misers" and "false" to humanity and the Christian faith, he quotes Bacon's maxim that "the power to do good is the true and lawful end of all aspiring. For good thoughts . . . are little better than good dreams, except they be put in act." Affirming a deep belief in both the certainty of individual progress and social progress, Raymond claims that "printing . . . has done more to improve individual character, to make men wiser and better, to inspire society with love of truth and regard for right, and thus to promote that general well-being in which true progress consists, than all the speculations of all the philosophers of the ancient world," a view that accords well with the attitude of the Collegian, who reads Tacitus for "his gossip" not his wisdom, and shares Truman's dislike of "musty old Seneca." Quoting Bacon, again, on language as "the footsteps and prints of reason," Raymond would have the scholar pursue Bacon's goal—to gain "greater power over nature and over man," through the study of the laws of thought and the arrangement of "Nature's divine machinery." Taking a view that is diametrically opposed to Melville's own mature choice of life, he attacks the "reclusive scholar," saying that "in this country, especially, no man can be wholly a private citizen; no man can throw off all public and all social duties. . . . Every man is of necessity . . . a politician." The American scholar has "no right to withdraw" from public duties. Although allowing for the "profounder and more exclusive devotion to solid learning" of a "higher class of scholars," not even they, he says, may "hold themselves aloof from the race but should remember ever that their true end is 'God's glory and the relief of Man's estate.'" Melville has caricatured in the figure of the Collegian this conception of the scholar's duty to apply his knowledge to the active life, possibly because Raymond in his own life may have appeared to have distorted it, using it as a justification of his own pursuit of power, prestige, and wealth in American public life.[25]

A further point in Raymond's address that links him and his attitudes with the Collegian is his espousal of an optimistic view of society. Citing the opinion of some thoughtful men that tendencies of American society are "evil and dangerous"—downward—and that "radicalism" is bringing all society "to one dead and unproductive level," Raymond says that this "gloomy representation of American society and life" leads some men to want the scholar to combat this radicalism and to bring society back to the old ways which experience has sanctified, and which ancestral wisdom has stamped "with approbation." Raymond, like the Collegian, who dislikes "gloomy fellows" and "ravens" who "sulk," sees "the effect of thus dwelling exclusively upon the darker and least promising symptoms of our social life" as injurious, because it tends to bring "scholars and the world into hostile relations, to implant distrust and defiance where common interests demand that sympathy, mutual confidence, and hopeful alliance, should unite both for a common end." He denies the correctness of this "condemnation" of American society, saying that it is yet young, and that its social evils are not yet rooted and chronic—a view which is, again, diametrically opposed to Melville's own mature views. Optimistically (though without mentioning slavery), Raymond says that the "disease" of social evil is not so rooted that the knife necessary to cut it away threatens the life of the patient, as it would in European society (and as many men more pessimistic than Raymond believed that the attempt to cure the disease of slavery in America would do). Quoting Bacon, for the third time, on the present as the "true antiquity of the world," he defines true conservatism as the Baconian principle of favoring the tested from the past, while welcoming the best of the new. He criticizes the crusade of distrust against the progressive spirit of the age, and affirms his trust in the "latent conservatism" of the American society. Scholars, he says, are apt, from their study and seclusion, to be overly "desponding" of the prospects of the country, a view that seems echoed by the Collegian's ready agreement with Truman's disparagement of "a gloomy fellow" (a "raven"), who, in Truman's words, is a "sulk" and a "recluse," who gets his gloomy ideas from "old plays" or "old books" and who "sets about stuffing himself with that stale old hay; and . . . thinks it looks wise and antique to be a croaker."[26]

Citing Bacon again, this time as a hero of the seventeenth century, Raymond argues against regarding that century as a whole as an admirable period, for he claims great and certain moral progress in this country, where "even in politics, virtue is essential to success." The present state "warrants that confidence" in progress made and "sympathy with the tendency of the times," the hopefulness and cheerful courage needed. His entire argument is against gloomy philosophers, who see better times and wisdom in the past, and it is for optimism about the present American society. Finally, Raymond claims that his views are the result of "observation and experience" in an active life, although he calls himself a "scholar," an "educated" man.[27]

This was Raymond in 1850. Although he edited and possibly wrote for *Harper's Monthly Magazine* in the 1850s, his literary-scholarly ambitions seem gradually to have faded away as the newly founded *Times* grew successful through his journalistic genius and the commercially advantageous business skills of his partners, George Jones and E. B. Wesley, the two banknote brokers who put up the capital for its establishment. He also became politically successful through his friendships with Seward and Weed. It is important to notice that politically, even after he helped to found the Republican party, Raymond remained in many ways a Whig conservative—a "Tory" to Greeley—and he distrusted and disliked intensely Greeley's socialistic ideas and most kinds of reform movement. He said early, in his delicately ironic tone, that he did not feel that he was "of those who 'feel personally responsible for the turning of the earth upon its axis,' nor did [he] deem it [his] special 'mission' to reorganize society."[28] Early in his career he had achieved journalistic fame in debate with Greeley in 1846–47, in an exchange of articles in the *Courier & Enquirer* and in the *Tribune* on the socialist-utopian theories of the Fourierite Albert Brisbane, whom Greeley defended. There probably is an allusion to Raymond's ironic rejection of any kind of socialistic "Association" or "Phalanx" in the Collegian's scornful rejection of any stock in the "New Jerusalem" to be built in Minnesota.

Raymond's personality and politics come together as being both conservative and "circumspect," as the Collegian is, in the following typical example of his written style:

> The world needs discretion as much as zeal, and although the latter generally usurps all the honors and glories of heroism, the former does a great deal the most toward carrying on the daily affairs of society and states. If everybody were discreet and nobody zealous, things would certainly go on much better than if everybody were zealous and nobody discreet. This form of statement, however, misleads—as it makes extremes the standard of comparison and judgment, which is never safe.

> Zeal tempered and guided by discretion, or discretion warmed and
> energized by zeal, is the true temperament for safe and successful con-
> duct.

His modern biographer, Francis Brown, comments: "It was a standard by
which Raymond, increasingly as he grew older, measured his own conduct."
In personality he lacked zeal and partisanship—"the power of passion"—as
Lyman Abbott phrased it. He was always "prudent" and possessed the ability
to see both sides of a question. Some saw him as "reserved, cold, and not a
little calculating." He was bookish and "remained in adult life the cold,
logical debater of the University." Brown writes of him that he was "inconsistent . . . and he scrapped on many occasions the aloof view of the scholar—
but he retained it sufficiently to impress those who did not know him well
as a complex personality whose devious ways could be best set down as those
of a trimmer."[29] Reform, political or social, was not in his blood, and to
some extent he must have denied it in others, for he saw the North-South
conflict always as a struggle for political power and only secondarily as about
the moral issue of slavery. One may add that, very likely, he would never have
welcomed the friendship of Benjamin Lundy, as John Quincy Adams did, but
he willingly joined the Republican party, when it was well on its way to
power on the antislavery issue.

With this biographical image of Raymond in mind, it is possible, then,
to read the curious double solicitation of the Collegian—first by Ringman-
Bryant and then by Truman-Weed—as alluding to the political positions
taken by Raymond in relation to the emergence in politics of the antislavery
movement: first, in the Free-Soil–Barnburner faction and, second, in the
formation of the Republican party in the period 1854–56. Melville portrays
Raymond first as impervious to the "sentimental," zealously moralistic solicitations of the antislavery movement as represented by Bryant in the editorial
position of the *Post* and as represented by Bryant's involvement in the Free-
Soil party and the Democratic Barnburner faction after 1846–47. Raymond
wrote of William Leggett, Bryant's abolitionist associate on the *Post*, after
his death: "Leggett was certainly a brave and gifted man. His abolitionism
was a result of a noble impulse, but I cannot join with Whittier in wishing
all young men to be like Leggett. The world needs discretion. . . ."[30]

In the later scene with Truman the allusion is to Raymond's rapid entrance into the newly formed Republican party in September 1855 (as soon
as Weed transferred his party mechanism and his efforts to it), an action
depicted in the Collegian's eager welcome of Truman and purchase of stock
in the Black Rapids Coal Company—which may possibly be a joke on the
"Black Republican" central committee which Weed ran (although the nominal

chairman was E. D. Morgan).[31] The conversation between Truman-Weed and Collegian-Raymond about the pessimistic "bears" whose "growling" brings down the value of Truman's "stock" alludes, I believe, through the stock-market imagery, to the frequent current predictions of danger to the Union in the formation of the new and admittedly sectional party. As background to the following polemical passage of Truman-Weed the reader should have well in mind the growing fear, expressed by more observant and wiser politicians than Weed, that the new political coalition that was "fusing" under the name "Republican" was not the answer to the sectional differences, but would only exacerbate them—which fear proved historically to be entirely true:

> "These same destroyers of confidence, and gloomy philosophers of the stock-market, though false in themselves, are yet true types of most destroyers of confidence and gloomy philosophers, the world over. Fellows who, whether in stocks, politics, bread-stuffs, morals, metaphysics, religion—be it what it may—trump up their black panics in the naturally-quiet brightness, solely with a view to some sort of covert advantage. That corpse of calamity which the gloomy philosopher parades, is but his Good-Enough-Morgan."

The "corpse of calamity" to which Truman-Weed applies the term "Good-Enough-Morgan" (a term meaning an excuse for a political attack, which originated in a remark of Weed's during the anti-Masonic movement in 1827) had in national politics increasingly for thirty years been the threat of secession—of the breakup of the American Union. Time and again, as David Potter writes, in *Lincoln and His Party in the Secession Crisis,* the South had cried "wolf" and gotten its way in political events, until the North practically and disastrously ceased to listen and heed the warning signals. John Truman, like Thurlow Weed himself, refuses to credit those "spurious Jeremiahs; sham Heraclituses," while the Collegian in this exchange, like Henry Raymond, detests "gloomy souls" who predict disaster. The Collegian's following speech expresses an almost mindless optimism, which is strikingly akin to the obliviousness of national danger that Potter describes as characteristic of the Republican leaders up to and after their election victory in November 1860—despite all of the South's warnings and those of the "Cassandras" of the North:[32]

> "Sitting on my sofa after a champagne dinner, smoking my plantation cigar, if a gloomy fellow come to me—what a bore! . . . I tell him it ain't natural. I say to him, you are happy enough, and you know it;

and everybody else is as happy as you, and you know that, too; and we shall all be happy after we are no more, and you know that, too; but no, still you must have your sulk." (p. 41)

Continuing their rapport, Truman-Weed scorns the wisdom of the "recluse," which he derives from seeing "old plays" (Weed preferred Dickens) or reading "old books" such as "musty old Seneca." He detests any man who thinks "it looks wise and antique to be a croaker" (*i.e.*, a predicter of disasters, especially political disasters). Like Raymond, again, in his political optimism, the Collegian joins in spirit with Truman-Weed's hopeful views: "I like prosperous fellows, comfortable fellows; fellows that talk comfortably and prosperously, like you." Four years, at least, before the secession crisis that led to the Civil War Melville is depicting in literary satire, as certain graphic artists also did, the limits of the political intelligence of two of the leaders of the Republican party. In retrospect the satire is hardly funny, nor must it have seemed so to him in later years nor to any readers then who comprehended it.

Typically, in January 1855, Raymond was charged with "trimming" in his office as lieutenant governor, to which he had been elected as a Whig, along with Myron Clark of the Temperance party as governor. Raymond traded and lobbied as a dutiful Whig to obtain the U.S. senatorship for Seward, which was Weed's objective also. As soon as this was achieved, the fusion between the Sewardite Whigs and the already active New York Republican organization could take place, which it did at Syracuse in September 1855. At this point Raymond became an active speaker and writer for the party; he attacked slavery extension and the "Slave Power" as being an ambitious political usurper—not on the moral issue of slavery. He called the new party "conservative," taking pains to discount the radical elements apparent in it. Raymond wrote the important "Address to the People," which opened the national organizational meeting of the Republicans on 22 February 1856, and which was adopted by the convention and widely reprinted. He appeared as a speaker at the Tabernacle meeting of the party in April with Bryant and Charles A. Dana, managing editor of the *Tribune.* Throughout this period he believed in "prudence" not zealous espousal of a cause, and usually he accepted Weed's experienced advice and political strategy. For example, although he favored Seward for president in 1856, as did Weed, he editorialized for Frémont for the nomination in June, when it became apparent both that Frémont was more "available" to "the people" at that time and that in order for Seward to win the presidency it was wiser for him to wait until 1860, when Republican chances to win the election seemed better than in 1856.[33] It is precisely this prudence which is alluded to in Truman's remark to the Collegian, "Prudent—you are prudent" (p. 56).

It has been necessary, in order to interpret fully the actions of the Collegian, to jump ahead in the discussion to chapter 9, "Two Business Men Transact a Little Business," and to take up his encounter with Truman, thus anticipating my interpretation of Truman as a caricature of Thurlow Weed, the New York political boss (see Chapter 7). Now, however, to follow the narrative we must return to chapter 6, where, after the last direct appearance of Ringman, there occurs the first appearance of the Man in a Gray Coat and White Tie, who is the second name on Black Guinea's list and is the fourth disguise of the Confidence Man. I shall offer evidence that the Man in Gray is a caricature of Theodore Parker, through whom Melville satirizes the pulpit-politician and his manipulation of the Christian doctrine of charity as it was used in the antislavery political movement.

7

The Fourth and Fifth Confidence Men (the
Man in Gray and John Truman) and Several
Antagonists (the Gentleman with Gold Sleeve-Buttons,
the Charitable Lady, the Elderly Quaker, the
Dried-Up Man, and Others)

The Man in Gray

The Man in Gray Coat and White Tie, the fourth guise of the Confidence Man, claims to be charity agent for a "Seminole Widow and Orphan Asylum," and appears in six encounters. He speaks up for Guinea's "worthiness," argues for trust generally, and successfully solicits money from two men (the Episcopal Clergyman and the Gentleman with Gold Sleeve-Buttons) and one woman (the Charitable Lady). Yet he is repulsed by three men (the Wooden-Legged Man, the Well-To-Do Man, and the Hard-Hearted Man). There is considerable evidence in appearance, personality and style that Melville intends to caricature Theodore Parker's public role as preacher, lecturer, pamphleteer, and soliciter of funds for the "Free Kansas" movement, which preceded the formation of the Republican party.

The Man in Gray—"the righteous man"—appears in chapter 6 as a "child of misfortune," like the Man with the Weed, but when more closely observed his face shows, rather, "much of sanctity"—*i.e.* he has a "holier than thou" look, as we might say today. This look is reinforced by observations that his face displays "latent though chastened {self-?} reliance," is "as long as my arm," and is "forlorn." His smile is "wan," and he seems humorless. In chapter 7, standing beside the Gentleman with Gold Sleeve-Buttons, his personality emerges as "unsprightly" and "soberly continent." He shows "animation" only when the Gentleman arouses his interest by suggesting a confederation of charities. Encountering the Charitable Lady (chapter 8), he displays "his original air, a quiescent one, blended of sad humility and demureness," and he shows "an air of melancholy exhaustion and depression," which attracts her attention. In his wan, sanctimonious, humorless physical appearance, not only does he resemble Parker, but he resembles the typical graphic caricature of the reformist clergyman in cartoons of the period.[1] Both his short stature and his inferior social class, irrespective of his profession, appear when Melville contrasts him to the rich Gentleman with Gold Sleeve-Buttons, beside whom he appears to be an "inferior, apparently, not more in the social scale than in stature."

His manner of persuasion varies from the "low, sad tone, full of deference," that he uses with the Charitable Lady—with whom he wishes to "mingle souls"—to the "not unsilvery tongue" and "pentecostal" gestures with the Gentleman. Mainly, however, with the Gentleman, with the Wooden-Legged Man, and with the Episcopal Clergyman his method of persuasion is rationalistic. For example, defending Black Guinea's genuineness he appeals to reason: "For I put it to you, is it reasonable to suppose that a man with brains . . . would take all that trouble . . . for the mere sake of those few paltry coppers . . . ?" His "prospectus" of the World's Charity—a comprehensive scheme to "methodize" the world's benevolence—parodies rationalistic schemes for social improvement. When the Gentleman objects that this sort of reasoning "seems all reasonable enough," but that it "won't do" with mankind, the "righteous man" answers: "Then mankind are not reasoning beings, if reason won't do with them." On the other hand, with the Charitable Lady, who is a widow, he uses emotion, appealing to her sentimental feeling for a "Widow and Orphan Asylum."

Stylistically, the speech of the Man in Gray exhibits a staccato movement of short or medium length clauses linked by commas or semicolons; frequent use of rhetorical questions; frequent use of "I," "we," and "you"; imagery and exempla from a wide range of geography and history (Rome, Hong Kong, Africa, London, Turkey); a striking figure from the New England pin industry; and, most obviously of all, a remarkable and consistent use of statistics in his appeal to the Gentleman in chapter 7.

The profession of the Man in Gray, as he presents himself, is that of a practical philanthropist—"no Fourier, . . . but a philanthropist and financier setting forth a philanthropy and a finance which are practicable." He claims to invent ways to "ease human suffering" (such as his "Protean" easy chair exhibited at the London World's Fair), and he seeks to methodize benevolent activities in order to make them more efficient. He would introduce "the Wall Street spirit" into charity. He is not a profound thinker, nor does he seek to convert personally anyone to Christianity. He seems to be a practical reformer, loosely connected to Christianity, who accepts the ways of the modern world and, "mindful of the millenial promise," believes that the "age of wonders" is not passed. His spirit of benevolence, characterized in agricultural imagery, goes over all the countries of the globe, "much as the diligent spirit of the husbandman, stirred by forethought of the coming seedtime, leads him, in March reveries at his fireside, over every field of his farm." Additionally, Melville characterizes him as the "righteous" man, contrasting him with the "good" man (the Gentleman). This "righteousness" is related to his appearance of "sanctity" and his casual assumption that "doing good to the world with a will . . . doing good to the world once for all and having done with it" by *his* rationalistic methods is the best thing for the world.

Many details of appearance, personality, type of argument, and style substantiate that the Man in Gray is a caricature of Theodore Parker (1810–1860), the Massachusetts ex-Unitarian preacher, lecturer, reformer, friend of the Transcendentalist group, "conscience" of the Republican party, and one of the most noted "philanthropists" of the period.[2] Of his fame as a preacher and lecturer T. W. Higginson wrote in *Contemporaries* (1899), "Probably [there was] no private man in the nation unless it were Beecher or Greeley whom personal strangers were so eager to see."[3] The white tie or cravat of the Man in Gray marks him as a clergyman.[4] Like the Man in Gray, in physical appearance Parker was described as "short . . . in figure," with features that were "quiet" and almost "bashful." Henry C. Wright called him a "little, plain, meek-looking man." His manner was described as "plain, modest, unassuming," more like that of a schoolmaster, farmer, or ploughman than a clergyman's.[5] Lowell depicts his farmer-like appearance and the effects of his eloquence in *A Fable for Critics*:

> There he stands, looking more like a ploughman than priest,
> If not dreadfully awkward, not graceful at least,
> His gestures all downright and same, if you will,
> As of brown-fisted Hobnail in hoeing a drill;
> But his periods fall on you, stroke after stroke,
> Like the blows of a lumberer felling an oak,
> You forget the man wholly, you're thankful to meet
> With a preacher who smacks of the field and the street.[6]

The comparison to a ploughman was fairly common, reflecting Parker's background as a farmer's son and a farmer himself as a youth before he went to Harvard. Emerson in his eulogy called him "a son of the soil."[7] Melville's comparison of the Man in Gray to the "noon sickleman" and to the diligent "husbandman" anticipating spring crops seems based on this association of Parker with farming. Another characteristic of Parker, his relative lack of humor, links him to the Man in Gray, who is "unsprightly" and "soberly continent."[8]

Concerning Parker's personal manner with men and women, his friend John Weiss speaks of his "thirst for affection" and for sympathy and friendship; he "would be loved by men" and "took a childish delight in human society."

He longed also for intimacy and could not understand why he was the "best-hated man in America." Weiss notes also that he was subject to "melancholy moods" frequently, as is the Man in Gray. He had, also, a known liking for the friendship of women. Of himself Parker wrote, "My companions of choice, and not necessity, are almost all women. I wonder at this; . . . I have always been intimate with eminent women, . . . and I number but few eminent men among my acquaintance."[9] Parker's craving for human sympathy, in particular that of women, seems to be ridiculed in the episode of the Man in Gray's solicitation of the Charitable Lady on the basis of their "mingling souls" (chapter 8).

As lecturer and orator Parker, like the Man in Gray, relied more upon factual and historical content and the rationality of his arguments and ideas for conviction than upon illustration, mimicry, and humor, as did Henry Ward Beecher, or upon the graces of presence and voice, as did his friend Wendell Phillips, who was in reputation a greater orator. According to a contemporary, George W. Bungay, "His face [is] dull, until he becomes animated before an audience," precisely as the Man in Gray rises from "a soberly continent air" to "animation" and a "not unsilvery tongue," as he warms to his argument with the Gentleman. According to a contemporary he displayed "a certain winningness of manner which attracts and gratifies the hearer." Though free of ostentation or artificiality he had power both of thought and composition as well as a "deep earnestness" that chained his hearers, as the Man in Gray holds the Gentleman as his auditor. Higginson describes his method as unadorned fact, often with a "sense of purpose and of power, [and] clear and lucid . . . delivery." Emerson notes his constant use of facts and his skill with them, as well as his logical method and his eye for historical relations. McCall in his essay on Parker as public speaker notes his heavy reliance on both intuition (conscience) and rational processes for his ultimate authority. He appealed to pride and love of mankind.[10] These aspects of his rhetoric are reflected in the Man in Gray's appeal to pride, when he says to the Gentleman, "That a Christian should talk so," and his appeal to love in asking the Charitable Lady, who has just been reading St. Paul's praise of love, to donate to the Seminole Widow and Orphan Asylum.

Stylistically, the conversation of the Man in Gray parodies some of the most noted characteristics of Parker's oratory and writings. McCall notes that he was very concerned about his audience and that it was the primary consideration in his style, accounting for the oral quality, for the staccato effect of his short, terse sentences, and the directness of address that resulted in a frequent use of "I," "we," and "you."[11] His sentences in his printed lectures tend to be made up of short or medium-length clauses linked by commas or semicolons; he has the habit of using the rhetorical question.[12] The wide range of historical and geographical references that the Man in Gray commands caricatures the constant habit of Parker, who was one of the most learned scholars of his day, of putting his scholarship to use in his speeches. Higginson suggests that his great learning might sometimes have impaired the quality of his thought.[13] Lowell, in *A Fable for Critics,* jokes at tedious length about Parker's learning, in the lines following those previously quoted: "And he talks in one breath of Confutzee, Cass, Zerduscht, / Jack Robinson, Peter the Hermit, Strap, Dathan, / Cush, Pitt . . . / Pan, Pillicock, Shakespeare, Paul, . . . " A work that displays well this aspect of his style is "Upon the Transient and Permanent in Christianity," but nearly any essay or speech reveals his broad range of reference to geographical and historical fact.[14]

Another strong stylistic mannerism noted by his readers and hearers was Parker's use of references to New England. This trait seems to account for the unusual simile, drawn from the specializations involved in the manufacture of a pin, in this passage: "Charity is not like a pin, one to make the head, and the other the point; charity is a work to which a good workman may be competent in all its branches. I invented my Protean easy-chair in odd intervals stolen from meals and sleep." Besides alluding to Parker's practical Yankee nature and background and to his much noted habit of overworking himself, this passage takes its figure from the New England industry of pinmaking.[15]

A final stylistic mannerism that connects most closely of all the style of the Man in Gray with Parker's oral and written style is the use of statistics. Weiss remarks upon Parker's love of statistics. Frothingham notes that his sermons "cost vast labor in compiling statistics." Higginson notes that he knew that New England people love "a philosophical arrangement and a plenty of statistics." Commager notes Parker's use of statistics in contrast to Charles Sumner's use of classical quotation. Albrecht calls him a New Englander who insisted upon facts, be they statistical, historical, or theological. Examples of Parker's addresses that are replete with statistics and tables are "A Sermon of the Perishing Classes in Boston" (1846), "The Mexican War" (1848), "The State of the Nation" (1850), "An Anti-Slavery Address" (1854), and especially "The Progress of America" (1854).[16]

Like the Man in Gray, and like some of the other New England reformers of the period, Parker was a philanthropist of the kind for whom Melville did not evidently have much respect.[17] He was a devout believer in rational schemes for reform. He rejoiced in the Fourierist movement because he felt "Our present form of society is irrational and unchristian."[18] He thought of himself as arousing "sentiment" through his sermons and addresses and then organizing the sentiment into the "idea," leaving the actual application of the "idea" to laws and institutions to the "political reformers." In chapter 7 the Man in Gray's invention of the "Protean easy-chair" seems to be a sharp satirical thrust at Parker's reform schemes, which might be interpreted as overeasy methods to ease the guilt of a New England conscience. The "Protean easy-chair" is "so all over bejointed, behinged, and bepadded . . . that in some one of its . . . accommodations . . . the most restless body, the body most racked, nay, I had almost added the most tormented conscience must somehow and somewhere, find rest." This notion of an all-purpose chair that might even give comfort to a "tormented conscience" points up by its absurdity the vanity of any easy earthly scheme to relieve the miseries of mankind, whether psychological, physical, or social. Disillusionment with oversimplified solutions to evils that have existed from the beginning of history is a pervasive Melvillean theme after 1848.

There is a strong possibility, also, that the Man in Gray's role as an agent for the Seminole Widow and Orphan Asylum may be an allusion to Parker's role as agent for the Massachusetts Emigrant Aid Society, which formed following the passage of the Kansas-Nebraska Bill (May 1854) and was connected with the disturbances in Kansas. Parker organized committees, raised money, circulated petitions, counseled politicians, preached, and lectured for this group.[19] During and after the presidential campaign of 1856 Democratic newspapers and public speakers were highly skeptical about the Kansas movement, treating the "troubles in Kansas," the formation of the emigrant aid societies, and the solicitations for "Funds for Widows and Orphans" as a "grand humbug that has been played off upon the people of the North." The entire Free Kansas movement was regarded from this political point of view as an exploitation of religious and philanthropic feeling by unscrupulous political villains. Singled out by Democratic editorialists for criticism were ministers such as Parker, Higginson, and Henry Ward Beecher, in particular, as clerical "frauds."[20]

Of Parker's efforts in politics in the middle 1850s and for the Republicans in 1856 Commager writes that he was "father-confessor and spiritual advisor to all the leaders of the Free Soil and Republican parties." He traveled all around the country, Commager writes, and men listened to his politics. "Only Beecher could command a greater audience, only Greeley was more widely read." Of the effects of his work Commager comments that he felt that his task as nonpolitical reformer was to create sentiment, to advance ideas, to suggest modes of action; he prescribed patterns for politicians to cut out. With this bent toward rational reform schemes, committees, exhortations, Parker was called the "conscience" of the Republican party.[21] It is this personal characteristic of rationalistic, programmatic speech and action combined with a highly individualistic and intuitive concept of absolute conscience that, I think, has been captured by Melville and caricatured in the Man in Gray as his impression of Parker's public personality. The "Seminole Widow and Orphan Asylum" may be read as a caricature of the Emigrant Aid Society and the "World's Charity," of the various benevolent organizations to which Parker gave aid and solicited the aid of others. Moreover, Parker had a secular millenialistic concept of the future of the United States as an industrial democracy. He accepted the Northern commercial values as the criteria of progress. He somehow assumed that spiritual values would go along with industrial development in the form of more schools, more churches, more lyceums, and more asylums. This acceptance of the inevitability of moral and industrial progress may account for the Man in Gray's desire for a World's Charity "quickened by the Wall Street spirit"—hardly the Holy Spirit.

As for the general characteristic of "righteousness," the connection between Parker and the Man in Gray is close enough to suggest that it may be just this personal attribute that determined Melville upon his choice of Parker for caricature as his clerical charity agent. "Righteous" and "self-righteous" are adjectives frequently used to describe Parker by friends and by those unsympathetic to him. Albrecht writes, "That he spoke always and only with self-righteousness even his enemies would admit." Even in criticizing the historian Prescott, Parker wanted "righteous history in which the historian would not only tell all, but judge all." The motive for his "passion for righteousness" was "to make the will of God prevail"—by his efforts and schemes. [22]

As the Confidence Man, the Man in Gray solicits five other characters, and in a sixth encounter he is attacked by the Wooden-Legged Cynic. To see what Melville is saying each one should be seen in some relationship to Parker, either as an individual in his or her historical context or as a social type who bore some relationship to Theodore Parker or to his type of radical cleric. It has been possible to identify either with some or with considerable evidence the following: the Episcopal Clergyman as Dudley A. Tyng (see Chapter 5), the Gentleman in Gold Sleeve-Buttons as Abbott Lawrence (see Chapter 7), the Charitable Lady as probably Lydia Sigourney (see Chapter 7), the Wooden-Legged Cynic as James Gordon Bennett (see Chapter 5), and the Hard-Hearted Old Gentleman as Lewis Cass (see next section). I have not yet been able to track down an identity for the Well-To-Do Gentleman "in a ruby-colored velvet vest," although for the moment he may be probably identified as some Whig or Democrat who did not join in the movement against the Kansas-Nebraska Act and who would therefore repulse Parker's efforts to solicit aid for a free Kansas. Men who were "Cotton" Whigs who might be models for this vignette would include Nathan Appleton, Robert Winthrop, George Ticknor Curtis, Rufus Choate, and Edward Everett. New York State Whigs would include D. D. Barnard and Washington Hunt. Massachusetts Democrats worth considering would include Caleb Cushing and Benjamin Hallett. Possible New York Democrats would include Marcy, Daniel Dickinson, and Charles O'Connor. Further research may reveal an individual associated with a "ruby-colored velvet vest" with a direct connection with Parker.

Taking up the characters slightly out of sequence of appearance, I propose that the scene in chapter 6 in which the Man in Gray discusses Black Guinea with the young Episcopal Clergyman and is challenged by the Wooden-Legged Man has as its background the New York City public context in which Parker had appeared for years as a lecturer on the platforms of the various antislavery societies and, in 1855, of the anti-Nebraska movement, where he was vociferously attacked by Bennett in the columns of the *Herald* and yet made a strong impact on an audience that had previously not been reached by his speeches on the Fugitive Slave Act and on slavery generally. I base my contention that he had an impact on the young Episcopal clergyman Dudley Tyng mainly on the textual evidence that Tyng's notable address, distributed in pamphlet form, displays throughout the influence of Parker's thought and politics. I have not yet uncovered evidence of a direct personal relationship either through newspaper accounts of meetings or through records in letters or biographies. That there was communication on some public level I am convinced, or that Melville, at least, believed or was given to believe that there was communication. More work needs to be done on this. That Bennett attacked Parker often in the *Herald,* just as the Wooden-Legged Man does the Man in Gray, there is abundant evidence in the pages of the *Herald,* as well as that the basis of his attacks was his skepticism about the motives of the men involved in the political antislavery movement, the anti-Nebraska movement, and the aid-to-Kansas movement. The Wooden-Legged Man questions the genuineness of Black Guinea, whom the Man in Gray defends, and suggests that not money but power is the motive of the "white scoundrel" whom he masks, just as Bennett imputed motives of power and patronage to the men who, in his view, exploited the slavery issue. In their dialogue Bennett's skeptical views of the humanitarian appeal of Guinea contend with Parker's philanthropic views for the soul of the young Clergyman (Tyng), and Parker wins, for the Wooden-Legged Man retires, leaving the field to the Man in Gray. After some little debate, the Clergyman gives him a "mite" for Black Guinea and something for the Asylum, just as Tyng joined the antislavery movement and gave up his parish in Philadelphia to join the political campaign for the Republican candidate in August 1856. It may be surmised from the statements in his address that he also contributed to the Kansas emigration aid effort.

The Well-To-Do Man and the Hard-Hearted Old Gentleman

The two characters who repulse the Man in Gray at the opening of chapter 6 are depicted in tiny vignettes that resemble in their minute definition of detail the graphic precision of the prints of Hogarth, where frequently in some small detail an entire character is revealed or a story is suggested. The first of these is the Well-To-Do Gentleman, who appears in a "ruby-colored velvet vest, and with a ruby-colored cheek, [and] a ruby-headed cane in his hand." This precise selection of physical details points, it seems evident, to a certain individual, perhaps as known widely through a portrait. For the moment he may be identified as some rich (because he is called "well-to-do" and has an expensive cane), well-living (ruby-cheeked) man who feels himself of high-social level, since his manner toward the Man in Gray's solicitations is haughty and he reacts with "pettish words" and "touchy disgust" to him, saying "You—pish. Why will the captain suffer these begging fellows on board?" His manners are not, however, especially good, for he "repulses" him "rudely." It seems likely, as suggested above, that Melville is caricaturing some (probably Northern) Whig or Democrat, although the former seems more likely for the following reasons. Since the next "gentleman" who repulses the Man in Gray is, I contend, an allusion to the Democrat Lewis Cass, it would be more artistically symmetrical to have these two gentlemen represent the conservative factions of each of the previously dominant parties than to have both gentlemen represent the same faction—though that is also possible. Moreover, it would more fully represent the whole political situation to show that both factions, which were previously alien if not hostile to one another, are now alike in their repulsion of the new party leaders seeking confidence. I suggest that Melville desired this kind of completeness in his pasquinade.

The second small-scale caricature in chapter 6—that of the Hard-Hearted Old Gentleman, who is "somewhat bulky"—points strongly to Lewis Cass (1782–1866), Michigan's Democratic leader, Jackson's secretary of war, senator from Michigan (1845–48 and 1851–57), Democratic presidential candidate in 1848, minister to France, and secretary of state for Buchanan. When he draws near to the Man in Gray and is solicited, he "scowls" and "swells his bulk out before him like a swaying balloon." The significant detail that connects him with Cass is that he is "bulky" and his bulk is compared to that of a balloon. Cass's public image in graphic prints hostile to him was that of a man with an enormous stomach, as can be seen well in a print of

1852, "Loco Foco Candidates Travelling on the Canal System," which shows Cass with a bulky protruding stomach, and in one of 1856, "Liberty the Fair Maid of Kansas—In the Hands of the 'Border Ruffians,'" which grossly caricatures the balloon-like bulk of his stomach (plate 12).[23] Cass was a Hunker Democrat who was not at all sympathetic to the anti-Nebraska movement nor to the proslavery zealots either. In a Senate speech on 12 and 13 May 1856, he attributed the troubles in Kansas to outside interference of both the New England Emigrant Aid Company and the Missourians who had crossed into Kansas Territory to vote illegally.[24] Whether he repulsed Parker or spoke of him personally has not been established.

In depicting the attitudes of both these gentlemen toward the Man in Gray it is evident that Melville is not especially sympathetic toward their repulsion of him, for they are both presented as unpleasant characters, wiser, perhaps, than the dupes of the Confidence Man, but not for that any more admirable. The reader must always keep in mind that satire intends to "present men as worse than they are," as Aristotle observed, and this includes both those toward whom the satirist, as a man, may feel more sympathetic and those toward whom he may feel less sympathetic.

In chapter 7 the encounter of the Gentleman with Gold Sleeve-Buttons with the Man in Gray is intended, the evidence suggests, to allude to the relationship of Abbott Lawrence, as representative of the Lawrence family (see next section) to Parker, as representative of the antislavery political movement, and forms a complex commentary on a fairly obscure chapter in Massachusetts politics. In chapter 8 the approach of the Man in Gray to the Charitable Lady satirizes, if this Lady does indeed caricature Lydia Sigourney (see section after next), the action of the political antislavery movement as it appealed to and exploited the sentimental religious sentiment of the "charitable ladies" of the period—of whom Lydia Sigourney was representative. I have not found any personal connection of Theodore Parker with Mrs. Sigourney.

The Gentleman with Gold Sleeve-Buttons

For the next character in the pasquinade, the Gentleman with Gold Sleeve-Buttons, an excellent case has been presented by William Norris in *American Studies* (1976) that he is modelled on Abbott Lawrence (1792–1855), Boston merchant, millionaire manufacturer, philanthropist, Whig politician, United States congressman from Massachusetts, and minister to England under Taylor.[25] Briefly summarized, the points of similarity include age (about "sixty"), appearance ("tall, rosy, between plump and portly, with a primy, palmy air"), and dress that is suggestive in its fine quality and purity of the inner goodness and purity of the man ("the fine covering had a still finer lining"). Norris sees similarities in Melville's description of the Gentleman's prevailing "good-ness" both of character and of fortune to contemporary impressions of Law-rence's personal and philanthropic qualities. He quotes from Melville's journal after a visit with Lawrence in London in 1849 Melville's description of him as "very kind, unaffected & agreeable," just as Melville describes the Gentle-man. Norris notes that Lawrence's wealth came from textile mills, which depended upon Southern cotton and hence upon slave labor, connecting this with Melville's writing that the Gentleman's hand and gloves are "spotless" because he has a "negro body-servant" to do "his master's handling for him." Norris's point is that Melville is expressing through the Gentleman's portrait his view that Lawrence's philanthropy was hypocritical insofar as he "received his funds, even indirectly, from slavery."[26] A further point he makes is that the descriptive detail of the Gentleman's especially clean bills, which he takes from his pocketbook—"crisp with newness, fresh from the bank"—alludes to the habit of Lawrence's older brother, Amos Lawrence (1786–1852) of dispensing in his charities only clean, crisp new bills, fresh from the bank for that purpose. Further, Norris connects Abbott Lawrence's sponsorship of part of the Great Exhibition of 1851 in London with the Gentleman's cu-riously digressive interest in that fair when the Man in Gray mentions it. Lastly he sees in the Man in Gray's pitch for a "World's Charity" a direct appropriateness to Lawrence's known interest in carrying on business in large schemes—by "wholesale" rather than "retail" methods, as exemplified in the founding of the textile mills at Lawrence, Massachusetts in 1845.

Norris's case for Melville's caricature of Abbott Lawrence is extremely good and may be reinforced by the following details. Sarah Maury's descrip-tion of him, cited by Norris for other details, mentions also that his features are "very handsome" and that he "has more repose of character than is usual in the men of America," traits reflected in the Gentleman's description as being "of more than winsome aspect" and as standing "apart and in repose."[27] Lawrence, as a native of New England would appropriately have the elm tree associated with him, as it is with the Gentleman twice in descriptive met-aphors, in which he is compared to "some full-leaved elm, alone in a meadow," in his look, and again to "the benign elm," when he seems "to wave the canopy of his goodness" over the Man in Gray. Further, Lawrence is treated satirically in two squibs in *John-Donkey* (1848), as the "great Boston Philan-thropist," the joke being his contribution to the "Feegee Mermaid Destitution Society," and again as giving a testimonial for a patent medicine being hawked by "Eliza Wright" (Elizur Wright), abolitionist speaker.[28] Next, if the reader is meant to see blended into the caricature of Abbott Lawrence some elements of other notable members of his family, as Norris suggests, then the case for the allusion to him, as representative of that family, is strengthened by the fact that his nephew Amos Adams Lawrence (1814–1886) was even closer to the Republican movement. A. A. Lawrence was the major financial backer, treasurer, and trustee of the New England Emigrant Aid Company—the "soul of the enterprise"—from its founding in 1854 by Eli Thayer as the Massachusetts Emigrant Aid Company until 1862, a contributor of funds for Sharps rifles, a supporter of political moves toward the free state of Kansas, and possibly a supporter of Frémont in 1856.[29] The three bills this character gives the Man in Gray would allude to A. A. Lawrence's contributions to "Free Kansas."

Yet closer, with regard to the Gentleman's cautiously positive response to the Man in Gray, another supporting fact is that, according to Allan Nevins, Abbott Lawrence, although a Cotton Whig, began shifting his political ground, as did some other Boston merchants, in response to the imminent passage of the Kansas-Nebraska Bill early in 1854, as is evidenced by his speaking in Faneuil Hall, 23 February 1854, against the bill. David Donald discusses the split in the Cotton Whig group into a Webster faction and an Abbott Lawrence faction in the late 1840s, during which Lawrence paid assiduous attention to Conscience Whigs, including Sumner.[30] This kind of politicking, intended to further Lawrence's vice-presidential ambitions in 1848, may possibly form part of the background for the portrait of Lawrence as willing to listen to and contribute to the radical solicitations of such a Republican as Parker. In joining the anti-Nebraska movement Lawrence would be moving toward the new party, although he died (1855) before being able to participate fully in it. This response, which would constitute a definite shift in his politics, is reflected in the Man in Gold's positive though careful response to the Man in Gray. That is, Melville is drawing attention, once again, to the strange bedfellowships that were appearing upon the American political scene under the pressures of the growing sectionalization. Just as the Man in Gray's solicitation of funds for the Seminole Widow and Orphan Asylum parodies Theodore Parker's solicitation of funds for Northern settlers in Kansas so the donation to him of money by the Gentleman with Gold Sleeve-Buttons alludes to the sympathy of Abbott Lawrence with the anti-Nebraska movement, and also, probably, to the contributions by Amos Adams Lawrence, his nephew, of time and money to the Emigrant Aid Company.

The Charitable Lady

Chapter 8 depicts the last encounter of the Man in Gray, which is a successful solicitation of a "Charitable Lady." Several elements of this woman's appearance, her sobriquet, her widowhood, her "excellent heart" and "affability," her internal conflict between "charity and prudence," and lastly her strikingly sympathetic response to a charity for Seminole Widows and Orphans ("those cruelly-used Indians") all suggest strongly that Melville is satirizing Lydia Huntley Sigourney (1791–1865), the "sweet singer of Hartford," the "American Mrs. Hemans," who was the best-known woman poet of her time.

Sigourney is described fairly late in life as a "prim little figure in black satin" and as a "short little body with 'soft patrician' hands." The "ubiquitous Mrs. Sigourney," as Frank Luther Mott, the historian of American journalism, terms her, was, besides being the most successful of women poets, an exemplar of "female" charitable activity, not always (or perhaps never) in a private way. The Duyckincks' *Cyclopaedia* notes that her "wide and earnest sympathy with all topics of friendship and philanthropy is always at the service of those interests." Early in her life, according to her biographer Gordon S. Haight, she resolved always to give one-tenth of her income to charity, which she apparently did, and, additionally, she constantly made and gave away clothing, taught children, visited the sick and poor, sponsored charitable groups, and supported missionary activities. Haight writes that "the Orphan Asylum, the Deaf and Dumb Asylum, the State Prison, the Retreat for the Insane were all objects of her benevolence." On the subscription list for her memorial after her death she was designated as the "Christian Benevolent Lady." Haight notes that she took an especial interest in benevolence toward American Indians, manifested early in a "Charity Society" for her "Forest Brothers," which she organized at the school that she operated in Hartford as a young woman, which sent and received letters from Indians and sent gifts and tracts. Moreover, uniting charitable with literary interests, her first successful long poem published was an Indian epic *Traits of the Aborigines* (1822), which treats the Indians as resembling the Hebrew patriarchs, admirable for their friendship, gratitude, reverence for age, and their piety, and concludes with a plea for missionary support, which will be registered in the "Lamb's book of life," as the Man in Gray registers the Lady's gift in his "book." She suggests, showing the same combination of prudence with charity as the Charitable Lady exhibits, that the conversion of the Indians would make the West safer for American settlers. This appeal to charity, Haight notes, came at a time of government policy to push the Indians westward and when a Society for the Civilization and General Advancement of the Indians had been rebuffed by Adams, Jefferson and Marshall. Sigourney's sympathies continued to follow the Indians, as the settlers pushed them westward, which she expressed in *Pocahontas* (1841), another verse epic.[31] Sigourney's charitable activity for the Indians is, I suggest, alluded to at the turning point of the encounter with the Man in Gray, when the Charitable Lady says, "And why did you not tell me your object before? . . . Poor souls—Indians, too—those cruelly-used Indians. Here, . . . how could I hesitate? I am so sorry it is not more" (p. 50).

Melville's Charitable Lady is "a plump and pleasant person," who is wearing half-mourning: "Her twilight dress, neither dawn nor dark [shows that] apparently she is a widow just breaking the chrysalis of her mourning." The husband of Lydia Sigourney was Charles Sigourney, a hardware merchant of Hartford, who died 31 December 1854, and for whom, curiously, she did not publish an elegy—as she ordinarily did for countless others. The usual period of mourning in the 1840s and 1850s was two years, so that if Melville were writing this chapter sometime during the summer of 1856, Mrs. Sigourney might well be likely to be "just breaking the chrysalis of her mourning."[32] It is possible that another direct allusion to Sigourney as she would appear to her vast reading public in 1856 may be contained in the description of the Charitable Lady's "thoughtful face" as retaining a "tenderness," as when "at evening . . . for a time the western hills shine on though the sun be set." She published a collection of essays on aging and the aged, *Past Meridian* (1854), in the preface to which she dedicates her work to those—including herself—"whose faces are toward the setting sun." The theme of the "parting sun"—which she fully exploits as a sentimental image for growing old— seems to be taken from the epigraph to her book, which she quotes from T. Buchanan Read: "The evening sun but fades away / To find new morning in the West."[33] None of the various essays seems to be particularly alluded to by Melville, but the general theme of one of Sigourney's most recent books—the sun that is past meridian and setting—lies, I suggest, behind his choice of descriptive imagery for the facial expression of the Charitable Lady.

It is not possible to read all of Sigourney's poems, thousands of which were published in annuals, magazines, and collections from 1815 until her death, but I have uncovered one, included in her *Poems* (1834), which takes as its theme the Pauline passage (I Corinthians 13) at which the Charitable Lady's finger is inserted in the "small gilt testament . . . in her hand, which she has just been reading." Sigourney's poem, "'Charity Beareth All Things,'" is about the Christian duty to go beyond the "natural," the "savage," and the "heathen" ethical injunction merely to love one's own to embrace the more difficult act of loving those who injure one—even him, "Who to the bosom of your fame doth strike / A serpent sting, your kindest deeds requite / With treachery."[34]

The pose of a lady holding a book, most often either a Bible or a copy of Milton's *Paradise Lost*, is a common one in late eighteenth and early nineteenth century portraits and the miniature of Sigourney as a young woman that was used for the print of her in her *Collected Poems* (1848) shows her holding an unidentified book.[35] It is possible that such portrait poses may have lingered on in lithographs of well-known women in the gift annuals of the second quarter of the century and that such a print of Sigourney may adorn one or more of them. She edited the *Religious Souvenir* for two years, 1836–38, and she contributed poems to many other gift annuals, none of which I have been able to consult in order to ascertain whether there might in fact be a print of her in later years holding a Bible.

There seems on the basis of present research to be no visible connection between Lydia Sigourney and the antislavery movement or any political movement, nor any between her and Theodore Parker, the Man in Gray. She avoided politics altogether as far as her public image as the ideal feminine literary figure went. She tried to present the model of a Christian lady, interested only in home, sentimental verse, and good works, although, as Haight depicts her, in reality she was a highly skilled promoter of her own social and literary reputation both in the United States and abroad, which she attained through multitudinous letters and gifts of her books, and through assiduous participation in the logrolling and mutual admiration activities of the "reputation mongers" of the literary world. Haight suggests that she owed her reputation, the pinnacle of which was the edition of her collected poems in 1848 in uniform binding and publication with those of Bryant, Longfellow, and Willis, to her choice of American themes early in her career and to her "Christianity." With small ability she made herself one of the most famous persons of her day and, besides, earned a living through her pen. Still, even at the peak of her fame she was regarded as the "little lady" attending regularly her "Charitable Society," and, in fact, she justified her own mercenariness in bargaining with her publishers about her work, by asserting as her motive that she wished to connect herself "with the ever soliciting & noble charities of the day."[36]

As a literary figure of dubious merit but of great social influence and as possibly the most famous feminine exponent of the sentiment of "charity" in public life, Lydia Sigourney would be a recognizable and vulnerable target for the satire of *The Confidence-Man,* and, even if no direct connection with the politics of the antislavery movement or with Theodore Parker can be found, she still may have been intended by Melville to represent the feminine religious sentiment of the period, to which the antislavery movement made a powerful appeal and which exerted its influence indirectly through men, who could vote.[37]

John Truman

An excellent case can be made that John Truman, the "man with the travelling-cap," who appears or is assumed to be present in chapters 9 through 13 and in chapter 15, is a caricature of Thurlow Weed (1797–1882), master lobbyist and Whig politician in New York State and national politics for more than forty years, founder and editor of the *Albany Evening Journal,* and cofounder of the Republican party, 1854–56 (plate 27). Two of the first descriptive adjectives used of Truman—"brisk" and "ruddy-cheeked"—apply also to Weed, whom his contemporaries described as having a "long, ruddy-complexioned face" and a lively and elastic manner.[38] Truman's "tasseled travelling-cap," seems to be an allusion to Weed's constant habit of traveling in his multifarious political activities, especially between Albany and New York City, between Albany and all parts of New York, and later between New York and Washington. Weed loved to travel and did so throughout the United States and Europe, making six transatlantic voyages, and writing letters about his travels to the *Evening Journal* sometimes.[39] In 1861 Melville himself in an attempt to call upon Weed in New York City for his help in obtaining a government appointment referred to Weed as "the bird [that had] flown back to his perch—Albany," when he missed seeing him.[40]

Adjectives used to describe Truman's personality are extraordinarily similar to those used about Weed. Truman is "brisk," "cheery," "good-natured," and shows "genial jauntiness." He values experience over speculation. He appears "animated," "yearning," the "soul of sociality," "fraternal," and "pleasant." He enjoys cards, wine—especially champagne—and cigars, as he saunters and chats with the passengers. He believes in "liberal constructions" of others' motives, and in the "refinedness and luxury of good feeling." Though he is compared to a "cockscomb" in his liveliness, yet he is "capable of philosophical and humanitarian discourse." He disclaims preaching, claiming to be an "equal and genial companion." Melville emphasizes in several passages his sociability. Truman dislikes "gloomy philosophers," "croakers," and recluses. The metaphor used to describe the effect of his speech is that of a "locust-tree sweetening the herbage under it," for it is the "wholesome accident, of a wholesome nature." Even after hearing the story of the vicious Goneril, he refuses to admit the "existence of unmerited misery" or to question Providence. He seems calm and impartial. Espousing a "sound and sublime . . . confidence," he insists upon putting the happiest construction possible upon the Goneril-Ringman divorce case. While drinking champagne with Roberts he is "half-serious" and "half-humorous." Descending to the emigrants' quarter of the *Fidèle,* he is compared to "Orpheus in his gay descent to Tartarus," while he "lightly hums to himself an opera snatch." His manipulative gifts appear when he moves "swift as a sister-of-charity" at the Miser's call for water, and when he follows this up with a request for his confidence and then for a hundred dollars. He utterly disclaims "self-seeking" or that he lives "for himself," yet he keeps mysterious exactly how "the gain [is] made" with the money entrusted to him, because to tell how would ruin him. He succeeds in every encounter, except in getting the Dried-Up Man to drink, smoke, play cards, or tell stories.

Weed's biographer Glyndon G. Van Deusen writes of him:

> It was a strong face, alert and confident. It reflected Weed's joy in living, his love of power and his zest for action. On occasion humor would lighten or compassion soften it. Friendliness was there, and charm, together with that touch of masterfulness that marks the administrator, the manager of men. . . . [His] persuasive, confidential manner was almost as striking as his face and figure. In conversation he was apt to tap the knee or grasp the arm or shoulder of the man to whom he was talking [see plate 27], and then pitch his voice low as though about to impart some weighty secret. Endowed with a vitality that was all the more impressive because it was controlled, the possessor of a restless, busy, scheming brain, he was a marked man among the politicos and his rooms at the City Hotel . . . were always crowded.[41]

He was, by all accounts, including his own in his *Autobiography,* compulsively sociable, good-natured, and generous—even to his political enemies. His grandson, Thurlow Weed Barnes, writes of him:

> In Mr. Weed's nature there was a certain wonderful quality which invited sympathy ?.d confession. Children, as well as men and women, made him their confidant. He was, in his day, a sort of 'father confessor' for the greatest and least among the people of New York. Presidents, governors, diplomats, speculators, clergymen, doctors, and lawyers sought him, when yearning to speak freely of their errors, perplexities, or expectations.[42]

A nearly identical capacity for eliciting social confidence—and confidences— is especially displayed in Truman's encounter with Roberts, when they fall "into that confidential sort of sympathetic silence, the last refinement and luxury of unaffected good feeling," in which Roberts proceeds to tell Truman the stories of the sick Miser, of Black Guinea, and of Ringman and Goneril, and to reveal his own inner doubts and confusions.

A reading of Weed's letters in the Barnes memoir discloses that the word "confidence" is almost a leitmotif of his expression, as it probably was of his conversation, and is of Truman's. Likewise, with the Collegian Truman plays the role of the genial, sociable companion—a lover of champagne and cigars, which parallels Weed's delight in and use of this sort of social relationship for itself as well as for political purposes: "He loved the creature comforts, good food, good wines and good cigars, luxuries that for the most part [early in his career] were beyond his means." A political friend wrote that he was "a noted and liberal entertainer."[43] Weed's *Letters from Europe and the West Indies: 1843–1852*, which appeared in the *Evening Journal* at the time, contain many accounts of his interest in food, liquor, and "segars."[44] In politics of this period it seems that to offer champagne, as Truman does to Roberts, was symbolic of a close personal and political relationship that usually involved lobbying. The high-minded and "pure" Charles Sumner, writing in 1852, termed an invitation he received to champagne on board the *Baltic*—whose owners were seeking a governmental subsidy—"the great man-trap set especially for members of Congress."[45]

Philip Hone, a very conservative Whig, thought Weed "somewhat of a radical," not comprehending his efforts to preserve the Whig party in a time of stress. Although Weed espoused antislavery with some moral fervor in his editorials for the *Evening Journal,* his motive was also (as Bryant claimed in the *Evening Post*) to popularize the Whig party in the North by capitalizing on strong antislavery feeling. His radicalism "was not based upon any deep discontent with the existing social order." Van Deusen emphasizes the double quality of his nature: "There were, indeed, times when he spoke and acted as a cynical manipulator of political forces. There were other times when he spoke and acted from the heart, and when his heart moved him he was a man of good will." McClure called him the "most astute politician of his day in any party."[46]

Striking evidence later in his life of Weed's great power to win confidence, as Truman does, is that he won the tribute of even the American Minister Charles Francis Adams, when he traveled to England during the war to influence English opinion for the Union cause. Van Deusen writes that "The Minister's son and secretary [Henry Adams] was similarly captivated." Henry Adams wrote of Weed:

> His mind was naturally strong and beautifully balanced; his temper never seemed ruffled; his manners were carefully perfect in the style of benevolent simplicity, the tradition of Benjamin Franklin. He was the model of political management and patient address; but the trait that excited enthusiasm in a private secretary [Adams] was his faculty of

> irresistably conquering confidence. Of all flowers in the garden of ed-
> ucation, confidence was becoming the rarest; but before Mr. Weed went
> away, young Adams followed him about not only obediently— . . . but
> rather with sympathy and affection, much like a little dog.
>
> The sympathy was not due only to Mr. Weed's skill of management,
> although Adams never met another such master, or any one who ap-
> proached him; nor was the confidence due to any display of professions,
> either moral or social, by Mr. Weed. The trait that astounded and
> confounded cynicism was his apparent unselfishness. Never, in any man
> who wielded such power, did Adams meet anything like it. . . . He
> thought apparently not of himself, but of the person he was talking
> with. . . . He was not jealous. He grasped power, but not office. He
> distributed offices by handfuls without caring to take them. He had
> the instinct of empire: he gave, but he did not receive.[47]

This extraordinary portrait of Weed's personality, authentic as far as history
knows, and consonant with that which Weed displays overwhelmingly to the
reader of his *Autobiography*, is uncannily close to that of Melville's fictional
character John Truman in the elements of apparent unselfishness, eliciting
confidence by its wholesomeness, its warm benevolence, its balance, its con-
geniality, its generosity, and in Truman's ability to "manage" the Collegian,
Roberts, and the Miser.

Further, the interested observation of the four men who are playing cards
in the cabin in chapter 10 finds a parallel trait in Weed as observed by the
Herald, in one of a series of editorials on the New York Central Railroad
monopolistic power grab in which Weed was involved, where Weed is seen
as "cunning and unscrupulous as ever, everywhere 'bobbing around' and
looking at the hands of the players" (*Herald,* 26 July 1856). Or more sympathetically as observed by Henry Adams:

> Management was an instinct with Mr. Weed; an object to be pursued
> for its own sake, as one plays cards; but he appeared to play with men
> as though they were only cards; he seemed incapable of feeling himself
> one of them. He took them and played them for their face-value; but
> once, when he had told, with his usual humor, some stories of his
> political experience which were strong even for the Albany lobby, the
> private secretary made bold to ask him outright: 'Then, Mr. Weed, do
> you think that no politician can be trusted?' Mr. Weed hesitated for a
> moment; then said in his mild manner: 'I never advise a young man
> to begin by thinking so.'[48]

Weed's own "trusting" quality, or at least the role of being a "trusting" person, perhaps had altered by 1861, when he visited the Adams family in London, but its prominence in his character in the early and middle part of his career and his genius for evoking trust in others make him a near-certain model for Truman, who "in pure goodness of heart, makes people's fortunes for them—their everlasting fortunes, as the phrase goes—only charging his one small commission of confidence" (p. 115).

Other aspects of Truman's personality that link him to Weed are his dislike of "gloomy philosophers" and preference for jolly fellows who enjoy drinking and social chat and do not predict evil. Van Deusen notes again and again Weed's strong preference for pleasant, affectionate companionship; his lifelong friendship for the optimistic New York politician Seward is especially illustrative. His failure through congenital optimism to credit the seriousness of the consistent Southern threats to secede throughout the 1840s and 1850s until after Lincoln's election points up the seriousness of Melville's critique of this kind of personality, especially when it becomes dominant in national affairs—as Weed's did at times. Another personal trait, Truman's desire to keep "mysterious" how the money entrusted to him by the Miser, in chapter 15, will bring "gain" to the investor is paralleled by Weed's passion for leaving unspoken exactly how favors would be done for the men who paid into his party war chests.[49]

As for style, certain qualities of Truman's style in the fairly long "philosophic and humanitarian discourse" with Roberts in chapter 13 resemble to some extent Weed's written style as revealed in the *Autobiography*: circumlocutiousness, a certain intellectual confusion, and a lack of grammatical accuracy and clarity, qualities for which his editorials in the *Evening Journal* were criticized by his peers.[50] The following nearly unreadable passage of Truman's discourse to Roberts, which is manifestly tangled in its syntax, must be intentionally representative of the style that Melville wished to parody:

[Truman] checked [Roberts], saying, that this would never do; that, though but in the most exceptional case, to admit the existence of unmerited misery, more particularly if alleged to have been brought about by unhindered arts of the wicked, such an admission was, to say the least, not prudent; since, with some, it might unfavorably bias their most important persuasions. Not that those persuasions were legitimately servile to such influences. Because, since the common occurrences of life could never, in the nature of things, steadily look one way and tell one story, as flags in the trade-wind; hence, if the conviction of a Providence, for instance, were in any way made dependent upon such variabilities as everyday events, the degree of that conviction would, in thinking minds, be subject to fluctuations akin to those of the stock-exchange during a long and uncertain war. (p. 72)

Another stylistic trait, Truman's quotation from Shakespeare's *Cymbeline* in his remark in chapter 11 that "Nature . . . in Shakespeare's words, [has] meal and bran; and, rightly regarded, the bran in its way was not to be condemned," is consistent with a trait, noted by Van Deusen, that "Shakespeare furnished [Weed] with more than one good epigram."[51]

Truman's professional role as president and transfer agent for the Black Rapids Coal Company is, the evidence suggests, a satirical comment upon the role that Weed played much of his life as the chief political boss—the wooer of funds and support and the dispenser of patronage and legislative favors—for successively the Anti-Masonic party, the Whig party, and the Republican party in New York State and at national conventions. Van Deusen describes the New York Whig Central Committee during Weed's ascendancy as the key to the Whig political structure that ran the party for a generation "making the important decisions on political strategy and tactics, gathering and disbursing the financial sinews of war." Weed's advice "would control the decisions of the Central Committee and he would act as the committee's agent" in transmitting its wishes to the Whig legislators. Weed's continued "dictatorial" relation to the party organization, after the Whig organization guided by him fused with the Republican organization at Syracuse in the summer of 1855, is, I suggest, alluded to by Truman's role as "president and transfer-agent" of the Black Rapids Coal Company.[52] The metaphor of "stock-jobbing" for the kind of political machinations taking place in Washington, for example, during the spring of 1856 was used by the Washington correspondent of Bennett's *Herald* (8 April 1856), writing of the total engrossment of that city in politics: "Politics has been turned into stocks, and has established a transfer office in this city."[53]

Truman's belief in "liberal constructions" of others' motives is reflected in Weed's personality. In the political strictures of his editorials he softened his criticism usually by attributing good motives. For example, when he rejected Henry Clay's compromise measures in 1850, he "softened his own refusal to accept Clay's project by a warm tribute to Clay's motives," and when he took issue with Webster's Seventh of March speech supporting the compromise, "He was careful to give the Senator from Massachusetts full credit for good intent."[54] This trait seems caricatured ludicrously in Truman's circumlocutious endeavor to see only good in both Goneril and Ringman, which concludes: "In brief, there were probably small faults on both sides, more than balanced by large virtues; and one should not be hasty in judging"

(p. 71). Similarly, Truman's curious mixture of beneficence and profit-seeking—in that he claims to make people's "everlasting fortunes," even while he clearly is a profit-seeking company agent—is reflected in Weed's curious mixture of benevolence and self-seeking as described by Van Deusen:

> The Lucifer of the Lobby was neither vicious nor antisocial in his intentions. He was, indeed, an influence for good in many ways. Skillfull as he was in adjustment and maneuver, masterly in the creation and maintenance of a political organization, the services that he rendered to the Republican party in the days of its infancy were little short of superb. John Bigelow, writing in 1858, paid willing tribute to Weed's disinterested and supremely valuable leadership. . . . The fact remains, however, that by the close of the eighteen-fifties Weed's pursuit of wealth, his close association with business interests, particularly the New York Central, and his failure to rebuke and cast off the spoilers and corruptionists who infested the capitol and hung about the 'Father of the Lobby,' were exposing him to assaults that were damaging to his personal reputation, as well as to his usefulness as a party leader.[55]

A single display of the personal traits of "coldness," "indifference," and "superiority"—which Truman makes in response to the Miser's hesitation—shows a different aspect of his personality for which there is, again, a precisely corresponding aspect in Weed's. Barnes notes that he disliked miserliness, quoting his saying that "avarice [is] the one vice I could not forgive."[56] Other small allusions that point to Weed as the object of Melville's satire are: (1) the comparison of Truman in chapter 15 to "Orpheus in his gay descent to Tartarus, lightly hum[ming] to himself an opera snatch," probably an allusion to Weed's known fondness for opera; (2) the critical remark of Truman that, "that corpse of calamity which the gloomy philosopher parades, is but his Good-Enough-Morgan." Weed inadvertently originated in his Anti-Masonic days this famous phrase for a politically-contrived fiction or "decoy," when in 1827 he was accused of having shaved or otherwise altered the corpse of an unknown drowned man to make it appear to be the murdered body of William Morgan, author of an exposé of the Masons. Weed, accused of exploiting anti-Masonic hysteria for political purposes, is reputed to have said to a group of Masons, who denied it was Morgan's body, that the corpse was a "good enough Morgan until after the election." The joke in Truman's remark resides in the fact that Weed is here caricatured as throwing the phrase back at the "gloomy philosophers"—the Democrats, who were constantly warning of the dangers to the Union of the antislavery agitation. Truman-Weed is saying, in effect, that they are using the danger of "calamity" to the Union

115

through secession solely in order to obtain votes to remain in office. A third slight allusion is the metaphor of the "locust-tree sweetening the herbage under it." The locust was a tree characteristic of central and western New York—Weed's home area.[57]

Weed was not extensively caricatured in graphic prints. An early and famous Democratic print by J. E. Freeman pictures him as "the Jolly Drummer" who "Beats Time for the Whig State Officers." Cigar in mouth, he leads a mock military procession that includes Governor Seward and Treasurer John C. Spencer, the point of the humor being that Weed, who did not hold any office, still had the power to command those who did and to make them "march" to his tune.[58] Another print is very relevant to the Truman caricature, although it appeared too late to influence Melville. It may even itself reflect Melville's work. "The Inside Track," printed in *Vanity Fair* before Lincoln's inauguration in 1861, shows Weed and Seward soliciting Lincoln's trust in them in the appointments to his cabinet. Weed grasps Lincoln's arm and says, "Trust to my friend Seward—trust to US. We'll compromise this little difficulty for you. But trust to US. Gentlemen from the country are often egregiously swindled by unprincipled sharpers. (Impressively) TRUST TO US!" (plate 27).[59] It is curious that the emphasis is so strong upon the word "Trust," unless it was clearly recognized by 1860 that Weed (and Seward) were regarded, at least from one point of view, as blatant exploiters of the psychology of "trust" or "confidence" in the same manner as Melville's Confidence Men were.

Truman's encounters with five other characters may each be regarded as commenting upon Weed's relations with another public figure or public group. That with Roberts-Wilmot comments satirically, the evidence suggests, on the Republican connections with the Free-Soil ex-Democrats, like Wilmot, who were drawn into the party as it formed in response to the Kansas-Nebraska Bill. Truman's sale of stock to the business-like Collegian-Raymond comments on Weed's dealing with Raymond in the period 1854–56, during which Raymond received the lieutenant-governorship and then became the writer of the "Address to the People" at the first national Republican organizational meeting. Truman's reading of the Elderly Quaker's ode (see next section) reflects Weed's response to the antislavery poetry of John Greenleaf Whittier as representative of abolition sentiment. His encounter with the Dried-Up Man, who is probably a caricature of Myron Clark (see section after next), a Temperance party leader, reflects Weed's role in Clark's nomination and election as governor of New York by the Whigs in 1855. Humorous implications derived from the pun on "weed" lie in Melville's use of the epithet "The Man with the Weed" for the Ringman-Bryant figure, the humor consisting in the perception of Bryant, the former Jacksonian Democrat, as in close political association with his ancient Whig enemy Weed. The strange political bedfellowships of the members of the newly formed Republican party was much commented upon. Likewise the possibility exists that Truman's mixed sympathy with and criticism of the Ringman-Goneril marriage and divorce situation reflects some publicly expressed attitude of Weed toward Bryant's (and other New York Barnburners') unhappy relations with the Hunker Democrats, though evidence is not presently available for this. Last, Truman-Weed's descent to the emigrants' cabin, where he finds the Miser and successfully induces him to invest his money in the Black Rapids Coal Company, may be read as a comment upon methods, either surmised by Melville or believed by him, that Weed used, or agents of his used, to induce the old Jacksonian Democrat, Francis Preston Blair, Sr. (see Chapter 8), to lend his wealth and his political prestige and power to the new party, as came to be represented by the address he wrote to be read at the organizational meeting in Pittsburgh. In considering these suggested interpretations of the confidence-soliciting encounters between characters in *The Confidence-Man,* the reader should remember that, like those of a graphic political print, the relationships of Melville's characters are fictions; they are not historical reconstructions of events. They comment upon history, or upon what the author believes to be historical events, but they are not themselves meant to be exact records of history.

The Elderly Quaker

The scene shifts in chapter 10 from the deck, where Truman met the Collegian, to the cabin, where the main activity is cardplaying: "whist, cribbage, and brag." Some passengers, however, are reading a printed poem that has been distributed by "a somewhat elderly person, in the quaker dress," who had "quietly passed through the cabin," as would a railway book-peddler distributing "puffs"—advertisements—for a book to follow, and had "without speaking, handed about the odes." It is a piece of "anonymous poetry, rather wordily entitled: 'Ode on the Intimation of Distrust in Man, Unwillingly Inferred from Repeated Repulses, in Disinterested Endeavors to Procure His Confidence.'" The poem engenders a conversation between John Truman and another passenger, "a little, dried-up man" (see next section), when Truman quotes the first two lines and uses them as the mainspring of an attempt to solicit this man's trust:

Alas for man, he hath small sense
Of genial trust and confidence.

117

If we are meant to assume that the distributor of the poem and its author are the same person, it would seem that the most likely topical allusion intended would be to John Greenleaf Whittier (1807–1892), Quaker journalist, essayist, politician (in the Massachusetts legislature in 1835), editor of the *Pennsylvania Freeman,* 1839–40, abolitionist tract-writer, and poet. Whittier, an astute, though quiet, politician, was one of the founders of the Liberty party, believing in the ballot as a way to end slavery, unlike his lifelong friend Garrison. As an editor of the abolitionist organ, the *National Era,* from 1847 to 1860, he used his poetry to arouse antislavery feeling and to change the current of public opinion. His early biographer, Samuel Pickard, wrote that seldom was there such an example of "the poetical and devotional temperament combined with preëminent political sagacity and business judgment" as in Whittier. Lewis Leary writes that he kept his hand in politics all of his life, even while feeling that his best talent was "quiet persuasion."[60]

Three traits of the Elderly Quaker, who is scantily described, suggest Whittier: his dress, his "somewhat elderly" appearance, and his "quiet passage through the cabin." Whittier was a devout Quaker, belonging to a strict Quaker family in Amesbury, Massachusetts. According to at least one observer he wore Quaker dress of the "strictest sort." Although Whittier would be only around fifty by 1857, he was a "sickly" man, having ill health from about twenty-five years of age, so much so that he retired from the editorship of the *Pennsylvania Freeman* in 1840, returned to Amesbury, and conducted his writing and political career privately from his home thenceforth. As for quietness, he was a dedicated advocate of nonviolence, never was a public speaker, and his friend T. W. Higginson wrote of him that he was very "shy, . . . reticent and quiet."[61]

The details of the poem which the Elderly Quaker distributes suggest strongly Whittier's poetry. The first two lines of the Ode (the title of which obviously parodies Wordsworth's "Ode: Intimations of Immortality from Recollections of Early Childhood"), quoted twice by Truman, are an iambic tetrameter (octosyllabic) couplet, a very characteristic meter of Whittier's verse. Lewis Leary notes, "A straightforward iambic measure, four beats to the line, precisely measured out with rhyme, or . . . blank verse such as Wordsworth did much better, most often served Whittier to express his earnest sense of human rights" or to write nature poetry. Further, "About one-third of his poems were written in four-stress lines, ordinarily in octosyllabic couplets." If a satirist wanted to parody Whittier, the iambic tetrameter couplet would be an easily recognizable metrical form to choose. As for the content of the Ode, the little Dried-Up Man calls it "queer" and compares it, in arousing in him—contradictorily—"trustful and genial" feelings, to "a sermon, which, by lamenting over my lying dead in trespasses and sins, thereby stirs me up to be all alive in well-doing." Whittier was quite capable of expressing private distrust, as in a letter to Lewis Tappan in 1849, where he wrote that, "I have scarcely charity enough to suppose that this marvellous conversion [of the Northern public to antislavery views] is altogether genuine & heartfelt." Nor is the Ode's curious rhetorical method of exhorting the desirability of trust by lamenting the existence of mistrust an uncommon rhetorical method of Whittier's antislavery poetry. For example, it is used as a method of exhortation to Massachusetts in "The Rendition," written on hearing of the rendition of Anthony Burns from Boston back into slavery in 1854:

> All love of home, all pride of place,
> All generous confidence and trust,
> Sank smothering in that deep disgust
> And anguish of disgrace.

He exhorts "Mother" Commonwealth to "rise," but, "Ah me! I spoke but to the dead; / I stood upon her grave." The rendition of Burns was, in fact, by all accounts the turning point of Massachusetts public opinion against the enforcement of the Fugitive Slave Law.[62]

With regard to the likening of the Quaker's distribution of the Ode to the distribution of book puffs, it may be noted that Whittier's abolitionist poems of the 1830s–1850s were self-confessedly written as propaganda—as attempts to change people's opinions on slavery. Henry Wilson wrote that he "prepared the minds of the people for political action." His poems were "puffs" for a cause. "He turned, he admitted, the crank of an opinion mill to grind out verses one so like the other that often only their titles distinguish them," according to his biographer Leary.[63] For Melville's other descriptive epithets (as an "angel," who has "snowed" verses, and as "sad Philomel") I have found no specific sources in Whittier's career.

The irony of Truman-Weed's using the Ode to test and enlist the Dried-Up Man's sociability becomes manifest in the latter's actual response to Truman's suggestions. Such trustful and genial actions as cards, wine, cigars, or a story he abruptly refuses. Thus, by failing to rise to the rhetorical intention of the Ode—which he had himself well described—the Dried-Up Man proves the actual assertion of the Ode—man's innate distrustfulness.

The Dried-Up Man

The little Dried-Up Man in chapter 10 receives only slight description. He looks "as if he never dined," and he says that he is "naturally numb in [his] sensibilities." Despite his claim that the Ode "works on [his] numbness not unlike a sermon," he refuses the sociable activities of cards, wine, cigars, and stories. The first three he never indulges in, and of the last he says that he "hardly thinks [he] knows one worth telling." This little vignette may be simply a type character-sketch of a "Dry" politician, yet it is possible that it alludes specifically to Myron H. Clark (1806–1892), who was a New York State politician and governor of New York, 1855–57. Clark was an ardent Temperance man—a "Dry"—during a period when the prohibitionist movement was strong. As state senator he pushed a prohibition bill through the New York Legislature, which was vetoed by Governor Horatio Seymour, a "Soft" Democrat and a "Wet." Because the American Temperance Union supported Clark and asked the Whigs to nominate him in 1854 and because as a Know-Nothing lodge member he appealed also to the Nativist vote, Thurlow Weed and the other Whigs were persuaded to nominate him for governor. C. H. Brown writes that he was nominated "largely through the machinations of Thurlow Weed working behind the scenes and providing free liquor and cigars in abundance." Van Deusen writes that "Weed had no great love for prohibitionist idol Clark," but in 1854 the Maine Law (Prohibitionist) men were powerful, and "the star of Myron Clark" was in the ascendant. He was strong enough to get the nomination on the Whig ticket, although it was necessary to balance him on the ticket with the non-Prohibitionist Raymond for lieutenant-governor. Of the nomination Weed wrote that Greeley through the *Tribune* had brought the people up to accepting a Temperance candidate, yet while Greeley "had shaken the temperance bush, Myron H. Clark would catch the bird." Nevins calls Clark a "reformer . . . and staunch advocate of the Maine law." Besides his Whig nomination, his Temperance support, and some Nativist support, Clark received antislavery support because he agreed to run on the "Auburn Resolutions," an antislavery platform drawn up by a fairly radical "fusionist" group after his nomination, according to Nevins. Clark later called this quadruple campaign the origin of the Republican party. [64]

This scene with Truman-Weed may be interpreted, if the Dried-Up Man is a caricature of Clark, as alluding to Weed's relations with Clark in New York politics in 1854. Following as it does upon Truman-Weed's successful encounter with Collegian-Raymond earlier, it deals, I would suggest, with the temporary coalition, engineered by Weed in 1854 between the forces of conservative but still antislavery Whiggery, as represented by Raymond, and the forces of equally conservative but Temperance-dedicated Whiggery, as represented by Clark. In this attempt the Ode dropped by the Elderly Quaker represents the influence upon New York politics of the antislavery agitation, through the pamphleteering and poetry of the abolition movement, as represented by Whittier. The little Dried-Up Man-Clark claims to be moved by the appeal to his feeling, but not apparently to the extent of entering very far into the intimate political relationship that Truman-Weed proposes by offering cards, wine, cigars, and stories, nor into the full and aggressive exploitation of the antislavery issue in politics, as would be represented by buying stock in the Black Rapids Coal Company. Truman does not even mention his stock to the Dried-Up Man. It should be noted, however, that Clark did later become a Republican and was appointed a revenue collector by Lincoln, according to the *Dictionary of American Biography*.

The Whist-Players

There is a transitional vignette in chapter 10 between the encounter of Truman-Weed with the Dried-Up Man-Clark and his next, with the Country Merchant-Wilmot, which probably alludes to a political situation as yet unidentified. Truman and Roberts become interested in the scene immediately before them in the cabin: "a party at whist; two cream-faced, giddy, unpolished youths, the one in a red cravat, the other in a green," playing with "two bland, grave, handsome, self-possessed men of middle age, decorously dressed in a sort of professional black, and apparently doctors of some eminence in the civil law." Merchant-Wilmot expresses suspicion of the two older men—fearing that they are "sharpers." Truman-Weed, true to his genial well-thinking nature, discounts this: "'You would not hint that the colored cravats would be so bungling as to lose, and the dark cravats so dextrous as to cheat?'" The depiction of political relationships as a card game is fairly common in prints of the 1830s and 1840s, as it was in English prints of the eighteenth century. It was especially apt for Henry Clay who was a gambler. See, for example, "A Political Game of Brag, Or the Best Hand out of Four" (1831), which represents Clay, Calhoun, Jackson, and William Wirt as playing cards—presumably for the 1832 presidential winnings, "All Fours, or Old Sludge" (1840) and "Political Game of Brag. Shew of Hands" (1848), showing four of the aspirants of that year: Taylor, Clay, Cass, and Polk (playing for Buchanan) (plate 2).[65] The whist game in Melville's scene may possibly allude to a particular situation—perhaps one in New York State or one nationally—but only further research will reveal what it may be.

8

The Sixth Confidence Man (the Herb-Doctor) and Two Antagonists (the Miser and the Sick Man)

The Miser

Melville's old Miser is described by Roberts-Wilmot in chapter 11 (p. 63) and again by Melville as narrator in chapters 15 and 20. To Roberts he appears as a "shrunken, old" miser. Later, his arm thrust out of his bunk is compared to a "wasted penguin-flipper," and he is "lean," his flesh being like "salted cod-fish, dry as combustibles." In chapter 21 Pitch calls him a "file." Most important for purposes of identity, his head is "like one whittled by an idiot out of a knot," since, as will be seen, in graphic prints the head of Francis Preston Blair, Sr. is caricatured in this peculiar shape. Further, the Miser's mouth is "flat [and] bony . . . nipped between buzzard nose and chin," and his cheek seems "like a wizened apple" (chapter 15). In his third appearance, in chapter 20, he is "a dried-up old man, with the stature of a boy of twelve," and he has "ferret eyes, blinking in the sunlight of the snowy boat."

The Miser wears "shrunken old moleskin," later specified as "an old white moleskin coat" (p. 82). According to the *OED*, moleskin may refer either to the skin of the mole used as fur or to cotton fustian. Since he is miserly, the cheaper cotton fabric, with its Southern associations, seems meant, and yet Melville probably also wishes to connote the rodent for later he uses "ferret" and "rat" to describe the Miser. His coat is rolled up as his "moleskin pillow," which resembles "a grimy snow-bank" (chapter 15). His "rumpled clothes of old moleskin" are referred to again in chapter 20. As a Pantalone, appropriately he carries "an old buckskin pouch" that contains "ten hoarded eagles, tarnished into the appearance of ten old horn-buttons," which he later gives to Truman-Weed.

In personality, the Miser clings to "life and lucre, although the one was gasping for outlet and about the other he was in torment lest death . . . should be the means of losing it." His mind is low, "never raised above mould." He has "no trust in anything, not even in his parchment bonds," which he had "packed down and sealed up, like brandy peaches in a tin case of spirits." His parsimony has driven him to take passage on the *Fidèle* in the cheapest emigrants' quarters, where he is sleeping on a bare plank.

Melville describes these quarters in considerable detail, for which the context remains puzzling. They are "dim and dusky" and "more to pass the night in than the day": "a pine barrens dormitory, of knotty pine bunks," that resemble "nests in the geometrical towns of the . . . penguin and pelican" in their "Philadelphian regularity." They are "pendulous," like the "cradles of the oriole." The place is like a "purgatory." As for the Miser's expression, throughout the two major scenes it is one "flitting between hunks [miserly] and imbecile—now one, now the other." A persistent motif of his conversation is his self-pity: "I am so old and miserable." He claims to have poor vision, no self-confidence, and little money—like the Pantalone dei Bisognosi of commedia dell'arte. He compares himself to "a poor, old rat here, dying in the wainscot." In sum, his main personal traits are his age, his sickness, his love of money, and his need to depend upon others, manifested in his first words from his bunk: "Water, water!" spoken in a "wail like that of Dives" from his bunk, when Truman enters his quarters.

The Miser's speech is quite distinctive in that it reveals his sickness, his miserliness, his self-pity, and a dialectal pronunciation. His voice is "disastrous with a cough," a "churchyard cough," that is sometimes "violent." A persistent motif of his conversation with Truman is this: "Ugh, ugh, ugh! Oh, I am so old and miserable. I ought to have a guard*ee*an" (pp. 84, 116, 117). He claims to have tried the Mammoth Cave in Kentucky for his cough: "Denned there six months, but coughed so bad the rest of the coughers— ugh! ugh!—blackballed me out." His speech is affected not only by his consumptive cough but also by his mood-swings from "imbecilic" excitement about Truman's propositions for investment to "hunkish" (miserly) panic. He readily uses "sarcasm" and slang, such as "Cant, gammon! . . . hum, bubble! . . . fetch, gouge!" He dwells repetitively on the number associated with his money and has a tendency to repeat words or short phrases in his excitement: e.g., "One hundred, one hundred—two hundred, two hundred—three hundred, three hundred" (p. 84); and "Stay, stay, . . . I confide, I confide," and "Nay, back, back—receipt, my receipt. Ugh, ugh, ugh! . . . My gold, my gold!" (p. 84) His speech seems to reflect a dialectal pronunciation when he calls the Herb-Doctor, "Yarb-doctor" (as does Pitch later), herbs, "Yarbs," Nature, "Natur," and, most distinctively, pronounces "guardian" as "guard*ee*an" each time he uses it. All these marks add up to a speech pattern that is decidedly provincial or dialectal.

He is first depicted by Roberts-Wilmot, who has seen him lying in his bunk and describes him in chapter 11 as a depressing spectacle—a case of a man who knows nothing but his physical life and his money and hence is an extreme example of a "want of confidence" in anything else. All of chapter 15 is devoted to Truman-Weed's solicitation of him and their conversation, in which he induces the Miser to give him a hundred dollars (ten eagles) to invest in an unnamed way, for the Black Rapids Coal Company is not mentioned to him by name. The kind of investment is "a secret, a mystery," one that will yield back "trebling profits." In this scene Truman-Weed mentions his "friend, the herb-doctor," who encounters the Miser in chapter 20 and sells him a box of the "yarb" medicine. Finally, in chapter 21 the Miser speaks with Pitch the Missouri Bachelor (for this caricature of Thomas Hart Benton see Chapter 9) who ridicules him for buying the Herb-Doctor's medicine: "You foolish old file you. He diddled you with that hocus-pocus, did he?" And in a last significant graphic vignette he is seen juxtaposed to the Herb-Doctor (for this caricature of Charles Sumner see Chapter 8) as a Siamese twin: The two stood together, the old miser leaning against the herb-doctor with something of that air of trustful fraternity with which, when standing, the less strong of the Siamese twins habitually leans against the other" (p. 122). Later, the Herb-Doctor leads him away to his berth. For each of these fictional relationships of Melville's Miser there is a significant parallel in the career of the senior Blair.

Many details link this severe caricature to Francis Preston Blair, Sr. (1791–1876), longtime editor of the *Washington Globe,* Jacksonian politician and leader in Democratic national politics for twenty-five years prior to his joining in the formation of the Republican party in 1855 and sponsoring Frémont's nomination. Blair was about sixty-five when Halstead described him thus at the Republican convention in Philadelphia: "He is a little old gentleman, thin, slender and feeble in appearance. . . . Then he is given a top-heavy appearance by the fact that his head is too big for his body, and his hat too big for his head."[1] Both Blair's unusual thinness and the peculiar shape of his head had for at least twenty years been the details by which he had been caricatured in many graphic political prints. Of the twenty-eight prints depicting Blair which I have examined, twelve show clearly a head that may well be described—like the Miser's—as resembling a whittled knot— that is, the head reveals a skull that is misshapen in its contours, being drawn somewhat to a point in back while excessively high and rounded above the forehead. Nearly all of these and many other prints show Blair's body as thin to the point of emaciation—deserving Pitch's metaphor, "file." Blair is most often depicted in profile, thus revealing well the peculiar shape of his skull, his thinness, and also sometimes showing a facial profile that may justly be described in Melville's terms as showing a "flat, bony mouth, nipped between buzzard nose and chin" (plates 1 and 2).[2]

Verbal descriptions bear out the graphic impression of Blair's physical appearance. McClure, who termed Blair "more nearly the founder of the Republican Party than any other one man," writes politely of Blair that he "lacked [the] finely chiseled face and outward intellectual signs" of his early associate Joseph Gales, while Blair's twentieth-century biographer, Elbert B. Smith, refers to his head as "egg-shaped" and "large," the weight of which "appeared tilted toward the rear," and calls him "skeleton thin" in old age. His lifelong friend, business partner, and financial advisor John C. Rives described him in 1855–56 thus:

> He is about five feet ten inches high, and would be full six feet, if his brain were on the top of his head instead of being in a *poll* behind it. He looks like a skeleton, lacks but little of being one, and weighed last spring . . . one hundred and seven pounds, . . . flesh he has none. His face is narrow, and of the hatchet kind, according with his meat-axe disposition when writing about his enemies. . . . We thought him very homely until we became well acquainted with him. . . . We still think he is as homely as one man in ten thousand.

Lastly, it is rather remarkable that a political enemy of Blair, after the war, writing in the Cincinnati *Commercial* in 1868, described him as an "idiotic-faced old man of a singular parchment ugliness" and with "wrinkles like a withered apple extending across his face transversely"—terms echoing Melville's adjectives about the Miser: "imbecile," flesh that "seemed dry as combustibles," and a cheek "like a wizened apple." Of his height Beman Brockway noted that though taller than Van Buren, Blair in the late 1830s was already so bent over, from his long hours writing while bent over his notepad on his knee, that Van Buren appeared the taller, a detail that suggests the Miser's "stature of a boy of twelve."[3]

I have not found any description of Blair's typical clothing that links it directly with the Miser's moleskin coat. Brockway mentions his wearing the "garb of a country farmer" and a "white hat."[4] I would suggest the possibility that his Southern background (Virginia, Kentucky, and Maryland residences) might account for white cotton "moleskin" clothing, since often in graphic prints white clothing, especially the costume of a planter, denotes a Southern person. Blair played the role of a farmer or planter at his Silver Spring estate.

The Miser's cough and apparent debilitation allude to Blair's chronic consumptive condition. His personality all his life was affected by his early tuberculosis and its lingering effects. W. E. Smith writes that his health was delicate from his youth, specifically his lungs. He was in such poor health that his wife's father predicted he would only live six months beyond his wedding day. Early in life he was "slight, with stooping shoulders and had very strong indications of consumption." Although he later developed vigor and endurance, he retained a fear of a recurrence of consumption (which

125

occurred in 1852), and he thought of himself as living on borrowed time and "prayed that he might reach forty." His lung condition also prevented his practicing the prolonged oratory demanded by law practice. He may well have been a persistent cougher.[5] Whether his mind was low—"Never raised above mould"—I cannot determine, nor was he miserly by his biographical accounts, but rather generous—especially to his relatives. However, there are hints of an unusual concern for money: E. B. Smith notes that his father's struggles with debt remained always a painful memory and that in his early years, until he was thirty, he was nearly always in debt; and W. E. Smith states that "thoughts of a possible return to poverty struck Blair with terror," even after he was a rich man. After the founding of the *Globe* and his success in holding Jackson's patronage and winning the congressional printing frequently and other government printing, he became a very rich man—telling Van Buren in 1845 that he believed that he was worth one hundred thousand dollars. He had the reputation, certainly, of wealth by 1845, and Bennett treated him as rich in an editorial in the *Herald* in February 1856. Beman Brockway recalled that Blair, whom he met in the late 1830s, talked a great deal about his farm, money, and land costs and saw money as the "controlling element in legislation"—which may reflect a miserly preoccupation with money.[6]

A personal trait of the Miser that points fairly suggestively to Blair is his dependence upon others and his self-depreciation, traits which resemble Blair's self-effacing dependence on Andrew Jackson in establishing himself in Washington and making his political and financial fortune there in the 1830s and 1840s. It is possible that Melville is satirizing Blair's famous fall from power when, after Jackson's retirement and Van Buren's loss to Polk at the 1844 Democratic convention, his newspaper, the *Globe*, which had been the administration organ for fifteen years, was ousted by Polk in favor of Ritchie's new paper, the *Union*. The Miser's motival complaint, "I ought to have a guardeean," would then satirize Blair's need to have a patron, since he was unable to retain power without a president such as Jackson or Van Buren to back him. When Blair entered the Republican party in early 1856, he was attacked by the Pierce administration newspaper, the Washington *Union,* for having his "intellectual faculties in decline," and especially for making use of Jackson's letters to him to attack the Democracy in his own published letter in the New York *Evening Post.* This letter, which achieved considerable influence, was dated 26 April, addressed to the Republicans of New York, and was entitled "A Voice from the Grave of Jackson!" It aroused a storm of denunciations that "old age was manifesting itself in 'garrulity and egotism'" and that Blair had only a "remnant of mind" left, possibly accounting for Melville's adjective "imbecile." William E. Smith notes that Blair was accused of being "a clinging ivy that had entwined itself about the sturdy oak (Jackson) and sucked nutriment from its power." Blair's accusations, in turn, that the Pierce administration was an imposter or "spurious Democracy" aroused great bitterness. It is possible that Melville reflects some of this bitterness in his caricature of Blair.[7]

As for speech mannerisms, the "churchyard cough" has already been linked to Blair's consumptive health. His rough and vigorous editorial style in the *Globe* is perhaps reflected in the Miser's use of "sarcasm" and slang, while the Miser's use of dialectal pronunciation strongly suggests Blair's Kentucky accent. For this, the best piece of evidence is contained in Beman Brockway's remarks that Blair was "a plain man" in manners and speech, that he had no polish or style, used "ordinary language," and seemed uneducated (though he was not). He spoke of his "taters," and he had a "southern and western style of expressing himself, which sounded outlandish to Yankee ears." He had a habit of emphasizing numbers and costs: "the *best* cost me fourteen dollars per acre, the *worst* twenty-eight"—revealing here, at least, a personal preoccupation with numerical figures, similar to the Miser's. Last, Brockway writes that Blair's "utterances were simple as those of an unpolished countryman who had never written a line for publication in his life." Brockway's report of his meeting with Blair depicts a character that seems very close to a model for Melville's Miser's speech habits, especially as regards the definite trait of using the dialectal pronunciations of "yarb," "natur," and "guardeean," all of which are listed in Richard H. Thornton, *An American Glossary,* as "provincial" pronunciations—the last being further characterized as used in the nineteenth century by "half-educated people." Although Melville may not ever have heard Frank Blair, Sr. speak, it is not at all unlikely that he would have some acquaintance with the personal traits of the man—again through his family connections with New York Democratic Regency politicians from his youth up.

A few other small details suggest that Blair is the model for the Miser. His reference to being at "Mammoth Cave" alludes to Blair's Kentucky background. The curious metaphor that Melville uses to describe how the Miser preserved his "parchment bonds"—"packed down and sealed up, like brandy peaches in a tin case of spirits"—may allude to Blair's custom of showing his pride in his Silver Spring estate by growing and gathering his own peaches and then having them packed in brandy to send to his friends, including Martin Van Buren at Kinderhook. E. B. Smith writes: "Peaches were apparently the most glittering ornament [at Silver Spring] and every fall Eliza spent long hours canning and brandying them for shipment in great quantities to distant children, relatives, and friends." It may be added that whether Blair's pride in his brandied peaches was known to the general public we do not know, but at least one recipient, Martin Van Buren, was a friend and old Democratic ally of Melville's uncle, Peter Gansevoort of Albany. Perhaps Melville ate some of the peaches. Another possible personal allusion is Melville's choice of a glass of water for the charitable act that Truman performs for the Miser. This may allude to the well-known story of Blair's founding of his estate in Maryland at a spring that he discovered by accident, which he named Silver Spring; after he had made it the central point of his gardens, he was always proud to offer the water to guests to drink. Lastly, the Miser's habit of keeping his money in gold in large amounts in a pouch that he carries with him may allude to Blair's lifelong hatred of the United States Bank, the campaign against which formed the principal political issue discussed in the *Globe* during the 1830s.[9]

Of the Miser's four relationships to other characters, three seem to refer to known public relationships of Blair. Roberts-Wilmot's knowledge of Miser-Blair alludes to the connection of David Wilmot with Blair as Free-Soil Democrats, which need not have been personal, but only that of cosupporters of Van Buren in 1848 and as comembers of the Republican National Committee, which issued the signed call on 29 March for the June convention in Philadelphia, and of the Platform Committee of which Wilmot was chairman.[10] Herb-Doctor-Sumner's (see Chapter 8) successful sale of medicine to Miser-Blair, again, has its analogue in the shared support of Van Buren in 1848 and the participation of Sumner with Blair in meetings in late 1855 and early 1856 intended to insure the nomination of Frémont.[11] Pitch-Benton's (see Chapter 9) scornful gibe at the Miser ("You foolish old file, you!") and his refusal to be taken in by the Herb-Doctor's medicines clearly allude to Benton's consistent refusal to join the antislavery political movement or to participate in the formation of the Republican party, even though Frémont was his son-in-law, and some of the promoters of Frémont had hoped thereby to induce Benton to join them. W. N. Chambers, Benton's twentieth-century biographer, writes that Benton counseled Blair "sternly" against joining the new party.[12] The graphic vignette in chapter 21 of the Herb-Doctor and the Miser linked together as "Siamese twins"—a common metaphor of the period for close political alliances—probably alludes to the intimacy of Sumner and Blair after the Brooks assault, when Sumner stayed as Blair's guest at the Silver Spring estate for medical treatment and recuperation.[13]

There is more difficulty in determining the precise context of Truman-Weed's approach to Miser-Blair, since Weed seems to have had no direct connection with Blair in the early stages of the party formation. Rather, Blair apparently was solicited into the party by Lewis Clephane, the business manager of the *National Era* and the organizer of the Republican Association of Washington in June 1855. He first asked Blair to attend the Pittsburgh meeting as a delegate, and when Blair refused, he used the stratagem of arranging for a "respectable" group of Free-Soil Quakers in Baltimore to organize a Republican Club and to choose Blair as their delegate to the Pittsburgh meeting. Blair was impressed by this apparently unsolicited support of him by Free-Soil Democrats in a slavery city and accepted it and went to the meeting, feeling as he did that he and his supporters were the true Democracy, while the rest of the "Doughface" Democrats were "Imposters." Clephane, also, engineered Blair's nomination as permanent president of the meeting, in which role Blair's address to the Republicans, arraigning President Pierce and the Southern Democrats, was read to the meeting, since he did not speak in public. He was caught up in the enthusiasm and sentiment of the convention and served on the Committee on Resolutions and Addresses and took a place on the National Executive Committee, as already noted.[14] It is possible that here—in joining the National Executive Committee— Melville surmised the delicate hand of Thurlow Weed, operating through the chairman of this committee, Edwin D. Morgan of New York. Morgan was a close associate of Weed in the organization of the new party in New York State. It is possible that Melville is using the Truman-Weed figure here in this maneuver as a type of the party executive and organizer—blending together Weed's real organizational power, Morgan's actual chairmanship, and the direct personal action in Washington of Clephane. The historical fact remains that Blair, an old-line Democrat, was induced to join with former Whigs such as Weed, Seward, and Morgan, with Know-Nothings such as Banks and Wilson, with antislavery Democrats such as Bryant and Bigelow, with Conscience Whigs such as Sumner, and with abolitionists such as Clephane, in the new party, and in this party Thurlow Weed very soon became one of the strongest active political agents.

The Sick Man

Two new characters are introduced in chapter 16: the Sick Man and the Herb-Doctor, who converse together on the deck of the *Fidèle*. The Sick Man (who is not to be confused with the Miser, who is also old and diseased) suffers a "chronic complaint" for which he has already tried three doctors, and yet he is induced by the Herb-Doctor to make one more trial of a remedy, the Omni-Balsamic Reinvigorator (pp. 86–94). He seems to be a caricature intended to represent the Whig party, which after a precarious existence of some twenty years was on the point of expiration in 1856. It is possible, additionally, that he caricatures some as yet unidentified elderly Whig, who, responding to Republican solicitation in the campaign of 1856, was influenced in part by Sumner's oratory, and who hoped to survive through the new political movement.

Withdrawn in a corner of the deck, he sits "wrapped about in a shawl." He is "cadaverous," "juiceless," "joyless"; he has a "livid skin" and a "sunken eye" and is compared to a "plant whose hour seems over, while buds are blowing and seeds are astir." At first he does not even answer the Herb-Doctor's inquiries but uses "feeble dumb show of his face" and a "dumb-show look" to communicate. When he does speak his voice, indicative of "consumption," is like "the sound of obstructed air gurgling through a maze of broken honey-combs," and in another place it becomes "husky." His personality reflects his sick condition. He is "unparticipating," "not warmed by the sun," is "tranced into hopelessness by a chronic complaint," is "impatiently querulous," and his "physical power [is] all dribbled and gone." He displays a "querulous look" and the "apathy of impotence." However, as the Herb-Doctor pressures him he is moved to "relent" and to give him a "long glance of beseeching." He is "hectic," "feverish," and "feebly wrings his hands." Although he laments that his previous confident hopes have often failed him, still he asks the "reason" for the herbs and would be "glad to be confuted."

The Sick Man's style reveals a curious mixture of medical and doctrinal terms, as if the style of some particular individual were being parodied. He denies wanting to seem irreligious, and because to deny the efficacy of the herb-medicine would be to deny "Natural Goodness" (*i.e.,* the natural goodness of man and of God), he allows himself to be talked into buying the medicine made of "natural" herbs. His three-part medical history forms the subject of his conversation with the Herb-Doctor. First, he has seen and taken the advice of "an eminent physiologist in Louisville, Kentucky, from whom he took "tincture of iron," to restore his lost energy—with no success. Next, he consulted "the great chemist in Baltimore," who prescribed a "respirator" and "a sort of gasometer," from which again he derived no help. Lastly, just six months ago, he consulted "the German doctor at the water cure," a follower of the hydrotherapist Vincenz Preissnitz—still with no success. Still hopeful, he buys six half-dollar vials of the Omni-Balsamic Reinvigorator.

The threatened dissolution of the Whig party was a commonplace topic of journalistic writing, speeches, and letters of the early 1850s. David M. Potter writes that, "The Whigs were badly divided in 1852 and their bisectional organization did not survive its defeat in this election." Of the Northern Whigs, Van Deusen writes that the New York Whig party "died" at Syracuse, 26 September 1855. Bryant uses the imagery of decrepitude for the few remaining Whigs in an editorial in the *Evening Post,* 11 October 1855. A *Herald* editorial (16 August 1856) terms the Old-Line Whigs "Fossil Remains—Petrified Men." Murat Halstead's reports of the conventions in 1856 notes that a fifth political convention was the last Whig conclave ever held, at Baltimore, 16 September, presided over by Washington Hunt and Edward Bates. Halstead editorialized of it that, "It is difficult to say whether this poor attempt to disinter and galvanize dead Whiggery is more ludicrous or melancholy."[15]

Two of the Sick Man's geographical references (to Louisville and to Baltimore) may allude to two of the final conventions at which the Whigs gathered in 1856 to nominate a presidential candidate. According to Andrew W. Crandall, the "Old-Line" Whigs, "galvanized into life by their own conservatism," were strongest in the border slave states, where some of them called a state convention in Baltimore, 29 April, while the *Louisville Courier* called for one in Louisville on 4 July. Crandall notes that the most significant group of Whigs was that in Massachusetts, where Old-Liners such as Robert C. Winthrop, Edward Everett, and Rufus Choate were a "brilliant residue" of the Webster Whigs (among whom Lemuel Shaw—though not a politician—should also be counted).[16] None of these men, of course, would be possible models for the Sick Man (if he be intended as an individual caricature), since none of them endorsed the Republicans—*i.e.*, bought Sumner's remedy, the new antislavery party. Choate, in fact, although a lifelong Whig, came out openly for Buchanan because he considered the Republicans "revolutionary" and disunionists; he published on 9 August in the Boston *Courier* an influential letter addressed to the Maine Whig State Central Committee, which was later reprinted in a pamphlet with a letter of similar import by George T. Curtis to the Massachusetts Whig State Central Committee.[17] Other Massachusetts Whigs endorsed Fillmore, not as the Know-Nothing candidate but as a former Whig president. Still, there were at least two older Massachusetts Whigs, Josiah Quincy and Joel Parker, who endorsed the new party's candidate, and one of these is worth consideration as a possible model for the Sick Man. Josiah Quincy (1772–1864), former Federalist and writer of the *Climenole* satires in the *Port Folio* and *Monthly Anthology*, mayor of Boston (1823–27), president of Harvard College (1829–45), and three-term United States congressman, began issuing political pamphlets against the Fugitive Slave Law after 1850, and in 1856 he published, first, a letter to E. Rockwood Hoar endorsing the Republicans and "was in line to make precedent for the new party," according to Crandall, and in August he published a reply to Choate's letter to the Maine Whigs which received a wide circulation.[18] Another possibility is Hamilton Fish (1808–1893), conservative New York Whig, governor of New York (1849–50), senator (1851–57), who came out for Frémont in September, which was quite late in the campaign, and published an open political letter to James A. Hamilton.[19] Further research should determine whether one of these men or some other notable Whig was Melville's satirical object—perhaps one who participated in the Louisville convention, the Baltimore convention, and who, perhaps, had even tried to retain power through the Temperance movement ("the water cure"), but who finally sought his political survival by joining the Republicans.

The Herb-Doctor

Melville's Herb-Doctor (or Man in the Snuff-Colored Surtout) appears in chapters 16 through 20, immediately after the departure of John Truman, who has recommended him and his medicines to the Old Miser. He is the sixth disguise of the Confidence Man and a very important figure both in what he represents and in the number and complexity of his relationships to other characters. He has dealings with five main antagonists: the Sick Man, the Invalid Titan, the Soldier of Fortune Thomas Fry, the Miser, and the Missouri Bachelor Pitch—as well as with assorted minor figures. His "true" character becomes a topic of discussion in the "Inquest," in chapter 18, by three other figures who appear as almost only voices. The evidence strongly indicates that Melville is satirizing Charles Sumner as the Herb-Doctor, and that he has dramatized his relationships to an old Whig politician (the Sick Man), to John Calhoun and Preston Brooks of South Carolina (in the composite caricature of the Invalid Titan discussed in Chapter 9), to George Law, a Know-Nothing politician (Thomas Fry; discussed in Chapter 9), to Thomas Hart Benton of Missouri (the Missouri Bachelor; discussed in Chapter 9), to Francis Blair, Sr. (the Miser; discussed earlier in this chapter), and to several other factions or persons with whom Sumner had dealings in his public career in national and local politics (the several minor figures).

The Herb-Doctor hawks three different kinds of medicine: the Omni-Balsamic Reinvigorator for the elderly sick, the Samaritan Pain Dissuader for both mental and physical pains, and a liniment for curing bone injuries and diseases. The type-character of a peddler of panaceas had been used earlier to satirize politicians in the comic periodicals, *John-Donkey, Yankee Doodle,* and the *Lantern* (parodying frequently their own patent medicine advertisements), since it was an obvious way to ridicule political rhetoric and oversimplified solutions, but I have not found any previous example of its use for the person whom I propose as the object of Melville's satire in his Herb-Doctor: Charles Sumner (1811–1874), United States senator from Massachusetts, 1851–74, a major antislavery orator of the late 1840s and 1850s, lyceum lecturer, and one of the founders of the Republican party (see plates 10, 11, and 28). The specific physical detail of his "snuff-colored surtout," as well as traits of voice, personality, oratorical style, and certain events and relationships to other characters strongly support this interpretation. Additionally, an important public event, the caning of Sumner in the Senate chamber on 22 May 1856 by Representative Preston Brooks of South Carolina, seems to be alluded to by the "sudden side-blow"—the "coward assault"—of the Invalid Titan upon the Herb-Doctor in chapter 17.

John Truman, referring to his "friend" the Herb-Doctor in chapter 15, had mentioned "his long snuff-colored surtout," and in chapter 16 this character first appears "in a snuff-colored surtout, the collar thrown back" (p. 86). David Donald, in *Charles Sumner and the Coming of the Civil War,* notes that Sumner chose his clothing carefully and at a time when most senators wore black frock coats his favorite costume was a "brown coat and light waistcoat, lavender-colored or checked trousers, . . ." "Snuff-colored" means, according to the *OED,* "brown, brownish," the color of powdered tobacco, which is snuff. That which people remarked upon was that Sumner's dress was unconventionally English—a lasting result of his trip to England and the Continent from 1837 to 1840. Two elements come together in this snuff-colored surtout. First, it is the appropriate costume for a traveling quack-doctor or of a showman, as is indicated by a reference to a puppet figure of a quack-doctor in Maurice Sand, *Masques et Buffons,* and by the costume of the showman in Hawthorne's story, "The Seven Vagabonds." Second, that Sumner happened to favor a brown-colored coat for public appearances may actually have suggested to Melville the idea that he might be represented as an herb-doctor selling medicines. As for the Herb-Doctor's "thrown-back" collar, there is a portrait of Sumner in Edward L. Pierce's *Memoir and Letters of Charles Sumner,* taken by Brady in 1869, which shows him with collar, lapels, and all, thrown back to display his watch and eyeglass—the characteristic pose that he assumed for speechmaking in the Senate.[20]

Melville's Herb-Doctor shows two bodily traits that characterized Sumner's typical method of delivering a speech. In chapter 16 he is seen with his "hand waving in persuasive gesture, his eye beaming with hope," while in chapter 17 he is seen "proudly raising voice and arm." Descriptions of Sumner's oratory noted the physical vigor of his delivery and that, in particular, "the most frequent gesture [was] that of swinging an arm over his head." Bungay wrote that he "swings his arms (especially when upon the platform)." The Herb-Doctor's "beaming eye" correlates with Harsha's observation that "when excited in debate, his eye brightens and becomes almost radiant with what is passing within." The Boston *Atlas,* after the Brooks assault, referred to his "eye, once so beaming, now languid." The Herb-Doctor's voice is described as "clear" and "flute-like." Contemporary listeners described Sumner's voice as "singularly sweet and melodious" and "singularly musical" and as "clear and powerful."[21]

The Herb-Doctor's manner and personality reflect in many significant details Sumner's public personality as reported by contemporaries. Melville's character is "cheerful," "benignly urbane," "manly, business-like"; he displays a "familiar cordiality," is not "frivolous" but has a "kindly heart," is "pathetic to the last," "calm," "affable," "forgiving," and yet he is "not unself-possessed," is "assured," and is "politely superior." The general picture of a man who is affable, yet conscious of his superiority, who is manly, urbane, polite—though not exuberantly genial and warm like Truman and the Cosmopolitan—and yet is capable of forgiveness under injury, emerges from Melville's depiction of the Herb-Doctor and is strikingly consonant with contemporary descriptions of Sumner's personality and with the portrait that emerges from his friend Edward L. Pierce's early biography and from David Donald's meticulously researched modern biography. Harsha, his first biographer, speaks of his "genial courtesy of manners" and his "kind disposition." Pierce quotes a contemporary observer of Sumner's first important oration, "The True Grandeur of Nations," in Boston in 1845, as saying that "he was the impersonation of manly beauty and power" and that he spoke "in cadences mellow and pathetic." As for Sumner's self-possession and his "superiority," his friend Whittier in "Sumner," a poem of praise, mentions, as if in response to criticism, his "slight defects" of "natural pride / Of power in noble use, too true / With thin humilities to hide / The work he did, the lore he knew," and his "assured self-estimate." His urbanity, the result of his socially successful trip to England and the Continent, was always noted, especially in contrast with the provinciality of the average congressman of his time. Bungay speaks of "the manly traits for which he is distinguished" and says that "his greeting [is] very cordial." In his eulogy of Sumner, Henry Ward Beecher said that he was of "a most manly type," and more critically that "by nature he was self-considering"; and that he "was so intense in his own convictions as to become arrogant, and impose his views upon others with a species of oratorical despotism." Pierce, most friendly about Sumner's faults, noted that he "delighted to talk of the noted persons he had met," and compares his "self-consciousness, self-esteem, self-poise" to that of other great men. Pierce quotes John W. Forney, in his *Anecdotes of Public Men* (1873), who mentions accusations of "arrogance," and a "certain self-sufficiency," which Forney claims were the result of a "consciousness of superior intelligence."[22]

There is one special personal trait of the Herb-Doctor that forcefully indicates that he caricatures Sumner. He consistently displays a "forgiving," "charitable" attitude toward those who are either coldly indifferent to him or who actually injure him. He is "not easily affronted" by the passengers' indifference to him in chapter 17, seeming to be "insensible to their coldness, or charitably overlooking it." When the Invalid Titan beats him, he does not

strike back nor does he seek "redress," claiming that "innocence is my redress." He is "patient under injury." This personal quality, which goes beyond
mere politeness and is quite unlike the typical masculine public behavior of
the period (duelling, caning, cowhiding, fists, pistols, or libel suits being
the more common response to real or fancied injury) was noted as remarkable
in Sumner. Pierce relates several incidents in which Sumner's response to
insults in the Senate and elsewhere showed either a curious indifference to
personal insult or an actual unawareness of malicious motives and feelings in
others. Rhodes writes that there was "nothing vindictive or revengeful in his
nature." It was most striking in the Brooks assault, where there was never
any suggestion of his seeking retaliation.[23]

Another peculiar trait of Sumner, somewhat inconsistent with his noted
urbanity but akin to his lack of a sense of humor, is noted by Julia Ward
Howe in her *Reminiscences* (1899) and described by Donald and may account
for the curiously grotesque approach that the Herb-Doctor makes to the Puny
Girl, who accompanies the Invalid Titan and seems to be his child. The
Herb-Doctor "cheerfully" and "trippingly" approaches this "nervous," gloomy
child, calls her "my little May Queen" and "with a half caper" sings "Hey,
diddle, diddle, the cat and the fiddle; / The cow jumped over the moon"
(p. 97). In his imperception of the child's irresponsiveness and of the Titan's
"heavy-hearted" gloom, Melville seems to be depicting a trait that Mrs. Howe
called Sumner's "grotesqueness of taste [which] made him the object of some
good-natured banter" and his lack of a "sort of imagination which enables a
man to enter easily into the feelings of others," and which "sometimes resulted
in unnecessary rudeness." Likewise, Donald notices his "stately attempts at
humor," his "elephantine humor" not always appropriate to its audience, and
in particular an occasion when he became the object of the laughter of the
entire Longfellow family as the result of an attempt to pet a calf—to which
this curious approach to the Puny Girl and his recitation of Mother Goose
may not impossibly be an allusion.[24]

Another peculiarity of the Herb-Doctor—the ambiguity of his motives
for his public actions—points to Sumner. The question of his character forms
the actual subject of dispute in chapter 18, which is entitled, "Inquest into
the True Character of the Herb-Doctor." Three men, who have been observing
his solicitations, his beating by the Titan, and his donation of two dollars to
a day laborer, question his motives: Is he knave, fool, or genius, or all three?
A "red-haired man," who carries a cane, sees him as a "knave," while a
"hook-nosed man," who quotes *Hamlet,* sees him as a "fool." Although neither
of these figures is presently identifiable, a third person, who believes that
"true knowledge comes but by suspicion or revelation," and who suspects
that the Herb-Doctor is "one of those prowling Jesuit emissaries," seems to

be a caricature of some Know-Nothing politician, as yet not identified. His suspicion that the Herb-Doctor is a "Jesuit" and the verbal play in the following exchange allude to the Native American platform of anti-Catholicism:

> "Do you know anything about him?" asked the hooked-nose gentleman.
> "No, but I suspect him for something."
> "Suspicion. We want knowledge."
> "Well, suspect first and know next. True knowledge comes but by suspicion or revelation. That's my maxim."

A Know-Nothing politician, who would dislike Sumner's lack of sympathy for his views, would naturally try to tar him with the brush of Catholicism, as the Know-Nothings did their other political enemies. Like the Herb-Doctor's, the ambiguity of Sumner's motives apparently remains still today for his biographers. Donald in his "Preface" stresses Sumner's "very complex personality" and the differences of opinion that have existed about his motives since his first public appearances in Boston in the 1840s. [25]

Another peculiarly personal trait of Sumner that is reflected in Melville's caricature of the Herb-Doctor is his habit of corresponding with European—especially English—friends and of mentioning them in conversation and letters. As Henry Adams sympathetically described it: "Mr. Sumner, both by interest and instinct, felt the value of his English connection, and cultivated it the more as he became socially an outcast from Boston society by the passions of politics. He was rarely without a pocket-full of letters from duchesses or noblemen in England." When the Herb-Doctor in chapter 19 hears Thomas Fry's name, he exclaims, "Any relation to Mrs. Fry? . . . I still correspond with that excellent lady on the subject of prisons. Tell me, are you anyway connected with *my* Mrs. Fry?" He is claiming a connection with Elizabeth Gurney Fry, the English Quaker prison reformer. Additionally, this little caricatural touch alludes to Sumner's early fame in the Boston Prison Discipline Society controversy with Louis Dwight, during 1845–47, which led to Sumner's being banned from Boston society. At the time of this quarrel about methods of imprisonment, Sumner's habit of referring to his correspondence with famous Europeans and his imputed desire for notoriety as a reformer were satirized in a comic paragraph entitled, "A Portrait in Aqua-Fortis," in *Yankee Doodle*—in the same issue that contains one of Melville's "Old Zack" satires. This squib, based on an article in the *Home Journal,* implies that Sumner has chosen "celebrity" as his profession—to "conspicuo-sify himself," and it ridicules him for alluding to his correspondence with the "Howards of Europe." The satire is harsh upon Sumner for his attack upon the secretary of the Boston Prison Discipline Society, who was Dwight.[26]

The style of the Herb-Doctor's longer speeches clearly parodies the principal noted traits of Sumner's oratory, which were: classical formality, a heavily Latinate vocabulary, long complex sentences, chains of logical reasoning, use of the rhetorical question, use of classical literary and biblical references, symmetry and balance, and the creation of memorable epithets and phrases. Harsha wrote of him that among rhetoricians he "stands in the foremost rank, and his style . . . will long be regarded as among the most perfect models" for the study and imitation of the student of oratory; and, "His composition abounds in an exuberance of classical allusions, which has been the subject of frequent and severe criticism." Higginson speaks of his long chains of rhetoric, erudite illustrations, his "florid Boston style." Adams wrote that "he was the classical ornament of the anti-slavery party." Less flatteringly, a "satirical lady" friend of Julia Ward Howe etched him as " 'the moral flummery member from Massachusetts, quoting Tibullus!' " Just as Sumner was faulted for his excessively long, Latinate sentences, the Herb-Doctor's opening speech might also be:

> And yet, when one is confident he has truth on his side, and that it is not on the other, it is no very easy thing to be charitable; not that temper is the bar, but conscience, for charity would beget toleration, you know, which is a kind of implied permitting, and in effect a kind of countenancing; and that which is countenanced is so far furthered. But should untruth be furthered?

One notices, also, here the emphasis of his rhetoric upon adherence to "truth" and "conscience," the latter term the key one of the Massachusetts "Conscience" Whigs—Sumner, Charles Francis Adams, Richard Henry Dana, Jr., Henry Wilson, Francis Bird, and others. And later in chapter 19 in reply to a long speech of the Herb-Doctor, which is complexly reasoned and heavily Latinate in vocabulary and sentence structure, the less literary Thomas Fry asks irritably, "What do you talk your hog-latin to me for?" (p. 112). Again, like Sumner, the Herb-Doctor likes to use literary quotations; one from Shakespeare's *Merchant of Venice* and one from Virgil's *Aeneid,* in chapter 16, and several from the Old and New Testaments. No other character in *The Confidence-Man* directly quotes from a classical poet.[27]

Sumner's literary ability to popularize memorable epithets and slogans is noted by Higginson, who calls him a great phrasemaker; and Donald writes: "A very high proportion of the antislavery men's armory of slogans came from Sumner's speeches: 'Freedom National,' 'The Backbone Party,'

'The Crime Against Kansas,' 'The Barbarism of Slavery' and the like." Other examples of phrases that he contributed to the political language of the period were "the Lords of the Lash and the Lords of the Loom," "The Remedy of Tyranny," and the "Remedy of Justice and Peace." Melville parodies Sumner's phrasemaking talent in the Herb-Doctor's catchy names for his medicines: the "Omni-Balsamic Reinvigorator," the "Samaritan Pain Dissuader," and in calling himself the "Natural Bone-setter." This last name alludes directly to a speech in 1850 in Boston in which Sumner said that the people should demand of their candidates "Three things at least. . . . The first is *back-bone*; the second is *back-bone*; and the third is *back-bone*." This phrase was turned against him after his election as senator, when for several months he failed to make the strong antislavery speech expected of him, and his "backbone" was questioned by his political opponents. Sumner undertook to answer the accusations. That the "back-bone" phrase became a catchphrase is seen in Sumner's caricature as "a baby without a backbone" in a graphic print satirizing a group of Massachusetts politicians, entitled, "The Massachusetts Baby Show" (185?). He is recognizable by his facial features, which are copied from daguerreotypes, and by a scroll he holds that reads "Libertas nationalis, servitas sectionalis,"—an allusion in Latin to his speech on "Freedom National, Slavery Sectional" in 1852.[28]

The main public event in Sumner's career that is alluded to in the episodes involving the Herb-Doctor is the famous assault upon him at his desk in the Senate on 22 May 1856 by Representative Preston S. Brooks of South Carolina—an event that was called by some the first blow in the Civil War (see plate 11).[29] Brooks beat Sumner for "insults" to his kinsman Senator Andrew P. Butler in his philippic "The Crime Against Kansas." Several details of the encounter in chapter 17 between the Herb-Doctor and the Invalid Titan (who I shall maintain in Chapter 9 is a composite caricature of John C. Calhoun and Preston Brooks) suggest that Melville intended the reader to perceive that that notorious event was being caricatured.[30] First, the Titan's angry interruption of the Herb-Doctor's "benevolent trade," which opens the scene of the beating, is compared to the moment when the stroke of "a great clock-bell—stunning admonisher—strikes one; and the stroke though single, comes bedded in the belfry clamor" (p. 99). It was widely reported in the press in the days immediately after the event that Brooks had waited in the Senate chamber until 12:45, when the Senate had recessed, and then approached and struck Sumner at or near one o'clock.[31] Second, the Titan carries a "swamp-oak stick." The cane with which Brooks struck Sumner was at first popularly believed to be of oak, though later it was revealed to be of gutta-percha.[32] That the Titan's stick is of swamp oak forms part of a complex of allusions in his description which point to South Carolina.

(Others are cited in Chapter 9.) Third, the Herb-Doctor "fancies" that the Titan's limp may be the result of a Mexican War wound—"buried bullet, maybe—some dragoons in the Mexican war discharged with such." Brooks was a veteran of the Mexican War, and his strokes on Sumner's head were compared by Garrison to "dragoon strokes which Brooks had learnt in the Mexican War."[33] Fourth, the unexpectedness of the blow, while the Herb-Doctor is busy reading aloud "a printed voucher" praising his medicine, reflects the unexpectedness of Brooks's attack upon Sumner—which followed immediately upon his appearance at Sumner's desk and his pronouncing of his name.[34] Fifth, the Titan's exclamation, "Profane fiddler on heartstrings! Snake!" echoes the violent language used by the Southern press and politicians about Sumner, as, for example, by Clement C. Clay of Alabama, who had called him in Senate debate "a sneaking, sinuous, snake-like poltroon."[35] Last, the Herb-Doctor's term for the beating, "this coward assault" (p. 100), echoes the newspaper term "coward assault" used in the *Times* account (23 May 1856) and by other papers and sympathetic speakers for the event.

The violent emotions provoked in the Titan by the Herb-Doctor's apparently innocuous solicitations resemble the kind of emotion that Sumner's speeches aroused in others, whether in his fellow Whigs, such as Robert C. Winthrop, early in his career, or in Southern leaders, such as Senator Butler (at whom he directed his criticism in "The Crime Against Kansas") and Brooks in the Congress. This emotional reaction Sumner apparently never quite understood, since he regarded his rhetorically powerful language as the kind that a great orator was supposed to use and which he claimed was not meant to be taken personally. He regularly lost friends because of blindness to the effects of his language upon other people. The Herb-Doctor's response to his beating, which is to use some of his own specific on his bruises and to say that he will not seek "redress," since "innocence is [his] redress," again reflects Sumner's nonresistance beliefs and his notable persistence in propagandizing his humanitarian and benevolent principles: "If that man's wrathful blow provokes me to no wrath, should his evil distrust arouse you to distrust? I do devoutly hope . . . for the honor of humanity—hope that, despite this coward assault, the Samaritan Pain Dissuader stands unshaken in the confidence of all who hear me!" Surely this scene, written we presume sometime in the months preceding the completion of the manuscript of *The Confidence-Man* in October of 1856, would call up in a reader's mind the most famous of all the personal attacks made upon any congressman in the antebellum period and the event which catalyzed Northern and Western sentiment to make the campaign slogan "Bleeding Sumner" equal in power to "Bleeding Kansas." Sympathy with Melville's satire, however, would be available only to those men such as Hawthorne, perhaps, or to Shaw and the

Curtises and other Massachusetts men who did not share the prevailing sense of outraged dignity which the assault provoked in New England.

The commentary that Melville seems to be making upon the event through caricature may perhaps be best suggested by the Titan's response to the Herb-Doctor's offer of his "remedy": "Some pains cannot be eased but by producing insensibility, and cannot be cured but by producing death." A common observation of the more pessimistic minds in the 1850s was that slavery was an illness of such magnitude that it could not be cured except by the death of the patient—the South. The moving portrait of the "invalid Titan in homespun" with his heavy walking stick of swamp oak and his "tawny and shadowy" countenance, whose "burdensome" step and "heavy-hearted" and "melancholy" expression indicate some great illness, grew, I believe, in Melville's hands from the commonplace metaphor of the period that slavery was a disease, an illness, for which the South was not originally responsible and which could not be cured by any measures open to man but only by Providence, God, or Destiny. When Brooks beat Sumner over the head at his Senate desk early in the afternoon of 22 May, it was generally felt to be more than one man responding to language that he considered insulting to his relative, Senator Butler; it immediately became an intensely symbolic event, as is reflected in the press, speeches, meetings, and graphic prints of it. To the North it became symbolic of the brutal power that the "Slavocracy" was believed to hold over the intellectual and moral spirit of the North. To the South it became symbolic of a manly, chivalrous response to accumulated personal, state, and regional slanders and provocations.[36] To Melville it appeared, it seems, as the response of a sick, perhaps dying, society to the useless remedies offered by a quack politician. Melville's satire of Sumner in this chapter is among his most sharp, powerful, and moving.

The assault on the Herb-Doctor is followed immediately in chapter 18 by the "inquest into [his] true character," which has been discussed earlier. It is worthy of noting that again, after the Brooks assault, as at the time of Sumner's election by the "Coalition bargain of Conscience Whigs and Democrats," his honesty was questioned by his opponents. Donald writes that they "from the beginning found something suspicious about his invalidism." It was charged that he was "shamming," as the aftereffects of the blows on his head lengthened into an illness of several months prior to the November election and eventually into years. Because he became an exploitable martyr for the Republican cause in the campaign of 1856 the validity of his subsequent illness (which Donald has researched in detail and has concluded was altogether genuine) was suspected by his enemies. As late as 1858, he was called "a charlatan, who, preceded by his servant in motley, with a trumpet or drum, cries his injuries and sufferings in the cause of freedom as saleable wares, for the purpose of putting money in his purse."[37]

Not all of the Herb-Doctor's relationships with other characters are presently decipherable, but suggestions can be made about some of the more important as follows: If the Sick Man, his first customer, the subject of chapter 16, is intended to caricature some elderly Whig politician, then the Herb-Doctor's success in selling him a box of six vials of Omni-Balsamic Reinvigorator represents Sumner's success in selling the political issue of antislavery in the new party to an old Whig politician, who had despaired of the Whigs' ever gaining power again. The relationship with the Titan and his "puny girl," in chapter 17, represents Sumner's relationship to some of his Southern congressional colleagues in Washington—a confrontation often of violence. The encounter, in chapter 19, with Thomas Fry, the "soldier of fortune," whom I discuss in Chapter 9 as a caricature of George Law, a New York presidential aspirant of the Know-Nothing party, is difficult to interpret precisely since not much has been written on Law, and I can find no specific connection between Sumner and him. However, Law did, apparently, go along politically with the switch to Frémont by his North American convention supporters, who had previously nominated N. P. Banks. And Law went Republican so far as to publish two letters against Fillmore, the national Know-Nothing candidate, which were widely circulated. Next, Sumner's political closeness to the elder Francis P. Blair, which is well documented, is satirized in chapter 20, where the Herb-Doctor sells the Miser a two-dollar box of his Omni-Balsamic Reinvigorator, and again in chapter 21, where the Miser leans, as "trustfully" as a Siamese twin, upon the Herb-Doctor's arm—a humorous comment upon the new alliance of the old Jacksonian Democrat Blair with the rising political power of the young ex-Whig and Republican—an alliance that lasted until the death of Sumner in 1874.

As for the encounter of the Missouri Bachelor with the Herb-Doctor in chapter 21, in which Pitch scornfully ridicules the latter's views, the satire reflects, I suggest, Benton's well-reported refusal to endorse the Republican movement, as he had been expected to do by some because Frémont was his son-in-law, although I have not yet found any direct historical connection between Sumner and Benton—such as a public exchange of letters or a debate. The differences in their views on the place of the slavery issue in politics may be reflected in the exchange between Pitch and the Herb-Doctor in their discussion of labor-hiring problems (p. 127). Pitch refuses to buy slaves, though from a slave state (just as Benton disapproved of slavery) not out of "philanthropic scruples"—as the Herb-Doctor suggests—but out of his detestation of servility, whether white or black. He accuses the Herb-Doctor of being "an abolitionist"—as Sumner often was—and the Herb-Doctor's response to this is a statement in which Melville seems to satirize Sumner's middle, compromising, "political" position on slavery. The Herb-Doctor denies being an abolitionist in the sense of a "zealot" (as would be Lundy, Garrison, or Phillips), and claims to be one only in the sense of

> A man, who, being a man, feels for all men, slaves included, and by any lawful act, opposed to nobody's interest, and therefore, rousing nobody's enmity, would willingly abolish suffering (supposing it, in its degree, to exist) from among mankind, irrespective of color. . . .

Such a speech read in the perplexing context of the 1850s—a period of conflicting state and national laws, of conflicting moral and property interests, and of conflicting feelings of hatred and love—should be read as ridicule of Sumner's imperceptivity of the nature of the problems that slavery posed in the eyes of so careful a studier of human nature as Herman Melville was. He places in the mouth of Herb-Doctor-Sumner words that summarize part of the problem and state obliquely its insolubility, as Melville saw it, in one sentence, even while making his character seem to be unaware of what he is actually saying. The Herb-Doctor has his cake of abolitionism (he feels for the slaves and would abolish suffering) and eats it, too (he would abolish slavery by a "lawful act, opposed to nobody's interest and rousing nobody's enmity")—an impossibility in the real world at that time. In these "picked and prudent sentiments" Pitch sees how such a "moderate" man may be used by the "wicked man." The satire here involves the charge that was leveled against the new Republican party that it was a concerted reach for power under the cover of philanthropic sentiment. The nonpolitical Abolitionists such as Garrison and Phillips made this charge, as did Douglass, noted earlier, after the 1856 election, and as did the strong Unionist, like Benton, who wanted the slavery issue left entirely out of politics.

In response to the Herb-Doctor's next question, whether Pitch, coming from a slave state is "without slave sentiments," Pitch deliberately puns on the phrase "slave sentiments," taking the meaning of it to be feelings of servility, rather than holding proslavery views. Accusing the Herb-Doctor himself of being servile, he asks whether *he* has a master or is "owned by a company," a remark that I take to be an allusion to Sumner's relationship to "Seward, Weed, Greeley & Co.," the Republican "firm," and I take the following to be a hit at Sumner's political ambitions: "'Come from Maine or Georgia, you come from a slave-state, and a slave-pen, where the best breeds are to bought up at any price from a livelihood to the Presidency.'" He echoes here a standard Unionist and Southern charge against Northern politicians.

Lastly, the encounter of Pitch with the Herb-Doctor may be viewed generally as that of the shrewd though rough personality of the Western politician Benton, familiar from childhood with the slavery problem, with the well-spoken but experientially naïve New Englander Sumner.

Of the minor figures with whom the Herb-Doctor has encounters I can identify only one with any evidence: the "man of the appearance of a day-laborer," who has a "bandage across his face" in chapter 18. The bandage, which conceals the "side of [his] nose," his "red-flannel shirt-sleeves," his "coat thrown across one shoulder, the darned cuffs drooping behind," his "pace that seemed the lingering memento of the lock-step of convicts," and his "clam-shell of a hand" all point to the type-character of "Mose," the New York City "B'Hoy." The B'Hoy was a character, based on the street life of the period, who appears in stage comedies, such as *Mysteries and Miseries of New York* (1848), *New York As It Is* (1848), and Ben Baker's *A Glance at New York* (1848), which starred F. S. Chanfrau, wearing a red shirt, plug hat and turned-up trousers. Mose is usually thus depicted in theatrical, comic, and political prints (plate 18).[38] Both Mose, the New York B'Hoy, and "Jakey," his Philadelphia counterpart, were drawn from the city firemen, who were as much rowdies and street fighters as community employees. The bandaged nose of Melville's character indicates that he has been in a fight, or "muss," as it was called in New York City slang.

Three examples of the red-flannel shirt that Mose typically wore may be seen in the following colored prints: "Dancing for EEls . . . In Catherine Mkt., N.Y." (1848); "Dancing for Eels" (1848)—a different print—depicting a scene from the play *New York As It Is* at the Chatham Theatre; and "Mose, Lize, and Little Mose Going to California" (1851).[39] Two political prints that illustrate the B'Hoy as holding his coat over his shoulder or his arm as Melville's figure does are: "The Political Mose," in *Young America* (1856) (plate 18) and "Dancing for Eels in the Charleston Market," in *Vanity Fair* (1860). Several prints in the New York *Lantern* in 1852 use the B'Hoy figure holding his coat over his shoulder.[40] The B'Hoy's penchant for fighting is used as part of the humor in "The Political Mose," where Lewis Cass, caricatured as the B'Hoy, says, "If I don't get a muss soon, I'll spile." Four prints that show the adaptation of the B'Hoy figure to political satire are the following: "The Democratic B'Hoy" (1848), in which Cass beats Taylor in a fight; "Who's Dat Knockin' at De Door" (1848), depicting John Van Buren as the B'Hoy trying to fight his way into the Democratic convention and being repulsed by Calhoun; the print already cited in *Young America,* "The Political Mose," in which Cass again appears as the B'Hoy spoiling for a fight; and the print already mentioned from *Vanity Fair,* published in connection with the Democratic nominations of 1860 in Charleston, South Carolina,

"Dancing for Eels in the Charleston Market," in which Henry A. Wise of Virginia is depicted as a B'Hoy watching Stephen Douglas dance for eels.[41] Other characteristics of the B'Hoy, which Melville does not use in his character, are his tall black "plug-ugly" hat, his rolled-up pants legs, and his black boots. The descriptive detail that his character has the "lock-step of a convict" alludes to the frequent jailing of the B'Hoys for street fighting, and the "clam-shell of a hand," to their localized connection with the New York City fish markets.

The Herb-Doctor's gift of two dollars to the B'Hoy, who steps forth eagerly, may possibly be a satirical thrust at Sumner's interest in prison reform. The point of contrasting the B'Hoy with the "unhappy-looking woman, in a sort of mourning," who sobs "behind [her] meagre bundle," but who is ignored by the Herb-Doctor, would be that men of Sumner's philanthropic type give sympathy and aid—on abstract principles of justice or charity—to those who do not really deserve it—*i.e.*, rowdies and ex-convicts—while they ignore the truly needy, who are too embarrassed to claim it (plate 10).[42] If this scene (which also includes an unidentified "demure-looking woman, in a dress rather tawdry and rumpled," who almost asks for the money being offered) alludes to some particular event of Sumner's career, it is as yet undiscovered, nor have I any suggestions for the identities of the women. There remain also unidentified in chapter 17 two very minor figures: a "sickly young man," who is a "new-comer, not from the shore, but from another part of the boat," who buys a bottle of the Samaritan Pain Dissuader; and "a cynical-looking little man, with a thin flaggy beard and a countenance ever wearing the rudiments of a grin," who holds "a rusty hat before his face." Since he "commands a good view of the scene," where, while the Herb-Doctor is plying his trade, he is struck by the Titan, this man may possibly be some congressional figure present during the assault on Sumner.

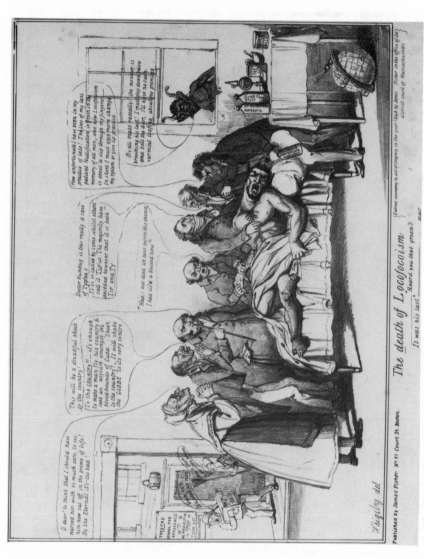

1. The Death of Locofocoism. Boston, 1840. Jackson, Blair, Levi Woodbury, Van Buren, Benton, unidentified, and Calhoun. Courtesy American Antiquarian Society.

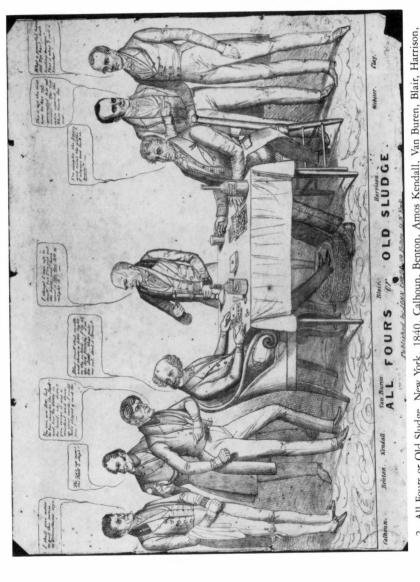

2. All Fours or Old Sludge. New York, 1840. Calhoun, Benton, Amos Kendall, Van Buren, Blair, Harrison, Webster, and Clay. Courtesy American Antiquarian Society.

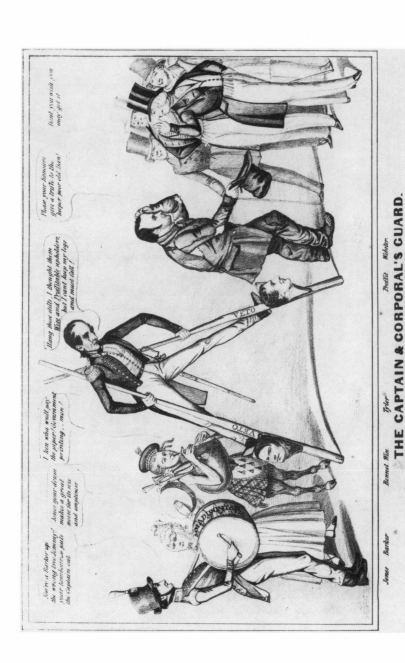

3. The Captain & Corporal's Guard. New York and Washington, 1841. John Beauchamp Jones, James N. Barker, Bennett, Wise, Tyler, George H. Proffit, Webster, various gentlemen. Courtesy American Antiquarian Society.

4. The Man Wot Drives the Constitution. New York, 1844. John Crittenden, Webster, Richard M. Johnson, Clay, Ladies representing peace and prosperity, Frelinghuysen, John Beauchamp Jones, Jackson, Tyler, and Van Buren. Courtesy American Antiquarian Society.

HINCKLEY SC.

THE NEW DAVY CROCKETT.

"I DID TO-DAY LOOK AT GENERAL KEARNEY WHEN HE LOOKED AT COLONEL FREMONT, AND I LOOKED HIM DOWN; I LOOKED AT HIM TILL HIS EYES FELL."—*Ex-Lieutenant-General Benton's Speech.*

5. The New Davy Crockett. *John-Donkey,* 1 (29 January 1848), 73. General Stephen W. Kearny and Benton. Courtesy Harvard College Library.

6. The Hurly-Burly Pot. New York, 1850. Wilmot, Garrison, Calhoun, Benedict Arnold, and Greeley. Courtesy Library of Congress.

7. The Presidential Harlequin. New York, 1851. Webster, Fillmore, and "Private Secretary" (unidentified). By permission of the Huntington Library, San Marino, California.

8. Barn-Burners in a Fix. New York, 1852. Van Buren, unidentified, Bryant, unidentified, John Van Buren, and Pierce. Courtesy American Antiquarian Society.

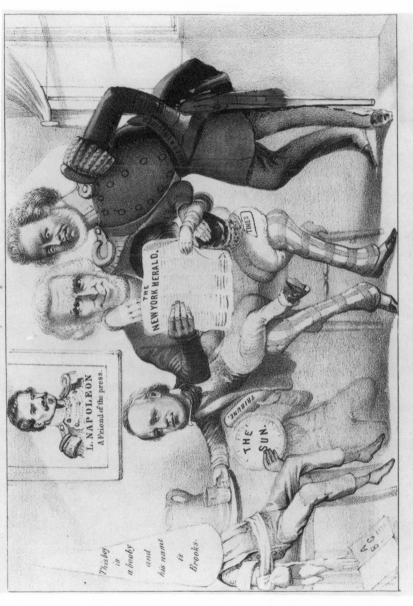

THE HAPPY FAMILY.

9. The Happy Family. From *The Old Soldier, Illustrated by His Son John*. New York: J. L. Magee, Vol. 1, No. 6 (1 June 1852). Erastus Brooks, Moses Yale Beach, Greeley, Bennett, Raymond, and James Watson Webb. Loose print by permission of the Huntington Library, San Marino, California.

I'M NOT TO BLAME FOR BEING WHITE, SIR!

10. I'm Not to Blame for Being White, Sir! Boston?, 1852?. Charles Sumner giving charity to a black girl. By permission of the Massachusetts Historical Society.

SOUTHERN CHIVALRY — ARGUMENT VERSUS CLUB'S.

11. Southern Chivalry—Argument versus Club's. New York?, 1856. Brooks caning Sumner in the Senate Chamber, 22 May 1856. Courtesy American Antiquarian Society.

12. Liberty, the Fair Maid of Kansas—In the Hands of the "Border Ruffians." New York?, 1856. Marcy, Buchanan, Pierce, "Liberty," Cass, and Douglas. By permission of the Stanford University Museum of Art, 81.27. Gift of the Committee for Art.

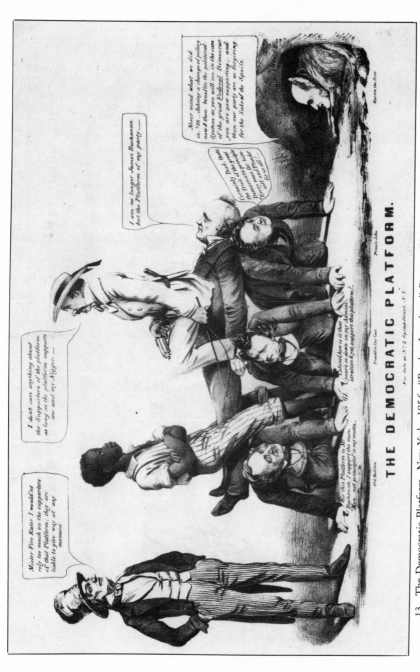

13. The Democratic Platform. New York, 1856. "Brother Jonathan," Benton, Pierce, and John Van Buren supporting Buchanan, who supports a black youth ("Slavery"), and a white planter. Martin Van Buren (*far right*). By permission of the Huntington Library, San Marino, California.

14. Col. Fremont's Last Grand Exploring Expedition in 1856. New York, 1856. Seward, Greeley, Frémont, Beecher, and a "Westerner" (Kit Carson?). By permission of the Huntington Library, San Marino, California.

15. The "Mustang" Team. New York, 1856. Two Unionist or Know-Nothing men, Greeley, Bennett, Raymond, a boy (unidentified), Frémont, Jessie Frémont?, and Webb. By permission of the Department of Special Collections, University Research Library, University of California, Los Angeles.

FANCIED SECURITY, OR THE RATS ON A BENDER.

16. Fancied Security, Or the Rats on a Bender. New York, 1856. Fillmore, John Breckinridge, Buchanan, Greeley, Frémont, William C. Dayton, George Law, Bennett, and Webb. By permission of the Department of Special Collections, University Research Library, University of California at Los Angeles.

KANSAS CRUSADER.

QUOTATION FROM A SPEECH OF REV. HENRY WARD BEECHER.

" WELL, SIR, IN REGARD TO THE RIFLES I PROPOSE TO COMPROMISE. *We will keep the weapons ourselves, but give you the contents.*"

17. Kansas Crusader. *Young America,* 1, NS (1856), 187. Henry Ward Beecher. Courtesy American Antiquarian Society.

THE POLITICAL MOSE.

Gen C——s.—If I don't get a muss soon, I'll spile.

18. The Political Mose. *Young America*, 1, NS (1856), 259. Cass as a New York B'Hoy. Courtesy American Antiquarian Society.

THE LION AND THE LAMB.

19. The Lion and the Lamb. *Young America*, 1, NS (1856), 295. Bennett embracing Greeley, reflecting his switch to Frémont in mid-June, 1856. Courtesy American Antiquarian Society.

PRESIDENTIAL TRIO.

AS PERFORMED BY THE NATIONAL MINSTRELS, FILLMORE, BUCHANAN AND FREMONT.

20. Presidential Trio. *Young America,* 1, NS (1856), 307. Frémont, Fillmore, and Buchanan. Courtesy American Antiquarian Society.

SETTLING VEXATION BY ANNEXATION.

JOHN BULL.—My dear Boy, if it comes to the worst, you'll see your Old Dad out of this plaguy French business, won't you?
JONATHAN.—Wal—can't say without seeing the boys first; I tell you what though—s'pose we ANNEX you, that'll settle this business right away!

21. Settling Vexation by Annexation. *Vanity Fair*, 2 (25 August 1860), 105. Great Britain ("John Bull") and the United States ("Brother Jonathan"). Courtesy Huntington Library, San Marino, California.

22. "The Irrepressible Conflict," Or the Republican Barge in Danger. New York, 1860. Lincoln, Greeley, Seward (being thrown out), Edward Bates, Weed?, Blair, Nathaniel Banks, "Negro" (slavery issue), a Northern Republican?, Raymond, James Watson Webb, and "Brother Jonathan." By permission of the Huntington Library, San Marino, California.

23. The Great Exhibition of 1860. New York, 1860. Greeley, Lincoln, black infant (slavery issue), Seward, Raymond, and James Watson Webb. By permission of the Huntington Library, San Marino, California.

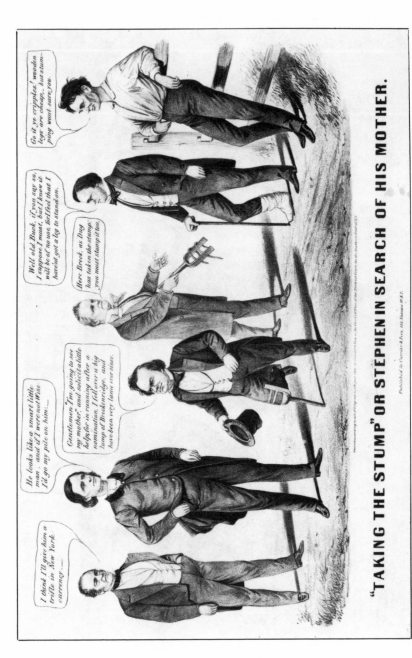

24. "Taking the Stump" or Stephen in Search of His Mother. New York, 1860. John Bell, Wise, Douglas, Buchanan, Breckinridge, and Lincoln. By permission of the Huntington Library, San Marino, California.

COMING 'ROUND.

LINCOLN.—I SAY YANCEY,—IF YOU'LL LET ME HAVE THESE STABLES IN PEACE FOR THE NEXT FOUR YEARS, I'LL GIVE YOU SOME OF THE BEST STALLS AND SEE THAT YOUR NAG IS WELL TAKEN CARE OF.

25. Coming 'Round. *Vanity Fair*, 2 (17 November 1860), 249. Lincoln and Yancey. Courtesy Huntington Library, San Marino, California.

26. "Like Meets Like." *Vanity Fair,* 3 (26 January 1861), 42. Lawrence M. Keitt of South Carolina and Garrison. Courtesy Huntington Library, San Marino, California.

27. The Inside Track. *Vanity Fair,* 3 (2 March 1861), 103. Greeley, Weed, Lincoln, and Seward. Courtesy Huntington Library, San Marino, California.

28. Worship of the North. Adalbert J. Volck, *Confederate War Etchings*, 1863?. Sumner, Greeley, Beecher, "black idol," "white victim," Lincoln, various cabinet members and generals, Harriet Beecher Stowe (*far right*). By permission of the Huntington Library, San Marino, California.

9

The Seventh Confidence Man (The PIO Man) and Three Formidable Antagonists (the Invalid Titan, the Soldier of Fortune Thomas Fry, and Pitch the Missouri Bachelor)

The Invalid Titan and the Puny Girl

Hawking the Samaritan Pain Dissuader to the passengers, the Herb-Doctor is confronted in chapter 17 with his most difficult potential customer—the Invalid Titan, who is to be interpreted, as stated earlier, as a composite figure representing South Carolina's role in national politics and based on at least two of South Carolina's political men of the period—John Caldwell Calhoun and Preston S. Brooks. He emerges from a landscape of rural sombreness, darkness, melancholy, and ghostliness, involving the more evil aspects of nature and history:

> For just then the boat touched at a houseless landing, scooped, as by a land-slide, out of sombre forests; back through which led a road, the sole one, which from its narrowness, and its being walled up with story on story of dusk, matted foliage, presented the vista of some cavernous old gorge in a city, like haunted Cock Lane in London.

His appearance contains references to "Carolina moss," cypress trees, and swamp-oak, all associated with South Carolina's flora:

> There stooped his shaggy form in the door-way, and entered the ante-cabin, with a step so burdensome that shot seemed in his pockets, a kind of invalid Titan in homespun; his beard blackly pendant, like the Carolina-moss, and dank with cypress dew; his countenance tawny and shadowy as an iron-ore country in a clouded day. In one hand he carried a heavy walking-stick of swamp-oak.

The Titan leads by the hand "a puny girl" of mixed ancestry, "not improbably his child, but evidently of alien maternity, perhaps Creole, or even Camanche." "Creole" may mean a person born in the Western Hemisphere (United States or Caribbean areas) of French, Spanish or African descent. The girl may be, then, either of half northern European descent through her father and half any one of these other descents, or she may be half northern European and half American Indian ("Camanche"). Her associations are more preponderantly Indian, for she wears moccasins and an "Indian blanket, orange-hued, and fringed with lead tassel-work." Graphic analogues suggest that she is a regional stereotype intended to represent Texas with its mixed population of Indian (specifically Comanche), Mexican, African, American, and European elements. In prints Texas appears as a woman, as, for example, in "Virtuous Harry, Or Set a Thief to Catch a Thief!" (1844), where Texas is a well-dressed woman, who claims to be of the same "blood" as Americans—a print clearly responding to accusations of mixed blood. In a contrasting print, "Matty Meeting the Texas Question" (1844), Texas is a savage-looking, dark-skinned, half-naked woman with Medusa-like hair, carrying a knife, manacles, whips, and pistols. She is borne aloft by Benton and Calhoun, who says, "Come Matty! We introduce you to the Texas Question. What do you say to her Ladyship?" Van Buren refuses Texas—slavery, ethnic mixture and all—while Polk accepts her for "that $25,000 a year." Calhoun was associated with the sponsorship of Texas because as Tyler's secretary of state he negotiated and concluded the annexation treaty in 1844.[1] The comparison of her to "a little Cassandra, in nervousness" probably alludes to Calhoun's constant prophesying of disaster to the South, unless it united in self-defense, for which a common metaphor was the classical figure of Cassandra, prophetess of the fall of Troy, who was not believed. The exact significance of Herb-Doctor-Sumner's comic dance and song before the girl and why he calls her his "little May Queen" remains uncertain, although "May Queen" may be an allusion to the Roman Catholicism of the Spanish-speaking population of Texas. In any case, they form part of his unsuccessful solicitation of the Titan and the Puny Girl and allude to Sumner's troubled relationship to Southern politicians.

The Herb-Doctor's claim of a previous acquaintance with the Titan on a Kentucky boat may allude to Sumner's single trip into the South in 1855, when he visited Cassius M. Clay in Kentucky.[2] His suggestion that the Titan might have a war wound—"some dragoons in the Mexican war discharged with such"—seems to be an allusion to Preston Brooks's service in that war, of which much was made after the Senate caning, as noted earlier. The next detail of description, the Titan's slanting posture, is, as suggested earlier, possibly related to the famous print, "Southern Chivalry—Argument Versus Club's," that appeared immediately after the assault and remains today one of the most powerful graphic prints of the period (plate 11). As a propagandistic image it both expressed much Northern feeling and provoked more. Although in Melville's chapter this posture of the Titan does not occur at

146

the very moment he is striking the Herb-Doctor—appearing as it does when they first speak together—still its curiously haunting effect lingers over in the reader's mind's eye to the violent moment when the Titan unexpectedly strikes the Herb-Doctor amid his "panegyrics." As noted above in the section on Sumner, the details of the timing of the assault, its suddenness, and the Titan's violent language all allude to the Senate incident, in which Brooks, reacting to Sumner's "Crime Against Kansas" speech as if it were a personal insult to his elderly relative, Senator Butler and to the state of South Carolina, attacked Sumner with the purpose of punishing him. In the intensity of his reaction to the "remedies" offered by the Herb-Doctor for "pains" that "cannot be cured but by producing death," the Titan reflects the career, although not the personal action, of Calhoun.

John Caldwell Calhoun (1782–1850) was United States congressman from South Carolina (1811–17), secretary of war under Monroe, vice-president under John Quincy Adams and Jackson, secretary of state under Tyler, and United States senator for seventeen years (1832–44 and 1845–50). He was termed by Harriet Martineau "the cast-iron man" for his strength of conviction and power of resistance to political forces that he regarded as inimical to Southern interests. He would be a natural representative of the antagonist side in the Melvillean examination of the question of the nature of mankind, and he would be a fit player of the cynical Pulcinella, critic of the Confidence Man's benevolent philosophy. According to his twentieth-century biographer, Charles M. Wiltse, Calhoun held a "realistic" view of human nature, derived from a Calvinistic background and from experience. He believed that the law of self-preservation requires man to pursue his own interests more than those of others, and that government was instituted to check this, but since the same human qualities exist in the governors and lead to abuse of governmental power, the internal structure of government itself must prevent abuse, whether the government be a monarchy, oligarchy, or of majority rule. In a constitutional government suffrage is not enough to prevent abuse of power by the majority; hence Calhoun evolved his doctrine of the "concurrent majority," in which each group within the nation would be obliged to yield its consent in order for the government to act. The concurrent majority would give to each part a negative upon the other. He held the "compact" theory of the American Constitution (the joint agreement of sovereign states), as opposed to the Marshall-Story-Webster theory of federal sovereignty derived from the people. He felt that the Constitution had provided sectional balance but that this was being lost in an evolution toward a numerical absolutism. He had formed his ideas by 1830, partly from Plato, Aristotle, Machiavelli, Hobbes, and Locke, but mainly, according to Wiltse, from his experience as politician and statesman. He was highly skeptical

147

about the motives of public men, believing that self-interest was stronger than patriotism or friendship. His speeches from 1847 on, which were widely read as the leading expressions of the proslavery argument, reflect his final attitudes as expressed in his posthumous *Disquisition on Government and A Discourse on the Constitution and Government of the United States* (1851).[3]

Several personal traits of Calhoun are reflected in Melville's Invalid Titan. First, his height, that of a "Titan" or "dusk giant," refers partly to Calhoun's actual height of six feet two inches and partly to his public image as one of the three "Titans," "aging giants," or "dying gods" of the Senate, along with Henry Clay and Daniel Webster. Willis in *Hurry-Graphs* (1851) mentions that he was "Tall, hollow-chested, and emaciated." Second, his "tawny and shadowy countenance" resembles Calhoun's "dark, scowling aspect," of disappointed ambition and fallen greatness as Hone describes it, and his "dark and Indian like [complexion, through which] there seemed to be an inner complexion of a dark soul shining out," according to another contemporary, Oliver Dyer. Third, the Titan's "burdensome" step reflects Calhoun's "feeble" step at his final very dramatic Senate appearance, when he was nearly at the point of death. Fourth, the Titan's melancholy, "heavy-hearted expression" and his unsociable personality reflect Calhoun's public personality as observed by contemporaries. He was noted for "a certain austerity"; he never joked and there were few instances of humor in his speeches: "Levity simply was not a part of the character of the man." Dyer writes that his "expression was firm, stern, aggressive, threatening," and he showed no ease, grace or charm as a public speaker. Martineau notes his "utter intellectual solitude." Magoon writes that his "iron features repel all thoughts of . . . glee." His twentieth-century biographer, Margaret Coit, notes a lifelong tendency to "melancholy."[4]

The Titan's speeches are laconic, consisting only of several short, simple declarative or interrogative sentences which reveal his hostility to the Herb-Doctor and his suppressed violent emotion. Magoon, in *Living Orators,* speaks of Calhoun's style as characterized by "short and pregnant sentences, disregard of oratorical conventionalities, and bold directness of diction," and as marked by "clearness, directness and energy." He uses no "gaudy rhetorical robes," and he speaks a "clear forcible laconic truth." His "erudition" is more from "solitary meditation, than from social converse, scientific research or literary recreation." Finally, like the Titan, he is "full of obstinate questionings." In this caricature of Calhoun Melville seems to have eliminated Calhoun's well-noted habit of philosophical and logical analysis but retained much of the general stylistic impression that his public speeches made upon his audience.[5]

Calhoun's public image in the 1850s was mainly that of his last few years as the senator from South Carolina, when he was dying of heart disease and tuberculosis. Wiltse describes him as a "grim-visaged realist" and as having the "hand of prophecy on him." Having no philanthropic theories, he saw self-interest rather than moral crusades behind the actions of the Northern and Western politicians. His prophetic powers were often commented upon and he was called a "Cassandra" for his predictions of disaster to the Union, if the Northern states continued to pursue their encroachments upon Southern rights and Southern power in the Senate. The most dramatic of all his appearances was his final speech in the Senate, 4 March 1850, in relation to the compromise. Wiltse writes that he was "emaciated and feeble, his sallow cheeks sunken, his long hair now almost white, his step short." Apparently "only the brilliant, flashing eyes and the grim straight lips remained of the old Calhoun," and like the Titan he appeared "ghostlike" as he sank into his seat. Unable to read his last long proposal for a solution to the sectional conflict, he asked his colleague Senator Butler to read it for him, but Butler, too, was unable, so that it was read by James M. Mason of Virginia. The speech contained only "cold, blunt realism": "Age had not softened him, disease had not dimmed his inner vision, experience had not left him any illusions as to the nature of man," Wiltse concludes.[6] Because of his close relationship to Butler, whom Sumner had insulted, and because he was the archetypal defender of slavery and bearer of the grievances and guilt of the Southern system—summed up in the metaphor of disease—and because of the physical and personal resemblance noted above, it seems likely that Calhoun is in part the allusion intended in the figure of the Invalid Titan. It is my contention that this historical image of him merged with the image of Brooks's assault on Sumner to produce Melville's Titan.

I have already pointed out the hint of military service in the Mexican War, which would constitute an allusion to Brooks's service in that war, and the image of the bell striking one o'clock, followed by the blow to the body of the Herb-Doctor in response to words spoken in public (as Sumner's speech was), as details which are intended to recall to the reader Brooks's assault upon Sumner in retaliation for what he regarded as a personal insult to his relative. Melville, I suggest, read this public incident, ominous and prophetic in its symbolic implications, as the response of a chronically diseased ("tremulous," half-crippled, "melancholy") invalid to the useless importunities of a quack doctor, who plays not only with the hopes and feelings of the chronically ill but purveys lies as he does so. Like Benito Cereno, whose condition on the *San Dominick* is misconstrued by the benevolent philanthropist, Captain Delano, the Invalid Titan's condition is misconstrued by the Herb-Doctor. In both the earlier story, *Benito Cereno* (1855), and in this scene in *The Confidence-Man,* the metaphors of invalidism, melancholy, and painful suffering stand for the Southern social system of African-American slavery, and Melville is depicting the deepening gulf of misunderstanding between the sections.

Calhoun himself, in words that Thomas Hart Benton called "memorable," compared the uselessness of crying, "'Union, Union, glorious Union!' in order to save the Union, to a physician crying, 'Health, health, glorious health!' to a dangerously ill patient."[7]

The Soldier of Fortune Thomas Fry

As stated earlier in connection with Herb-Doctor-Sumner, there is reason to believe that Thomas Fry, the begging Soldier of Fortune in chapter 19, caricatures George Law, a presidential aspirant in 1856 of the Know-Nothing party—called also the "Americans," "Native Americans," "Indians," or "Hindoos." Law's close association with several American filibusters of the 1850s—"soldiers of fortune" who sought American expansion into Cuba and Central America—make him very apt to be caricatured as Melville's "Soldier of Fortune."

Fry, dressed as an ex-soldier "in a grimy old regimental coat," with a "rag of a cap," claims to be a wounded ex-soldier of the Mexican War. He has "the hard ironic eye of one toughened and defiant in misery," while his face is "grim and wizened," "unshaven . . . like a ogre," and displays "a morose ogreness." He is a cripple, whose "interwoven paralyzed legs, stiff as icicles" are "suspended between rude crutches." His body movements are those of a cripple; his "whole rigid body, like a ship's long barometer on gimbals, [swings] to and fro, mechanically faithful to the motion of the boat." Near the end of the scene he again "rocks himself," subsiding from "his hard rocking into a gentle oscillation." When approached, he "nervously increas[es] his swing (his custom when seized by emotion) so that one would have thought some squall had suddenly rolled the boat and with it the barometer." Later, he "stumps" after the Herb-Doctor and "with his horny hand catches him by a horn-button." He is compared to a "hyaena," when he "claws" the Herb-Doctor. His voice varies from a seemingly natural gruffness and a laugh that is "startling" through a joviality that he puts on when he begs—expressed in "hi, hi!" cried "like a fellow in the pit of a six-penny theatre"—to a voice "convulsed" with emotion when the Herb-Doctor has impressed him with his generosity. He has a "wild laugh."

Fry's personality is described as prevailingly "half-moody, half-surly," "hard [and] ironic," "sneering," "morose," and "sarcastic," only momentarily relieved when, after collecting some funds by begging, he seems "gleeful" and laughs. He undergoes a marked change near the close of the chapter, in response to the kindness of the Herb-Doctor, becoming "soothed." His style is that of a plainspoken, somewhat unsocial and self-defensive man, accustomed to independence if not isolation. The story of his life is told to the Herb-Doctor in brief, declarative sentences, with only a few metaphorical ornaments chiefly drawn from naval and sea imagery (*e.g.*, "like a canal-boat splashing into the lock," and ". . . drifting down stream like any other bit of wreck"). His profession, he claims, was that of an artisan—a "cooper" or barrel maker—and he displays "the most illiterate obduracy," as if he lacked education altogether. The story that he tells of his being kept in jail as witness to a crime and his being unable to raise bail seems to be intended by Melville as an illustration of injustice to the Northern white workingmen and to be calculated to reveal the abstract nature of Herb-Doctor-Sumner's political principles. The horrors of Fry's jail experience would seem to demand the sympathetic interest of a politician interested in prison reform, yet the Herb-Doctor is shown failing to credit the truth of Fry's tale.

His role as Soldier of Fortune and certain details of his description may be linked to George Law (1806–1881), canal contractor, transportation promoter, self-made millionaire, sponsor of expansionist schemes, and would-be politician in the 1850s in New York City. According to the *Dictionary of American Biography* and *Appleton's Cyclopedia,* Law was born in New York of Irish immigrant descent, and though a man who read a great deal he was not educated. He worked as a hod carrier, stone cutter, and mason, which may be reflected in Fry's "horny hand[s]," though I have not found that he was a cooper. By 1830 he was making considerable money in canal, lock, and aqueduct building in various states, a career which seems to be alluded to by the descriptive imagery of the "canal-boat splashing into the lock." From 1834 he lived in New York, displaying great engineering and financial ability in the construction of the Croton Waterworks and the High Bridge. This work and the expansion of the Harlem Railroad—doubling its value— and construction work on the Mohawk and Hudson Railroad may be reflected in the unusual metaphorical image drawn from construction work which Fry uses in a speech to the Herb-Doctor, when he says that he wishes to "drill [the Happy Man], drop the powder, and leave him to explode at his leisure." Law achieved his greatest fortune and fame when he went into ocean steamship navigation with his ships the *Neptune,* the *Oregon,* the *Ohio,* and the *George* and profited from federal mail subsidies. In 1847 he took over the federal contract for the New York, New Orleans, Havana, and Chagres Mail service of the United States Mail Steamship Company. This career in navigation would account for Melville's choice of naval and sea imagery in the descriptive passages already cited. His financial support of the filibustering expeditions of Narciso Lopez in Cuba, 1850–51, and of C. F. Henningsen and William Walker in Nicaragua in 1856 would account for Melville's caricature of him as a "Soldier of Fortune." The Mexican War background that Fry claims was typical of filibusters, such as General John A. Quitman, who tried for years to get up an invasion of Cuba.[8]

Law came most directly into the public eye in connection with politics when in 1852 he exploited the popular issue of American prestige in Cuba by insisting on sending into Havana harbor his steamship *Crescent City*, with a purser on it who had been banned by the Cuban captain-general. For this act of bravado, he was taken up by the anti-Catholic Know-Nothing party, while his shipyard workmen named him "Live-Oak George" in admiration. In February 1855 he was endorsed for president by the Pennsylvania Legislature, and he was a contender at the Know-Nothing convention in Philadelphia in February 1856, where he ran second in the voting to Fillmore. As a result of the bolting of the Northern states' delegates, a second meeting—of the "North Americans"—was held in New York in June, which was, as noted earlier, a convention manipulated by Greeley and Weed—"at work busily as beavers and sly as moles"—in order that Banks be nominated, who would then withdraw in favor of Frémont. According to Banks's modern biographer, Fred H. Harrington, Banks's own man Isaac Sherman and three other "North Americans," including George Law, were in on the deal. According to Isely, the Republican Executive Committee Chairman, E. D. Morgan, and Law made a deal that the "North Americans" would informally nominate Banks and William F. Johnston, and then, when Banks withdrew, the Republicans would name Johnston for vice-president. Law kept his end of the deal, but the Republicans did not.[9] Fry's appearance on crutches would represent, then, in a symbolism like that of the political prints, Law's "stumping" as the Know-Nothing candidate until defeated by Fillmore and then the liability that loss represented.

According to Crandall, the historian of the origins of the Republican party, Law's supporters in New York State were the "pure-blood Know-Nothings," led by James W. Barker, and were in competition with the "Silver Grey" ex-Whig faction that favored Fillmore. Law had wealth, ambition, and more backing than Fillmore, including Bennett's New York *Herald*, yet Fillmore won the nomination. Although Law was still a leader at the bolters' convention, he was enthusiastic for Banks, and his name was not this time presented for president at all, apparently. He became chairman of the special committee formed to consider the Republican proposal that the "North Americans" cooperate with them, and he wrote the response to this invitation which was read aloud to the Republican convention on its second day. Law moved to support Frémont and on 3 July he published a letter in pamphlet form which called Buchanan a "tool of the South" and said that he knew from the *Crescent City* affair that Fillmore would not protect Americans and had been thrust upon the Know-Nothing convention by the slave oligarchy. This letter and another, displaying some personal animus toward Fillmore, were considerable assets to the Republican campaign. His importance to the Republican cause is represented in an anti-Republican cartoon, "Fancied Security; Or, The Rats on a Bender" (1856), where he is a rat climbing into the government grain-bin (plate 16).[10]

Evidently, then, Law's political movements are consonant with Fry's relationship to the Herb-Doctor, if we take the latter to represent, not specifically Sumner, but the Republican movement generally. First, Fry appears as a solicitor of public confidence in himself, just as Law solicited votes for himself as a Know-Nothing aspirant. Then, he yields to the persuasions of the Herb-Doctor and buys his medicine—*i.e.,* endorses the Republican views and candidate.

There are some other descriptive details that link Fry with Law. Fry's "grim and wizened" face, resembling that of an "ogre," is not incompatible with the public image of Law. Halstead describes him as a "ponderous old fellow," his face as "masses of florid flesh," and his hair (in a bust displayed at the first Know-Nothing convention) as "shaggy, wild bristle, like the mane of a rampant lion," though in reality, he writes, it is "formidable" only in quantity and "not stormy in appearance." Also, he resembled, to Halstead's eyes, a "heavy pork merchant." A cartoon of Law in the *Lantern,* "The American Gulliver Bringing in Cuba," shows Law with a fringe beard and a mane of hair. He appears big and fierce and possibly might be called "ogreish," but not "wizened," as I understand the word. He appears decidedly "ogreish" in two prints later than 1856.[11] Law's lack of education and his workingman's background are reflected in Fry's uneducated speech and his "illiterate obduracy" in response to the Herb-Doctor's "hog-Latin . . . address." Fry's New York City background and Melville's comparison of his cry, "Hi, hi!" to that of a "fellow in the pit of a six-penny theatre" also reflect Law's background.

Read politically the contrasting stories that Fry tells to justify his begging may be linked to political campaign issues in 1856. The main story, that of the injustice done to him—a workingman of Anglo-Saxon descent—when he witnessed a crime, for which the richer and better-connected criminal escaped punishment, would represent the appeal that the Know-Nothing party made to urban workingmen in New York and Massachusetts, who feared the competition of both the Irish and the German Catholic immigrants, while they envied the earlier settlers who had risen in wealth and social status.[12] The earlier story that he tells, that he is a wounded veteran of the battle of "glorious Contreras," would represent the political value of military fame gained in expansionist ventures—such as the Mexican War or as Law's chauvinistic defiance of Spanish (and Catholic) power in Cuba in the *Crescent City* incident. Further research on Law's fairly obscure career, on James W. Barker, and on Know-Nothing politics in New York City, 1854–56, should either reinforce his identity as the model for Thomas Fry or negate it for some other man.

Pitch the Missouri Bachelor

In the next four chapters (20–24) Pitch, "A Missouri bachelor, a Hoosier gentleman," appears and dominates the scenes with his aggressive personality, which is based on a "general law of mistrust." He may be identified, with considerable evidence, as a caricature of Thomas Hart Benton (1782–1858), one of the dominating figures of the American Senate and American politics from 1820 to 1850. Ranked by his contemporaries with Clay, Webster and Calhoun as a powerful force in the nation's destiny, Benton, after serving as a colonel in the War of 1812, was senator from Missouri for thirty years, Missouri's representative from 1853 to 1855, a Jacksonian Democrat, a non-believer in humanitarian reform, yet opposed to slavery extension and a deadly enemy of the Southern slavery-extensionists. As the Herb-Doctor says of Pitch (and Pitch agrees), that he is "though living in a slave-state without slave sentiments," so was Benton, although from Missouri, not a defender of slavery. Details of Pitch's character that link him most evidently to Benton are his Western "Davy Crockett" style costume, his distinctive style of speaking, his externally ursine personality and several of his attitudes—most notably his skepticism about mankind.

Pitch's physical appearance is described as "eccentric-looking" and "ursine," and by several other metaphors from the bear. He has a "grim stubble-chin" and is "all raccoon." His costume is that of a western backwoodsman, typified by that worn by the "Davy Crockett" figure on stage and in prints: a "shaggy spencer of the cloth called bears-skin," a "high-peaked cap of raccoon-skin, the long bushy tail switching over behind," "rawhide leggings," and carrying as implement "a double-barrelled gun."[13] His voice is a "growl" like "bruin in a hollow-trunk," and he has apparently a western or country accent similar to the Miser's, using "Yarbs" and "natur" and the solecism "go lay down." A repeated gesture, which is indicative of his aggressive personality and which may have been a stage gesture of the comic back-woodsman, is to "click" or "snap" his rifle lock. Other gestures are to "smite [the] folds of [his] bear-skin," to wag the raccoon tail of his cap in the Herb-Doctor's face, and to thrust out his arm "paw-like," all associating him with animals of western or frontier life.

An important aspect of his personality is suggested by the name "Pitch," which indicates his claim to consistency of principle: he says that he will "stick to what [he] says." Another aspect is his being a "bachelor," *i.e.,* independent of responsibilities. Another, suggested by the imagery of aggressive beasts, by his rifle and his "Spartan manners" and sentiments," is that he likes to take a military posture. Additionally, he is suspicious, "morose," irreverent, "impulsive," "insulting," "surly," "like a snapping turtle," and "disdainful." He is a "solitary." Yet Melville hints that his apparent aggressive misanthropy may be a bit exaggerated or put on for appearance, since his expression of "half-cynic, half wild-cat" is grotesquely excessive, "which [makes] its sincerity appear . . . dubious"—*i.e.,* he may be kinder than he appears and only be playing the gruff role. The Herb-Doctor calls him a "humorist"—a wag." And the Cosmopolitan says that he found his "heart . . . an inviting oyster in a forbidding shell," and that his "outside is but put on." Besides this, Pitch seems fairly well educated, claiming to use both philosophy and his reading—in addition to experience—as his guides. He is "not less acquainted, in a Spartan way . . . with philosophy and books than with woodcraft and rifles." Finally, an allusion to his previous history is made by Charles Noble, who thinks that he is not a Missourian by birth but years ago came West "a young misanthrope from the other side of the Alleganies, less to make his fortune than to flee man" (p. 192). It will be seen that nearly all of these personal traits were seen in Benton's public image.

Pitch's style in conversation, likewise, bears strong resemblances to Benton's, as will be seen. It is abrupt, forthright, severe and iconoclastic. He has a habit of repeating "Sir" and repeating similar words and phrases in a singularly distinctive prose rhythm. For example: "Fact, Sir, fact," and "You can't, sir, can't," and "A rascal, sir . . . a rascal" (pp. 123, 124, 137). In conversation with the PIO Man he is "contemptuous," distrustful, calling his views "Gammon," and commanding, as if addressing his dog, but still he uses the characteristic address, "Sir," and the repetition of words and phrases. This style of speech is displayed with the Cosmopolitan, although he seems less aggressive and domineering with this character. A typical example of Pitch's speech is this to the Herb-Doctor:

> "Sir, in the passion-fits of nature, I've known birds fly from nature to me, rough as I look; yes sir, in a tempest, refuge here," smiting the folds of his bearskin. "Fact, sir, fact. Come, come, Mr. Palaverer, for all your palavering, did you yourself never shut out nature of a cold, wet night? Bar her out? Bolt her out? Lint her out?"

And this to the PIO Man:

"Hold, come back, sir; back here, back, sir, back! I tell you no more boys for me. Nay, I'm a Mede and Persian. In my old home in the woods I'm pestered enough with squirrels, weasels, chipmunks, skunks. I want no more wild vermin to spoil my temper and waste my substance. Don't talk of boys; enough of your boys; a plague of your boys; chilblains on your boys."

Lastly, his metaphors are drawn mainly from farming, plantations, horses, and machinery.

Pitch's views generally are exemplary of his principle of distrust of mankind, in which he is a potent advocate of the thesis that mankind of all shades of skin are unworthy of trust. He relates anecdotal examples supposedly drawn from his experience to defend his claim that his "confidence [is] in distrust." Curiously, in conversation with the PIO Man the main theme of Pitch's response to his effort to get Pitch to hire a boy on his property is that machines would be better to do the work than human beings, an attitude that reflects, in terms of bitter humor, I suggest, the current national argument in the political context about what kind of labor should be used in developing the western United States—free laborers of European descent or African-American slave labor—in particular in developing Kansas and Nebraska. Whether Benton ever actually suggested that the use of machinery would be a solution to the argument over what kind of labor to introduce into the new areas I do not yet know.

Although Thomas Hart Benton's physical traits are not incompatible with Pitch's, yet the appearance of Melville's character is more dependent upon the western theatrical and graphic "backwoodsman" type than upon Benton's actual physical appearance. And, indeed, there was precedent in graphic prints for using a backwoodsman costume for Benton, as was used earlier for Clay. Clay is caricatured as "The Hunter of Kentucky" in a Crockett-type costume (coonskin hat, leggings, and rifle) in 1844. Nearer in time and person is a caricature of Benton in 1848 in a cartoon in *John-Donkey*, entitled "The New Davy Crockett," showing him in a fringed frontier coat (a "spencer") and leggings, holding a rifle and displaying a fierce and pugnacious expression (plate 5). The theme of this print is the Frémont court-martial in 1848, in which Benton took the side of his son-in-law and aggressively defended him publicly against the charge of disobedience to his superior officer, General Stephen W. Kearny. At the time, Benton was much ridiculed in the comic papers for claiming that by the fierceness of the expression of his eye in a courtroom confrontation he had forced Kearny to drop his eyes. This cartoon demonstrates clearly that Benton's contemporary public image was one of an aggressive, dominating, and blustering personality—much like the commedia dell'arte Capitano, the theatrical convention upon which I have claimed Pitch's character is based and of which the stage "backwoodsman" is a variant. Adding to Benton's strong military associations, which make him apt to be cast as a frontier fighter or as a theatrical Capitano, was his attempt in 1847 to become lieutenant-general (general-in-chief) of all the American armies in Mexico, an attempt that failed despite President Polk's support. He was satirized in *Yankee Doodle* for this, as "General Tom Thumb," in a cartoon, "First Exhibition of Gen. Tom Thumb Benton," where he is viewed with contempt by Generals Santa Anna, Winfield Scott, and Zachary Taylor, and in another, "Design for a Statue to be Erected to Himself by Gen'l Tom Thumb Benton."[14] Benton is a constant subject of satire both in prints and in literary pieces throughout the period of *Yankee Doodle*'s publication, 1846–47, so it may be assumed as certain that Melville was familiar with his public image, as we know he was with that of Taylor.

In personality Benton was notable for his "painful honesty and dogged consistency" both in his hard money policy in the 1830s and in his thirty-year effort to keep slavery agitation out of Missouri. He is characterized by Magoon as "eminently laborious, imperious, and democratic in his habits of spirit and style" and not "infrequently betrayed by strong feeling into imperious action, in public speech"—as is Pitch. He prided himself on being a solitary, his most famous remark in the 1830s being, "Solitary and alone I set this ball in motion" (the Expunging Resolution to remove the Senate's censure of Jackson for removing federal deposits from the United States Bank). "Sometimes [he was] too fractious for a dignified Senator," and yet his apparent egotism was regarded as better than a hypocritical modesty that might mask selfishness. A sketch in *John-Donkey,* "National Zoological Institute, No. 2," depicts him as an obstinate old animal with a terrible mane, who snaps at his fellows. William E. Smith, Blair's biographer, characterizes Benton, who was a relative, lifelong friend, and political ally of Blair, as "imperious, pugnacious, and overbearing," and as tactless, and notes his "vanity . . . egotism . . . austerity [and] dictatorial attitude." Yet "fearlessness" was his most dominating characteristic. Benton's modern biographer, William N. Chambers, writes that he had "great muscular energy, physical bulk, and pugnacity." Also, he had "a trigger-touchy sense of personal honor, which involved him in fights and pistol duels." In one quarrel he and his brother nearly killed Andrew Jackson, who later became a political friend, and he did kill another man in a duel—an act he regretted all his life. He was "temperamentally as aggressive as a Missouri bobcat," Chambers writes.[15]

However, again precisely like Pitch, Benton had a double aspect to his personality. Although in public he was "austere and little given to the amiable arts," yet "this street lion was a house lamb." At home he was "easy, charming, affectionate, delightful, courtly." Friends and enemies recognized his "familial devotion," his capacity to listen as well as talk, and his "warmth" as a host. This double aspect of Benton's personality is, I think, depicted in Pitch's switch from his surly, cynical, domineering, and morose attitude to the "indulgent . . . artless . . . companiable" aspect of his nature by which he is betrayed by the PIO Man's wiles into hiring a boy from him. Again, like Pitch, Benton took pride in his mainly self-acquired learning and was remarkable in his conversation and speeches for his learning in literature and history, a quality reflected in the wide range of references Pitch makes in his arguments. Lastly, the event from Pitch's past history surmised by Charlie Noble—that he came West to flee man—alludes to a formative event of Benton's life, when at the age of eighteen he felt compelled to leave North Carolina and to make a new start in the West as the result of expulsion from the University of North Carolina for the theft of money from several fellow students.[16] The common rumor of this youthful crime probably lies behind Pitch's pointed reference to "St. Augustine on Original Sin [as] my text book," since it may be remembered that Augustine dwells, in *The Confessions*, Book II, upon his theft of pears at the age of sixteen as an example of "gratuitous evil, having no temptation to ill, but the ill itself."[17]

Pitch's distinctive speaking style more clearly imitates the widely parodied speaking style of Benton than does the style of any other character in *The Confidence-Man* parody the individual being satirized, with the possible exception of the parody of Emerson's style in Winsome's speeches. Benton was "resolute and daring in debate, sometimes to a reckless degree." It was "hard for him to endure restraint" and he was subject to "anger." He was "a powerful, polemical speaker" and one who "insistently demanded the facts, facts, facts, concerning any issue." He was capable of using the cant term "Gammon" about the Kansas-Nebraska Bill. Most significantly for our purposes he had the mannerism of using the Senatorial "Sir" constantly and of repeating certain words and phrases in a peculiarly distinctive rhythm. This stylistic trait of his was so well known that George Templeton Strong could, quoting Hamilton Fish, mimic Benton speaking in 1854 on the Kansas-Nebraska Bill, in his *Diary* thus:

> "'Did you ever see a dog, sir, in the month of July or August, which had been shot through the head about a fortnight before? The condition of that animal, sir, after that accident, is the condition of the bill you mention. Putrefaction, sir, and decomposition, and tendency to annihilation, characterize alike the dead dog and 'the dead bill.'"

The repetitive use of the apostrophe "Sir," and the carefully structured rhythmical and verbal repetitions were evidently easily caricatured traits of Benton's conversation. An even better example is found in Halstead's report of the 1856 Democratic convention in Cincinnati. Benton, "Hot for Buchanan," says:

> "This administration is most weak and corrupt, sir—corrupt and weak, sir. The President [Pierce] don't know his own mind for one hour, sir— not for one hour. Look at our foreign relations. There is more danger of the peace of the world being disturbed than you are aware, sir, more than you are aware of, sir.
> "The passions of the people are fearfully aroused, sir—fearfully aroused. Mention the name of Douglas and every bad passion is aroused—every one aroused, sir. He is a political filibuster, sir, he could not carry a free state. The North is incensed, very justly incensed at his conduct, sir. This thing of slavery agitation was all settled, sir, until he broke it up. The angry feeling of the North is very just, sir.
> "As for Buchanan—never a leading man in any high sense, sir—but a man of fair talents, and a very pure man in both his public and private life, sir. He is a man of peace, sir—eminently a man of peace. The effect of his nomination would be to restore peace to the country, sir."

I have quoted thus much from Halstead's version of Benton's conversation, both to illustrate his style and to indicate his political views at the period of the 1856 nominations and elections. Melville's caricature of his public personality is stylistically unmistakeable. [18]

In all three of Pitch's conversations—with the Herb-Doctor, the PIO Man, and the Cosmopolitan, and in his remarks to Miser-Blair, Melville makes allusions to Benton's relations with representatives of the antislavery political movement as it emerged in the formation of the new Republican party in the 1850s. Sumner in the Senate, Greeley at the *Tribune,* and Henry Ward Beecher in his Plymouth Church pulpit were all exponents of the humanitarian spirit, of the benevolent view of man, and of the "faith" or "confidence" in man that Benton's principles and experience as a boy and man of Southern birth and his own self-knowledge, perhaps, led him to deprecate. In response to the Herb-Doctor's views of the benevolence of nature and of man, which he terms "your Confession of Faith," Pitch upholds a confession of faith in natural depravity—the doctrine of "Original Sin," for which St. Augustine is his "text book." I cannot find that Benton cited St. Augustine frequently, but his own early career, with his record of theft, and his observation of all the quarrelling, duelling, feuding, and general violence of western life in Tennessee, and his own shooting and stabbing affray with

Jackson, who had been formerly and was later his friend, and his killing of a young man in a duel—all surely show the experience of a man aware of sin. And against the Herb-Doctor's view of the benevolence of nature, when Pitch cites the flood that carried off his plantation, Benton might have cited the frost that killed his entire cotton crop in one night, as well as other early disasters that he was accustomed to recount dramatically to his children. [19]

Pitch ridicules the Miser in chapter 21 for buying medicine from the Herb-Doctor thus: "You foolish old file you! He diddled you with that hocus-pocus, did he?" This seems to allude to the fact that Benton "sternly" counseled Blair, his old Democratic political ally, against joining the new party. It is possible also that when he tells the Miser to "Go lay down in your grave, old man," he is alluding to the caricature of Blair as a "galvanized corpse" in the 1830s. However, Benton was personally sympathetic to Sumner after the Brooks attack, commenting that the attack was part of "a conspiracy; yes, sir, a conspiracy"—"these men hunt in couples, sir." So, as suggested above, this scene with Herb-Doctor-Sumner does not reflect individual historical relationships but rather Benton's negative relationship to the antislavery movement as represented by Sumner. He refuses the Herb-Doctor's medicines just as Benton refused the solutions to the sectional crisis that the new party offered. [20]

I have already discussed at length in Chapter 8 Pitch's conversation with the Herb-Doctor in chapter 21, when he accuses the salesman of being an abolitionist. Pitch here reveals the same dislike of slavery that Benton felt. Benton did not want to see slavery extended into the territories, because it would, in his opinion, only extend what he regarded as an insoluble problem. Founding his views of the institution on his reading as a student in 1804 of St. George Tucker's edition of Blackstone's *Commentaries,* he cited in his *Thirty Years' View* (1855) Jefferson as being against keeping the African-Americans in the United States, because prejudice was ineradicable, and because their memory of the evil done to them would always remain a menace—clearly a tacit acceptance of evil in human nature as exemplified in both human groups. Benton felt that nature had made real distinctions between "races," a notion which may be reflected in Pitch's repeated citation of evils done by nature to man. He also felt that the "incurability of the evil is the greatest objection to the extension of slavery," saying "I deem it an evil and would neither adopt it nor impose it on others." [21]

As a pessimistic but not despairing Unionist Benton suspected the motives not only of the Northern abolitionist agitators but of the Southern slavery advocates as being aimed at disunion: "Truly the abolitionists and the nullifiers [proslavery men] were necessary to each other—the two halves of a pair of shears, neither of which could cut until joined together. Then the map of the Union was in danger; for in their conjunction that map was cloth between the edges of the shears." Benton's negative view of both extremes of the sectional conflict reveals an earnest, passionate skepticism about the kinds of men engaged in political life. He distrusted John Quincy Adams and John C. Calhoun with equal vigor.[22] It is this double-pronged distrust evident in Benton's political speeches and writings that Melville depicts through Pitch, making him an articulate and vigorous exponent of the mistrusting side of the question as to the nature of mankind. Like the Invalid Titan, who I have contended represents Calhoun's even more dramatically pessimistic view, Pitch believes that some evils cannot ever be cured, the tendency of boys of any nation or color to steal and to malinger being one of them and the servility of mankind another. He says to Herb-Doctor-Sumner, who was a potential presidential candidate in 1856 and whose senatorial election in 1851 had been termed by its opponents a venal "bargain":

"Come from Maine or Georgia, you come from a slave-state, and a slave-pen, where the best breeds are to be bought up at any price from a livelihood to the Presidency. Abolitionism, ye gods, but expresses the fellow-feeling of slave for slave."

The PIO Man

The agent of the Philosophical Intelligence Office (the PIO Man), who is described by Black Guinea as "a ge'mman wid a brass plate," and who is the seventh guise of the Confidence Man, appears only in chapter 22, "In the Polite Spirit of the Tusculan Disputations." His identification as a caricature of Horace Greeley is one of the most certain that can be made in Melville's "man-show." He is "a round-backed, baker-kneed man in a mean five-dollar suit, wearing collar-wise by a chain, a small brass plate, inscribed P.I.O.," who, "with a sort of canine deprecation, slunk behind." The image of a public figure—usually an editor or a politician—as a dog wearing a collar appears in political prints, where it may signify various attributes of the dog: fidelity, servility, obedience, guardianship, hunting function, etc.[23] His dog-like air, emphasized by the brass dog collar, is reiterated several times: he "whines," he "crouches," he seems to "wag his very coat-tails behind him." The Missouri Bachelor Pitch calls to him "as if to his pointer." He emits "canine whines and groans." The shabbiness of his clothing is consistently emphasized also: his coattails are "shabby"; he makes "a shabby bow"; he tucks out of sight "his frayed cravat-end"; he tries to assume "as genteel an attitude as the irritating set of his pinched five-dollar suit would permit"; he extends "his threadbare leg." In chapter 23 Pitch recalls him as a "threadbare Talleyrand," an "impoverished Machiavelli," a "seedy Rosicrucian," whose boot heels are "worn." Lastly, in chapter 24, the Cosmopolitan, referring back to him, mentions his "inferior coat."

The PIO Man's voice and manner are especially self-deprecating and obsequious in the first part of his conversation with Pitch. He "whines," "slinks," "crouches," is "obsequious"; he calls Pitch repeatedly "Respected sir"; he bows "as grateful for permission" to talk; he "ducks and growls" as if he had the "spinal complaint of servility." He is "demure," making a "plaintive dissent," and "lowly"; he asks if he can in his "small, quiet way" submit certain "small, quiet views" to Pitch. As he talks, however, and gains Pitch's attention, he rises in dignity, although Pitch still has to ask him twice to "stop flunkying." Still he abates "in humility as he [gains] in the argument," and he rises "in eloquence as his proselyte" sinks into conviction.

The intention of the PIO Man is to ingratiate himself by a deferential approach, to gain a hearing for the ideas upon which he claims his employment office is founded, and then to persuade the Bachelor to hire one of his "boys" as a servant. In the course of this, he propagandizes his benevolent view of the nature of mankind against the Bachelor's misanthropic view. He begins by encouraging Pitch to expound in his vehement manner *his* ideas. He appears to be shocked by Pitch's very pessimistic view of the depravity of boys and men. To Pitch's shocked disbelief, in turn, he claims to believe that mankind "present as pure a moral spectacle as the purest angel could wish." The PIO Man discounts as simple misjudgment any evil that the Bachelor claims to have observed in each of the thirty-five boys he has hired previously.

Presently, having gained by his obsequious modesty the attention of the Bachelor, the PIO Man proceeds to expound the "strictly philosophical principles" upon which his office claims to be founded. His "quiet theory" teaches him "to proceed by analogy from the physical to the moral." What he means is that instead of reasoning from experience and observation of individual actions and from human history, as the Bachelor has done, he simply takes an analogy from the natural world of physical nature and uses it to construct the view of mankind that he wishes to impose. For example, using a "horticultural" figure, he says: "Like the bud of the lily, [the manchild] contains concealed rudiments [of] points at present invisible, with beauties at present dormant." Alternatively, upon the analogy of the downy chin of a boy that "sprouts" into a beard in the man, he reasons that to a boy who evinces no "noble" qualities should be given "credit for his prospective" noble qualities; the noble quality will sprout like the beard. In the third physical analogy, like baby teeth that, "deficient in goodness," drop out and are replaced by "sound, even, beautiful and permanent ones," so the boy's "transient moral blemishes" will drop out to be replaced by "sound, even, beautiful and permanent virtues." In a fourth analogy from nature, the PIO Man cites the transformation of a caterpillar into a butterfly, for he believes that "a youth of one character can be transformed into a man of an opposite character." He cites for this the life of St. Augustine, which makes a very telling impression on Pitch, who has just admitted that Augustine "on Original Sin" is his "text-book." The PIO Man finally moves in strongly with his fifth and last analogy from nature—that of the change of the "silky husk" into the "solid" ear of corn—an analogy that wins over the Bachelor, for he has observed just such a change in his own corn crop, when he had despaired of its fruition. With the promise of a boy with a "sound mind" and "sound body," the agent wins the "conditional confidence" of Pitch and, next, his complete confidence. I have gone into considerable detail here because I believe that Melville is satirizing both the "principles" that the PIO Man holds (the natural evolution of the individual and of mankind toward the good) and his method of reasoning by analogy from natural fact to moral experience—not to mention his personal hypocrisies.

Horace Greeley (1811–1872) founded the New York *Daily Tribune* in 1841 and edited it and the *Weekly Tribune* and *Semi-Weekly Tribune* from then until his death.[24] Politically, he shifted from being a Clay Whig during the 1840s to the Republican party during its founding in 1854–56. Throughout his career he was a powerful force in city, state, and national politics through his newspapers—especially the *Weekly Tribune,* which had a national circulation—through other publications, and through personal influence. According to Isely, he achieved the zenith of his power during the formative years of the Republican party.[25] Greeley's appearance was among the most well known of his time and was voluminously satirized in journals and prints (see plates 6, 9, 14, 15, 16, 17, 22, 23, 27, and 28).[26] James Watson Webb, rival editor of the New York *Courier & Enquirer,* attacked Greeley thus in 1844:

He is a philosopher. . . . He seeks for notoriety by pretending to great eccentricity of character and habits, and by the strangeness of his theories and practices. . . . He lays claim to greatness by wandering through the streets with a hat double the size of his head, a coat after the fashion of Jacob's of old, with one leg of his pantaloons inside and the other outside of his boot, and with boots all bespattered with mud, or, possibly, a shoe on one foot and a boot on the other, and glorying in an unwashed, and unshaven person.

Greeley's reply, depreciating himself as a "humble" man, the "son of a poor and humble farmer," was that the story of his carelessness of appearance had "from its origin in *The Albany Microscope*" sunk "at last to the columns of the *Courier & Enquirer,* growing more absurd at every landing."[27] Rourke writes that "rough verbal sketches of his odd figure were scattered over the country," and that "perhaps few public men have been so frequently photographed and painted; from the early fifties onward he sat again and again for one or another form of portraiture."[28] An early series of comical literary sketches, accompanied by drawings, satirizing Greeley as the "New-Light Reformer," called "The Untranslated Don Quixote," ran in *John-Donkey* in 1848.[29] This fairly sophisticated series ridicules chiefly the split between Greeley's idealistic cant and the realities of his daily life—especially his business transactions. In the 29 January sketch Greeley's use of analogies from the physical world to make his editorial points is parodied. Particular emphasis is laid upon his belief in mankind's capacity to become perfect, "if all the usages of society, which only interfere with progress, were got rid of."[30]

Three aspects of Greeley's appearance especially noted by his contemporaries are reflected in the conception of the PIO Man: the cheapness and carelessness of his clothing, his peculiarly shambling walk, and his high-pitched nasal, or "whining" voice. His clothing, by which he was (and still is) easily recognized in sketches and cartoons, such as those already cited, was from his early years in New York described as rustic, dilapidated, slouching and cheap, as is that of Melville's character. Parton writes of him as a young man that "he never manifested, on any occasion, in any company, nor at any part of his early life, the *slightest* interest in his attire, nor the *least* care for its effect upon others." A characteristic anecdote told by Parton concerns a "five-dollar" suit—linking him directly with the PIO Man. Greeley, as a young man, had been teased about his dress, but still he clung to his "linen roundabout, his short trowsers, his cotton shirt, and his dilapidated hat. Still he wore no stockings, and made his wristbands meet with twine." One evening he appeared dressed in a complete suit of "faded broadcloth, and a shabby, over-brushed beaver hat. . . . The coat was in the style of a swallow's tail." Greeley was "metamorphosed into a decayed gentleman by a second-hand suit of black, bought . . . for five dollars." Parton adds, "This five-dollar suit was a failure. It had been worn thin. . . . A week's wear brought out all its pristine shabbiness, and developed new." Later in life, when Greeley had become famous as an editor and lecturer, Parton writes of him: "Mr. Greeley's attire is in a condition of the most hopeless and . . . elaborate disorder." More minutely descriptive, based on contemporary observation, is Hale's summary:

His clothes, if anything, became even more wayward: one trouser leg usually hung inside his country boots, while the other flopped down over it; his collar and string necktie had a way of slipping around to one side; his worn jacket pockets bulged with clippings, letters and manuscripts.

Constance Rourke describes Greeley during his lawsuit with Fenimore Cooper:

> Somewhere he had picked up an old light drab coat of Irish frieze and a battered hat of similar toneless hue; the garments were long since outdated . . . his collar riding up or retreating from sight.

When derided about his costume his defense was "plaintive, bold, yet obscure." He disclaimed perversity, "grew pensive, even drooping," and "declared that when he came to New York he was only a poor farmer's boy, and had made his way without assistance." He deliberately kept his shabby costume and made it into an asset, as Rourke shrewdly comments, "not only for a reason which Barnum down the street would have understood, but because . . . his appearance was somehow a sculptured emblem of the moment," for he "looked the avowed rustic, the homely sage. . . ."[31]

Concerning Greeley's peculiar posture and walk Parton quotes a friend's description of him as a young man as having "a slouching careless gait, leaning away forward as he walked, as if both his head and his heels were too heavy for his body," and as a "bent and shambling figure." Later, appearing in a lecture hall, he is described by Parton as he "wags his hasty way to the platform," recalling Melville's phrase, "wag his very coat-tails." In both editions of Parton's biography there appears a sketch, "Young Greeley's Arrival in New York," in which he appears to be "baker-kneed" like the PIO agent in his left leg.[32] There are two political prints that show well Greeley's "baker's-knee": "A Member of the Press Going to the Worlds Fair and the *Fare* he Received after He Got There!" (1851) and "The Rival Babies: A Comedy in one act . . . ," in the *Lantern* in 1852.[33] Rourke writes of him in the 1840s: "Tall and gangling, he still stumbled as he walked, as though he were pushing forward on a blind errand." Hale writes that Greeley had described himself in 1841 as "slouching in dress; goes bent like a hoop, and so rocking in his gait that he walks down both sides of the street at once," and a reporter wrote "of his body, swaying backwards and forwards, as if it were impossible for him to stand perpendicular and erect." Harriet Beecher Stowe wrote of him later in life: "He . . . is shambling, and bowed over in carrying himself." Prints that illustrate especially well his bowed-over posture are: "Great Speech of Clay. Bran Bread is Riz!!" (1847) and "Managing a

Candidate" (1852).[34] The PIO Man's crouching, groveling, ducking posture, his round back, his wagging gait and baker-knee seem intended to satirize not only Greeley's doglike servility of manner but his actual physical appearance.

Of Greeley's distinctive voice, Parton wrote that he had "a strange voice, highpitched and whining," and as a youth "he had a singular, whining voice," similar to that Melville gives the PIO Man. Later in life, while giving a lecture, Greeley is described thus:

> The voice of the speaker is more like a woman's than a man's, high-pitched, small, soft, but heard with ease in the remotest part of the Tabernacle. His first words are apologetic; they are uttered in a deprecatory, slightly-beseeching tone; and their substance is, 'You mustn't, my friends, expect fine words from a rough, busy man like me; yet such observations as I have been able hastily to note down, I will now submit, though wishing an abler man stood at this moment in my shoes.' An impressive or pathetic passage now and then, which loses none of its effect from the simple, plaintive way in which it is uttered, deepens the silence.

The plaintiveness, the self-deprecation, the quietness are all reflected in Melville's caricature. Hale, using contemporary sources, writes: "If he stopped acquaintances or they stopped him, he broke into his high, squeaky, nasal voice, bantering, asking insistent questions." And, "His voice remained 'weak and husky'—and squeaky, too,—no matter how much he tried to train it for the platform." Of his lecture manner, Rourke writes that "His voice had remained a high trembling falsetto, weak and querulous, without persuasion or appeal." Besides these details of voice, contemporaries noted his "meek," "benign," "angelic" expression, accentuated by flaxen hair and a pale complexion, which suggested to the shrewder observers that this was "a disarming personality, but also a somewhat deceptive one":

> Wherever he went, he bore with him an air of benevolence and simplicity. Yet [in 1856] he had also been engaged on a political maneuver of extraordinary sophistication. Some men who knew what he was up to thought him devious. Others called him plain dishonest. Two of those whose political fortunes became most involved with his operations—Stephen A. Douglas and Abraham Lincoln, . . . were not always sure that they understood the editor's motives at all.

He was often compared to Benjamin Franklin, the Talleyrandish diplomat who wore an air of homespun simplicity, too, and Greeley often alluded to this model. Whittier called him "sage and bland, our later Franklin."[35]

Greeley's religious denomination throughout his adult life was the Universalist Church. He stated his conviction publicly in 1855 that God "will, in his own good time, bring the whole human race into a state of willing and perfect reconciliation to himself and obedience to his laws,—consequently one of complete and unending happiness."[36] He held the fundamental tenet of Universalism, which is the "illimitable love and goodness of God, assuring triumph over evil in human society as a whole and in the life of every individual." The Winchester (N.H.) Profession of 1803 held that God "will finally restore the whole family of mankind to holiness and happiness."[37] His Universalist conviction, pithily expressed in the phrase "There's a good time comin', boys"—which was widely attributed to him—is reflected in his generally optimistic, ameliorative, reformist attitudes toward individuals and society. His whole life was dedicated through the pages of the three *Tribunes* and his lecturing and political activity to publicizing reformist causes of one sort and another: Fourierism, labor associationism, temperance, vegetarianism, the antislavery movement, the land distribution reform movement, manual training schools, abolition of the death penalty, abolition of flogging in the navy, and even communism—via the London reports in the *Tribune* written by Karl Marx. Optimism guided not only his attitudes toward societal reform, as a "Christian Socialist," but was the source of his confidence that individuals could reform, as his many loans and kindnesses to unfortunate friends testify.[38]

Not only could Melville know well Greeley's appearance, voice, and attitudes, but he owned a copy of Greeley's lectures, *Hints Toward Reforms* (1850). He alludes to the title of this on four occasions when he depicts the PIO Man as desiring to "hint" his views (pp. 132, 136, 141, 143). Its effusive dedication sums up Greeley's attitude of "trust":

> To the Generous, the Hopeful, the Loving, who, firmly and joyfully believing in the impartial and boundless goodness of our Father, *Trust,* that the errors, the crimes, and the miseries, which have long rendered earth a hell, shall yet be swallowed up and forgotten, in a far exceeding and unmeasured reign of TRUTH, PURITY, AND BLISS. *This Volume* is respectfully and affectionately inscribed by The Author.

In the essay, "The Emancipation of Labor," Greeley states a view identical to that of the PIO Man:

> I see no reason why the wildest dreams of the fanatical believer in Human Progress and Perfectibility may not ultimately be realized, and

each child so trained as to shun every vice, aspire to every virtue, attain the highest practicable skill in Art and efficiency in Industry, loving and pursuing honest, untasked Labor for the health, vigor, and peace of mind, thence resulting as well as for its more palpable rewards, and joyfully recognising in universal the only assurance of individual good.

In "Life—the Idea and the Actual," he writes: "Say what we will and justly may of the incurable depravity of Man, as evinced in the universality of Sin and Crime, this world is better and more hopeful than it has been," and in the same lecture: "To realize profoundly that the individual is nothing, the universal everything—to feel nothing a calamity whereby the sum of human virtue or happiness is increased, this is the truest wisdom." And of progress:

> Yes, a brighter day dawns for us. . . . Wiser in its very follies, less cruel and wanton even in its crimes, our Race visibly progresses toward a nobler and happier realization of its capacities and powers. Compared century with century, this progress is not so palpable, since what is an age to individuals, is but a moment in the lifetime of the Race; but, viewed on a larger scale, the advance becomes cheeringly evident. . . . The ages of darkness—of unconscious wandering from the path of Right and Good . . . are rapidly passing away.[39]

Greeley's views would have been eminently laughable to Melville, who wrote with caustic irony to George William Curtis in September 1857, "I have been trying to scratch my brains for a Lecture. What is a good, earnest subject? *Daily progress of man towards a state of intellectual & moral perfection, as evidenced in history of 5th Avenue & 5 Points"*—when Fifth Avenue was in a state of urban decay and Five Points was the crime and prostitution center of New York City.[40]

The specific objects of the satire in chapter 22 are, besides the doctrine of the general goodness of mankind—which is common to all Melville's Confidence Men—the PIO Man's optimism that the individual boy will naturally outgrow his early vices and the method by which he persuades the Bachelor to agree—the "analogical method." This method of reasoning "by analogy from the physical to the moral" seems to be Emersonian in its immediate origins, though it is Stoic and Neoplatonic in its ultimate sources. Emerson's essay *Nature* (1836) disseminated the theory that "Particular natural facts are symbols of particular spiritual facts":

> Every appearance in nature corresponds to some state of the mind, and that state of the mind can only be described by presenting that natural

appearance as its picture. . . . Man is an analogist. . . . The most
trivial of these facts, the habit of a plant, the organs, or work, or noise
of an insect, applied to the illustration of a fact in intellectual history
or in any way associated to human nature, affects us. . . .[41]

This "radical correspondence between visible things and human thoughts" is
subject to a dangerous interpretation: the use of such perceived analogies
between the physical and the spiritual as bases for reasoning about the structure of reality—in particular human moral experience. Such experience,
though it may safely be illustrated by analogies drawn from material nature,
should not be construed in terms of analogies drawn from material nature
but studied in and for itself as a separate object of science. The PIO Man's
thinking illustrates the habit of using such analogies as a way of construing
reality to defend an optimistic view of human nature. He carries the Emersonian notion of man as an analogist to caricatural extreme. He adduces five
different "natural facts" from "natural history" not to *illustrate* what he or
others might have observed in human moral experience but actually to *ratio-
nalize* about that moral experience—to give it structure and coherence. This
is using natural fact to "symbolize" spiritual fact with a vengeance; it is the
negation of the lessons of human history for the sake of a superficial coherence
and easy generalization.

To depict the PIO Man's peculiar kind of thinking emphatically Melville
has him use five different analogies: the change of the lily bud into a flower,
of the downy chin into a beard, of baby teeth into permanent teeth, of the
worm into a butterfly, and of the husk into the ear of corn—all to argue for
the "natural" evolution of a wicked child into a good adult. Although I have
not yet found the specific editorial or lecture in which Greeley uses a similar
analogy to expound his view that the individual "naturally" evolves toward
the good, the tenor of his thought, the influence of Emerson on it, and the
evidence that he was satirized in 1848 in *John-Donkey* for precisely this kind
of error in reasoning suggest that it is this sophistical characteristic of his
mind that led Melville to caricature Greeley as one of his public Confidence
Men, who delude their audience through sophistical dialectic. Greeley, like
the PIO agent, puns "with ideas" as another man may "with words"—*i.e.,*
on the basis of a similarity between some natural fact (*e.g.,* the change of
the worm into the butterfly) and some moral or spiritual event (*e.g.,* the
possible change of a bad boy such as St. Augustine, into a good man), he
substitutes the implicit certainty of the first for the highly problematic certainty of the second. The PIO Man's type of reasoning is a speculative
confidence game, similar in its intellectual deviousness—its pseudorational-
ity—to the "magical con games with the common language" that the twen-

tieth-century philosopher Eric Voegelin has discerned in Hegel's word play with the terms *Geist* and *Wesen* in *Phaenomenologie*: "The game is rigged; you can't win once you let yourself be sucked into accepting Hegel's language."[42] The Bachelor is taken in, even though he himself discerns that the PIO Man is a punster with ideas.

A further connection with Greeley may be found in the name of the PIO Man's agency. Although one meaning of "Intelligence Office" is, as Hershel Parker notes, an employment agency, "intelligence" itself meant in newspapers of the time simply "news" of any kind.[43] In the *Tribune*, for example, there is "Commercial Intelligence," which means "commercial news" and "Law Intelligence," which means "legal news," besides others. "Intelligence Office" may, then, allude to the *Tribune* and its function as a purveyor of "Intelligence" of all sorts. Moreover, in qualifying his title as agent of a "Philosophical Intelligence Office," Melville is, I suggest, alluding to Greeley's well-known and much satirized pretensions to being a man of philosophical principles and to running his paper to expound those principles. His propagandizing in editorials and in the selection and presentation of news itself for various social causes earned for him early the sometimes contemptuous, sometimes jocular nickname "The Philosopher."[44] It may be noted also that the meaning "employment agency" for "Intelligence Office" may allude to the habit of newspapers—Greeley's in particular—of advocating certain candidates for public office in their editorials and by granting news space for speeches—"selling the candidate" as we call it today. The PIO Man sells the Bachelor a boy to work for him—in whom he may have "confidence"—much as Greeley's paper "sold" its readers political candidates in whom they might have "confidence." The word "confidence" is a cliché in editorials and political speeches for the desired relationship between voter and candidate.[45] The depth of Melville's scorn for such papers may possibly lie behind Pitch's contemptuous riposte to the fawning agent: "As for Intelligence Offices, I've lived in the East, and known 'em. Swindling concerns kept by low-born cynics, under a fawning exterior wreaking their cynic malice upon mankind."

Thomas Hart Benton's connection with Greeley is alluded to in this chapter as if it followed a pattern: solicitation by Greeley, followed by Benton's scorn of him, then by his acquiescence in Greeley's offer, followed by a resurgence of skepticism and a final rejection of Greeley's solicitations. There is some similarity though not a precise one in the general pattern of Benton's and Greeley's relations from about 1854, when Greeley, a Whig, wrote favorably of Benton, a Democrat, in his feud with David Atchison for the Missouri senatorship, even treating him as of presidential caliber. Greeley praised Benton fulsomely in an editorial 11 May 1854, for his opposition to the Kansas-Nebraska Bill; and Isely writes that in 1856 when Greeley wished to win the good graces of the Jacksonian group of Democrats—of whom Benton was perhaps the most prestigious—for the new Republican party, he published an ingratiatingly solicitous letter in the *Tribune* to Benton (6 March). Benton's response was quite negative and remained so, even when the Republicans nominated his son-in-law.[46] There appears in the currently available evidence no analogue to Pitch-Benton's temporary duping by PIO Man-Greeley.

10

The Eighth and Last Confidence Man (Frank Goodman the Cosmopolitan) and His Antagonist (Charles Arnold Noble)

Frank Goodman the Cosmopolitan

The entire second half of *The Confidence-Man* (chapters 24–45) is dominated by the character Frank Goodman the Cosmopolitan, who in a series of encounters with eight other characters on the *Fidèle* plays out the last disguise of the Confidence Man. Considerable evidence indicates that Frank Goodman is a caricature of the most popular and famous American preacher of his day, the Liberal Congregationalist Henry Ward Beecher, and that Beecher follows upon Lundy, the "Negro" (as representative of the slavery issue), Bryant, Parker, Weed, Sumner, and Greeley, as being seen by Melville as a public confidence man soliciting belief in himself and in his ideas.[1] In discussing his use of Beecher's public image in the depiction of Goodman it is necessary to anticipate my conclusions and those of other scholars as to the identities of the characters with whom Goodman converses, evidence for which will be offered later.

Goodman corresponds to the "ge'mman in a wiolet robe" on Black Guinea's list of references, since he appears wearing a "vesture" [vestment or robe] barred with various hues, that of the cochineal [reddish purplish or violet color] predominating." The word "vesture" hints at clerical dress, while the international mixture of styles is symbolic of his role as a "Citizen of the World," as is his "Nuremburgh pipe" with its "porcelain bowl painted in miniature with linked crests and arms of interlinked nations." Bird allusions are present, also, for Pitch compares his appearance to that of a "toucan fowl"—from the "Brazils," because of the "parti-hued, and rather plumagy aspect" of the man. Only certain details of Goodman's costume can be linked presently to Beecher's personal appearance and more work remains to be done on this aspect of the caricature.

As for Goodman's complexion it is healthy, glowing, and rosy as, by all reports, was Beecher's. Comparing his cheek to a "rosy pipe-bowl," mellowed by the "essence" of the tobacco in it, Melville writes that it looked "as if something similar of the interior spirit came rosily out" on it. Yet both "rosy

pipe-bowl, or rosy countenance" are lost on that "unrosy man, the bachelor."
Goodman is evidently clean-shaven, as was Beecher all his life, for in the
barbershop scene (chapter 43) there is no mention of moustache or whiskers,
and the Barber seems to lather Goodman's entire face: he "lathered him with
so generous a brush, so piled up the foam on him, that his face looked like
the yeasty crest of a billow, and vain to think of talking under it. . . . He
must keep his mouth shut."

Goodman exhibits four types of body gestures, two of which Beecher is
recorded as having exhibited habitually. Evidently, he likes to touch people,
for three times he lays his hands upon Pitch and once upon Noble (chapters
23, 25). Second, in chapter 24, he stands "at rest, sideways and genially, on
one hip, his right leg cavalierly crossed before the other, the toe of his vertical
slipper pointed easily down on the deck." Third, in chapter 24, he is pictured
as thrusting out both vertical palms for double shields," symbolically defending himself in argument. Last, when getting set for a long explanation he
stands with "his left hand spread, and his pipe-stem coming crosswise down
upon it like a ferule" (chapter 24). As for Goodman's voice, it seems to be
angelic, for when he first accosts Pitch it is "sweet as a seraph's" (chapter
23), and upon entering the barbershop he says in a ministerial manner, "Bless
you, barber," to the dozing Barber, "in tones not unangelic" (chapter 42).

The Cosmopolitan's personality, as revealed over the 21 chapters in which
he appears, is perhaps best summed up, although flexible within a given
range, as prevailingly warm, kind, brotherly, frank, and genial—all characteristics of the publicly observed temperament of Henry Ward Beecher. The
terms used to characterize Goodman most frequently are "genial" and "frank."
He stands "genially," puffs his pipe in a "charitable" manner, is "not . . .
swift to take offense," is "not unamiable," "beams," espouses a "fraternal
and fusing feeling," is self-characterized as "warm and confiding," and he
seeks a "fraternal" relation with Pitch. With Noble he is less exuberant, is
very attentive during the Indian-hater narration, is "grave" and "gentle," and
yet by his manner and his call for a "charitable" interpretation of Pitch's
character and by "frankly" offering his hand to Noble, he leads up to their
beginning a "boon-companionship." His "surrender" to Noble's offer of wine
in the barroom is highly emotional, Goodman suggesting that their "friendship at first sight" resembles "love at first sight" (chapter 29). While drinking
with Noble he deliberately introduces the theme of "geniality," of "charity,"
and of "humor," behaving throughout in a genial, charitable, and humorous
manner. He maintains his "easy sociability" throughout chapter 30, being
"gravely social" and showing "quiet forbearance." He asks for a "charitable"
interpretation of Polonius' character and exploits the theme of geniality as he
draws closer to Noble in boon-companionability. In chapter 32, after he

performs his magic trick with the coins, throwing off suddenly his role of a suppliant and transforming Noble back from a frozen rejection of his request for a loan, he says "I am something of a funny man," and he eyes Noble "in tenderness." He maintains his "mild" demeanor until Noble leaves (chapter 35).

With Mark Winsome Goodman alters his manner somewhat; he becomes more dignified, "blunt," "deepening in seriousness," and "cautious," though remaining very friendly and sociable. Showing a remarkable flexibility of feature and body control as he describes the rattlesnake, "he seemed so to enter into [the] spirit—as some earnest descriptive speakers will—as unconsciously to wreathe his form and sidelong crest his head, till he all but seemed the creature described" (p. 213). The same extraordinary ability to mimic was noted as one of Beecher's greatest gifts in public speaking, as will be evidenced below. Though still "mild" he exhibits "renewed earnestness," and he eyes Winsome "ruminatingly." With the Crazy Beggar, he is "kind and considerate," reproaching Winsome for his coolness (chapter 36). With the Disciple Egbert, Goodman plays the role of an eager but practical student, suggesting modestly that they enact a "common case" in order that he may understand Winsome's principles. Like an actor, again, he flexibly assumes "a serious and care-worn air, suitable to the part to be enacted" (chapter 38). He throws himself into the role of "Frank" who needs money throughout chapter 39, showing the skills of an accomplished actor as Beecher did frequently. After hearing in silence the story of China Aster (chapter 40), he responds, still in the role of the pleading friend "Frank," to Egbert's enactment of the role of the hardhearted friend "Charlie." Suddenly, in a mobile turnaround he throws off the role "he had assumed," and he rejects the philosophy of Winsome as "inhuman," unfeeling, and uncharitable in its application to real cases. Goodman's mobility of expression and attitude, a prerequisite of acting ability, is underlined by Egbert's farewell thought about him—a recollection of Shakespeare's lines beginning "All the world's a stage. . . ." (chapter 41).

With the Barber, in chapters 42 and 43, Goodman reassumes his benignly jovial manner, but he increases in argumentativeness and in confidence, as if he felt either socially or spiritually superior—the latter being suggested by his "Bless you," opening the chapter, and by the fact that his voice "seemed a sort of spiritual manifestation" to the Barber. At first he argues with "cautious kindliness, feeling his way," and he is "dispassionate, if not deferential," but after being shaved he radically shifts his manner:

> Hard to say exactly what the manner was, any more than to hint it was a sort of magical; in a benign way, not wholly unlike the manner, fabled or otherwise, of certain creatures in nature, which have the power

of persuasive fascination—the power of holding another creature by the button of the eye, as it were, despite the serious disinclination, and . . . earnest protest, of the victim. (pp. 264–65)

Goodman's inexplicable, "magical" personal power over the Barber disappears as magically the moment the Barber is alone again.

In the final scene in the gentlemen's cabin Goodman's personality exudes "cheeriness" like "a sort of morning," but flexibly, again, he tones it down upon seeing the Old Man reading. He is courteous and serious while reading the Bible; he still claims to "love man" and to "have confidence in man." He is deferential and gentle with the Old Man and "gravely" conversational, regarding him at the close of the book with "sympathy," as he leads him away into the darkness in a "kindly" manner. With the Juvenile Peddler he is benign and tolerant. In sum, although his manner adapts with the skill of an accomplished actor to his interlocutors, his basic personality appears to be warm, kindly, benign, affectionate, tolerant, convivial, and frank. All of these characteristics were noted of Beecher, and none is present that was not attributed to him except Goodman's inclination to drink and smoke. These latter are, I think, called for by the fictional scene in which Melville has placed his caricature for the purposes of the satire—a social and political scene in which liquor and tobacco (and often gambling) were appropriate.

The most striking characteristics of Goodman's rhetoric and style are these: (1) the use of story ("parable"), illustration, or anecdotal example; (2) dramatization of a hypothetical case using mimicry to make a point; (3) the emotional, nonintellectual, nature of his themes; and (4) the use in his sentences of alliteration and balance in the coupling of opposites. All of these appear in Beecher's published work and in descriptions of his preaching and lectures. Perhaps the best examples of Goodman's use of illustration as argumentative technique are the earliest in chapter 24. Arguing with Pitch about the need to be philanthropic not misanthropic with others, he tells "a little story" about the "woman of Goshen," which Pitch calls "a parable," and he suggests that he might even tell "another story about an old boot in a pieman's loft" to support further his belief that one should give up the "too sober" view of life. In chapter 28, arguing still for the value of wine, he relates the "fable" of the man who drank any kind of wine, thinking "the sham article . . . better than none at all," which he suggests illustrates "as in a parable, how that a man of a disposition ungovernably good-natured might still familiarly associate with men," though he thought most men falsehearted. If the text is examined for further examples, it will show that Goodman consistently draws on his actual experience, upon everyday human actions, habits, and beliefs to support his arguments rather than on philosophical inquiry, logic, books (even the Bible), or historical or statistical evidence. Goodman, apparently, as a "mature man of the world" draws upon the world's experience and his own in it to make his arguments for "confidence" in man and Providence (chapter 23). This rhetorical method is, as I shall show below, consistently and uniquely—for his time—characteristic of Beecher's preaching and lecturing.

As for Goodman's use of the dramatization of a hypothetical case as a rhetorical device, requiring the ability to mimic others, the most striking examples are in the two long encounters with Noble and with Egbert. In the first of these he takes on the role of a gentleman friend who is "in want . . . of money," evidently in order to test Noble's professed friendship. In the second, he proposes with Egbert's agreement to test Winsome's philosophy by a hypothetical "case" in which there are two friends, one of whom seeks a loan from the other. The entirety of chapters 39, 40, and 41 consist in his playing the role of "Frank," the indigent friend, in search of a loan from his bosom friend "Charlie," played by Egbert. Flexibly, after the "rupture of the hypothesis," he returns to his own character. Beecher was famed for his method of dramatizing hypothetical situations to illustrate his doctrines— among the most famous being his dramatizations of slave auctions.

Goodman's themes are those of the heart, of feeling: philanthropy, charity, good humor, confidence, conviviality, friendship, and the like. Although the solicitation of trust is common to all the Confidence Men, the peculiar emphasis of his appeal is upon his own personality and feelings as exemplary of what all men ought to be. He holds his "fraternal and fusing feeling" as the emotional standard for all mankind. Further, Goodman's style when he speaks in his own voice displays a marked habit of alliteration and rhythmical balance and contrast, *e.g.*: "A cosmopolitan, a catholic man; who, being such, ties himself to no narrow tailor or teacher, but federates, in heart as in costume, something of the various gallantries of men under various suns" (p. 151). And: "Let me tell you too—*en confiance*—that while revelry may not always merge into ebriety, soberness, in too deep potations, may become a sort of sottishness" (p. 152). And: "Talking of piemen, humble-pie before proud-cake for me. This notion of being lone and lofty is a sad mistake" (p. 153). And: "Ah, did you but know it, how much pleasanter to puff at this philanthropic pipe, than still to keep fumbling at that misanthropic rifle" (p. 156). And: "Give me the folly that dimples the cheek, say I, rather than the wisdom that curdles the blood" (p. 276). And lastly: "Neither by land nor by water, am I ever seriously disquieted, however, at times, transiently uneasy; since with you sir, I believe in a Committee of Safety, holding silent sessions over all, in an invisible patrol, most alert when we soundest sleep, and whose beat lies as much through forests as towns, along rivers as streets" (p. 284).

Goodman's beliefs and ideas are simply stated, for they are similar fundamentally to all the previous Confidence Men: the natural goodness of man ("in man a ruling principle of kindness"), the belief in progress ("the advance of the humanitarian spirit"), and the belief in the goodness of Providence ("in the universe a ruling principle of love"). Besides these, the special emphasis of his discourse is on the *pleasures* of human sociability ("How much pleasanter to puff at this philanthropic pipe than still to keep fumbling at that misanthropic rifle")—a sociability which is, he claims, "according to natural law." Goodman also stresses national and racial tolerance ("No man is a stranger"), reverence for the "nobility" of man ("Man is a noble fellow"), and pervasively in his encounters the theme of brotherly love as expressed in conviviality, the "charitable" interpretation of others' motives—thinking no evil of them—and "confidence" in the good intentions of others—returning good for apparent evil—as a way of life. It has already been noted that "love" for the Cosmopolitan is pure impulsive feeling detached from reason, authority, or historical experience. He compares "love" to the love of wine, and this curious metaphor pervades the ensuing conversations, carrying with it stronger overtones of the religion of Bacchus than of the Christian notion of Christ as the "true Vine." Other important beliefs he reveals are in the value of humor (not irony or satire, however), in the press as a "dedicated principle of beneficent force and light," and in the association of beauty with goodness: "that beauty is at bottom incompatible with ill."

In appearance, personality, rhetoric, style, and ideas Frank Goodman almost certainly caricatures Henry Ward Beecher (1813–1887), who was in Melville's lifetime the most popular and renowned preacher in the United States. He was also a lyceum lecturer, a political speaker for the Republican party, and a journalist who wrote extensively on all kinds of subjects for the Brooklyn-based religious weekly, the *Independent*. Beecher published twenty-four books, including a novel *Norwood* (1867). The son of Lyman Beecher, of Puritan descent, and the brother of Harriet Beecher Stowe, Henry Ward was educated at Mount Pleasant Classical Institution, at Amherst College, and at Lane Theological Seminary in Cincinnati. After holding two pastorates in Indiana he moved to the New York area in the fall of 1847 to take over the newly established Plymouth Church in Brooklyn, where he remained until his death. He was extremely well paid and well loved by his numerous congregation, so much so that in 1850 they gave him a "Grand Tour" of Europe, from which he returned an art enthusiast. During a career of forty years his audiences at Plymouth Church always ranged between 2500 and

3000 in attendance twice every Sunday, while on the lyceum circuit he drew consistently larger audiences than any other American speaker. During the early 1850s he did not preach abolitionism (nor had he earlier), but he wrote on antislavery themes in the *Independent* and attained such influence that his article, "Shall We Compromise?" (21 February 1850) was regarded as a national event. He also offered Plymouth Church to Wendell Phillips, when the Rynders mob drove him from the Broadway Tabernacle in 1850. In the middle 1850s, after the strong Northern reaction to the Kansas-Nebraska Bill, he plunged into the antislavery movement in a spectacular way, especially in his famous "Great Speech" of 1855, in which he pictured the North-South conflict in irreconcilable terms, and when he started the fund for Sharps rifles—which came to be called "Beecher's Bibles"—for Northern settlers in Kansas (see plates 14 and 17). In May 1856, in an extemporary speech at a mass meeting in the Tabernacle protesting the Brooks-Sumner caning, he further enhanced his antislavery reputation, extended his power as an opinion maker, and began a career of great political influence which continued all his life, although he never ran for political office. He joined the newly formed Republican party, and he spoke for Frémont and Dayton during the canvass two or three times a week to eight thousand to ten thousand people each time. He claimed later that his especial task was to win over the "Silver Grey"—New York Old-Line Whigs—from Fillmore, who was the Know-Nothing and Whig candidate. During the War, when he both supported and criticized Lincoln, his greatest help was a series of lectures in England in 1862–63 on behalf of the North. He edited the *Christian Union* and gave the prestigious Yale Lectures on preaching in 1872.[2]

For his flamboyant style of preaching and for his extraordinary emotional power over vast audiences Beecher was widely ridiculed and lampooned. Bennett, for one, called him a "clerical thespian" in a *Herald* editorial, 12 May 1856; *Young America* called him "the low comedy man on the clerical stage"; Henry W. Bellows, pastor of the Unitarian Church to which Melville later belonged, spoke of his "union of moral philosopher and comedian," and he was frequently caricatured in anti-Republican cartoons in 1856 (plates 14 and 17).[3] His name became almost a leitmotif for humor in the pages of the comic periodicals in the middle and late 1850s. Thomas Nast caricatured him in 1863 as the "Rattlesnake Charmer" of the Confederacy, an allusion to his "magical" rhetorical gifts. A *Vanity Fair* writer sums up much previous satirical opinion in complaining dryly of his "Sabbath harlequinades" and concluding that "Motley in the pulpit on Sunday interferes with the week-day interests of a humorous publication"—such as itself.[4] Later in life, his reputation with most of his congregation survived even the scandal of a six-month trial in 1874 for "alienation of affections" brought by his former friend

Theodore Tilton concerning Tilton's wife Elizabeth—an event for which he was much ridiculed.

Before discussing the many personal and stylistic links between Goodman and Beecher, it should be noted that the very type-name Melville gives his character—the "Cosmopolitan"—evokes the historical type to which Beecher consciously belonged. "Cosmopolitan" or "cosmopolite" meant in the eighteenth and nineteenth centuries, according to the *OED,* a person of philanthropic feelings and public actions. More importantly, in this period and earlier, it might carry very negative connotations in a political context. For instance, it was used very pejoratively by James T. Austin in his Faneuil Hall speech in 1837 defending the mob killing of the abolitionist journalist, Owen Lovejoy, in Alton, Illinois (the speech in reply to which Wendell Phillips made his speech on the murder of Lovejoy which brought him his first oratorical fame): "Suppose now, some new cosmopolite, some man of philanthropic feelings, not only toward man but animals, who believes that all are entitled to freedom as an inalienable right, should engage in the humane task of giving freedom to these wild beasts of the forest. . . ."[5] Negative connotations for "cosmopolitan" are borne out by the uses cited in the *OED* and should be kept in mind in appraising Melville's choice of this sobriquet for one of his most important characters. I am not saying that Melville shared the political attitudes of Austin but that he expected his readers to be aware of the pejorative connotations of "cosmopolitan" in a satire on political themes. It should be noted further that the name "Goodman" carries with it the associations—whether positive or negative—of New England Puritanism. It was in the seventeenth century a title for a Puritan man, as exemplified in Hawthorne's story "Young Goodman Brown." Beecher was proud of his Puritan ancestry and one of his most popular lectures was in praise of "Puritanism."

The Cosmopolitan's clothing, besides being appropriately "cosmopolitan" in its multinational aspects, alludes to Beecher's dress in several ways. The use of "vesture," which can mean "vestment" or "clerical robe," hints at a religious profession. Further, after Beecher's European trip in 1850 he became notorious for his love of personal display and especially of fine fabrics, carpets, bright silks, cushions, and velvet drapes in his study. Rourke writes that "Color affected him like an appetite." Hale speaks of him as reportedly "garishly garbed." He collected stuffed birds, especially hummingbirds and birds of paradise for their colorful feathers, a personal taste that seems reflected in Pitch's descriptive term "toucan fowl" and Goodman's "plumagy aspect." Beecher's tactile pleasure in caressing fine fabrics, which was a marked change from the Beecher family's Puritan background, is alluded to in the Cosmopolitan's first speech, as he touches Pitch's shoulder: "Whoever in our Fair has fine feelings loves to feel the nap of fine cloth" (p. 149). Both a portrait painted before 1851 and a photograph with his sister Harriet show him wearing a coat with a velvet collar. A New York *Times* report (31 May 1856) of a speech of his alludes to his wearing his "claret-colored squash hat." Relevant to his personal tastes is a remark of his friend Thomas Knox that he loved rugs: "Of every nationality, hue, and fabric . . . giving an air of most leisurely abandon and cosey comfort." A short literary satire in *Vanity Fair* in 1862, "B. B. B.," describes Beecher playing a billiards match with P. T. Barnum, while wearing a colorful costume, smoking a briarwood pipe, and drinking rum.[6] Nearly all Beecher's biographers note his radical break in dress and belongings with the Puritan plainness of his father Lyman Beecher and his espousal of the "ample" philosophy of luxuriance in the beauty not only of nature but of the fine and decorative arts.

Beecher's complexion was described by several observers as "ruddy" and "healthy," consonant with Goodman's "rosy" cheek. Howard calls him "florid" and "rosy-cheeked." He was clean-shaven, as Goodman is, all his life. He had wide blue eyes and a firm mouth with "humor lurking and almost laughing in the corners." Moore characterized his expression as "pure and elevated, almost like the angels' faces that we have seen in dreams," phrasing curiously suggestive of Goodman's angelic aspect as he appears to the Barber. Of his voice one observer writes that it was "full of music" and another that it was "richly melodious" and especially effective on the "low and tender keys."[7] With regard to typical body gestures while appearing as a speaker: his admirer, Augusta Moore, who collected passages from his sermons in *Notes from Plymouth Pulpit* (1859), describes his standing "one foot crossed over the other, and supported upon its toe"—a "manoeuvre certain to be repeated almost constantly," a movement which is similar to Goodman's stance "at rest, sideways and genially, on one hip, his right leg cavalierly crossed before the other, the toe of his vertical slipper pointed easily down on the deck." He liked to touch people, as Goodman does. The other two gestures—thrusting out his palms vertically and bringing down his pipestem crosswise on the open left palm—are both gestures Beecher may have learned as typical elocutionary gestures in school, where he was trained in elocution by John E. Lovell, author of *The United States Speaker.*[8]

Beecher's personality was described by nearly all observers as "frank" and "genial," as "friendly," "unconventional," "original," "highly emotional," or "grandly positive." Other terms used to express its quality were "enthusiasm," "personal magnetism," "philanthropy," "catholicity," "tolerance," "sympathy," "unresentfulness," "lovableness," "perennial humor"—all of which are aspects of Melville's characterization of Frank Goodman. Beecher's sister Harriet wrote to George Eliot, "My brother is hopelessly generous and confiding. His inability to believe evil is simply incredible. . . . [He] spoke no slander, no, nor listened to it." Goodman introduces himself to Pitch as "warm and confiding" and consistently appears generous both in his opinions and his actions. Moore describes Beecher as "frequently humorous," as "free and genial." Lyman Abbott, who knew him well, said that his wit and humor were "invariably tempered by genial good-feeling," and that his manners were "frank, cordial, and kind." Knox, another friend, writes that he was "never very ministerial in his deportment" but was "so frank and genial" that all his congregation loved him and that "his spell was magnetic." Howard quotes the letter of a lifelong friend which describes Beecher when he first came to New York in 1847 as having (like Goodman in approaching Pitch) a "free, brusque address and direct approach" and (again, like Goodman in his kindness to the Crazy Beggar) Beecher's "love could cover all offenses, his pitying all excuses." It was said by Theodore Parker that he had "a genius to be loved" and captivated men without an effort. One of these seems to have been Whitman, for he said after a visit with Beecher, "He was more than commonly cordial, and I hope I was, too, for I felt more than commonly drawn to Beecher."[9]

Another striking trait of Goodman which appears to be modeled upon Beecher is his flexibility of mood. Moore writes thus of the mobility of his temperament: "He has numberless diverse moods and aspects. . . . Never was human face more variable . . . 'on different days he looks like a different man.'" Beecher's remarkable capacity to shift, as Goodman does, from warm, frank geniality to a more serious, "grave," and "tender" mood is thus described by Abbott: "He will pass instantly . . . from hilarity to reverence and from reverence back to hilarity again. . . . He is catholic, broad, of universal sympathies, of mercurial temperament, of instantaneous and lightning-like rapidity of mental action." Beecher displayed the same kind of sensitivity to his audience and impressibility that Goodman shows in each of his encounters, when he adapts himself to the person and mood of his interlocutor. Howard writes: "Ever impressible, and as full of intuitions as a woman, he felt the presence of men and women. Time and again, the tenor of his discourse altered at the sight of a face. Incidents of the moment often shaped the discourse of the hour."[10]

Like Goodman, who remarks, "I for one must have my fellow-creatures round me, thick, too—I must have them thick," Beecher wished to be surrounded physically by his people, so much so that he cut away the usual isolated pulpit and in the church that he designed for himself he had the platform brought forward into the midst of his audience, so that he might be, as he said, in the "center of the crowd, and have the people surge all about me!"[11] Again, like Goodman's love of nature and man and his defense of humor and drollery, Beecher's "poetic sympathy with nature and humanity," his "native sense of artistic beauty," and his "lurking love of fun and frolic" are noted by a reviewer of his "Star Papers" in *Harper's Monthly* (1855). He "makes little account of the clerical starch, which we used to deem as essential to the New England parson as the black coat and white cravat." His book reveals a "gamesome gladness" and "a cheerful, appetizing tendency." Moore defends his humor against charges that he was a "clerical Buffoon," while Hibben notes that his humor might be "crude, sometimes almost vulgar" and that he disapproved of Garrison because he lacked "good-natured benevolence [and] . . . a certain popular mirthfullness" that Beecher possessed. The *Berkshire Eagle* (17 August 1855) reviewed a local lecture of his on the "Importance of Cheerfulness, or the Relation of Mirth to the Intellectual Faculties," in which he defended cheerfulness and wit. Like Goodman, who upholds humor as a "blessed thing" (p. 184), Beecher held that if a man is gifted with mirthfulness, it should be allowed to burst forth in "sheaves of light and fancy" and not be regarded as a violation of the sanctity of his office.[12]

Beecher's personality as viewed by his admirers, who numbered in the hundreds of thousands, was, Barrows writes, like "a sunburst of genial humor and Christian charity." Of his personal generosity, which was noted by many observers, Amory Bradford, for example, writes that, "His own charity surpassed any that he preached"—a trait that Goodman shows even toward the cold personalities of Winsome and Egbert. R. DeW. Mallary, a member of Beecher's Plymouth Church congregation, recalled "how fond he was of reading the thirteenth chapter of First Corinthians." Reinforcing this association of Beecher with the Pauline chapter that furnishes the theme of charity for *The Confidence-Man* is the fact that the one-line inscription placed, when he died, on his tombstone in Greenwood Cemetery, Brooklyn, was, "He thinketh no evil," the first of the five passages excerpted from 1 Corinthians 13 by the Deaf-Mute when he writes upon his slate.[13]

Finally, Goodman's "catholic" nature seems to allude to Beecher's religious tolerance, which was described thus late in life by one of his early hearers:

> He was just as liberal then to all other denominations as he was when he died. He never said anything against any other creed. I've heard him say he'd like to sit beside the Roman Catholics in heaven. And he not only never spoke any harm of others, but he also never thought any harm of them. He was the most unsuspicious man I ever met. He made the best of everybody.

When he died various Christian denominations and the Jewish synagogues of New York eulogized him thus: "His love for mankind included all races and religions." The rabbi of Temple Emanu-El in New York said: "This typical American was the perfect citizen of the world"—the same characteristic as Melville's Cosmopolitan, who claims to be "a cosmopolitan, a catholic man . . . a true citizen of the world" (p. 151).[14]

Not only in appearance and personality, as evidenced in the foregoing, but in rhetorical method and speech style, Frank Goodman seems to be a deliberate caricature of Beecher. The main characteristic of Beecher's rhetoric as noted by contemporaries was his consistent habit of using concrete illustrations to make his points, just as Goodman uses his little stories, parables, and fables. Lionel Crocker writes in an analysis of his habits of public speaking that Beecher's most significant contribution to the sermon in America was that he changed it from being logically argumentative to being primarily illustrative: "The use of illustrations is the most distinctive single feature of Beecher's presentation." Oliver Wendell Holmes praised his "felicitous facility of illustration, his familiar way of bringing a great question to the test of some parallel fact that every body before him knows." His typical procedure was to settle on a theme for a sermon, then seek out illustrations in daily experience and reading to illuminate it. Even in his early sermons he played down the traditional Presbyterian rigor of logic and theological argument typical of his father's preaching.[15] An especially pertinent example of the technique, which shows also Beecher's use of imagery from commercial life— the comparison of belief in God's grace to "confidence" in a commercial letter of credit—is found in Augusta Moore's *Notes from Plymouth Pulpit* and may stand for many others:

> Suppose I were to set out on a pilgrimage to Jerusalem, and before I started were to go to Brown Brothers & Co., and obtain letters of credit for the cities of London, Jericho, etc. Then, with these papers which a child might destroy, which would be but ashes in the teeth of flame, which a thousand chances might take from me, I should go on with confidence and cheer, saying to myself, 'As soon as I come to London I shall be in funds. I have a letter in my pocket from Brown Brothers & Co., which will give me five hundred dollars there; and in the other cities to which I am bound I shall find similar supplies, all at my command, through the agency of these magic papers and pen strokes of these enterprising men.' But, suppose that instead of this confidence I were to sit down on shipboard, and go to tormenting myself in this fashion: 'Now, what *am* I to do when I get to London? I have no money, and how do I *know* that these bits of paper which I have with me mean

anything, or will amount to anything? What shall I do? I am afraid I shall starve in the strange city to which I am going.' I should be a fool, you say; but should I be *half* the fool that that man is who, bearing the letters of credit of the Eternal God, yet goes fearing all his way, cast down and doubting whether he shall ever get safe through his journey? No fire, no violence, nor any chance, can destroy the checks of the Lord. When he says: 'I will never leave thee, nor forsake thee,' and 'my grace shall be sufficient for thee,' believe it; and no longer dishonor your God by withholding from him the confidence which you freely accord to Brown Brothers & Co. [16]

In style, theme, imagery, tone, and terminology this passage from one of Beecher's sermons is suggestive of Melville's Confidence Man in his last disguise as Frank Goodman, especially in the rhetoric he employs in his last encounter with the Comely Old Man.

For the sources of his persuasive power over men and women Beecher put first the study of his audience—of mankind. An account of him in the *Times* (9 June 1856) refers to his power residing in "his intimate knowledge of human nature." He said, "If I know my own business—and the presumption is I do—it is to hunt men and to study them"—a curious metaphor considering that Melville caricatured him as the Confidence Man, a hunter of men for demonic reasons. According to Crocker, not books but people were his sources—their motives, desires, and conduct, and people crowded to hear him because he knew the motives of his fellow men. Abbott writes of him: "The study of human nature is not only an integral part but an essential part of his preparation for the pulpit." Howard notes that he "found his most instructive books among his fellows rather than in cloistered libraries." [17] This quality informs the representation of Beecher as the Cosmopolitan so deeply that it goes beyond caricature to become portrait. Throughout the long series of encounters with men varying as widely as the Barber and Winsome, Goodman-Beecher listens more than he talks with his interlocutors; he studies their speech, faces, and motives with a quiet intensity, and he sees through them with consummate skill, even while he seems protected himself, as Beecher apparently was, against the disillusionment and bitterness that the perception of evil in others most often engenders.

The most striking resemblance of all between Beecher's platform style and Goodman's rhetoric is in Goodman's ability to mimic and to dramatize a subject by enactment of a hypothetical case. Beecher's use on the platform of mimicry and of theatrical techniques led to his being frequently called an actor. Fred W. Hinrichs said he "was as much an actor as a preacher." Moore in her preface to *Notes from Plymouth Pulpit,* recounts a "cold, polished, cynical man of the world" once saying, "I go to hear Henry Ward Beecher with the same feelings that I go to witness the performances of Burton"—the great comic actor on the Philadelphia and New York stage, who may have acted the title role in the performance of John Brougham's entertainment "The Confidence Man" at Burton's Chambers Street Theatre in 1849. Moore mentions that Beecher often aroused "irresistible laughter" and was called, as noted earlier, by sophisticates "a clerical buffoon." The Duyckincks' *Cyclopaedia* (1856) records the contemporary opinion that his type of mind and style trenched "close upon the dividing line between licit humor and lithe buffoonery." *Vanity Fair* published a squib on him as "The Reverend Roscius" in 1861. Knox writes, "His play of feature and his mimetic skill were so remarkable that it was often said of him that he would have been a wonderful actor." Seward is reported to have said of him after hearing him preach in 1854: "It was a noble speech—sermon it was not. . . . He is a man who seems, in going through a discourse of an hour, to act a dozen parts, from the deepest tragic to the broad comic." Rourke writes that "An incomparable mimic . . . he could echo the very inflections of the other voice. . . . He could imitate with exactness the gait and speech and usual movements of a drunkard, a blacksmith, a fisherman, a wood-cutter." Nearly all his biographers cite the extraordinary effect that his dramatic enactments of slave auctions created. Barrows writes of one of these: "He extemporized there on the stage the auction of a Christian slave. The enumeration of his qualities by the auctioneer, and the bids that followed were given by the speaker in perfect character. He made the scene as realistic as one of Hogarth's pictures and as lurid as a Rembrandt."[18] This unusual dramatic ability is not only exhibited in Goodman's frequent changes of mood and when he sinks himself into the role of "Frank" the indigent friend in the little playlet of the "Hypothetical Friends" with Egbert, but the reader's attention is drawn to it especially in the following passage in chapter 36 from the scene with Winsome, in which he expresses his "confidence in the latent benignity" of the rattlesnake: "As he breathed these words, he seemed so to enter into their spirit—as some earnest descriptive speakers will—as unconsciously to wreathe his form and sidelong crest his head, till he all but seemed the creature described." Finally, a friend said of Beecher, "In the use of words he was a necromancer," a characterization parallel to the depiction of Goodman's power over the Barber in chapter 43, "Very Charming," when Melville speaks of his "magical" manner and "power of persuasive fascination" and his "irresistible persuasion."[19]

In the political context, among other functions, Cosmopolitan-Beecher represents the "pulpit-politics" of the 1856 presidential campaign—the influence especially of the New England ministry upon the founding and progress of the Republican party. As Rhodes writes, "The zeal of many preachers broke out in the pulpit, and sermons were frequently delivered on the evils of slavery, the wrong of extending it, and the noble struggle freedom was making on the plains of Kansas."[20] This influence was disparaged by the partisans of Buchanan and Fillmore. For satirical purposes, both in Melville's work and in the graphic satire of the period, the response to this influence became focused upon Beecher in particular, because of his charismatic powers, although Theodore Parker and T. W. Higginson and others, such as Dudley Tyng, shared it. Undoubtedly Beecher was the most caricaturable, although as discussed earlier, if the identifications offered for the Episcopal Clergyman and the Methodist Minister are correct, such relatively minor men as Tyng and William Brownlow of Tennessee were, in Melville's eyes, participants in the same censurable activities.

That Melville disliked clergymen who carried their politics into the pulpit is apparent, as noted earlier, in his poem, "The Age of the Antonines." He writes as if emotionally envious of this period of Roman history, calling it a "halcyon Age" and the "zenith of time / When a pagan gentleman reigned," and when "No demagogue beat the pulpit-drum / In the Age of the Antonines." He wished that "We [might] read in America's signs / The Age restored of the Antonines."[21]

Lastly, with regard to the characterization of Goodman-Beecher as a demonic figure, an anti-Republican campaign poster associates Beecher with serving the Devil. The poster, noted earlier, advertises a steamer named the "Black Republican" to depart November 4, 1856, for "Salt River," which will carry along with its Captain (Frémont), "Holy Rifle" Beecher as Fireman; and it announces that besides him "A great number of 'Political Parsons,' who have *stolen the Livery of Heaven to serve the Devil in,* will be on board."[22] The humorous intention of this poster, although on a much lower level and simpler than Melville's handling of the topic, is not altogether unlike his in *The Confidence-Man* in its association of the Devil with a Republican minister. Readers have always picked up the consistent hints that the Confidence Man, in each of his disguises, is a devil figure. What I suggest is that Goodman-Beecher, as a "political parson," participating in the formation and campaigning of the new party, which was based upon the sectional antislavery principle, appears to have likewise stolen the livery of Heaven to serve the Devil in. He may be interpreted, then, as the embodiment in dramatic form of the Melvillean perception that a good man or a good cause may in its activism become subservient to an evil end. This perception is repeated by him in several different ways but most succinctly in his poem, "Fragments of a Lost Gnostic Poem, of the 12th Century":

(Stanza 2)
Indolence is heaven's ally here,
And energy the child of hell:
The Good Man pouring from his pitcher clear,
But brims the poisoned well.

Melville's choice of the name "Goodman" for his major embodiment of the Confidence Man has yet another dimension. He states the perception quite explicitly and prosaically in the "Supplement" to *Battle-Pieces*—his prose commentary upon the Civil War and its causes: "Nor should we forget that benevolent desires, after passing a certain point, can not undertake their own fulfillment without incurring the risk of evils beyond those sought to be remedied."[23] The good intentions of Beecher as an antislavery sermonizer and platform speaker receive, I believe, the criticism that in seeking their fulfillment they may end by bringing about a greater evil than the one they intend to remedy—*i.e.*, a civil war in which slavery may not be ended for African-Americans but extended and consolidated. The slaves may be brought into a worse condition than formerly and the Union of the States may be destroyed. With the hindsight of history it may be hard for us to see that Melville saw a man such as Beecher thus, but the evidence for the caricature is there and the caricature of Beecher fits Melville's discursive statements about the "Good Man" and his potentially counterproductive "benevolent desires."

Charles Arnold Noble

In the next eleven chapters (25–35) an extended dialogue between the Cosmopolitan and Charles Arnold Noble takes place—the longest single interchange between two characters in *The Confidence-Man*. The setting is first the porch of a cabin and next a bar with some little tables on deck, where the two men attempt to establish a genial "boon companionship."[24] Goodman's and Noble's attempt to become friends alludes, in the historical context that I have tried to define, most generally to the North-South sectional relationship and its problem of mutual trust. The series of chapters in which they converse about many subjects culminates in Goodman's surprising announcement that he is in "want of money" (chapter 30). When his request for a loan of fifty dollars is abruptly refused (chapter 31), he proves not really to need it, since he already has at least that amount in cash in the form of ten "half-eagles" (chapter 32). Friendship withered, their encounter ends feebly with Noble anxious to leave and Goodman the psychological winner, even if unsuccessful in his loan request (chapters 32–35). Within this section there are two interpolated tales: that related by Noble of the Indian-hating Colonel John Moredock, which throws considerable light on Noble's character, and that of the Gentleman-Madman Charlemont, illustrative of Goodman's forgiving character. Having already interpreted Frank Goodman as a caricature of Henry Ward Beecher, the charismatic leader of Northern antislavery public opinion, I shall offer evidence that Charlie Noble caricatures William Lowndes Yancey, the charismatic leader of Southern opinion in the middle and late 1850s (see plate 25).

The physical setting in which the Cosmopolitan first meets his new acquaintance suggests to the reader that he should look for allusions to the southern United States. Noble is seen standing in a semicircular porch opening, near the deck of the *Fidèle,* which is "lit by a zoned lamp swung overhead, and sending its light vertically down, like the sun at noon. Beneath the lamp stood the speaker [Noble]." The lamp may be read as an allusion to the hot sunny climate of the South, which was one of the main sectional differences always noted in controversial literature. This initial indication of Noble's Southern origin is confirmed later, when he testily reacts to Goodman's defense of "the sons of the Puritans" by remarking defensively in return: "And who be Puritans, that I, an Alabamaian, must do them reverence?" (p. 192).

Noble's physical traits are described by Melville in an even more involuted manner than usual (p. 158). He is "neither tall nor stout, neither short nor gaunt"—that is, he is middle-sized. He has "a body fitted, as by measure, to the service of his mind." He seems not to be remarkably good-looking, for he is "less favored perhaps in his features than his clothes." His skin seems to be coarse, for the "fineness of the nap [of his coat] seem[s] out of keeping with something the reverse of fine in the skin." He has "singularly good" teeth, which some would think are "too good to be true"—that is, they may be false teeth and, possibly, an indication to the reader that Noble is older than he wishes to appear. Later, it is mentioned that he has "sallow hands."

Noble's clothing is "less [beautiful] in the fit than the cut"—a hint that his clothes do not fit well, although they may possibly be rather good quality, for Melville speaks of the "fineness of the nap" being out of keeping with the "reverse of fine in the skin." Additionally, he wears a "violet vest," which sends up "sunset hues" to his face, and he later displays a "shirt-frill."

Of body-gestures only four are notable. He tries to roll about "like a full pipe [cask] in the sea," when asking Goodman to drink (p. 180); he slaps his hand on the table in anger (p. 196); throughout the scene with Goodman he constantly refills his companion's glass but not his own; and when angry with Goodman's loan request, he jumps up suddenly from the table and tosses out his foot in anger (p. 203).

Noble's personality is a sensitive, emotional one—prone to quick anger, uneasiness, and testiness bordering upon violence. In the initial description Melville observes that his face "betokens a kind of bilious [testy, choleric, impulsive] habit," which is confirmed by his subsequent behavior and by the use of the adjectives "nettled" (p. 192), "resentful" (pp. 192, 198), "excited" (p. 196), "testy" (p. 197), "touchy" (p. 198), "eager," "impetuous" (p. 202), and "nervous" (p. 205). In offering opinions he shows almost excessive "earnestness" (p. 196). He tries, however, to mask this "habit" by a "curiously interesting . . . warm air of florid cordiality, contrasting itself with one knows not what kind of aguish sallowness of saving discretion lurking behind it" (pp. 158–59). Reemphasizing this and analogizing his manner to his clothing, Melville comments that "the manner flushed the man, . . . in the same fictitious way that the vest flushed the cheek" (p. 159). Throughout the scene with the Cosmopolitan the reader feels that Noble is playing the role of a "cordial" *bon vivant,* trying to get him drunk in order to carry out some ulterior plan, possibly gambling, possibly a loan request. Most readers have felt this and hence have taken Winsome's accusation that Noble is a Mississippi riverboat "operator" (gambler or speculator) at face value. Whether he is a gambler or not is not entirely clear, since he never makes any overt move, but certainly he does display a false personality of generous "geniality" and bonhomie and a forced "lyric" mood, which his more genuine testiness, "saving discretion," and dislike of certain kinds of men breaks through—especially in his remarks on the virtues of Indian-hatred, on Polonius, and in his sharp and angry rejection of Goodman's loan request. Also, although he claims that he does not distrust the purity of the wine that he orders and which they drink, yet he drinks very little of it and makes a wry face at the taste of that little, as if suspicious of its quality.

Most revelatory of Noble's essential character is his great interest in the man-hating Missouri Bachelor Pitch and his outspoken admiration of the Indian-hating Colonel Moredock, which introduces the reader (and Goodman) to him:

> "Rather entertaining old 'coon [Pitch], if he wasn't so deuced analytical. Reminded me somehow of what I've heard about Colonel John Moredock, of Illinois, only your friend ain't quite so good a fellow at bottom, I should think." (p. 158)

Quite evident in his telling of the history of Moredock is that Charlie Noble *admires* men who display "devout" ethnic hatreds, such as Moredock's murderous hatred of Indians. He is eager to tell about Moredock ("With all my heart," p. 160), and he calls the day in his boyhood when he saw Moredock's rifle and when he may have seen the man himself a memorable day. Melville allows the significance of Moredock's intense Indian-hating and Indian-killing to be clearly pointed out by the philanthropic Goodman, even while Goodman himself is struck with "incredulity": Moredock, he says, "was either misanthrope or nothing; and his misanthropy the more intense from being focused on one race of men" (p. 177). Goodman sees the meaning of the story clearly as an exemplum of motivated "racial" hatred. Considering the political context of *The Confidence-Man* and its themes as I have interpreted it, I wish to suggest that Melville may have retold this story of a western American's motivated—almost glorified—race-hatred through the *persona* of his major Southern character Charlie Noble for the purpose of showing Noble's capacity to make a *tu quoque* rhetorical argument, one in which Noble implicitly defends Southern race prejudice by paralleling it to Western race prejudice. Noble is, to use the modern term, a "racist." Additionally, other traits of character that Moredock reveals, such as self-reliance, bravery, solitariness, realism, resoluteness, selfless devotion to a cause, and courteousness all appear to Noble admirable and hence imitable.

Curious details about Noble's voice that Melville mentions are a "latent squeak," when he tries to sing the verses about wine (p. 180), and "a strange kind of cackle meant to be a chirrup" (p. 182) that he emits over the port wine that he has ordered. As for his actual social status the only descriptive indication is the remark that he has "the air somehow of one whose fortunes had been of his own making" (p. 159), which would seem to suggest that he is a self-made man. His manners seem "bluff" and "cordial." Winsome later warns Goodman that he is a "Mississippi operator"—which is not necessarily true.

Noble is not only a voluminous talker but a conscious rhetorician. He gives a precise exordium to his lengthy monologue, dividing it into his "first theme," which is Indian-hating, and his "next and last" theme, the Indian-hater Moredock (p. 162). His own speaking style (as distinguished from his imitation of James Hall's style, while retelling Hall's story of Moredock) reveals a pronounced tendency to omit the subject of the sentence, especially when it is a pronoun (e.g., "Had a little skrimmage," p. 158; "Knew too much," p. 161; "Never so deceived in a man in my life," p. 203). In his anecdote of the memorable day in his boyhood he employs Defoe-like circumstantial particulars in order to make his story seem authentic, which suggests that he is a consciously realistic teller of anecdotes. Also, he can mimic the style of another narrator—Hall—and has a good memory for others' stories. He likes to quote poetry, singing two verses from Leigh Hunt's "Bacchus in Tuscany," and reciting a "panegyric on the press," in the form of a loose parody of Old Testament encomiastic style, which is probably Melville's own composition in the manner of other parodies of this sort that appeared in the comic periodicals frequently as political satire.

Noble's ideas are few, yet in a social situation he seems willing for his own purposes to talk about many things—the press, wine as a social bond, tobacco, humor, "surly" philanthropists and "genial" misanthropes, Shakespeare's Polonius and Autolycus, conviviality, and especially about Moredock the Indian-hater.

In several personal traits, in his Alabama loyalty, in his non-humanitarian ethical stance Charles Arnold Noble so closely resembles William Lowndes Yancey (1814–1863) that he may be interpreted as a caricature of this militant Alabaman, who was a lawyer, editor, legislator (1841–43), United States congressman (1844–46), Democratic politician and was, most importantly, as the author of the States' Rights "Alabama Platform" of 1848, the leading proslavery orator, pamphleteer, and political journalist in the sectionalist movement that led up to the secession of the Southern states during the winter of 1860–61. The "Arnold" in Noble's name would allude to the traitorous intent of Yancey, as viewed by a Northerner. From midway in his career Yancey was recognized as a militant exponent of the Southern rights interpretation of the Constitution and was always named among the leading "Fire-eaters." Halstead called him "Prince of the fire-eaters" in 1860. Emerson D. Fite wrote that "No man ever put the arguments of the South more powerfully." Dumond writes that "without Yancey's brilliant oratory and indefatigable labors there would have been no secession, no Southern Confederacy." And Malcolm C. McMillan writes that "Many historians . . . agree that, by leading the disruption of the Democratic Party, one of the few remaining national institutions, in 1860, Yancey contributed more than anyone else to the election of Lincoln, Southern secession, and the timing of the Civil War (see plate 25). [25]

In physical appearance Yancey seems, like Noble, not to have been distinguished by height or personal beauty. Halstead describes him at the Democratic convention in 1860 as "middle-sized." Henry S. Foote, political contemporary, describes his face as "well-shaped, but neither strikingly handsome or the reverse." Yancey's only full-length biographer, John W. DuBose, notes that his head was "neither large nor small, but remarkable for the symmetry of the contour." It was noted by observers that while he was orating "his countenance [became] ablaze with that peculiar halo which was wont to surround it in his most earnest effects," while another description, cited by Clement Eaton, mentions his "countenance aglow." Some attributed this to drink. It is possible that this "peculiar halo" or "glow" may be reflected in Melville's ascription of "sunset hues" to Noble's face. As for clothing, Rhodes writes that his dress was "picturesque" and in "a pronounced Southern style," yet present research does not yet disclose whether this would mean a "violet vest" and "shirt-frill" such as Noble wears. But closely linking Noble to Yancey are two different prints (reproduced in Shaw, *Abraham Lincoln: The Year of His Election* and in Clement Eaton, *The Mind of the Old South*) which show him wearing suits apparently so ill-fitting that the sleeves almost cover his hands. Moreover, this detail of Yancey's personal appearance is reinforced by Foote's observation that his clothes "did not always fit him as well as they might have done." I cannot find that Yancey wore false teeth or had a coarse or "sallow" complexion, but a sallow complexion was a frequent Southern white characteristic because of the prevalence of malaria. Nor do I find that he displayed in his oratory any of the particular gestures that Noble does— only that his stance was limited, his gestures few but impressive, employed to "mark a climax or drive home a conviction."[26]

The strongest indication that Noble caricatures Yancey is his temperament. Noble's "bilious [testy, impulsive, choleric] habit," which is reinforced later by the adjectives "testy," "excited," "touchy," and "impetuous," and by gestures such as pounding his hand on the table in anger and "tossing" out his foot in anger, resembles Yancey's well-known fiery temperament, which was not, be it noted, entirely unique to him but was stereotypical of the Southern white man, both as self-characterized and as viewed in the North. Significantly, Clement Eaton chooses Yancey as the most powerful representative of the type of the emotional, impulsive, rash Southern man in his chapter, "The Voice of Emotion," in *The Mind of the Old South*. He quotes William Gilmore Simms as saying, "We Southrons . . . are creatures of impulse and prejudice," and another contemporary as remarking of Yancey that he excelled in all that was "fierce, stormy, vituperative, denunciatory, impetuous and scornful"—all adjectives that might well be applied to Noble's character as drawn by Melville. Thomas H. Watts, a political opponent and personal friend, wrote of him: "Yancey's fiery temper sometimes got the better of his judgment." Perhaps to Melville and others the fact that Yancey had shot and killed his wife's uncle in a dispute in 1838 and had fought a duel with the Whig congressman, Thomas L. Clingman, of North Carolina in 1845 over Clingman's alleged insult of the Southern Democrats in a congressional speech, would show sufficiently a "bilious habit"—a choleric temperament. In defense of him on a manslaughter charge for the killing it was said, DuBose reports, that he wore a pistol habitually because of a habit, "acquired in carrying it while passing through the Indian country of the West."[27] The duel with Clingman was an "affair of honor" in this period, yet duelling was not a code that all gentlemen felt obliged to honor; it was more customary in the South than in the North. It was often cited by Northern critics of Southern society as a symptom of the "barbarism" and indulgence of anger and violent behavior encouraged by the slave system. Testiness of temper, haughtiness, hair-trigger expressions of violence, and courage formed part of the stereotype of the "chivalric" Southern gentleman and Yancey's history and temperament fit well into the type as seen by Northern and Western eyes. [28]

Again resembling Noble's personality, Yancey at certain times wore an air of great cordiality and good humor in public, that was striking enough to be noted three times by Halstead at the Democratic conventions in 1860, as well as an air of "perfect sincerity," similar to Noble's earnestness. At Charleston in April he appeared to be a "mild and gentlemanly man, always wearing a genuinely good-humored smile and looking as if nothing in the world could disturb the equanimity of his spirits," and at the very moment of the destruction of the Democratic party on 30 April, he "was smiling as a bridegroom," and finally, at the Seceder's convention in Baltimore in June, Yancey "who always wears a surface smile, twisted about in his seat with the unrest of intolerable felicity, laid his head first upon one shoulder, and then upon the other, and glowed with satisfaction," at the establishment of a Southern party. Yet beneath this smiling surface was "a man of strong impulse and deep emotions." According to DuBose, "There was a visible suppression of feeling, a curbing of force latent in the man," and according to Foote: "Occasions sometimes arose when, either having lost his accustomed power of self-control or deeming it expedient to make some display of the stormier energies with which he was endowed, he unloosed all the furies under his command upon some noted antagonist, and did and said things which those who witnessed his sublime ravings never again forgot." The fictitiousness of Yancey's surface good-humor correlates with that of Noble's apparent cordiality. However, I can find no attribution to him of the adjective "saving discretion," which Melville gives to Noble, unless Foote's further observation that Yancey "had studied men closely and had looked deeply into the motives and purposes of those with whom he had held intercourse or whose movements in public life had specially attracted his attention," might be so interpreted. Lastly, Noble's claim to enjoy wine, even while he makes a wry face at the taste of it and fails to drink much of it, might just possibly allude to Yancey's stated dislike of the "common stuff of commerce" in liquors and his preference for the pure "mountain dew" that was sent him as a gift by his friend Benjamin Perry. [29]

Noble's sympathy with men who display strong prejudices is very evident in his interest in Pitch, the Missourian, who claims to hate all men, and in his admiration of Moredock, who hates Indians, and is a trait that is consonant with Yancey's twenty-year obsession with defending and extending the slave-system founded upon a devout belief in the intellectual and moral inferiority of the African-Americans and the rightness of slavery for them. Yancey's views on Indians I have not yet been able to discover, but as I have already suggested, it is possible that since the theme of Hall's story is ethnic hatred and the hero of it an Indian-killer, Melville may intend to evoke the similarity of Western Indian-prejudice to Southern African-prejudice by having Noble, his caricature of a Southern man, use a well-authenticated history of Western prejudice as a rhetorical device in defense of Noble's own Southern prejudice. Like the proverbial pot and the kettle, Noble is saying, in effect: "Look, we Southern whites—'Saxons'—are not unique in our prejudices. You, too, (*tu quoque*) have your prejudices. In fact, you are even more violent than we are, for your 'heroes' systematically hunt down and exterminate another race, while we only subjugate and, in fact, improve another race." At this point it should be remembered that his interlocuter caricatures Henry Ward Beecher, who was regarded as partly a Westerner, even though of New England birth and education, because he had moved to Indiana as a young man and had spent his early career there and made a name for himself before moving to Brooklyn in 1847. If Melville's purpose is, as I have suggested earlier, to evoke the similarity of Western Indian-prejudice to Southern African-prejudice, it seems, then, that he wishes to depict the real strength of ethnic animosities in men such as John Moredock and, if my identification of the caricature is correct, men such as Yancey. Meanwhile, Goodman-Beecher, who professes not to believe in the real existence of such ethnic animosities, is revealed as being either a naïve fool for not believing in their reality, or a knave for pretending not to, when he really is quite aware of them. In the historical context the same criticism can be and was made of the Republican party leaders in the 1850s. If they in their humanitarian rhetoric did not recognize the reality of the pervasive attitude of the American of European descent toward the African-American, they were indictable as fools, while if they did recognize it and even, perhaps, shared it, then, they were dishonest—knaves—in pretending that it did not exist.

As for Noble's voice, to which Melville ascribes a "latent squeak" and a strange kind of "cackle," there is no evident correlation, thus far, with Yancey's voice, which in his public speaking was praised for the opposite qualities of being "musical" and "silvery" and was, according to Halstead, "remarkable for its power." It is remotely possible that the "cackle" and the "chirrup" are allusions to the emblem of the Democratic party—the rooster—more particularly to a young specimen of it such as Yancey, who was associated with the "Young America" branch of the party.[30]

In social status Yancey was, like Noble, a self-made man. After the death of his father, he was relatively poor as a child and was raised in Troy, New

York, by his stepfather, an antislavery Presbyterian minister and teacher. His single attempt at plantation life, when he married a wealthy woman in 1835, collapsed in the panic of 1837 and ended tragically in 1839 with the accidental poisoning of nearly all his slaves. Prior to that and from then on he made his living by his efforts in law and journalism. His chief fame and political power—intermittent as it was—came from public speaking in defense of Southern rights and for Southern unity, an area in which he acted to a large extent as an independent political force—an additional "self-made" aspect of his career that may be reflected also in Noble's "air somehow of one whose fortunes had been of his own making." He never cooperated well with the ordinary party men. Finally, with regard to personality, Yancey's manners were, like Noble's, "frank and unassuming."[31]

Yancey's public speaking style was not unlike Noble's. Noble's device of stating his two-fold theme at the beginning of his account of Indian-hating and of Moredock is like Yancey's rhetorical habit of carefully stating his theme or themes in his exordium. DuBose writes that "one exordium was of two sentences, of nearly equal length . . . in which he stated the argument he was about to make." His style was characterized by "strength rather than beauty, by directness rather than finesse," as is Noble's. Several writers noticed his "logic" and his "earnestness," and the absence of elegance, of metaphor, and of poetic imagery, although he did quote poetry, as Noble does. Relatively few gestures were noted; he seemed to suppress his feelings and curb his force; yet, as noted by Foote above, he could unloose his "stormier energies" when required. He marshaled facts to support his position, just as Noble adduces the detailed story of Moredock's life and opinions to support his view that "Indian-hating still exists, and, no doubt, will continue to exist, so long as Indians do" (chapter 25). DuBose quotes a friend as saying that Yancey was always "deeply in earnest, and . . . he spoke truth as if it were truth, and as if he felt, in the deepest recesses of his heart, the full measure of the words he used." Last, it may be noted that Yancey, like Noble, was given to very lengthy speeches, even beyond four hours, and to monologues. Halstead notes that at the Charleston convention in April 1860 Yancey asked for extra time and at the Seceders' convention in Baltimore in June 1860 he was "guilty of that terrible offense . . .—too much speaking. . . . The people left the hall by hundreds; yet he spoke on as if unconscious that . . . he was boring them." And in her diary Mary Boykin Chesnut reveals his reputation for loquacity in her surprise that Jefferson Davis had sent Yancey to England in 1861, asking, "Who wants eloquence? We want somebody who can hold his tongue. People avoid great talkers, men who orate, men given to monologue." Like Yancey's, Noble's speeches are lengthy; his relation of the Moredock story and its "metaphysics" of Indian-hating requires fourteen pages in the edition of *The Confidence-Man* by Elizabeth Foster—the only longer monologue being Egbert's story of China Aster.[32]

A topic of the conversation between Goodman and Noble in chapter 30—the character of Shakespeare's Polonius and the meaning of his advice to Laertes (*Hamlet,* 1.3)—may possibly be a specific allusion to Yancey's attitude toward James Buchanan, elder statesman of the Democratic party, if Noble be taken to represent Yancey not only as an individual but also as representative of the political ideas and attitudes of the Young America branch of the Democratic party in the 1850s during the ascendancy of the radical proslavery imperialist, George Sanders. Like its counterparts in Europe— Jeune France, Giovane Italia, and Disraeli's Young England—it was militant in its opinions, dogmatic in its views, inclined to sarcasm and sharpness in its rhetoric and sponsored a satirical periodical to express its views: *Yankee Doodle; or Young America* (1854–56). The New York *Herald* referred to Yancey among a group of younger Democratic Southern politicians who think James Buchanan "an old fogy" and a "time-server," and would prefer younger men like Breckinridge (17 July 1856). In chapter 30 Noble's insistently emotional response to Polonius as "the fly-blown old fop," the "bowing and cringing, time-serving old sinner," the "discreet, decorous, old dotard-of-state," and "the ribanded old dog" (p. 196) seems to reflect Yancey's association with the Young America faction, which introduced into Democratic political rhetoric the term "Old Fogy" for party members who were of the older generation—men such as Lewis Cass and James Buchanan.

Among the "Old Fogy" notions that Yancey himself was pleased to dispense with, one was the natural rights of man. In a speech at a Southern Commercial Convention after the Dred Scott decision in 1857, quoted by DuBose, he called two of the Founding Fathers, Jefferson and Monroe (whom he claimed otherwise to esteem) "old Fogies" because of their expressed humanitarian views on the "ethics of slavery." He went on proudly to claim that the influence of Young America, as he saw it, was in part responsible for the Supreme Court decision in the Scott case:

> I say that the old fogies of that day [Jefferson's] entertained opinions in relation to slavery, which we of this day are unanimously agreed were not sound. And Mr. Monroe, in signing that Missouri compromise, which the Supreme Court of the United States, under the influence of Young America, and the ideas which have sprung up within a few years past, in that great decision . . . have declared that those old sentiments were wrong; that Mr. Monroe was wrong; and therefore when that Virginia statesman put his name to that Missouri compromise, he put

his name to a law which that decision has said was a law which made us unequal in the Union, and therefore was unconstitutional.

Yancey continues, in a startling simile, to compare the introduction of the new ideas of his faction, which he claims are embodied in the Dred Scott decision (chiefly the notion that slavery is a blessing), to the introduction of the new "message" of Christianity by St. John and by Jesus, terming the Pharisees and chief priests "the old fogies of that day": "It [Christianity] was a new idea and broke like a thunder-clap over old fogydom of that time," as his ideas shock the old fogies of his time. It would appear, then, that opinions which Stephen Douglas, the former shining light of Young America, could not accept (e.g., the Taney Court's interpretation of the Constitution as guaranteeing the extension of slavery into new territories and denying that an African-American could ever be a citizen) were regarded by Yancey as the new and exciting truths which Young America had militantly brought to the American consciousness. I suggest that Melville in depicting Noble-Yancey as earnestly contemptuous of Polonius—"the discreet, decorous, old dotard-of-state"—is alluding to the contempt expressed by Yancey and other Young America factionalists for older Democrats who found it hard to accept the full implications of the proslavery principles enunciated by the younger Southern members of the party—and for James Buchanan, the presidential candidate in 1856 in particular.[33] As for the allusions possibly lurking in other topics of the conversation in chapter 30—the press, wine, tobacco, humor, Shakespeare's Autolycus—I have, at present, no conjectures but only suspicions that contexts will be found for them, perhaps in the debates of the Temperance movement or some other area of public controversy.

There are several parallelisms of Yancey to Beecher that make them similar in their representative functions for their respective sections. The most important is that each had become during the period in question the most widely known and powerful public speaker (both as the expresser of and the maker of public opinion) of his respective section. Yancey was to the South what Beecher was to the North—the great manipulator of mass feeling. DuBose writes that "at no time in his career was [Yancey] ever found in attendance on a political meeting that a general outcry did not arise from it demanding a speech from him." Precisely the same thing is said of Beecher and happened most notably at the meeting in the New York City Tabernacle in May 1856, after the Brooks assault on Sumner, when Beecher was called from his seat as an auditor and virtually compelled to speak. DuBose speaks of the hundreds of addresses "by which Mr. Yancey shaped the public opinion of the South," while Beecher's biographers reiterate his speechmaking efforts and his power over audiences not only in the New York area but all over the

North and West. Similarly, again, Yancey was treasurer of a fund for the benefit of Jefferson Buford's group of Southern Kansas settlers "for the advancement of the Southern cause there," according to DuBose, while Beecher collected funds in support of Kansas settlers from the North and West. In interpreting the representative character of these two major sectional caricatures it must be emphasized that, apparently, it is not in roles as statesmen, writers, thinkers, or inventors of new ideas, but as master sensors of public feeling and master verbalizers of common opinions that Melville chose them to represent their respective sections in the longest confrontation of characters in *The Confidence-Man.*[34]

The importance of Yancey in the national scene at this time (although he reached the peak of his fame later when he toured the North in 1860) must be stressed because he, like several others whom I claim that Melville is satirizing in *The Confidence-Man,* has been buried from the view of the average reader of Melville's work by the Civil War and its consequences. Raymond of the *Times,* in an important exchange of public letters with Yancey in 1860, called him "the author and the head" of the disunion movement, writing that while Calhoun "planted the seeds of it in the intellects and the ambition of . . . the rising statesmen of the South," because his doctrines were "too abstract for general appreciation," since his death the "apostles of his creed" have propagated it and "no one man . . . more zealous" than Yancey in this work. On his side, like the antislavery advocates on theirs, Yancey saw himself as the apostle of a creed, political in its intentions while "religious" and "moral" in its appeal. Although other Southern extremists were powerful through their writings, notably Robert Barnwell Rhett of South Carolina and Edmund Ruffin of Virginia, in the movement toward secession, it was Yancey who both reflected and shaped Southern opinion in his public speaking. Charles M. Wiltse, the modern biographer of Calhoun, attributes to him, more than to any other man, the creation of the Confederacy.[35]

The importance of Yancey's role as Southern spokesman by 1860, when he toured the North and West campaigning for the Constitutional Democratic nominee, John C. Breckinridge, is evident in two prints that appeared in *Vanity Fair.* In the first of these, "Scan. Mag. at Washington" (29 September 1860), Yancey is caricatured in female dress as "Nancy of Alabama," eagerly listening to "Miss J. B." (President Buchanan in female dress), who has come to her kitchen to gossip. Miss J. B says: "Yes my dear, and they do say, Steve Douglas is going to sell out to Old Abe, and Old Abe's to give him ever so much money and quicksilver, besides the whole town of Chicago. But I wouldn't mention it for anything." In the reproduction of this in Shaw, *Abraham Lincoln: The Year of His Election,* Shaw suggests that this print comments on the various efforts to fuse tickets during the four-way campaign of

1860. The parrot in a cage in "Nancy's" kitchen, who cries "Brecky wants a cracker," seems to imply that Breckinridge is Yancey's personal possession at least in the eyes of the public. Another *Vanity Fair* print that reflects the public notion of Yancey's influence is "Coming 'Round" (17 November 1860), after the election of Lincoln (plate 25). It depicts a stable called the "White House" in which Lincoln, dressed as the groom in charge, says to Yancey, who is dressed as a jockey and is holding the bridle of a horse labelled "Fugitive Slave Law": "I say, Yancey, if you'll let me have these stables in peace for the next four years, I'll give you some of the best stalls and see that your nag is well taken care of." The Northern belief in Yancey's power over Southern feeling and action at this critical time is implicit in the print. Whether or not he actually possessed such power, what is relevant to our concerns is that by 1860 the North generally recognized his ascendancy as a spokesman, which I suggest Melville perceived four years earlier and is the reason why he caricatures him as the representative sectional type in the central confrontation of political opponents in *The Confidence-Man*.[36]

11

Two Antagonists (Mark Winsome and Egbert the Disciple) and Their Antagonist (the Crazy Beggar)

Mark Winsome the Mystical Master

With the transition from Charlie Noble to Mark Winsome the Mystical Master, which takes place in chapter 36, Melville's Cosmopolitan encounters a different kind of antagonist—one who is, like himself, nominally an admirer and lover of mankind but one who, inconsistently, twice shows distrust of certain kinds of men, although not of Goodman himself. Winsome, who at first sight easily believes Goodman to be a "beautiful soul" simply because of his "beautiful" appearance, evinces deep distrust of two other men—Noble, who has just left the scene, and the Crazy Beggar, who appears while he and Goodman are talking. Since Winsome has long been identified as a caricature of Ralph Waldo Emerson (1803–1882), and since more recently the Crazy Beggar has been recognized as a caricature of Edgar Allan Poe, and since Charlie Noble seems, as I have argued, to be one of Yancey, it appears that Melville is satirizing the attitude of Emerson (and through him of other New Englanders) toward Southerners, for both Poe and Yancey were representative Southerners—the one in literature and the other in politics and oratory. The foundation of Winsome-Emerson's distrust of Noble-Yancey is merely hearsay ("He is suspected . . . as a Mississippi operator"), and of his distrust of the Beggar it is "a damning peep of sense" which he thinks he sees and which to him indicates "scoundrelism" in the Beggar. Neither excuse betrays any attempt on Winsome-Emerson's part to extend to either of these men the same kind of trust that he accords to his new acquaintance Goodman, which is based solely upon his "beauty," or to Egbert, the disciple whom he regards as a reflection of one aspect of himself and who caricatures Henry David Thoreau. I think that Melville is satirizing in this complex pattern of acceptance and rejection the failure of certain New Englanders, specifically the Transcendentalist believers in the "divinity" of man, such as Emerson and Thoreau, to be consistent with their own beliefs and to extend their trust and affection to their white Southern "brothers"—sinful as they may have considered them to be. This trust is what men such as Edward Everett expected of them when he wrote, conscious of his own moral limitations, that he thought Southern white men as "good Christians, as good patriots, as good men as we are." And after the war, it will be remembered, Melville wrote in the "Supplement" to *Battle-Pieces* about the need for brotherly love toward the Southerners of European descent "who stand nearer to us in nature" than the Southerner of African descent.[1]

As noted in chapter 1, that Melville caricatures Emerson in the figure of Mark Winsome was recognized as early as 1938 by Yvor Winters in his essay on Melville in *Maule's Curse* and has since then been supported by Egbert Oliver, Elizabeth Foster, and by most scholars of Melville's work.[2] Considerable supplementary evidence that I have found, of which the following details seem worth citing, confirms and broadens their pioneer work.

Just as Winsome is "tall" and "angular," so Emerson was described as "tall and slender," over six feet, and displayed "angular movements of the hands and arms." Where Melville describes a brow "placidly thoughtful" in Winsome's appearance, Oliver Wendell Holmes describes in Emerson an "expression . . . calm, sedate, kindly, with [a] look of refinement" and Bungay writes that he was "intellectual-looking." Although Emerson's age does not tally with Winsome's, since he would be about fifty-three in 1856 instead of being "perhaps five and forty," yet Emerson was frequently described as looking younger than his actual years. Bungay, writing in *Off-Hand Takings* (1854), of Emerson at that time places him as "between forty and fifty years of age," when he was actually over fifty. Emerson's eyes, similar to Winsome's eyes of "pellucid blue," are described by Holmes as being of the "strongest and brightest blue" and by Emerson's family as "absolutely blue." Emerson's dress, according to a younger friend Charles Woodbury, showed nothing exceptional; "Anything that excited remark in dress and demeanour he avoided by instinct," just as Winsome's disciple's costume—"modelled upon his master's" and hence descriptive of Winsome's also—is "neat, with just enough of the mode to save it from the reproach of originality" (p. 225).[3]

Winsome's double-aspect of "shrewdness and mythiness, strangely jumbled"—"a kind of cross between a Yankee peddler and a Tartar priest" (p. 212)—reflects a similar quality in Emerson, for which Oliver cites Lowell's and other contemporaries' observations of Emerson's face and character. There may be added Woodbury's remark that his look "portrayed by turns the sagacity of the man of affairs and the 'vision' of the clairvoyant." And Edwin P. Whipple, the lyceum lecturer and rival on the platform of Emerson, claimed in his "Some Recollections of Ralph Waldo Emerson" to have been the first to call Emerson a "Greek-Yankee—a cross between Plato and Jonathan Slick." Whipple also mentions alternate epithets to his, expressing the same observation, such as a "Hindoo-Yankee—a cross between Brahma and Poor Richard," and that there are many other competitors for originating these "epigrammatic impertinences." Another personal trait of Winsome, his

"kind of farmer dignity," is similar to Emerson's resemblance to an "inquisitive farmer" and his showing a "rustic curiosity and simplicity" to his friend
John Burroughs.[4]

Additions to Oliver's citations of contemporary sources that noted Emerson's coldness of personality, which is obviously caricatured in Winsome's
"preternaturally cold, gemmy glance," his seeming "purely and coldly radiant
as a prism," in his predilection for "iced-water," in the "icicles" in his look,
and in his "frozen nature" (pp. 214, 216, 217, 219, 253), are the following.
Emerson's literary executor, James Elliot Cabot, mentions that he lamented
but excused his own "coldness" to Margaret Fuller. Holmes cites Lowell's
observation that majesty "seemed to hedge him round" and asks, "What
man was he who would lay his hand familiarly upon his shoulder and call
him Waldo?" and writes that "his ideas of friendship, as of love, seem almost
too exalted for our earthly conditions, and suggest the thought as do many
others of his characteristics that the spirit which animated his mortal frame
had missed its way on the shining path to some brighter and better sphere
of being." Such a reaction in a contemporary of Emerson suggests also Melville's comparison of Winsome to "Raphael"—the Archangel (p. 223). Franklin Sanborn, on first meeting Emerson in 1853, describes him "talking in
the same cool, profound, impersonal way in which he wrote." Woodbury
writes of Emerson as Concord's "clear, cold, solitary flame"and later of a
gesture in lecturing as "a slight movement of the hand, repelling as from the
cold pole of a magnet." Isaac Hecker, of Brook Farm and the Paulist Order,
wrote of transcendentalists generally and possibly of Emerson in particular
that "a Transcendentalist is one who has a keen sight but little warmth of
heart," and "It is his lips and head that speak, not his tongue and heart."[5]

Other traits of Emerson that parallel Winsome are the following. Where
Winsome regards Goodman "scholastically," so Holmes notes of Emerson
that his "personal appearance was that of a scholar, the descendent of scholars." As for Winsome's trait of "artistically eying the picturesque speaker
[Goodman] as if he were a statue" (p. 213) and his interest in his beauty,
Whipple in his "Recollections" writes, "The sense of beauty was so vital an
element in the constitution of his being that it decorated everything it
touched." Again, Winsome's "infantile intellectuality" is observed less satirically in Emerson by Holmes: "His whole look was irradiated by an ever
active inquiring intelligence." Winsome's "prism-like" and "gemmy" quality
seems to reflect what Holmes notes of Emerson's speaking: "An hour passed
in listening to that flow of thought, calm and clear as the diamond drops
that distill from a mountain rock, was a true nepenthe for a care worn soul."
And more closely similar, Woodbury notes that his "bearing had a certain

translucency." Lastly, like Winsome, who is "constitutionally obtuse to . . . pleasant drollery," so Emerson, according to Woodbury, rarely laughed.[6]

As in nearly all the other caricatures in *The Confidence-Man,* Melville's uncanny sensitivity to style—both written and spoken—is manifest in his parody of Emerson's style. He applies to Winsome's style of speaking the adjective "oracular" and "calm energy," while of Emerson's speaking style John Albee writes that he "spoke in a mild, peculiar manner, justifying the text of Thoreau, that you must be calm before you utter oracles," and that "he sometimes expressed himself mystically and like a book"—an apt description of Winsome's way of speaking. Winsome's pretentious quotation of a Greek word for the English word "favor" reflects Emerson's passion for the Greek language that was noted by Woodbury in his *Talks with Ralph Waldo Emerson* (1890). Winsome's display of rare learning in his quotation from an uncommon source in Proclus's commentary on Plato satirizes Emerson's richness of literary and philosophical allusion, which placed his discourse far above the head of his average listener. He was almost uniformly criticized for being "obscure," "too learned," or "mystical." Wichelns in his study of Emerson's oratory notes the "unfamiliarity" of his examples "brought from sources the auditor had never read, never heard of." Woodbury observes that even in conversation Emerson was "held in duress by his own thought" and his conversation was mostly a "monologue of oral reflections which seemed to be addressed to a widely read and thoughtful audience and which always exacted much of the listener." As for the "abstruseness" of Winsome's "occult" philosophy, which Goodman claims seems "above the comparatively vile uses of life," likewise Franklin Sanborn claims that to him, a practical reformer and friend, "The highest things in [Emerson] are almost inaccessible; nobody knows what his real philosophy is." A sharply negative—and Southern— view of Emerson's style was that of a writer in *De Bow's Review* in 1861, who could almost be describing Melville's parody of Emerson, for he saw the style as "affectedly, studiously, and elaborately involved and obscure."[7]

More minutely considered, Winsome's style in its central passages mimics Emerson's habit of writing in sentences that convey a single thought or intuition not always developing out of what precedes or into what follows. Good examples, which also display the "oracular" quality, are: "Pharaoh's poorest brick-maker lies proudlier in his rags than the Emperor of all the Russias in his hollands . . . for death, though in a worm, is majestic; while life, though in a king, is contemptible (p. 218); and (displaying parody also of Carlyle, who was a powerful influence upon Emerson), "If still in golden accents old Memnon murmurs his riddle, none the less does the balance-sheet of every man's ledger unriddle the profit or loss of life"; and "Man came into this world not to sit down and muse, not to befog himself with vain subtleties, but to gird up his loins and to work"; and lastly (displaying, also, the combination of the mystical and the practical in Emerson), "Mystery is in the morning, and mystery in the night, and the beauty of mystery is everywhere; but still the plain truth remains, that mouth and purse must be filled" (p. 223). Emerson's habit of composing his paragraphs and essays in clusters of loosely linked, self-reliant, intuitive statements—called aptly "mental saltations" by Albee—and the "oracular and epigrammatic" character of his prose make him easy to parody by a master of prose style such as Melville.[8]

An important aspect of Emerson's character, which involves simultaneously style, thought, and personality, is the remote distancing of himself from others whether in his rhetorical relationship to his audience, or in his intellectual accountability, or in his affections. This quality is peculiarly captured in the exchanges between Winsome and Goodman in their opening scene and in the discussion of the rattlesnake. Of Emerson Wichelns writes that there always seemed to be "a distance between the speaker and his hearers." Also, he gradually released himself from "that intellectual accountability to his peers which every writer and speaker—on the higher levels at least—customarily acknowledges" and also he "released himself from close social responsibility" to ordinary citizens. He also disliked argument or logical defense of his views and had a "dislike of the wrangling process of debate" with others.[9] If one associates his personal coldness, noted earlier as an emotional trait of Emerson, with his remoteness from his audience as a speaker, and with his moral doctrine of self-reliance, which does not presuppose any strong feeling of accountability on the part of the individual to society, a complex of character traits emerges which seems clearly parodied—with satirical exaggeration—in Melville's portrait of Winsome engaged in conversation with the warm, friendly, emotionally involved—and socially "accountable"—Cosmopolitan-Beecher. Winsome's grotesque fascination with the "beautiful creature, the rattlesnake," which charms him because it is totally "unaccountable," is "exempt from knowledge and conscience," and lives "the care-free, joyous life of a perfectly instinctive, unscrupulous, and irresponsible creature," carries to an extreme a central element in Emerson's thought and character—an aestheticism that is both a personal predilection and a philosophical assumption of most of his thought, stated early on in *Self-Reliance* (1841): "The only right is what is after my constitution; the only wrong what is against it." The habit of conforming moral right and wrong not to an absolute and independent standard but to personal feelings and habits—"my constitution"—is an aesthetic habit of adjustment of which Emerson is the great American example and exponent.

Emerson's remoteness and lack of emotional give and take is an oratorical trait diametrically opposed to Beecher's warm involvement with his audience discussed earlier, as is his relativistic aestheticism to Beecher's Christian evangelical commitment. Both temperamental characteristics enter into the contrast of characters that Melville dramatizes in the Goodman-Winsome conversations. In view of this contrast it is interesting to notice that Wichelns, writing almost ninety years after Melville's contrast of the two public speakers, chooses also to contrast them and judges that "Emerson, in short, was no Beecher." [10] In the caricatures of both men Melville is dealing not with physical appearance alone or with style alone but with the essential character as expressed in physical appearance, style, and the public intellectual positions of the two men. The power of his characterizations becomes all the more deeply evident, then, when the reader realizes who they are and thereby perceives through the fictional characters and the actions they perform Melville's commentary upon the men themselves who are caricatured.

Several details in the caricature of Emerson link it closely to the assumed period of the writing of *The Confidence-Man*. The topic of "Beauty," besides being an important one in Emerson's thought, was, according to his letters, the subject of a lecture (first given in March 1855), that Emerson took with him on his lecture tour during the winter of 1855–56. During the period 18–21 February 1856, he was in the Berkshires, and on 13 March according to his pocket diary he gave a lecture in Pittsfield. Foster in her notes states that the *Berkshire Eagle* on 7 and 14 March noticed his lecture but does not say whether the newspaper mentioned the topic or reported the content. I have not yet found any report of it. Though it is not possible to claim that Melville heard Emerson lecture on beauty at this time or any other, it is certainly possible that as a result of his lecturing at that time on that topic his ideas on beauty would be "in the air" as something to be talked about by people with literary and intellectual interests in Pittsfield and in the Berkshire towns generally. Melville may have been swayed by the current interest aroused by Emerson's lecturing to choose this aspect of this thought as the opening focus of his intellectual satire rather than some other aspect. An additional link directly to this period is Emerson's quotation in his *Journal* "*SO*" of a passage from Proclus on Plato's theology in Thomas Taylor's translation, *The Six Books of Proclus . . . on the Theology of Plato* (1816). Emerson drew directly upon his notebooks for lecture material all his life; and so it is possible that he may even have mentioned Proclus's commentary on Plato in one of the lectures given in February and March in the Berkshires. [11]

There is evidence in Emerson's writings to show that he intensely disliked and distrusted not only Southerners like Poe who defended the slave system but Northern men who defended Southern rights under the Constitution, at the same time as he admired, liked and trusted Northern men of pronounced antislavery views. Thus, his attitudes are perfectly consonant with Winsome's distrust of Noble-Yancey and of Crazy Beggar-Poe and his trust of Goodman-Beecher and Egbert-Thoreau. In the same section of his *Journal* during 1856 as the reference to his reading of Proclus Emerson, turning to the current political controversy about slavery and reacting specifically to the caning of Sumner, expresses strong distrust of and dislike of certain Southerners— Robert Toombs of Georgia and Preston Brooks—and of their Northern "sympathizers," of whom he names the New York Democrat Isaiah Rynders, the distinguished Boston lawyer and orator Rufus Choate, the conservative Whig lawyer and U.S. congressman Robert Winthrop, and the Boston lawyer George Hillard, a Whig and former friend of Sumner. He writes scornfully that, "refined Boston upholds a gang of Rhynderses, & Toombses, & Brookses . . . the Choates & Winthrops, and . . . the Hillards we see through them very clearly." The same lack of a universal compassion and trust that Cosmopolitan-Beecher observes as a trait in Winsome-Emerson and which Emerson shows in these remarks had appeared earlier in his *Journal* during 1851 in some thoughts about his own motives for hating slavery and Southern slaveholders and for hating men like Webster and Everett. He writes, "The absence of moral feeling in the . . . white man is the very calamity I deplore. The . . . captivity of a thousand negroes is nothing to me." And he notes again in his *Journal* during 1852–53 that some abolitionist feeling (whether his own or others' is unclear) is founded on dislike of the brutality of slave-holding *in the white man*—equating that violence with the black man himself: "Brute instinct rallies and centers in the black man." It appears that it was not compassion for the blacks or trust of them but his and other Northerners' personal shame and suffering—their wounded pride—which the Fugitive Slave Law aroused that was the motive to much antislavery indignation as expressed in his address, "The Fugitive Slave Law," given in 1851, where he says that he feels "mortified," "dishonored," and "discredited" as a citizen. He takes to himself in his shame the imputed guilt of the legal and political leaders whom he sees as failing in honor. He certainly would have included Lemuel Shaw among those who failed his own ideals, along with men such as Webster, who was Shaw's lifelong friend and associate, and Everett, for he writes in his *Journal*, "What a moment was lost when Judge Shaw declined to affirm the unconstitutionality of the Fugitive Slave Law!"—alluding to the Sims case in April 1851. [12]

Concurrently with his privately expressed views Emerson carried his antislavery attitudes with him on the public platform during the winter lecture season in 1854–55, when, according to the editors of his *Journal* for this period, Susan Smith and Harrison Hayford, he took only two lectures to present to the public—both on slavery. One was the address of 3 May 1851, first given to the citizens of Concord in response to the Fugitive Slave Law, and the other first given in January 1855, entitled "American Slavery." In the first he is emphatic concerning the basely self-interested motives of the Massachusetts magistrates, judges, and government officials who upheld the law and enforced it, seeing in their acts only "party feeling" and "monied interests." He denies that Webster had any honor or moral perception and throws out a challenge to the judges of his state to "feel the spirit of Coke or Mansfield or Parsons to read the law with the eye of freedom."[13] Although he did not repeat this exclusive emphasis upon current political matters in the 1855–56 season, yet anyone aware of Emerson as a public lecturer probably would be aware by this time of his anti-Southern animus and of his strong criticisms of the Massachusetts political and legal figures who had upheld enforcement of the Fugitive Slave Law in that state in the famous cases of Shadrach, Sims, and Burns. After the caning of Sumner in late May Emerson spoke again on the public platform in his address, "The Assault upon Mr. Sumner, Speech . . . in Concord, May 26, 1856," and again in September at a Kansas Relief meeting in Cambridge, where he claimed that in that conflict, "All the right is on one side." He supported Kansas relief by attending the meetings in aid of it in Concord, gave liberally to the cause, and spoke there and elsewhere when called upon. Evidently he favored the Republican party, for he was appointed as alternate delegate to the Republican convention, and his friend Whittier urged him to go in place of George Boutwell, former Democrat and "Coalition" governor of Massachusetts.[14] Presumably, Emerson favored Frémont in the November election. Likewise presumable, then, is that he would favor the activities of men such as Beecher in speaking for the Republican cause, even though he did not choose himself to campaign, having long ago decided to leave that kind of public activity to other men. Hence, it appears from the evidence that there is nothing in Emerson's expressed attitudes that would contradict and much that is consonant with his being the model for a figure who appears to admire and trust Frank Goodman, a character identifiable with the antislavery preacher Beecher, and who distrusts Charlie Noble, one identifiable with the proslavery Alabaman Yancey, and who distrusts and rejects the Crazy Beggar, identifiable with the proslavery Virginian Edgar Allan Poe.

As for Emerson's attitude toward Beecher personally there is some evidence. In February of 1855 he heard Beecher lecture on "Patriotism" and described him in a letter as "admirable for his sense, & his aims, and not less, for his health," adding—perhaps with a touch of envy—"He has the vigor of ten men." In his *Journal* for 1852–55 he listed Beecher along with Greeley, Parker, and Horace Mann as "our four powerful men in the virtuous class in this country."[15] These four are the men that he trusted and admired in public life; and it is remarkable that two of them—the Republican leaders Greeley and Parker—are the models for two of the disguises in which the Confidence Man appears in Melville's book prior to the time when he appears in his last guise, in which he is a caricature of Beecher, the third of the four men.

Lastly, Winsome's trust and admiration of his disciple Egbert clearly alludes to and represents Emerson's relationship to his friend and admirer Henry David Thoreau. Thoreau's pronounced antislavery views will be evidenced later in this chapter and Winsome-Emerson's relationship to Crazy Beggar-Poe discussed in the following section.

Crazy Beggar-Poe

Midway in chapter 36, while Goodman and the mystic Mark Winsome converse, the Crazy Beggar appears "peddling a rhapsodical tract," which Goodman buys (but does not read) and Winsome scorns to purchase because he never "patronizes scoundrels" (p. 219). Harrison Hayford has shown with conclusive evidence in "Poe in *The Confidence-Man*," that the Beggar is a caricature of Edgar Allan Poe (1809–1849), the Southern poet and critic. The Beggar's action tests the real humanity of each of the other men, and in doing so forms in the historical context a part of Melville's commentary upon Emerson's attitude toward the South as revealed in his relationships with two representative Southerners and upon Beecher's attitude toward Southerners. Although I have little to add to Hayford's citations of contemporary descriptions of Poe's appearance and personality and their reflection in the description of the Beggar, I would like to amplify his discussion of the meaning of the Beggar's relationship to Winsome and Goodman.

Hayford notes the Beggar's similarity to Poe in his "slenderness," his broad brow, his "raven" hair, his paleness, his "buttoned-up frockcoat," his refined and gentlemanly manner despite poverty, his air of "dethronement," his "haggardness," his "inspired" look, and his pride—all details reflected in contemporary observations of Poe. Likewise, he parallels with good reason the Beggar's "rhapsodical tract . . . setting forth his claims to some rhapsodical apostleship" to Poe's ambitious pseudophilosophical prose poem *Eureka,* which he read in an "inspired" manner in New York in 1848 according to one observer. [16] Small details that may be added to those cited by Hayford are that Rufus Griswold, Poe's inimical and mendacious biographer, mentions in his obituary notice of Poe in the *Tribune* in 1849 Poe's "tattered frockcoat" (identical to the Beggar's "tattered . . . frock-coat") and that after an interview he was sent to a bath from which he returned a "gentleman," implying that Poe was "dirty" as the Beggar is. Likewise, Poe's hair was apparently curly, as is shown in his portrait in Arthur Hobson Quinn's *Edgar Allen Poe,* resembling the Beggar's "raven curls."[17] Although not every detail of Melville's cameo caricature is thus far traceable to contemporary sources, the allusion to Poe is as unmistakable as that of Winsome to Emerson.

Seeking the historical context of Winsome-Emerson's attitude toward Beggar-Poe, Hayford recalls Poe's career-long quarrel with the Boston literary and intellectual world ("Frogpondium" as he called it), his "Boston reading fiasco" of 1845, and his sharp critique of the Transcendentalists, yet does not see any reason why Melville would "saddle Emerson with any of the onus of all this." He notes Emerson's remark about Poe to William Dean Howells in 1860 in which he referred to Poe as "the jingle man." To his account of the Emerson-Poe differences should be added Emerson's remarks to Woodbury that Poe had "an uncommon facility for rhyme, a happy jingle," "that Forceythe Wilson was a better poet," and that Poe "might have become much had he been capable of self-direction."[18]

To understand this encounter it is significant that Melville first notices in the Beggar that he has "one glimmering peep of reason," despite his palpable craziness, and then has Winsome-Emerson reject his solicitations precisely for this personal trait—which Winsome terms "a damning peep of sense" and claims is "damning [because] sense in a seeming madman is scoundrelism" (pp. 219–20). Again, Griswold's obituary sketch, which did more even than Poe's own notorious bad habits to create an unfortunate public image of him, may form some background for Melville's caricature. Griswold attributed to Poe a "shrewd" character and "sharp" intellect, which, he claimed, Poe was incapable of using in any practical way to help himself get ahead in the New York literary world. Winsome's rejection of the Beggar for the combination of a "peep of sense" or "reason" with apparent madness is probably intended simply to make the ironic point that Winsome is rejecting a character who actually resembles himself in his combination of the "mystical" and the "practical" but who is remarkably less successful at doing so. It may not be irrelevant, additionally, to recall that Amos Bronson Alcott, whom Emerson called a "capuchin or divine mendicant," was a most improvident man and perhaps the most mad-seeming of Emerson's Transcendentalist friends. He might well qualify as a madman in the pure state— with no "damning peep of sense." Emerson repeatedly helped Alcott financially and sponsored a fund-raising event for him and his family.[19] Melville may, then, be alluding to Emerson's sympathetic attitude toward Alcott in contrast with his unsympathetic one toward Poe.

Another possibility as background for Winsome's rejection of the Beggar may be that Melville saw Emerson the optimist rejecting Poe the pessimist. Hubbell writes that Poe had "little sympathy with reformers" and was "too much the pessimist to share the optimism of Emerson and Lowell." He became almost a symbol during his lifetime of the man who saw habitually the dark side of nature and life, especially through the fame of the publications of and his readings of "The Raven," a poem in which the central figure is a "croaker" or bird of melancholy and woe. Moreover, Poe became after his death in 1849, especially through Griswold's scandalous obituary, the archetypal melancholy and distrustful man. Griswold wrote that Poe felt he was already "damned," always bore a "controlling sorrow," and that "harsh experience had deprived him of all faith in man or woman."[20] Poe's posthumous public image makes him not only an excellent representative of the "no-trust" side of the argument in *The Confidence-Man* but also in the historical context a fitting exponent of the view of nature and man for which Emerson's philosophy had no use.

Another not impossibly relevant element in the background of the Emerson-Poe confrontation may be Poe's published critique of Emerson, which may well have added to Emerson's distrust of the Southerner. Poe disposed of him in a condescending tone as one of "a class of gentleman with whom we have no patience whatever—the mystic for mysticism's sake," in his series of critical paragraphs called "Autography" in *Graham's Magazine* (1841–42). Poe continues in the same tone:

> Quintilian mentions a pedant who taught obscurity, and who once said to a pupil 'This is excellent, for I do not understand it myself.' How the good man would have chuckled over Mr. E.! His present *role* seems to be the out-Carlyling Carlyle. *Lycophron Tenebrosus* is a fool to him. The best answer to his twaddle is *cui bono?*—. . . to whom is it a benefit? If not to Mr. Emerson individually, then surely to no man living.

After praising briefly Emerson's "composition of occasional poems in which beauty *is* apparent *by flashes,*" he comments upon his handwriting that it is "bad, sprawling, illegible and irregular—although sufficiently bold," and that "this latter trait may be and no doubt is, only a portion of his general affectation."[21] Melville has just prior to the entrance of the Beggar been satirizing Emerson as a pedantic Dottore, as a "mystic," as pretentious and obscure, and as imitative of Carlyle, sharing apparently for the sake of his literary intentions in *The Confidence-Man* Poe's view of Emerson's limitations.

Finally, perhaps the simplest explanation for the rejection of Crazy Beggar-Poe by Winsome-Emerson is that Melville, observing the strong New England sectional bias against the South in Emerson, as revealed in his antislavery speeches, attributed to this bias his dislike and rejection of Poe as a man, a poet and a Southerner. Jay Hubbell in *The South in American Literature* chooses Emerson to illustrate the extent to which sectional controversy and bias kept the New England writers from understanding antebellum Southern literature. Noting that Emerson, at least, had seen something of the South during a visit for his health to Charleston and St. Augustine in 1826–27, he goes on to discuss Emerson's change from an early strongly expressed dislike of reformers—including abolitionists—to a virulent distrust of the slaveholding South. He writes that "the serene and philosophic Emerson was swept along by the tide exactly like lesser men." By the time of the Sumner-Brooks caning Emerson considered the South "a barbarous community," where "life is a fever, man is an animal, given to pleasure, frivolous, irritable, spending his days in hunting and practising with deadly weapons to defend himself against his slaves and against his companions brought up in the same idle and dangerous way." He came to accept, Hubbell adds, "the Abolitionist legend of a barbarous South." Yet apparently Emerson did not denounce in public individual Southerners except Brooks, and he gave them credit for courage.[22] Still, Winsome-Emerson's distrust of Crazy Beggar-Poe is consonant with my interpretation of the overall pattern of Melville's satire within the historical context of the sectional controversy. By 1856 Emerson, as a New Englander, had come to distrust and hate Southerners (and their Northern sympathizers) despite his professed belief in the natural divinity and goodness of mankind. He was inconsistent in his attitudes. Unlike Beecher who could hate the sin and yet love the sinner, Emerson hated the sinner on principle when he saw evidence of the sin; hence, Poe like Yancey would fall under the ban of his exclusion.

The Beggar is the second of three figures who appear on the *Fidèle* (the first being Charlie Noble and the third the Juvenile Peddler in the last chapter), who perform a function like that of the Confidence Men themselves: they wish to win confidence—to sell themselves or their ideas. In this function they set up a counterpoint to the Confidence Men and represent, I believe, Melville's depiction of the roles of certain Southern men on the national stage as seekers of trust for their point of view. The point of view represented is that of the belief in the irreducible evil in the nature of man. Yancey held this view deeply, as did Poe, whom Baudelaire praised for his affirmation of the natural wickedness of man, and as did Henry Wise of Virginia, probably caricatured as the Juvenile Peddler (see Chapter 12). The distrust of mankind adumbrated in the sign hung up publicly by the Barber in the first scene of the book and which motivates such Southern and Southwestern figures as Titan-Calhoun and Pitch-Benton emerges fully as the motivating force in the caricatures of Noble-Yancey, Crazy Beggar-Poe and Juvenile-Wise. They do not merely respond to the Confidence Men's solicitations as do the previously introduced antagonists, but they actively *solicit* confidence in return from the Confidence Men themselves and from other Northern and Western figures such as Winsome-Emerson and Old Man-McLean. Noble-Yancey deliberately tries to sell himself as a friend and boon companion to Goodman, just as Yancey tried to sell his view of Southern rights to Northern minds; Crazy Beggar-Poe approaches both Goodman and Winsome in an effort to sell his tracts to them, just as Poe tried to establish himself as a writer with something important to say to Northern minds; and the Juvenile Peddler-Wise enters the cabin and tries to sell his useful products to Goodman and the Comely Old Man (see Chapter 12), just as Wise and other Southern politicians tried to retain their power in the North by bargaining through the party system.

Egbert the Disciple

The character Egbert (chapters 37–41) has especially puzzled readers for fifty years, ever since Egbert Oliver first suggested that it was a caricature of Henry David Thoreau (1817–1862), Massachusetts poet, naturalist, and Transcendentalist. Certain elements of Egbert's description and dialogue have seemed to him and to other readers to point to Thoreau as model. However, Elizabeth Foster and others have dissented from this identification. Foster offers her judgment, in an excellent discussion of Emersonian thought in the introduction to her edition of *The Confidence-Man,* that Winsome and Egbert represent respectively Emerson's "metaphysics" (his "abstract philosophy") and his "ethics" (its "practical effect"), and that Melville was dramatizing in these two characters the dualism in Emerson's work which had been commented on from Lowell's *A Fable for Critics* (1848) to the present. In her notes she disputes Oliver's identification of Egbert with Thoreau, noting that Thoreau's usual appearance was quite the opposite of Egbert's, whom Melville describes as a "well-dressed, commercial-looking gentleman" (p. 222). This latter point is one of several stumbling blocks in associating Egbert with Thoreau. Hershel Parker generally supports the connection of Egbert with Thoreau, citing additional evidence of points of contact—literary and personal—between him and Melville, including those by way of Evert Duyckinck, Horace Greeley, Hawthorne and *Putnam's.* [23]

Besides those that Oliver notices there are several more resemblances of Thoreau to Egbert. Significant details cited by him are that Egbert is introduced as a "promenader," perhaps an allusion to Thoreau's habits of walking and hiking; that he is characterized as a "disciple of Winsome several times (including in the title of chapter 38), clearly an allusion to the common public view of Thoreau as a disciple of Emerson; that Egbert is about fifteen years younger than his "master" (thirty to the latter's forty-five), just as

Thoreau was about fifteen years younger than Emerson; that his "costume seemed modeled upon his master's," just as Thoreau's, according to Franklin Sanborn, appeared modeled upon Emerson's; and lastly that Egbert's conception of friendship resembles remarkably Thoreau's as expressed in the section on friendship in "Wednesday," in his *A Week on the Concord and Merrimack Rivers* (1849). To these may be added others. Just as Egbert seems "lithely to shoot up erect . . . like one of those wire men from a toy snuffbox," so was Thoreau characterized by his erect posture. George F. Hoar in his *Autobiography* writes that he was called "Trainer Thoreau" by the boys of Concord because he "had an erect carriage which made him seem something like a soldier." The role of the "practical disciple" of the "mystical master" Winsome-Emerson seems more applicable to Thoreau than to any other of Emerson's numerous followers. Emerson said of him that he gave him "in flesh and blood and pertinacious Saxon belief . . . my own ethics." Like Egbert's "shaved chin," Thoreau's was "clean shaved" most of his life, according to his biographer Joseph Wood Krutch, although late in life he grew a beard to keep his throat warm. Although Melville does not use the adjective "shrewd," he suggests this trait in Egbert when he describes his face as showing "something" that hints that he might put even so "profitless" a thing as mysticism to profitable account; Thoreau's friend Franklin Sanborn, in his biography, observes that Thoreau's face reminded him of "some shrewd and honest animal's . . . woodchuck or fox."[24]

More important as suggesting that Egbert caricatures Thoreau is Melville's emphasis upon the imitativeness of his dress, which "seemed modeled upon his master's" (p. 255) and of his voice—which, when he speaks, sounds as if his master speaks through him as a "ventriloquist" (p. 252). Sanborn in his biography observes of Thoreau: "In his tones and gestures he seemed to me to imitate Emerson, so that it was annoying to listen to him," adding that he "looks like Emerson, too—coarser, but with something of that serenity and sagacity which E. has." In his *Recollections* Sanborn quotes another observer, Ednah Littlehale, as remarking that Thoreau by 1848, when he was thirty, was "all overlaid by an imitation of Emerson; talks like him, puts out his arms like him, brushes his hair in the same way, and is even getting up a caricature nose like Emerson's." Woodbury , speaking of Emerson's powerful personality, writes that "Thoreau felt the perilous singling [out] until his mode of speaking and tones caught the trick of Emerson's so nearly that the two men could hardly be separated in conversation." In sum, as Emerson's twentieth-century biographer Walter Harding writes, his contemporaries "thought of Thoreau not only as a disciple but also as an imitator of Emerson. . . . It was a bugbear Thoreau had to live with for the rest of his days," which hurt his reputation severely.[25]

Winsome's emphasis on Egbert's "discipleship" and his "glancing upon him paternally" seem, also, to have as context a quality in the Emerson-Thoreau relationship that Woodbury describes thus: "Of no one did Mr. Emerson talk so often and tenderly. . . . Emerson made Thoreau; he was the child of Emerson, as if of his own flesh." Emerson, he writes, called him "my Henry Thoreau" until "the disciple became as his master, adopting his accent and form, realizing his attractions and antipathies and knowing his good and evil." Woodbury continues: "Thoreau was the more concentrated and sinewy of the two; and, once beginning to carry out the parent's discipline and thought into his own life, he was uncompromising." Egbert as "practical" disciple seems clearly to be a caricature of this paternal-filial aspect of Thoreau's career. Moreover, it is interesting that the coldheartedness that Melville chose to depict in both men and summarizes in Goodman's final comment on their "frozen natures," Emerson himself saw as a fault in Thoreau (as well as in himself) when he commented, according to Woodbury, that "his fault was that he brought nothing near to his heart." John Weiss, a Harvard contemporary, writes dryly of Thoreau, after his death, that he was "cold and unimpressable" and that his face "lacked affectional emotions" and that although he could meditate well on friendship, he "soon learned to do without friends." Lastly, Egbert's "inconsistency" in first asserting man's freedom of "will" and then man's determination by "some chance tip of Fate's elbow in throwing her dice" (p. 251)—which "amazes and shocks" Goodman—has its context in Thoreau's own inconsistency of thought, as well as in Emerson's notorious remark on "a foolish consistency" as the "hobgoblin of little minds" in *Self-Reliance*. Harding speaks of Thoreau's essential eclecticism, noting that he changed his mind as he grew older and never unified his thought. [26]

Additional personal traits that suggest Thoreau as Egbert's model are the following. Although Melville does not use the adjectives "brusque" or "disputatious," Egbert reveals qualities that may be so characterized in his conversations with Goodman. Thoreau was described by Emerson as "brusque in manner" and "pugnacious" about trifles. Sanborn in *Recollections* speaks of his "background of pugnacity and disputation." Another trait, Egbert's claim that he never accepts loans seems reflected in Thoreau's claim that he refused ever to "be indebted to any person pecuniarily," as recorded by Sanborn. Again, Egbert displays a quality of sharp, uncharitable assessment of self and others that appears reflected in Thoreau as observed by Emerson: he "had a great contempt for those who made no effort to gauge accurately their own powers and weaknesses," and he cites as a *bon mot* of Thoreau's his remark, "Good heart, weak head." Likewise Egbert shows a self-centered, unyielding, unsympathetic, negative rigidity in his response to Goodman which seems related to the egotism noted by many in Thoreau and characterized by Sophia

Hawthorne as "arrogance of manner," and by Hawthorne, himself, who knew Thoreau intimately, as an "iron-pokerishness—an uncompromising stiffness,—in his mental character." Hawthorne saw him as the "most unmalleable fellow alive—the most tedious, tiresome, and intolerable . . . the narrowest and most notional." Again, Henry James, Sr., after meeting him described him as "the most childlike, unconscious and unblushing egotist it has ever been my fortune to encounter." Emerson in his funeral oration said of Thoreau that, "It cost him nothing to say No." Likewise, just as Goodman finds no pity in Egbert's response to his appeal when he plays the role of a lifelong friend in their "hypothetical case," so R. L. Stevenson found "no trace of pity" and "constitutional indifference" in Thoreau's works. Lastly, some of Egbert's sardonic humor, as revealed in the remark, for example, "Are you a centaur?" (p. 230) in the exchange with Goodman, may be a reflection of a similar quality in Thoreau, as noted by his biographer Canby.[27]

As for style, one of the few similarities of Egbert's to Thoreau's is Egbert's long monologue in which he tells the story of China Aster, since apparently Thoreau, according to Canby, had a "habit of lecturing his friends in monologues" which was derived from his loquacious mother.[28] I am inclined to think that the interpolated tale is part of Egbert's overall characterization within the theatrical convention of the stage Yankee, for, as recorded in stage histories, the Yankee was given to long, rather dry, storytelling.

Despite the many details that point to Thoreau as the subject of the satire in the figure of Egbert, there are several stumbling blocks to asserting with certainty that this is the correct interpretation. First, Egbert's role as a "thriving young merchant, a practical poet in the West India trade" (p. 224), which is anticipated by his description as "a well-dressed, commercial-looking gentleman" (p. 222), simply does not square with any contemporary observations of Thoreau's appearance and personality that present research has unearthed, while nearly all descriptions reveal quite the opposite public view of his role and general sartorial appearance. Thoreau seldom or never could be described as "well-dressed" as Egbert is, for apparently during most of his life he was dressed in very practical and rough clothing suitable for outdoor work or for walking, hiking or boating. Sanborn writes that "the fashion of his garments gave him no concern, and was often old, or even grotesque." As seen by W. D. Howells he wore "fashionless trousers being let down too low" and wore "homespun." This aspect of his costume conflicts with that of Egbert's, even while the fact that his "costume seemed modeled upon his master's" does seem to allude to Thoreau's copying of Emerson's dress, as recorded by Sanborn and cited by Oliver. More conflicting still is the fact that Thoreau's public role as a writer and speaker was anti-commercial on principle. Hawthorne saw him at about twenty-five as having "much of wild original nature still remaining in him" and as repudiating "all regular modes of getting a living," while Stevenson wrote of his attitudes that "nothing, indeed, can surpass his scorn for all so-called business," a view that is borne out by nearly every observation on his career, by his letters, and by his published work. He was notably inept in the commercialization of his writing. Further, none of the qualities that Hawthorne notes in him of desiring to lead "a sort of Indian life," or his "keen and delicate" observation of and intimacy with nature, or his "deep and true taste for poetry" are apparent in Egbert. On Thoreau's capacity for true friendship—almost as if in contradiction of Melville's satirical characterization—Channing, his lifelong friend, said of him that he "meant friendship, and meant nothing else, and stood by it without abatement, not veering as a weather cock with each shift of a friend's fortune."[29] A last personal detail that does not point to Thoreau is Egbert's age, which is twice mentioned as "about thirty" (pp. 222, 225); Thoreau would be about thirty-nine in 1856.

Perhaps an even more powerful indication that Egbert may not caricature Thoreau is his speaking style (leaving aside his narration of the China Aster story—the style of which he disclaims, p. 233). Egbert speaks in a brisk, "business-like," plain manner. He uses very blunt, short sentences, with very little sensory imagery, and a dry hard wit. Among the few metaphors he uses are those of an "old man and a cow," of the "ocean" and a "wader," and of a railroad train. His only literary references are to Solomon's *Proverbs,* to Winsome's "Essay on Friendship," and to Shakespeare's *As You Like It.* He relates the moralistic tale of China Aster. In strong contrast, Thoreau's written style is a carefully molded, consciously artistic one, employing the Emersonian habit of stringing together asyndetically sentences that express a single intuition or perception. It is condensed, elliptical—frequently to the point of obscurity—dense with connotative language, and "nutty"—to use Thoreau's own word about it. He cultivated a mannerism of turning commonplaces on end in order to surprise or shock the reader or merely to appear original—a habit criticized by Emerson as a "trick of rhetoric . . . of substituting for the obvious word and thought its diametrical opposite."[30] His prose is especially rich in sensory observations used descriptively and as metaphors, in references to all aspects of the natural world which forms his principal subject, and in analogies between man and nature. His literary references are to a remarkably wide range of literature (both verse and prose), religion, and philosophy—especially the oriental—and show his considerable learning. Whether one examines the works published in 1849 (which would include *A Week*) or by 1856 (which would include *Walden*), these general traits of his style are present. Melville does not seem concerned at all to parody that style, which he would be presumed to be—consistently with the other caricatures in *The Confidence-Man*—if indeed Egbert were meant as a caricature of Thoreau.

My efforts to find a model for Egbert, applying the same methods of identification as I have used in all the other figures in *The Confidence-Man*, have not, then, conclusively confirmed Oliver's original suggestion, but they have not yet yielded any better candidate among Emerson's circle of friends and followers. He had many disciples, among them, for example, William Ellery Channing (1818–1901), of whom Hawthorne writes in his *Notebooks*: "He is one of those queer and clever young men whom Mr. Emerson . . . is continually picking up by way of a genius."[31] He had close personal friends in business or the professions, who were "thriving"—men such as George P. Bradford, John Murray Forbes, Abel Adams, and Samuel G. Ward. However, despite considerable research into these and other possibilities, no better candidate than Thoreau has emerged and it has proven necessary for the time being to base my interpretation of the chapters involving Egbert on the hypothesis that he is a highly distorted caricature of Thoreau—perhaps one based on a personal impression or on a second hand, "inside," impression of him.[32] Such an impression might have derived, perhaps, from Thoreau's and Melville's friend Hawthorne or from Duyckinck, or might, perhaps, be based on impressions left in New York City literary circles by Thoreau during his brief stay on Staten Island May through December 1845, when he lived with Emerson's brother and tried to establish himself in a literary career in New York. This hypothesis assumes that Melville for some unknown reason chose not to parody Thoreau's written style and leaves open the possibility that there may have been some grounds for Egbert's style of speech in Thoreau's personal manner of speaking or lecturing.

A major question to answer is this: Why does Melville caricature Thoreau, if Egbert be intended to allude to him, as a "thriving young merchant . . . in the West India trade," when Thoreau's character and thought were directly opposed to trade and to business, and the only commercial activity of his life was his development of a new pencil that enabled his family's graphite and pencil business to survive and prosper? Is Melville saying that, given Thoreau's temperament, he should have been a merchant? Is he illustrating the "practical" aspect of Thoreauvian-Emersonian thought by caricaturing Thoreau as a merchant (even knowing he was a writer and amateur naturalist), saying by implication that the practicality of his thought would permit him to be—should he want to be—a thriving merchant in trade? The caricatures of the protagonists in *The Confidence-Man* usually make sense in that the fictional role chosen by which to satirize the historical person fits his or her historical role. For example, Bryant the poet of graveyards and death, is appropriately caricatured as a "man in mourning"; Parker, the abolitionist preacher, as a

charity soliciter and projector; Weed, the political power broker, as a commercial broker; Sumner, the idealistic statesman, as a seller of herbal remedies;
Greeley, the newspaper editor and political entrepreneur, as an employment
agent, and so on. Likewise those of the antagonists usually fit their historical
roles. For example, Douglas, the popular politician, as a gregarious barber;
Blair, the rich old journalist, as a rich old man; or Lawrence, the millionaire
textile magnate, as a rich planter (a "Lord of the Loom," as a "Lord of the
Lash"). In nearly all cases Melville seems to be using the fictional role as an
appropriate metaphor for what he thinks the real activity of the historical
person is. That is, he uses it as a means of satirical characterization of the
man or woman's actual public function. He presents them in the traditional
satirical way as worse than they are—but similar—in order to draw attention
to their vices. However, in the instance of Egbert, there seems to be no
similar relationship between the fictional role of a merchant and Thoreau's
public role, which, so far as the usual view goes, was that of a fairly unconventional litterateur—the Hermit of Walden Pond—and critic of society—
even a Diogenes—particularly of its commercial activities. Of other writers
of this period (one thinks of men such as Nathaniel Parker Willis and women
such as Lydia Sigourney) one might say that he or she "traded" in literary
skills and productions, but Thoreau by all accounts was notably lacking in
the ability to commercialize his literary work. His early essays were poorly
paid for, his *Week on the Concord and Merrimack Rivers* sold so badly that he
had to repurchase most of the edition from his publisher, and *Walden* was
only a moderate success. It does not seem likely that he could have been
regarded by Melville as a "thriving young merchant" in the writing trade. If
Egbert alludes to Thoreau, what kind of "trade," then, could Melville be
satirizing?

Lecturing was for Thoreau apparently no more financially successful than
writing, yet he might have been regarded by some as a successful seller of
antislavery convictions. There is the remote possibility that "West India trade"
might mean propagandizing the issue of emancipation. The British emancipation in 1833 of their West Indian slaves was constantly held up to
Americans by the antislavery societies as an incitement to shame for the
existence of Southern slavery. Emerson's address in 1844, "On the Anniversary
of the Emancipation of the Negroes in the British West Indies," which
Thoreau aided in publicizing by ringing a church bell in Concord and later
in getting it published, achieved considerable renown. Thoreau's own antislavery views were well known through his letter of praise of Nathaniel P.
Rogers, who was editor of the antislavery periodical *Herald of Freedom,* published in the *Dial* in 1843–44; through his letter to Garrison on "Wendell
Phillips before the Concord Lyceum," published in the *Liberator* in 1845;

through his refusal to pay his poll tax and subsequent jailing in 1846; and through his Concord lyceum lecture in 1848 on "The Relationship of the Individual to the State" (published in 1849 as "Resistance to Civil Government"). On 4 July 1854, he spoke on "Slavery in Massachusetts," protesting the arrest of Burns and his return to Virginia. Though it may be only a remote possibility, yet I can offer no other or better solution presently to the problem of the caricaturing of Thoreau as a "merchant in the West India trade" than the suggestion that Melville in selecting the fictional role by which to satirize Thoreau saw him very narrowly as a significant and successful lecturer and writer in the antislavery movement—a "merchandizer" of humanitarian and abolitionist views, and that he chose to ignore Thoreau's lecturing and writing on other subjects—with the exception of the topic of friendship. His views on friendship—expressed in the long digression in *A Week*—Melville evidently chose to single out as caricaturable, not only as derivative of Emerson's view of the subject but also as a narrowly self-serving view of human relations which he believed characteristic of Thoreau. The suggestion that I am making here, strange as it may seem to us at this late day, is that Melville, for the satirical purposes of *The Confidence-Man,* focused upon Thoreau as a professional seller of benevolent ideas—under the metaphor of a merchant in "the West India trade"—whose "goods" (antislavery benevolent notions) are manifestly contradicted by his personal practice, which he justifies by a rarefied (Transcendental) theory of friendship that precludes by its logic ever giving "help" to a friend. I cannot at this time suggest any better solution to the problems that the hypothesis that Egbert is a caricature of Thoreau presents.

After being introduced by Winsome to Goodman, Egbert, as Melville's thirty-eighth chapter title tells the reader, "Unbends and Consents to Act a Social Part"—the title itself apparently a comic comment on Thoreau's stiff posture and social exclusiveness. His encounter with Goodman-Beecher is complicated by the fact that it exists on two levels. On the first Egbert simply accepts Goodman as an acquaintance of his master, whom he has been asked to instruct in the practical applications of Winsome's philosophy. On the second he deals with Goodman only as Goodman enacts the fictional role of "Frank," the childhood friend of himself (in the role of "Charlie"), in their dramatization of a "hypothetical case." Within their little playlet Egbert-Thoreau is asked to treat Goodman-Beecher as he would treat a childhood friend who had lost all his wealth and needed financial help. What is revealed by this device is that in Winsome-Emerson's philosophy true friendship can subsist only between financial equals. When this equality disappears friendship does too. As a satirical comment on the Emersonian-Thoreauvian concept of friendship this seems fairly clear if somewhat stringent. The political applications in the historical context are less easily available to us; yet the general pattern of *The Confidence-Man* would suggest that they are there.

What seems to be happening is that Goodman-Beecher, who is the representative of evangelical love entering political action as a speaker for the Republican party, is testing the charitable responses of a dry egotistic New England "practical" Transcendentalist, who should be, in the historical context, ostensibly on the same side—that of the antislavery cause. Goodman-Beecher has just found out in the encounter with Winsome-Emerson that he personally is acceptable—on aesthetic grounds—to Winsome, while Beggar-Poe, a Southerner, is not and is rejected. In this second test of a typical New Englander, by means of the hypothetical case of childhood friends—where one might most of all expect acceptance and trust—he finds that Egbert-Thoreau, the practical and "commercial" side of New England character, will not treat as a friend (love or consider as a spiritual equal) any man who is not his equal financially. Melville is contrasting Beecher's profession of warm, all-embracing humanitarianism and his message of universal charity with Thoreau's version of transcendental friendship—a selfish, self-reliant egotism, as evidently he saw it manifest in Thoreau. Egbert's negative response to Goodman's plea is consonant, moreover, with Thoreau's refusal to participate in party politics, even when the new Republican party came to represent the antislavery cause. Unlike Emerson, who did descend to political action for the Free-Soil party in 1852 and favored the Republicans in 1856, Thoreau did not join any antislavery societies or any political party whatever, distrusting as he did all organizations of church or state. According to Krutch, "he never lost his distrust of organized movements."[33] His individualistic eschewal of any government whatever is, one may hazard the interpretation, satirized as the heartless, worldly, self-interested and self-protective wisdom of Egbert.

12

The Cosmopolitan and His Final Antagonists (the Barber, the Clean Comely Old Man, the Juvenile Peddler, and the Irish Voice)

William Cream the Barber (Second Appearance)

The Cosmopolitan Frank Goodman holds the stage for twenty chapters, encountering eight major characters and dominating thus nearly the entire latter half of *The Confidence-Man*. In relationship to the other characters both in conversation and in action he functions generally as the representative of the moral and religious sentiment of trust in mankind that Melville saw fueling the antislavery movement as it emerged into mass political action in the formation of the sectional Republican party. The scenes in which he converses with Winsome-Emerson and with Egbert-Thoreau should be interpreted generally as commentary upon the relationships of the Republican political faith—the Confidence Man's consistent role—to the New England Transcendentalist intellectual movement. Cosmopolitan-Beecher, possibly because of Beecher's innately social temperament, appears as consistently loyal to his philanthropic principles, while the Yankee Transcendentalists are revealed as inconsistent—if not hypocritical—in their espousal of humanitarian views which they do not apply in practice. The implications of Winsome-Emerson's distrust of Noble-Yancey and of Beggar-Poe seem to be that while a man like Beecher would be faithful as a "Good Man" to his professed doctrine of charity, even toward the Southerners Yancey and Poe, Emerson and Thoreau, professed believers in the natural divinity of man and its humanitarian implications, really confine acting on that belief to the narrow scope of acceptable New England friends, denying the natural bond of benevolence with Yancey and with Poe, or with anyone who is not a financial and spiritual equal.

It has not yet been possible to establish in the historical context of Beecher's career and writings any personal relationship to Yancey or to Poe, on the one hand, or to Emerson or Thoreau on the other, which might disclose a specific topical context for Goodman's dealings with Noble and the Beggar and with Winsome and Egbert. Is there, for example, a specific historical context for the fact that Goodman-Beecher accepts Beggar-Poe's tract and gives him a coin? Evidently, he pities him as a poor man, although he does not read the tract, only promising to do so later. It is possible that Beecher in the *Independent* or even in a lecture (not likely in a sermon) spoke some kind words about Poe or about his works, but as yet I have found no connection between the two on a personal basis. Nor have I yet found what he may have said or done in relation personally to Yancey, Emerson, or Thoreau.

In the context of the sectional controversy, it seems likely that Beecher did not hold the same kind of moralistic repugnance for the slaveholding Southerner that Emerson did. Goodman is benignly sympathetic to Noble-Yancey, establishes a "boon companionship" of wine and cigars—symbolic of a political relationship with him—and then by playing the game of asking for a loan of fifty dollars he sees through Noble's pretentions and reveals Noble's self-interest at the same time as he displays his own financial superiority. Likewise, with Beggar-Poe, whom he does not test in the same way as Noble, he appears benign, buys his tract—as an act of charity—and thereby lives up to his own professed humanitarian principles, but he does not bother to read it. Again, Goodman-Beecher appears kind to a Southern figure, his tolerance being contrasted with Winsome-Emerson's unkind rejection of Beggar-Poe. His amused observation of Winsome and less amused testing of Egbert in order to reveal to the reader the heartless practical implications of Winsome-Emerson's Transcendental philosophy seem to indicate that Beecher was viewed by Melville as superior in humanity and Christian love to both Emerson and Thoreau. It does not appear to mean, however, that Beecher is any less dangerous to the American political community than the other two men, only that he is more consistent with his own professed humanitarianism and is, besides, a man of an entirely different temperament.

Similarly, in the two chapters (42–43) following those in which Goodman encounters the two Transcendentalists, there seems to be no direct public connection, so far as my present research goes, between Beecher and Stephen A. Douglas, who, caricatured as the Barber, reappears in an encounter with Goodman in the barbershop of the *Fidèle*. As discussed earlier in Chapter 4, the Barber's initial skepticism and concluding distrust of Goodman, which sandwich his "magically" induced episode of trust in the middle of the scene, reflect the basically skeptical attitude of Douglas toward the antislavery movement generally and his animosity toward Northern political preachers specifically after their attack upon him and his Kansas-Nebraska Bill in 1854–55. It is possible that further research may reveal some particular newspaper altercation or a platform confrontation between Douglas and Beecher, overlooked in the sources that I have presently consulted, which would be the specific topical context of the Beecher-Douglas scene.

With reference to the more general historical context, I suggest that the differing attitudes of North and South on the interpretation of the Constitution and the extended dialogue in speeches and print on the slavery question form the specific historical context to which Melville is alluding in his depiction of their temporary establishment of an "agreement" according to which the Barber will "trust" Goodman and other customers for the price of a shave—an agreement which Goodman subsequently repudiates. It is possible, if the reader takes the Barber here to represent the Southern point of view— as Douglas frequently did—that his entering into the written agreement with Goodman alludes to the formation of the contractual obligations between the states that occurred in the writing of the Constitution. If so, it would appear that Melville in this suggestive scene is commenting upon the Southern assertion that the Northern states had broken their contract with the South in the refusal of some of them to carry out the provisions of the Constitution as the South interpreted those provisions. The refusal of certain Northern states to accept and enforce the Fugitive Slave Law was read by many conservative Whigs and Democrats in both North and South as a repudiation of their Constitutional obligations and hence as implying the release of the Southern partners from the obligations on their part to the contract. If Melville is alluding to this political-legal context, then Goodman's cavalier dismissal of his obligations and of the agreement—interpreting it as he pleases—would allude to the Southern accusation that the North had not lived up to its Constitutional obligations, while the Barber's final tearing up of their agreement at the end of chapter 43 would reflect the growing Southern loss of faith in the North and in the federal Union.

The Clean Comely Old Man

In the final chapter of *The Confidence-Man,* "The Cosmopolitan Increases in Seriousness," Melville introduces the last two important antagonists of his Confidence Man and of the Cosmopolitan's particular line of argument for trust in mankind. One of these, the Clean Comely Old Man, who sits reading the Bible in the gentlemen's cabin and who is led out into darkness at the end, is, I suggest, a caricature of John McLean who had been a United States Supreme Court justice since 1828 and was a potential Republican candidate for president in 1856. I shall argue that Melville is dealing with McLean's loss of the nomination and, through it, with the ushering out of the political spirit that McLean represented—a peculiar blend of Old-Line Whig financial caution with Christian-Methodist confidence—by the new spirit of Republican, Christian-humanitarian optimism that Henry Ward Beecher had come to represent. The second important figure in this chapter—the Juvenile Peddler who joins in their midnight conversation—represents, I suggest, Southern proslavery political extremism of the kind that led to secession and, possibly, specifically Henry A. Wise, senator and governor of Virginia, who was a dominant figure in the Democratic party and was a proponent, like Yancey, of the "heretical" faith in states rights and slavery extension, and who became later a Confederate leader. The Juvenile Peddler's conversation with Cosmopolitan-Beecher represents, I contend, yet another encounter of a representative Southern with a Northern figure—this time with a slight hint of sinister collusion between the two figures suggesting the danger to the Republic of both.

To begin with the setting. In the gentlemen's cabin where the entire final scene takes place there is a "solar lamp," which is decorated with "the image of a horned altar, from which flames rose, alternate with the figure of a robed man, his head encircled by a halo." This lamp, by which the Old Man sits reading the *Fidèle*'s copy of the Bible, is interpreted by Elizabeth Foster with good iconographic reasons as an allusion to the "light" of the Old and New Testaments.[1] At the end of the scene (and of the book) the Cosmopolitan extinguishes this lamp and "with it the waning flames of the horned altar, and the waning halo round the robed man's brow." In the darkness that ensues (a darkness evocative of the "Universal darkness" that "buries all" at the end of Pope's satire *The Dunciad*) he "leads the old man away." His action raises the question why a character who is a caricature of Henry Ward Beecher, the most celebrated evangelical Christian preacher of his day, should be depicted putting out a lamp that symbolizes the Bible— a lamp which "the commands of the captain required . . . to be kept burning till the natural light of day should come to relieve it." The text seems to suggest that Beecher was regarded by Melville as a threat to the very foundations of the religion that he professed and preached, an authorial attitude of considerable satirical sharpness. Yet it is one that proved prophetically accurate, for Beecher's preaching of romantic Christian liberalism and his later acceptance of Darwinian evolutionism became a powerful force in the gradual decline of orthodox Congregationalism and fundamentalist reliance on the Bible.[2]

Under the lamp sits "A clean, comely, old man," whose head is "snowy as the marble" of the table at which he is reading, and whose countenance is "like that which imagination ascribes to good Simeon, when, having at last beheld the Master of Faith he blessed him and departed in peace" (p. 273). That is, his face resembles, as I read the passage, that of Simeon, the man who had come "by the Spirit into the temple" to see Christ before he should be permitted to die (Luke 2:26–32), as he is represented in the numerous graphic depictions of "The Presentation of Jesus in the Temple." If one examines some of the notable examples of this scene produced by artistic "imagination" in the graphic religious art of painters important in Melville's period and most likely to have been known to him, one discovers that Simeon's iconography called for a benign-looking countenance with a high and broad forehead rising into a semibald area on top, long flowing white hair on either side, and a long flowing beard.[3] This Old Man has also a "hale look of greenness in winter," and his hands are "ingrained with the tan, less apparently, of the present summer, than of accumulated ones past." He seems to be about seventy—"three-score-and-ten"—years of age and looks like "a well-to-do farmer, happily dismissed, after a thrifty life of activity, from the fields to the fireside." His personality appears unsophisticated, for he is characterized as "fresh-hearted" as at the age of fifteen and seems like those "to whom seclusion gives a boon more blessed than knowledge," for they will go "to heaven untainted by the world, because ignorant of it," resembling "a countryman {who} putting up at a London inn, and never stirring out of it as a sight-seer, will leave London at last without once being lost in its fog, or soiled by its mud." The point of this simile is that the Old Man's appearance is that of a pure and innocent man. However, it is hinted and borne out by his subsequent behavior that he is not so "clean" and fresh-hearted as he seems to be.

To continue, not only is he reading the Bible at this late hour on the boat, but he is a habitual reader of it, for later he says that "Man and boy, I have read the good book this seventy years." He is "kindly," "anxious," considerate of others, concerned about the welfare of the Juvenile Peddler, yet he is selfishly alarmed by the boy's hints of possible theft, suspicious of counterfeit bills, and is "lawyer-like" in examining his own bills. He switches from suspicious, perplexed scrutiny of the bills to a "rapt look" when thinking of the need to place "trust" in the Bible, and then back again to anxiety about his physical safety on the boat as he prepares to retire. He is forgetful.

The Comely Old Man's speaking style is not marked by any striking mannerisms, but is carefully polite, courteous, and just a little formal, while his plainness, simplicity, and lack of witty humor are contrasted sharply with the quick wit and double entendres of the Juvenile Peddler.

The overall picture presented is that of a pious Protestant evangelical Christian, who practices Bible reading as a habit, attends church, and is a believer in "that Power which is alike able and willing to protect us when we cannot ourselves." His acquaintance with the Bible is limited to the Protestant text, for he is not aware of what is written in the Apocryphal book *Ecclesiasticus,* the "Book of Wisdom" of Jesus the Son of Sirach, a text that has always formed part of the canonical Bible of the Roman Catholic Church. He would discount the Apocryphal books, especially the "Book of Wisdom," with its warnings against deceptive friends and its message that would "destroy man's confidence in man." And yet in his actual behavior, not in his professions of what he believes, he clearly is perfectly aware of the need to distrust mankind, for he buys from the Peddler a "Travellers' Patent Lock" for his cabin door and a money belt for his cash, and he accepts gratefully and puts to use immediately the "Counterfeit Detector" given him by the boy. Melville is giving the reader, then, yet another caricature of a man with a double personality, resembling Roberts-Wilmot and Pitch-Benton in this— and resembling many politicians then and since. On the one hand, the Old Man displays a shrewd, cautious, money-conscious American temperament, while on the other he shows a Protestant Christian devotion to the Bible and apparent purity of character. This double natured personality, reinforced by several personal details resembles closely the portrait of the Ohioan John McLean (1785–1864) that emerges from the main historical study dealing with his career, Francis P. Weisenburger's *The Life of John McLean, A Politician on the United States Supreme Court* (1937).[4]

Two portraits of McLean (pronounced McLain), reproduced in Shaw's *Abraham Lincoln: The Year of His Election,* show a high broad forehead extending into a bald dome and hair which, although not white, flows down on either side to touch his collar. However, unlike the typical Simeon of Christian iconography, McLean shows no beard. The well-disposed Sarah Maury described him in 1846 as "Tall and dignified," with a fair complexion, light blue eyes, and as somewhat bald. He had, she thought, an "expression . . . of the noblest moral character," and had an "amiable" and benevolent personality. When she saw him in church praying, she thought he showed a "graceful benignity," suggestive of the Old Man's "benign" curiosity toward the Cosmopolitan. His modern biographer, Weisenburger, quotes a description of McLean as a "large man with a head of similar proportions, in later years bald in front but covered on each side by a long mop of rather dishevelled hair." He had a Roman nose, full lips, a firm jaw. He was "stalwart and great-looking," according to some, while others saw "not much evidence of intellectual magnitude, [nor] . . . of moral grandeur" in his appearance. Whether McLean's hands might have been tanned like the Old Man's from his youthful labors on his father's farm in Ohio or from circuit riding I have not discovered, but his health was apparently good enough to permit his thinking of the presidency in 1856 and even in 1860, so it seems likely that he appeared "hale" even at his advanced age.[5] He would be over seventy in 1856.

McLean's career displays a personality that is in its traits of apparently benign, somewhat naïve, virtue, coupled with shrewd caution, similar to that which the Clean Comely Old Man exhibits. According to Weisenburger, he nourished presidential ambitions for thirty years while serving on the Supreme Court, from before the election of 1832 until that of 1860. With a minimal frontier education, he had studied law after working on his father's farm until he was sixteen, and although he was Ohio's representative in Congress at the age of twenty-seven, his career after he resigned that office in 1816 was mainly as an administrator and a judge. Because of help that he had given to elect President Monroe, he was appointed postmaster-general in 1823, a position that he held with nearly universal esteem for efficiency and honesty through the administrations of Monroe and John Quincy Adams until 1829, when Andrew Jackson appointed him associate justice of the Supreme Court mainly in recognition of the importance of the West, Weisenburger writes, and not for his juridical talent. Throughout his postmaster-generalship he maneuvered constantly for political position and for useful alliances. President Adams came to suspect McLean's political acts and "double-dealing" only gradually, writing in his diary that his conduct was "that of deep and treacherous duplicity." McLean was capable of smooth words coupled with disloyal or hostile actions and played the double game so well that Adams could find no action for which to dismiss him. As early as this period he was accused of "religious cant and hypocrisy"—as the Clean Comely Old Man might well be. He politicked for the presidency in 1832, while on the Court, even considering the Anti-Masonic nomination, for which he was favored by Thurlow Weed and others. His efforts in 1836 included the purchase of a newspaper, but he did not succeed, nor did he receive any bid in 1840. In 1844, taking a position "aloof" but eager, he lost out to Clay, and in 1848 his strength bowed to Taylor's.[6]

Crandall, in his *History of the Republican Party,* writes that McLean appealed to the "Old Conservative" stratum at the convention in 1856 and was "the central figure" in their effort to place a candidate. He was a "Northern man with a conservative record." According to Weisenburger, McLean's presidential prospects "reached high tide in 1856" within the new Republican party, since his attitude on the slavery issue, although not quite good enough for Greeley, was good enough for men like Edwin M. Stanton, Joshua Giddings, and Lincoln, while certain leaders in the old Whig party were willing to support him in the new party. Webb of the New York *Courier & Enquirer* spoke at the convention for him and many conservative Republicans liked him, as did former members of the Know-Nothing party. However, for Greeley he was not sufficiently "sound on the goose" (politically orthodox), nor did Charles A. Dana, ex-Brook Farmer, Greeley's editorial aide and representative of the new political spirit, favor him, calling him an "old fogy" and a "marrowless old lawyer." Prior to the convention in June, while Greeley, Seward and Weed were "straining every nerve to defeat" McLean, others such as Lincoln and Thaddeus Stevens pleaded for him. On an informal ballot he received 196 votes to Frémont's 359, which McLean felt was a "base betrayal of confidence." Stanton, Giddings, and others thought that McLean could have beaten Buchanan, which Frémont did not. McLean bitterly complained about Frémont's inexperience and about the money that freely flowed to secure his nomination and he saw him as controlled by Blair, Greeley, Wilson, and Weed—"all of whom were corrupt" in his view. He had "no confidence" in Fillmore either.[7]

Thus we have the portrait of a habitual "politician on the United States Supreme Court"—as Weisenburger entitles his biography—who was on his other side termed "a grave respectable man, pure and safe" and who had been converted to Methodism as a young man, became a well-known Methodist layman, published in 1846 a series of articles on the Bible and "the Bible and the Sabbath," and was in 1849 honorary president of the American Sunday School Union. He was "kind" and generous and had an "unsullied personal life," so that of him a friend could say that he "had barely enough of the dross of human nature in him to identify him with humanity." A temperate man himself, he yet could write realistically that "A very large proportion of the wire workers in politics are hard drinkers themselves, and those of them who do not drink would on no consideration give up the influence of intoxicating spirits, in political operations." Weisenburger further characterizes McLean as displaying an unassuming demeanor and modesty which concealed his ambition. Some saw in him selfishness and a bending of principles to that ambition. Interestingly, Weisenburger likens him to Sumner and to Joshua Giddings in being "a moralist rather than a realist"—who saw inconsistency in others, while "blind to waverings of his own conduct." Melville's Comely Old Man seems totally unaware of his own inconsistencies of professed belief and performed actions.[8]

As associate justice on the Supreme Court for thirty years, McLean gave his opinion on several important slavery cases, including *Jones v. Van Zandt* in 1847 and the Dred Scott case in 1856. Robert Cover, a modern historian of several judges who handled slavery cases, in *Justice Accused,* treats him as a "formalist" in a somewhat overly simplistic "moral-formal" contrast of judgmental patterns and links his earlier attitude on slavery questions with that of Justice Joseph Story, a friend of McLean's, and that of Lemuel Shaw. Yet, Cover quotes Salmon P. Chase as saying of McLean that he was "sound on slavery, politically and personally, if not judicially," implying a conflict of a judicial head with a political and moral heart. In the Van Zandt case his opinion, according to Cover, showed a "reverence for imagined rights under the Constitution" and a great fear of anarchy, not unlike that of Shaw in the Sims case. Likewise, McLean wrote letters defending judgments in the early 1850s that upheld the Fugitive Slave Law, for he cautiously felt that conscience was "not always a sure guide." In the Dred Scott case, however, directly in the period of our interest in him and at the time when Northern public opinion was rapidly sectionalizing on the slavery issue, McLean dissented from Taney and the Southern point of view, appearing thus to change with changing public opinion in the North. Moreover, he was widely accused of leaking Court discussions to the *Tribune* and of giving a dissenting view in favor of Scott's freedom only in order to enhance his own political chances for the Republican nomination. After the decision in 1857 his dissenting opinion was termed by some readers of it a "stump-speech" to prove his antislavery views and a bid for Northern political favor.[9]

McLean's later combination of an optimistic Christian-Methodist, antislavery attitude, flowering into Republicanism at the right political moment, with a certain cautious conservatism that appealed to the Silver Grey Whigs entering the party seems reflected in Melville's Comely Old Man. The Old Man trusts Goodman-Beecher and claims to share in his belief in the "good news" of the Gospel (p. 273), in his discounting of the pessimistic apocryphal "wisdom that curdles the blood," and in the "guardianship" of "a Committee of Safety" over them and the *Fidèle*, just as McLean by making himself available to the Republicans offered his "trust" in the Republican platform and its spirit. He even appears to have changed his views on the interpretation of the Constitution with reference to the rights of African-Americans in writing his opinion on the Dred Scott case and in making known the fact that his views would be sympathetic to the Republican cause even before that case was decided by the Supreme Court. On the other side of his character McLean's caution and conservatism on this issue, as shown in the earlier Van Zandt case and on other cases in the 1850s, seems to be reflected in the Old Man's relationship with the Juvenile Peddler, who represents the slave interest, for there he agrees to buy the devices for keeping money safe that the boy sells. He purchases the "Travellers' Lock" and a money belt, both items which I take to symbolize the Fugitive Slave Law and its enforcement, which were reputedly the price exacted by the Southern politicians under threat of withdrawal of Southern trade, repudiation of the debts owed the Northern banks and merchants, and ultimately of secession. That is, if we interpret the "Mahogany Door" which the Peddler holds up as alluding to the threat of secession, then the lock and the money belt would represent the Fugitive Slave Bill and its enforcement, this symbolic complex of details constituting a commentary on the relationship of the political power of the slave interest, as represented in the Peddler, to the political power of the Northern banking and commercial interests (both conservative Whig and conservative Democrat), represented by the old Whig John McLean. (For further commentary on the relationship of Old Man-McLean to Peddler-Wise see below.)

The caricature of the Clean Comely Old Man, besides alluding to

McLean, seems to be representative of a general type, the "Silver Grey Whig," or "Old-Line Whig," or "Straight Whig"—all designations for a faction of the dying Whig party which held conservative views on the interpretation of the Constitution (*e.g.*, enforcement of the Fugitive Slave Law) and on the safety of money (*e.g.*, not endangering trade and banking relations with the South). It is apparently because McLean was representative of this group that he held as much power as he did at the Republican convention, where as already noted, he received 196 votes in an informal first ballot to 359 for Frémont, who was backed by the new spirit and "new creed" of "Free Soil, Free Speech, *etc.*" It was apparently owing to the exertions of certain younger politicians, in combination with Weed and Greeley that McLean lost out. John Bigelow, associate of Bryant on the *Evening Post* and the former Know-Nothing Nathaniel Banks, as well as Gamaliel Bailey of the abolitionist Washington *National Era* and the Blairs, were all initiators of Frémont's candidacy. Against the wave of publicity which they skillfully created and the attractiveness of Frémont as a romantic adventurer and soldier-explorer, McLean's chances dimmed. Halstead, in his report on the convention, adapting the terms "Young America" and "Old Fogyism" from the Democrats to Republicanism, saw McLean as an Old Fogy and rejected him. Writing of his favorite, the Ohioan Senator Chase, Halstead wrote:

> Numbers of delegates elected as Chase men have been captivated by the star of Fremont. The counsels of Horace Greeley and Thurlow Weed have turned them over. These New York politicians, wish to keep Mr. William H. Seward nicely pickled away to turn up some time auspicious to him . . . New York politics is here, as everywhere, in the market [*i.e.*, buying and selling]. The young men have been enlisted in the Fremont cause, and the old fogies have gravitated to John McLean. The politicians of the East are for Fremont, because they think he will win. The prestige of coming victory is with him, and the camp followers are at his heels, of course. Pennsylvania wants the conservatism of Buchanan outdone, and McLean to do it, and New Jersey backs her, and one-third of the delegation of Ohio endorses her. Out of the sixty-nine delegates of Ohio, McLean has twenty-four. [10]

Halstead goes on to accuse the McLean movement of being an attempt "made by the antediluvian Whigs who have been placed in Congress by the Republican movement, to reorganize the defunct Whig Party under a thin disguise of Republicanism, to consist solely of talk about the Missouri Compromise." But now, Halstead felt, "it will be killed outright and forever," despite the efforts of the "old Whigs, with moss on their backs, of Pennsylvania and New Jersey—those who were pretty fairly up in the ranks twenty-five years ago, and have been lagging ever since." Despite a letter of withdrawal from McLean, his "friends" persisted in placing him in nomination, only withdrawing him after he lost on the informal first ballot. As Halstead saw the operations of the convention on this day, both his favorite, Chase, and the Old Fogy McLean—both Western in origin—were eased out by "politicians of the East"—by whom he meant Weed, Greeley, F. P. Blair, Sr., Banks, and others. This perception of the operations of the Republican nomination is, I think, alluded to by Goodman-Beecher's escorting out of the Old Man and by the Peddler's curious remark to him: "Is the wind East, d'ye think?"[11]

To Halstead his favorite, Chase, represented a purer form of antislavery feeling, while McLean represented merely the old Whig party trying to stay alive within the Republican movement: "Venerable Whiggery made a stronger effort here to rejuvenate than I would have believed it could have done, had I not observed the operation. But the name of Judge McLean could not save it." Moreover, he saw the nomination of Dayton—a conservative Whig—for vice-president as "a concession to the ulta conservative, or McLean men." In other words, the picture one draws from Halstead's on-the-spot observations is that McLean was "ushered out"—to use a modern metaphor—by the Eastern politicians and by the mass feeling for Frémont, which seemed spontaneous but had actually been engineered by Blair, Andrew Jackson's master publicist, and other journalists. Halstead's description of the surge of feeling that took over the delegates is interesting for his use of the term "faith," in which if we substitute the term "confidence" can be seen something like the feeling with which the last chapter of *The Confidence-Man* is concerned:

> The members of the convention had much faith in the power of their cause, and knew that they represented a vast host of intelligent men. They had faith in themselves and faith in their candidate. From the first there was no mistake but Fremont would be the nominee, and there was a very deep and solemn conviction in a large majority of the delegates that he was not only a good man but THE MAN. The faith in him was very remarkable, and was, to me, to a great degree unaccountable. It seemed . . . that a popular instinct, such as sometimes, on great occasions, leaps chasms in logic . . . had found in Fremont the man for the times. A feeling of faith in Fremont gathered strength every hour of the sessions of the convention.[12]

The Juvenile Peddler

Although some of the details of appearance and personality suggest that the model for the Juvenile Peddler, who appears in the final chapter in conversation with the Cosmopolitan and the Comely Old Man, may be the Southern political leader, Henry A. Wise, it is more certain that he is a type figure representing the Southern "slave interest" (or "slave power" or "slavocracy"). The Peddler has usually been seen by readers as an aesthetic contrast or counterpart to the Deaf-Mute of the opening chapter and as representing the opposite extreme of witty, worldly wisdom from the Deaf-Mute's silent, un-worldly kind of truth. I would suggest that he also represents the principle of self-interest carried to its extreme of proslavery opinion and become a political principle—contrasted with the philanthropic attitude of abolition, which the Deaf-Mute represents. In his encounter with the Cosmopolitan he represents yet another example of the Southern sectional political movement, which was chiefly Democratic, in an encounter with the sectional Republican spirit represented by Goodman-Beecher. In relationship to the Comely Old Man (who I have suggested caricatures Judge John McLean of the United States Supreme Court, a Whig-Republican contender for the presidency) he represents the political power of the slave interest exercised through the party system upon certain Northern politicians. In yet another aspect, the Juvenile Peddler symbolizes the revolutionary (anarchic, to some eyes) spirit of secession for the sake of states' rights and slavery extension which had been stigmatized, for example, by Benton, as early as 1835 as "heresy" and by the Republicans later as both "revolutionary" and a "heretical" faith, and that led in 1861 to the founding of the Confederate States of America. [13]

The peddler is a boy, whose face has "a polish of seasoned grime" that causes his "sloe-eyes" to "sparkle . . . like lustrous sparks in fresh coal" (p. 277). That is, his skin is dark as coal. In several of the prints of this period a figure representing a slave state or the slave states is depicted with a dark or black complexion referring to its population of African descent. Examples are "The Oregon and Texas Question" (1844), in which Texas appears as a dark-skinned woman, and "The American Twins—North and South" (1860), in which the Southern man has dark skin. [14] The boy's "sloe-eyes" suggest the sloeberry bush, a plant widespread in the South, used in making sloe gin. The boy's smile reveals his "leopard-like teeth"—possibly another allusion to the African origin of much of the Southern population— while the comparison of his smile to that of the "wild beggar boy" of the

Spanish painter Murillo is probably an allusion to the Southern political interest in the Spanish-speaking and Spanish-owned portions of Central and South America and the Caribbean (especially in Cuba) and to the "slavocracy's" interest in annexing some of these territories. The Spanish association is reaffirmed later by the metaphor of the *auto-da-fé*, drawn from the Spanish Inquisition, which Melville uses to describe the Peddler's costume. The African association is reaffirmed when he leaves the scene "with the air of a young Caffre [Kaffir]" (an African of a Bantu tribe)—perhaps also an allusion to the widely bruited possibility of the reopening of the African slave trade in the Southern states, or, should they secede, in a new confederacy. [15]

The Juvenile Peddler's clothing consists in "the fragment of an old linen coat, bedraggled and yellow" and a ragged "red-flannel shirt." The rags of the shirt, "mixed with those of his yellow coat," appear to "flame about him like the painted flames in the robes of a victim in *auto-da-fé*" (pp. 276–77). The red-flannel shirt obviously connotes the revolutionary political impulse, abroad internationally with renewed vigor since 1848, while the reference to the victims of the fires of the Spanish Inquisition suggests that the Peddler is meant to be associated with some kind of religious or political heresy—which, in this context, I believe to be that of the Southern point of view on the meaning of the Constitution, as seen by Northerners. Next, the boy is "bare-footed," which is perhaps an allusion to the comparative commercial poverty of the South, and, lastly, he has "no allotted sleeping-place" on the *Fidèle,* perhaps an allusion to the slave interest's increasing restlessness within the Union.

The Juvenile Peddler carries with him among his travelers' conveniences "a miniature mahogany door, hinged to its frame," without a lock, which he uses to demonstrate the "Travellers' Patent Lock" that he carries to offer for sale. He also sells money belts and gives away "Counterfeit Detectors" to customers who purchase seventy-five cents worth of his wares. If the Peddler be intended as a caricature of the Southern slave interest as a political force, it may be possible, as suggested earlier, that the "door" he carries represents the constant threat of secession—of going out of the Union—that was used by Southern politicians for many years, it was claimed, as a bargaining tool to get their way in Congress. If this interpretation be correct, then the money obtained for the "Patent Lock" that he sells to the Old Man to lock his door and thus safeguard his "cash" (p. 279) might represent whatever concessions were made or were conjectured to have been made by Northern conservative and moneyed interests (such as the Old Man caricatures in the person of John

McLean) to the Southern slave interest in order to keep it from pressuring for withdrawal from the Union and thus taking the Northern money that had been loaned to and invested in the South with it. That the Fugitive Slave Bill was such a concession was an accusation leveled frequently by Northern antislavery politicians. A concession demanded in 1856 was that Kansas be taken in as a slave state. Likewise, the money belt that the Peddler sells to the Old Man may represent some additional safeguard—perhaps individual agreements between planting interests and banking interests—which Southern leaders sought to obtain from Northern conservatives. Lastly, the "Counterfeit Detector," with which the Old Man examines his three-dollar bill on the "Vicksburgh Trust and Insurance Banking Company" (pp. 280–82) appears to allude directly to the problem of the safety of funds placed in Southern banks. The Old Man is highly suspicious of the value of this bill drawn on a Mississippi bank, while Goodman blandly asserts, "The bill is good; don't be so distrustful" (p. 282), reflecting Republican optimism.

Both of the Juvenile Peddler's body gestures reinforce his association with slavery considered as a vested interest or an institution with political force. Upon leaving, he scrapes back "his hard foot on the woven flowers of the carpet, much as a mischievous steer in May scrapes back his horny hoof in the pasture" (p. 280)—a gesture that links him with the black slave considered as animal property (similar to the earlier image of Black Guinea as a "steer" when the Drover places his hand upon his head). Likewise, when the Peddler leaves, he flourishes his hat and leaves "with the air of a young Caffre." Both similes identify the Peddler himself with the black slave as valuable property at the same time as he represents the white master (for the boy apparently is of European descent) as acting for and identical with his property interests. That is, the Peddler's character, unlike that of the black man, Black Guinea, which is distinct from that of the white Drover's, is an amalgam of the two elements. He represents simultaneously the black slave and the master as an economic and political unit, operating, as Melville depicts them, from a position of economic inferiority (for the Peddler is relatively poor) and instability (for he has "no allotted sleeping-place" on the boat).

The foregoing are, then, some of the reasons for interpreting the Peddler as a representative or type-figure of the Southern "slavocracy" group interest, and by extension, of the political power that it laid claim to through its threats to secede and establish independence, as that interest and its threat might have appeared to Melville in the summer of 1856. There are, furthermore, some reasons for believing that he may be alluding in particular to Henry Alexander Wise (1806–1876), U.S. congressman 1833–44, minister to Brazil under Tyler and Polk, governor of Virginia 1856–60, and Confederate general during the war. In his political career, Wise began as a Democrat—a Jackson man—but shifted to the Whig position when the president removed the government deposits to the state banks. He became associated again with the Democrats when he joined Tyler's "Corporal's Guard"—firm supporters—in the mid-1840s and became a leader there during the administrations of Pierce and Buchanan, in both of whose nominations and elections he was deeply involved. He consistently defended slavery, though never believing it beneficent (see plates 3 and 24). [16]

The association of the Peddler with Wise is most strongly suggested by the several punning witticisms on the words "wise" and "wisdom" in the various interchanges between the boy, the Old Man, the Cosmopolitan, the Perverse Man, and the Irish Voice in the last chapter. The theme of "wisdom" first appears in the Cosmopolitan's inquiries about the meaning of the "Wisdom of Jesus, the Son of Sirach" and his discussion of "ugly" wisdom with the Old Man (pp. 275–76). It is taken up again in the comments of the Perverse Man that "wisdom" should be sought "under your blankets"—i.e., in sleep—and of the Irish Voice that they should not burn their fingers "with the likes of wisdom" (p. 276). It is resumed after the Juvenile Peddler's entrance in his enigmatic and provocative comment that he will "never get so old and wise" (p. 277) as to play with toys—a remark that the Old Man and the Cosmopolitan oblige him to clarify by revealing that he has sold "more than one old man a child's rattle" at the "fair in Cincinnati last month." They toss the words "wise" and "wisdom" back and forth in a last exchange in which Goodman suggests that since the boy seems "pretty wise," he ought to "sell [his] wisdom and buy a coat." Then, the boy claims that he has already done that and that his coat—ragged and bedraggled as it is—is all that he could buy with "the price of [his] wisdom" (p. 278). Henry A. Wise's name had been the subject of punning in graphic prints throughout the 1830s, when he was most conspicuous in Congress in investigating corruption in the Van Buren administration and in his running battle with John Quincy Adams over the introduction of petitions dealing with abolition. Two prints prior to 1856 that pun on "Wise-wise" are "A Bull Chase, 'The Words of the Wise, are as Goads'" (1839), in which Wise goads Levi Woodbury, the subject of his House investigation; and "The Captain & Corporal's Guard" (1841), in which President Tyler stands upon two stilts, labelled "Wise" and "Proffit," and calls them "Wise & Proffitable" supports (plate 3).

A later print that puns on his name is "'Taking the Stump' or Stephen in Search of His Mother" (1860), where he says of Douglas, "If I were not Wise I'd go my pile on him" (plate 24). [17]

Furthermore, it is possible that there may be an allusion to a specific political action of Wise during 1856 in the Peddler's remark that he had sold "more than one old man a child's rattle" at "the fair in Cincinnati last month." Different accounts of the internal machinations that led up to and continued at the Democratic convention in Cincinnati in May of 1856 indicate that crucial to the nomination of Buchanan and to the defeat of Pierce's and Douglas's hopes was the support of the Virginia delegation, which was led by Governor Wise. It was suggested at the time and later that a deal was made at the convention by which Buchanan was supported at an important moment by the Virginia delegates. Hesseltine and Fisher write in their introduction to Halstead's reports on this convention that "Virginia's leaders broke the Southern phalanx by deserting Pierce and drawing closer to . . . Buchanan." In a note, they add that Robert Tyler, writing on 13 June 1856, to his father, the ex-president, said that Buchanan was clearly indebted to Virginia for the nomination: "Mr. Wise is in truth the Warwick of the hour." Bennett's *Herald* accuses Buchanan of paying his "pound of flesh" to the Democratic "Shylocks at Cincinnati" by promising to pay later by accepting Kansas as a slave state (3 August 1856). Furthermore, after the convention and in later years it was rumored by John Bigelow of the *Evening Post,* who reported the convention, that a deal had been made by one of Buchanan's men through which in exchange for the nomination Buchanan would promise that should he be elected, and should the Republicans win in 1860, and should the Southern states secede while he was president, he would do nothing to prevent them from leaving the Union. [18] With this political context as background, it is possible to read the Peddler's remarks that he had sold "more than one old man a child's rattle" at the "fair in Cincinnati last month" and that "these old men . . . were old bachelors" as allusions to such a rumored deal between Wise and Buchanan. It will be recalled that Buchanan was a lifelong bachelor and was caricatured in several prints in that role. "Bauble" or child's "toy" was a metaphor for the presidency. [19]

As for the fitness of Wise to be the specific model for a caricature, which more generally should be interpreted as representing the political power of the slave interest, Roy Nichols in *The Disruption of American Democracy* notes that by September, when as a result of the Maine election, which Frémont won, the Democrats feared he would win nationally, Wise took two public actions which made him appear an extremist even to the point of revolution. He wrote to his fellow Democratic governors of the South inviting them to an emergency conference at Raleigh, and the next day he ordered the Virginia militia into readiness. To a kinsman he wrote, "If Frémont is elected there will be a revolution." A *Herald* editorial comments on a rumor that Wise, Davis, and other fire-eaters planned a "coup d'état in the red republican style," if Frémont was elected (6 September 1856). David Potter in *The Impending Crisis* notes the constant threat of disunion, if Frémont were to be elected, as a Democratic campaign theme of Southern leaders throughout the summer and early autumn of 1856. He cites the threats of *De Bow's Review*, Robert Toombs, James M. Mason, John Slidell, Jefferson Davis, and Andrew P. Butler, and notes Wise's call for a convention of Southern governors as a dramatization of the will of many Southerners to secede if necessary.[20]

There are only a few personal details that connect the Juvenile Peddler with Wise, but they are worth mentioning. Several observers mention his "dark and brilliant eye" or his "piercing eyes," which perhaps are reflected in the Juvenile Peddler's sloe-eyes that "sparkle." An early description of Wise in Congress at thirty by a reporter notes that "He dresses like an old man, though his general appearance is very youthful." Whether he still could be so described in 1856 I have not found, but the detail is suggestive of the "old linen coat" and the "grown man's cast-off beaver" hat that the boy wears. Again, like the Peddler, who has heard much "ill" of himself with his "sharp ears," Wise heard much ill of himself, especially during his verbal battles with John Quincy Adams in Congress and on account of his involvement with the Graves-Cilley duel (in which Congressman Jonathan Cilley of Maine, who was Hawthorne's friend, died), for which he received "much opprobrium," according to his biographer Meade. The personality and rhetorical style of the boy show some of the same characteristics of wildness and wittiness, of humor and mimicry, and of tactless defensiveness that were attributed to Wise. His grandson, Barton H. Wise, notes that he had a habit of contradicting in debate for the sake of debate and a love of paradox. Philip Hone found him "entertaining" in debate and noted his "comic power." According to Eaton he used much "humor and mimicry" to appeal to his hearers. Likewise, the Juvenile Peddler uses mimicry to ridicule the Old Man, echoing his "Go, child—go, go!" with "Yes, child,—yes, yes" (p. 280), and throughout his appearance he is witty, sarcastic, contradictory, and quick in repartee based on paradox. Again, just as Wise was thought by Northerners to be quite erratic and was called by Philip Hone "the wild-cat of Virginia" and thought to be "either crazy or has not so good an excuse for his conduct" in the Congress, the Peddler mystifies the Old Man, who wonders at his "strangeness" and whether he might not be "sort of simple." Also, Hone typed Wise as the "most inflammable" among "the combustibles" of the South, writing that Wise "vomits fire like the Dragon of Wantley."[21]

Lastly, it may be noted that as a defender and exponent of "worldly wisdom," of which the premise would be the conviction of the natural depravity of man, the Juvenile Peddler in both capacities—as alluding to Wise and to the slave interest generally—functions appropriately. A basic premise of the defense of the slave system was the belief not only in a natural incapacity of the African-American to govern himself but in the impossibility, because of natural human wickedness, of the two kinds of people—black and white—living peacefully together without the subordination of one to the other or the extinction of one by the other. The pessimistic, melancholy view of mankind, which underlies all of the "No-Trust" characters in *The Confidence-Man* is especially evident in the figures that I have interpreted as Southern or as Southern sympathizers: the Barber, the Drover, the Wooden-Legged Man, the Invalid Titan, the Puny Girl, Charlie Noble, the Crazy Beggar and last of all in the Juvenile Peddler.

In his actions, as I have already suggested, the relationship of the Peddler to the Cosmopolitan alludes to the relationship of the Southern sectional movement—in its hard core slave-interest political aspect—to the Republican antislavery movement. The Peddler's "wink expressive of a degree of indefinite knowingness" about the Cosmopolitan's real but hidden nature as a deceptive character, contains a hint that they understand pretty well what each is about, and it reflects, as I suggested in an earlier chapter, the not uncommon perception in the period that the two opposing political movements appeared in their effects, if not in their intentions, to be in collusion in their destructive activity as far as the existence of the Union was concerned.

The Irish Voice

Also heard in the final scene of the book, while Goodman, the Old Man and the Peddler converse, are two "voices," who make interjectory comments from the surrounding berths in the gentleman's cabin. The first of these is a "perverse man," who is mentioned early in the chapter as desiring that the light of the solar lamp be put out so that he can sleep, and who speaks again four separate times. The themes of his comments are: skepticism of biblical confidence; and the "wisdom" of sleeping. Rather importantly, he seems to offer a definition of the Confidence Man as one who, in the words of Jesus the Son of Sirach, "speaketh sweetly with his lips," and will "speak thee fair" and yet "if thou be for his profit he will use thee"—words that are directly applicable to the fair and sweet words of Goodman-Beecher (pp. 272–76). The identity of this voice—an important one to a full understanding of the last chapter of *The Confidence-Man*—remains enigmatic on the basis of present research.

The second voice that overhears the conversation in the cabin and also comments from a berth may be identified by its Irish "brogue" and by the import of its comments as very likely an allusion to Michael ("Mike") Walsh (1815–1859), the Irish-born Democratic politician, workingman's advocate, and journalist, who founded and edited in New York City a weekly journal, *The Subterranean* (1843–47) and represented the "Hell's Kitchen" area of the city in the New York Assembly in the late 1840s and in Congress (1852–54). [22] In the first of the two comments that the Irish Voice makes he addresses Goodman-Beecher and Old Man-McLean: "Arrah, and is't wisdom the two geese are gabbling about all this while? To bed with ye, ye divils, and don't be after burning your fingers with the likes of wisdom." And later, when the young Peddler, who has entered the cabin, laughs at the Old Man, the Voice asks: "What do the divils find to laugh about in wisdom, begorrah? To bed with ye, ye divils. . . ." (pp. 276–77). Because this Voice first calls Goodman-Beecher and Old Man-McLean "geese" and then "divils," it is apparent that Melville intends the reader to perceive that the Irish Voice is skeptical of the Republican movement, as represented by Beecher and McLean, considering them either fools, as geese are, or wicked (knaves), as devils are. Yet the Voice terms Peddler-Wise likewise a "divil," indicating skepticism of the good intentions of the Southern extremist faction which the Peddler represents. The political attitudes implied, the sarcastic tone of the comments, and the significant personal detail of the Irish brogue all link this voice to Mike Walsh.

A "radical Democrat who championed the common [white] man," according to his biographer, Robert Ernst, Michael Walsh made a career out of attacking in colorful language in speeches and in print "dishonest demagogues" and "political vultures"—especially those of Tammany Hall. His stylistic choice of "denunciatory" editorials, "coarse invective," and "witty exaggeration" and his frequent use of the terms "fools and knaves" to designate his opponents are consistent with the tone and language of the Irish Voice. The Democratic politician Forney called Walsh a "satirist by nature" and said that as a "destructive critic" he had no peers, though he had no constructive proposals to make about government.[23] The Irish Voice, like Walsh, offers no more constructive suggestion than that the cabin's occupants not "burn [their] fingers with the likes of wisdom" and get "to bed" immediately and go to sleep.

Walsh took generally a proslavery stance, yet he did not favor the extreme Southern view that desired expansion of slavery or secession. Like Daniel Dickinson and Edwin Croswell, he was a Hunker Democrat. He hated the Barnburners and the Free-Soil movement (Van Buren in particular), and later he was a "Hard" Democrat—who after the "Soft" Democrats, such as Marcy, welcomed back the Barnburner defectors, refused to do so. Throughout the 1840s he shared Calhoun's views on slavery, favoring an alliance of wage earning Northern Democrats with the planter aristocrats at that time although Calhoun favored a planter alliance with capital not with Walsh's workers. Speaking in the House in 1854, he still reflected views similar to some of Calhoun's and Fitzhugh's, claiming that the only difference between the black slave and the white "wage-slave" was that one had a master without asking for him, while the other had to beg for the privilege of becoming a slave. One, he said, was the slave of an individual; the other, slave of an "inexorable class." He thought the North quixotic and insincere to worry about the slaves, when poverty was ignored in the North.[24] Yet, when it came to the expansion of the Southern system—the goal of the Southern extremists—Walsh was critical of them also, speaking in favor of resolutions against slavery extension, and Forney reports that Walsh was "especially severe upon the airs of the chivalry of the South" and had "no patience with them." Thus, Walsh's political stance is altogether consistent with the Irish Voice's negative view of Peddler-Wise, the representative of Southern extremism. In the House, Walsh evidently "gloried" in giving negative votes generally.[25]

Walsh's character and views were undoubtedly known to Melville early, as a resident of New York City and as the brother of a Democratic politician. Gansevoort Melville had been "popular" as an orator with the Irish in New York and was actively involved in the New York City Democratic efforts in 1844 to sign up Irish voters for the party, even at the risk of illegally naturalizing them by the hundreds. This was at the same time as Walsh was establishing his newspaper and was winning his way in the party, in his attempt to break the barriers of the Tammany Hall electoral system for the

Irish immigrants. Later than *The Confidence-Man,* in his *Journal* (written while traveling in Europe and the Near East from October 1856 to May 1857) Melville refers to Walsh as if familiar with him and interested in him as a public character. Evidently the Cornish engineer of Melville's steamer the *Smirne* informed him that he became acquainted with "Mike Walsh on board this boat last year." Walsh, Melville was told, had made a speech in Trieste to some engineers, which had impressed the *Smirne*'s engineer. "He was out at elbows & borrowing money," Melville relates second hand. According to Walsh's biographers, by this time he had been defeated for Congress in the 1854 election and had gone to Europe on business; he was reputed also to have become an alcoholic.[26] As a performer in Melville's "man-show," Mike Walsh is one of the very minor but highly colorful—verbally—members.

13

The Political Commedia

Like the harlequinades discussed in Chapter 1 and like the graphic art that was political in its intent discussed in Chapter 3, Melville's pasquinade is a commentary on political persons and events. Yet it is extraordinary in its complexity of allusion and in the quality of the argument analysed. As we have seen, it centers the bulk of its references, though not all, upon the political movements of his early maturity—roughly the period 1846 to 1856. As already pointed out in Chapter 2, it was during these years that the slavery issue, which had been relatively quiet since the Missouri Compromise, reappeared in Congress with Wilmot's introduction of the proviso named for him and the consequent debates, continuing with the debates about the enactment of the Compromises of 1850 and with the passage of the Kansas-Nebraska Act in March 1854, which repealed the Missouri Compromise and aroused intense Northern reaction to the possibility of the extension of slavery into Kansas and the breach of "faith" that Northerners felt this represented. The immediate background of most of the personal caricatures that Melville has created in *The Confidence-Man* is the founding of the new political party during 1854–56 upon the issue of the Northern sectional opposition to the extension of slavery. During this period Northern (and Western) public opinion was influenced by antislavery arguments in the press, in the pulpit, and in political speeches to move away from commitment to the Constitutional tolerance of slavery in states where it had been established and from indifference to the problem of extension of it to an attitude of open detestation of it and fear of its extension into new territories and states. It is with this alteration in the state of the public mind—North, West, and South—that *The Confidence-Man* is concerned and with the men and women who influenced the formation of public opinion through the public media. It might almost be said that *The Confidence-Man* is about the formation of public opinion and that one of its major themes is propaganda and the effects of propaganda in the exacerbation of the sectional controversy.

We may surmise that the first impetus to writing *The Confidence-Man* was Melville's observation that all of the chief public actors in the antislavery movement, from the gentle Lundy to the ebullient and charismatic Beecher, might be conceived as manipulators of philanthropic feeling. He would have, then, connected this observation with that of the existence of a new American character type—the "confidence man"—who had appeared in the newspaper accounts of William Thompson's fraudulent activities in 1849, had furnished material for editorial moralizing in *The Literary World* and other periodicals, and had become a staple news item in the *Tribune,* the *Herald,* and other papers (directly juxtaposed, incidentally, with antislavery and proslavery editorials) in the 1850s. This new American example of an old criminal type gave birth to an American theatrical type-character in John Brougham's stage farce, "The Confidence Man," through whom an entire series of public figures could be satirized. Just as a confidence man manipulates social situations and language to control the responses of others, so the antislavery (or any other) orator employs social situations and language to control political responses of others. If some of the chief actors in the antislavery movement were to be dramatized as a series of confidence men, their relationships to other persons in the public scene could also be dramatized and illustrated by the enactment of the typical fraudulent intrigues of such a type-character. The next step would be for Melville to presuppose or hypothesize the idea of a single master personality underlying the various examples of the fraudulent activities, and this personality he could have discovered in the function of the Harlequin mask in the Pantomimes. Directly from the stage, Harlequin had become a usable metaphor for any person who underwent a succession of changes of appearance, style, belief, or attitude. It had likewise been used in graphic prints for politicians who readily changed their public stances to suit their constituents or their interests. The dramatic device of the successive intrigues of the Harlequin mask could, then, through the use of the American type-character of a Confidence Man, dramatize the growth and effect of the antislavery movement upon American public opinion if the movement were conceived as the successive actions of a series of manipulators of public opinion. The mask of Harlequin-Confidence Man could appear from scene to scene in different disguises, each one caricaturing through specific allusions the public appearance, speech, and actions of a particular individual in the movement.

The richness of this dramatic conception would become fully realized when in opposition to the Harlequin-Confidence Man a variety of public responses to the antislavery movement could be depicted as the dramatic antagonists to Harlequin's protagonistic actions. Many shades of public response to the philanthropic argument as expressed by representative individuals and types could be depicted (ranging from the most negative and resistant to the most positive and confiding) in the several other comic masks who were traditionally Harlequin's antagonists: Pantalone, Dottore, Capitano, Pulcinella, and Pierrot. These antagonists could satirize contemporary individuals or factions through the same allusive techniques. Through adaptation of the six traditional comical satirical type-characters, then, Melville could generalize about the public figures as he saw them—seeing one series of them as examples of trickster types and other groups as either potential dupes of the trickster or as unpersuadable critics of him. He could, also, particularize them in terms of their personalities by means of caricature of physical details and by parody of style and ideas.

Melville's adaptation of traditional comic theatrical character-types to American character-types and of theatrical and graphic techniques of topical allusion in his caricatures of individuals results in a work of fiction that is as extraordinary in its originality as it is complicated in its interpretation. It is a work in which nearly every one of the many characters (omitting the most minor appearances) exists on three levels: first as a generic type of humanity for which a theatrical mask in commedia dell'arte had been developed; second, as an American or regional variant of the more general human type; and third, as alluding to or being a caricature of a specific contemporary individual. It is possible to read the book solely on the level of the comic interaction of the character-types—both generic and national—as knaves and fools *sub specie aeternitatis*. I read it thus in my earlier interpretations of it.[1] However, as shown in the foregoing chapters, to miss the level of the contemporary topical references—the caricatures of individuals on the public stage—is to miss the satirical commentary Melville is making on American politics in a time of national crisis—on the knaves and fools (as he saw them) in the public life of his time. Melville has, of course, integrated all three levels of characterization in his creation of his characters. It is only for purposes of literary analysis, leading to fuller appreciation of his meaning, that we must distinguish the generic types (the masks of commedia dell'arte and Pantomimic origin) and the national and regional (American variants of the generic types), as well as the specific historical caricatures that the characters embody. In my essay, published in 1974, "Harlequin-Confidence-Man: The Satirical Tradition of Commedia Dell'Arte and Pantomime in Melville's *The Confidence-Man*," I have shown to what extent nearly every one of the characters in *The Confidence-Man* is informed by a commedia dell'arte mask and, in many cases, also, by an American or regional type-character. These conclusions need only be briefly recapitulated here.

By all indications the Confidence Man himself is modeled upon the Harlequin mask. Precisely like the stage Harlequin he switches from one disguise to another, appearing as an American ethnic, professional, or regional type, even while alluding to seven (or possibly eight) different Americans involved in contemporary or slightly earlier politics. As the antagonist of Harlequin, the mask of Pantalone informs a series of nine characters: the Barber, the Drover, the Country Merchant Henry Roberts, the Gentleman with Gold Sleeve-Buttons, the Miser, the Sick Man, Charlie Noble (probably),

Egbert the Practical Disciple, and the Clean Comely Old Man. There are, besides these, several minor figures who seem to belong to this type: the Well-To-Do Man, the Hard-Hearted Man, and probably the Dried-Up Man. In each case the character is a man who has money or is in some way associated with the ownership of property. There are only three figures in *The Confidence-Man* who correspond to the Pierrot mask, but they are memorable characters: the Deaf-Mute, the Crazy Beggar, and the Juvenile Peddler. Of the four main Dottore roles, two are clergymen, one is a college student, and one purports to be a mystical philosopher: the Episcopal Clergyman, the Methodist Minister, the Collegian, and Mark Winsome. Pulcinella is the mask to whom correspond the Wooden-Legged Man and the Invalid Titan, while, finally, Melville's Capitanos are the Missouri Bachelor Pitch, aggressively brandishing his shotgun, and Thomas Fry the Soldier of Fortune.

My earlier elucidation of the theatrical analogues for the type-characters that Melville has adapted in *The Confidence-Man* and, in this book, the search into the history and biography of the period for the originals for the caricatures (set forth in detail in Chapters 4 through 12) permit us to discern a pattern both in the historical context that forms the subject of his satire and in his attitude toward that subject. What emerges from the identifications of the caricatures is a pattern in which the rise of the antislavery movement and its emergence into partisan political action as the Republican party are satirized as the confidence-soliciting actions of a series of Harlequin-type characters, while the various responses to this political movement on the American scene are depicted as the various responses to Harlequin-Confidence Man of a series of Pantalone-type, Dottore-type, Capitano-type, and Pulcinella-type characters. Each of the eight Confidence Men demonstrably caricatures a man (or in Guinea's case not a man but the political issue of slavery as represented in the figure of a black ex-slave) involved in the antislavery movement as it emerged first in the journalistic work of Lundy, next in the partisan political exploitation of the philanthropic sentiment aroused by the issue of slavery, and then in the journalistic and political actions of Bryant, Parker, Weed, Sumner, Greeley, and Beecher—all major figures in the founding of the Republican party. The cases for the identifications that I have proposed for these caricatures are, as stated earlier, of varying strengths. Black Guinea, for example, may eventually be shown to be not a stereotype only but also a caricature of an individual who used the slavery issue for political purposes (e.g. Seward), while several of the relationships of the Herb-Doctor-Sumner and of Cosmopolitan-Beecher to other characters are still problematic. But, unless for each of them a better historical candidate is found and an entirely different pattern discerned in the successive Confidence Men (or the idea of caricature rejected altogether), we are obliged to conclude that Melville is depicting the emergence and action in American politics of the new sectional party in the 1850s as that of a magisterial confidence man at work—sometimes successfully, sometimes not—amid a crowd of passengers on a Mississippi steamer.

Likewise clearly outlined, though not yet in every detail entirely satisfactorily referrable to the historical context, is a pattern of responses to the Harlequin-Confidence Man by other type characters (Pantalone, Dottore, and Capitano) which forms a commentary on the various responses of other political groups and individuals to the emergence of the new party. The pattern of encounter enacted over and over between the Confidence Man and his antagonists has been shown to correspond in nearly all cases (in some more strongly than others) to an actual historical relationship on the public stage between an antislavery or Republican politician and some other public figure.

Each of the Pantalone figures represents the response of another faction, usually as represented in an individual, to the Republican movement, as follows. Just as the Drover skeptically mocks Black Guinea, so did the Southern slave-interest group, represented by Fitzhugh's views, deride the African-American claim to equality and the antislavery plea for sympathy and justice for the slaves. Just as the Country Merchant Roberts gives sympathy to Guinea, so did David Wilmot take up the antislavery extension cause in his introduction of the proviso; and just as he listens sympathetically to Ringman-Bryant's story, so did Wilmot, a Democrat, join the Barnburner and Free-Soil movement in which Bryant was a leader. And just as Roberts buys into Truman-Weed's Coal Company, so did Wilmot join the Republican party. Just as the Gentleman in Gold Sleeve-Buttons listens sympathetically to Man in Gray-Parker's schemes, so did Abbott Lawrence listen sympathetically to the antislavery cause as it politicized in the new party, of which Parker was spokesman, and so did his nephew Amos A. Lawrence donate heavily to the New England Emigrant Aid Company for which Parker was soliciter of funds. Just as the Hard-Hearted Man and the Well-To-Do Man repulse the Man in Gray, so did Cass and other Hunker Democrats and Old-Line and Silver Grey Whigs repulse the Republican movement of which Parker was spokesman.

Likewise, just as the Old Miser is induced by Truman-Weed to contribute his gold eagles to him and by Herb-Doctor-Sumner to buy his medicine, so was Blair, the old Jacksonian Democrat, induced into the new party by its promise of renewed political power for him. Just as the old Sick Man is induced to buy the medicine of Herb-Doctor-Sumner, so were certain old Whigs, anxious to regain power, lured into accepting the doctrines of the new party of which Sumner was the chief oratorical and congressional ornament. Just as Charlie Noble shows an apparent willingness to seek a deal (establish a "boon companionship") with Cosmopolitan-Beecher, and then, finding out his own self-interest, roughly repulses him, so did Yancey as representative of deep South slave-interest and sectionalism first seek advantageous commercial ties with the North and West and abruptly break off, when the relationship failed to be supportive. Just as Egbert is not taken in by Cosmopolitan-Beecher's pleas for a loan (in the guise of "Frank"), so did Thoreau not join in the Republican political action although he claimed sympathy with the slave. Just as the Barber is solicited for his trust, so was Douglas solicited for his adherence to the new movement. Last, just as the Old Man is led out into the dark by Cosmopolitan-Beecher, so was McLean led into another political defeat by the Republican leaders.

Similarly, three of the Dottore characters stand or act in relationship to the Harlequin character as did their historical models in relationship to the Republican party movement. Just as the Episcopal Minister trusts Black Guinea enough to go search for his sponsors in order to convince other passengers and also trusts Man in Gray-Parker, so did Dudley A. Tyng espouse the antislavery issue and give credence to and lecture on the party and the Kansas movement in which Parker was a prime mover. Just as the Collegian is not a willing listener to Ringman-Bryant and yet is eager to buy into the Black Rapids Coal Company, so Raymond of the *Times* was not sympathetic to Bryant's Barnburner Democratic views yet readily joined the Republican party once Weed had transferred his strong Whig organization into it. And last, just as Mark Winsome is attracted to Cosmopolitan-Beecher's personality but palters over doing him a "favor," so Emerson, although he admired Beecher and other Republican leaders such as Greeley and Parker, did not actively speak for the Republicans. And just as Winsome rejects the apostleship of Crazy-Beggar-Poe, so did Emerson hate and despise most Southerners. (The parallels between the actions of the Methodist Minister and the public actions of Brownlow are, as noted earlier, not yet entirely established.)

The relationships of Melville's two Capitanos to his Harlequin-Confidence Man figures, like the foregoing also, correspond to public political relationships. Just as Pitch the Missouri Bachelor ridicules Miser-Blair for buying Herb-Doctor-Sumner's medicines, so did Benton ridicule Blair for joining the Republicans. And just as Pitch argues with, momentarily trusts, and finally distrusts PIO Man-Greeley, so did Benton dispute with Greeley about the slavery issue and did not, although expected to, join the new party. (The temporary trust he shows in hiring one of PIO Man-Greeley's servants has not, as yet, an historical parallel established.) Just as Fry the Soldier of Fortune listens to Herb-Doctor-Sumner and trusts him enough to buy his pills, so did George Law listen to Republican solicitations after his own political loss in the Know-Nothing party and agree to endorse the nomination of Frémont.

247

Each of Melville's American Pulcinellas in his highly critical response to Harlequin-Confidence Man's solicitations reflects the strongly hostile attitude of a man (or men) to the Republican party. Just as the Wooden-Legged Cynic sharply distrusts Black Guinea's pleas and publicly scorns and attacks him, so did Bennett question and attack the antislavery cause both in its early abolitionist stages and in the Republican movement—seeing it as a stalking-horse for self-interested politicians such as Seward, Weed, Greeley, and Raymond. Just as the Invalid Titan utterly mistrusts and then brutally attacks the Herb-Doctor-Sumner, so did Calhoun and, later, another South Carolina representative, Preston Brooks, resist any Northern remedy for the slavery problem and in the assault on Sumner (and in other Southern acts of violence in Washington), physically express their hostility to the antislavery movement generally.

Lastly, Melville's two characters whom I have interpreted as informed by the Pierrot mask, stand at the beginning and the end of the pasquinade as framing and contrasting embodiments of the contrasting "truths" that the American political scene offered to Melville's eyes: the optimistic, philanthropic message of the antislavery movement and the opposing pessimistic, self-interested message of the proslavery rebuttal. Just as the Deaf-Mute chalks up his philanthropic message on his slate and is rejected by most of the passengers and disappears, so did Lundy at the start of the antislavery movement in the 1820s present his humanitarian message in his *Genius of Universal Emancipation,* then receive a generally negative response from the American public, and die in 1836—to be followed by the renewal of his effort by other antislavery activists. Just as the Juvenile Peddler speaks a worldly, self-interested message and sells useful "conveniences" to Old Man-McLean, so did Wise and other sharp Southern politicians, such as Soulé (who later became secessionists) offer worldly, commercial, self-interested arguments in defense of the Southern system and were listened to by conservative Northern Whig politicians like McLean, who, however, lost power under the impact of the Northern Republican movement in 1856.

The various antagonists to the Confidence Man I have interpreted as representing the responses of both individuals and factions to the political and philosophical persuasions of the antislavery movement and the new party. These responses range from outright rejections of the solicitations of the movement to acquiescences in it for varying motives. The antislavery movement, further, it will be argued in the following chapter, seems to have been seen by Melville as both an expression of, and the manipulation of, a mainly Northern belief in the natural goodness of mankind and in an optimistic interpretation of the Declaration of Independence and of the Constitution in those terms. While he apparently saw the Republicans as positing as their "faith" a belief in the natural goodness of mankind, Melville saw the various negative responses to the new party—whether Democratic, Silver Grey, Cotton, or Old-Line Whig, Hunker Democratic, Know-Nothing, Temperance party, or fire-eating secessionist—as manifestations of more or less pessimistic beliefs in self-interest as fundamental to human nature and to the organization of human society, and in the Declaration and the Constitution interpreted in those terms. These widely differing interpretations of the "Founding Faith," which were increasingly articulated as the self-understandings of two differently constituted societies, diverged historically toward an apparently irreconcilable conflict. I will offer the view that Melville evidently saw, as did several of his contemporaries, the Republican optimistic belief, which required theoretically the same "trust" in the capacity for self-government of a man of African descent as it did of a man of European descent, as being in conflict with the mainly, though not exclusively, Southern belief which pessimistically denied that "trust" to any man of African descent. Moreover, with regard to the issue of the trustworthiness of the African-American and his right to citizenship—represented in the rhetorical structure by Black Guinea's "case"—Melville evidently saw the political use by the Republicans of this issue as a test case for the belief in the natural goodness of mankind as being, in fact, a rhetorical and political trap being set for unwary American voters in 1856.

As Melville presents them, Black Guinea and each of his claimed sponsors, as well as his forerunner, the Deaf-Mute, are depicted in the fiction as confidence men, and it is suggested that they are human agents of a demonic evil pervading American public life. On the other hand, the antagonists' mistrust of Black Guinea and his sponsors, which is variously Southern, Western, or Northern when it appears, is satirized as narrowly misanthropic, demonically infected with race hatred, dangerously anarchic, or as tragically selfish and limited in its aims. Melville's pasquinade appears, then, to be a *politically* nonpartisan judgment of the confrontations of political factions and extremes in a malign atmosphere of demagogic sophistry.

14

The Political Argument

Touching construction of a pact,
A paper pact, with points abstruse
As theologic ones—profuse
In matter for an honest doubt;
And which, in end, a stubborn knot
Some cut but with the sword. . . .
(Clarel, IV, V, 87–92)

In the preceding chapters it has been shown that Melville's fictional "stage," like a comic Pantomime on topical themes or like a graphic print on a contemporary political situation, is constantly making allusions to the public political and social scene. Like these other kinds of satire, *The Confidence-Man* is a statement about contemporary history; it says something about its time. Although I do not claim to have identified with certainty all the caricatures or the many allusions, it is possible on the basis of those for which good cases have been made here and by other scholars to sketch the outlines of Melville's analysis of the current historical-political situation, since the central terms and concerns can be identified and defined.

An important reflection on American political beliefs that Melville makes *in propria persona* and not through a fictional *persona* is found in his poem, "The House-Top," written about the draft riots in New York City in July 1863. In this poem he makes a direct comment upon the prevailing American "faith" concerning the nature of man and contrasts it with actual practice. He describes hearing "the Atheist roar of riot" and reflects that "man rebounds whole aeons back in nature" on such occasions, requiring that "Wise Draco come, deep in the midnight roll / Of black artillery, . . . / In code corroborating Calvin's creed / And cynic tyrannies of honest kings." He concludes, pointing to the disparity of ideal and actual human behavior:

> He ["Wise Draco"] comes, nor parlies; and the Town, redeemed,
> Gives thanks devout; nor, being thankful, heeds
> The grimy slur on the Republic's faith implied,
> Which holds that Man is naturally good,
> And—more—is Nature's Roman, never to be scourged.[1]

As he sees it, then, the American Republic's political faith assumes that man is naturally good and that the individual citizen, like the citizen of ancient Rome, should always be above the indignity of scourging. Melville evidently saw this trust in the innate goodness of the natural man as a central assumption of the political faith of his time. By the light of the "Republic's faith" the doctrine of the Declaration of Independence that "all men are created equal" and are "endowed with inalienable rights, among which are life, liberty and the pursuit of happiness" had been read and interpreted as the foundation of antislavery thought and action. Yet associated with the "faith" and creating a significant internal contradiction and potential for dispute was the written compact of the United States Constitution, with its duties in regard to the returning of fugitive slaves and its guarantees of certain property rights—including property in man, thus denying implicitly any faith in the natural goodness of the African and his descendants. By the light of the same "Republic's faith," however, the Southerner saw no contradiction in the Constitution's slavery provisions, because the faith, in his interpretation, did not include the African as "Nature's Roman"—*i.e.* as a citizen. It is this peculiar blend of political-religious faith, containing internal contradictions and differing interpretations, centering upon the question of the natural goodness of the black man, and the language associated with it that furnishes Melville with the terms of a political analysis, not unique to him, that shapes the rhetorical postures and groupings of the dialogues of *The Confidence-Man.*

Growing out of the philological dispute in the historical context about how to construe or interpret the meaning of the words in the Declaration and in the Constitution was the question of the meaning of the Republic's "faith," because more than one interpretation of it had been brought forward to guide political action in the several states. Proponents of the faith interpreted one way were most of the reformers and the antislavery politicians, orators, and journalists of the North and West, some of whom, undoubtedly, merely saw the antislavery issue, based on faith in human goodness and human rights, as a means to personal power. Webster had observed early that the slavery issue could be used as a powerful political theme by both good and evil men, and Rufus Choate had termed it a "capital on which a patriotic man, or body of men, may not trade."[2] Proponents of the faith interpreted in a different way, in which natural goodness and natural rights were assumed to be predicated only of men of European descent, were most politicians, orators, and journalists of the South, and those sympathetic to this interpretation in the North and West. These men, too, for various motives, sought power on the issues of property rights and states' rights based on their interpretation of the Declaration (though some disregarded it as a Jeffersonian effusion) and of the Constitution. The political culmination of the conflict in interpretations occurred in the founding of the Republican party in the mid-fifties, with its platform asserting its opposition to the extension of slavery, which was an expression of the Northern interpretation *vis-a-vis* the Southern as expressed in the Democratic platform. The legal culmination was the Supreme Court opinion read by Chief Justice Taney in the Dred Scott case, generally understood as a definitive triumph for the Southern interpretation that the doctrine of natural rights did not apply to the black man. In *Clarel* (1876) Rolfe, the character most representative of Melville, thinks back upon "that evil day" in 1861 when North and South rose in armed conflict, "Touching construction of a pact, / A paper pact," containing "points abstruse / As theologic ones" which were "profuse / In matter for an honest doubt" (IV, V, 87–90).[3] It was these "points abstruse / As theologic ones" concerning the construction of the United States Constitutional pact which perplexed with mounting urgency all thinking persons during the years of Melville's growth to maturity (especially men in positions of judgmental responsibility such as his father-in-law Lemuel Shaw) and which I believe are the source of the formulation of the question that gives the structure of *The Confidence-Man*: Is any man, black or white, to be trusted to act for the good of another? Or, phrased slightly differently: Is any man entitled to the trust that the American "faith" in man seems to require?

From the beginning of the nation the inconsistency between the "founding faith," interpreted as applying to all men, and the letter of the Constitution with its provisions for slavery and its implicit denial of the natural rights of certain "persons" held "to service" and its tacit affirmation of the property rights of the slaveholder, was present in the national consciousness both as a moral and a political problem. On the one hand, in time, in the antislavery movement the "faith" based on the Declaration gradually took the form of invoking a "higher law" than the Constitution, which was variously called the "moral law," "conscience," "natural law," or "Christian charity"— still always carrying within it the eighteenth-century Enlightenment premise of the natural goodness or benevolence of mankind. This historical movement produced at its extreme positions outright rejection of the Constitution, in which some such as Phillips and Garrison demanded disunion of the states or burned the Constitution, while others such as Lysander Spooner, for example, tried to reinterpret the Constitution as nonsupportive of slavery. On the other hand, on the proslavery side a fragmentation of opinions took place, some upholding slavery only because the Constitution recognized it and it was the law of the land, and some because they believed it either good or necessary in itself. Of those who accepted slavery as necessary because of the Constitutional obligation some questioned or denied any faith in natural benevolence, holding the older and more pessimistic view of the nature of mankind as true. Of these some cited the classical Aristotelean assumption expressed in his *Politics* of natural differences and inequalities of which any state for its own safety must take cognizance, while others drew upon the Augustinian-Calvinistic belief in natural depravity and held a view of the state similar to the classical view. Both these defended the Constitution and the Union but were accused by the believers in the creed of human rights and in human goodness of "infidelity" to the "founding faith" as interpreted by themselves. Yet a third group on the proslavery side consisted of those who claimed to keep the "faith" in natural rights with its underlying premise of natural benevolence and the right to liberty but denied that any person of African birth or descent was meant to be included in the political society formed by the Founding Fathers or was subject to either its rights or its obligations. The "faith" for men such as Taney in the Dred Scott opinion that he wrote was based upon a radically different interpretation of the nature of mankind and hence of the Declaration and the Constitution than, for example, that of Sumner. For these differing interpretations of the spirit and the letter of the Constitution the religious terms "faith" and "heresy" were frequently used in a manner analogous to their use in the history of Christian thought. Like the contending Christian sects, who each laid claim to the true faith in Christ but differed in their interpretations of the meaning of the Christian message, and who each called the other "heretic," so the differences in interpretation of the meaning of the "Founding Faith" led to mutual accusations of "heresy" in political interchanges.

By 1856 the conflicting interpretations of the faith became concentrated upon the specific political issue of the extension or nonextension of slavery into the Kansas-Nebraska Territory. Each party seized upon this issue as a means of testing the "fidelity" of the people to its own interpretation. The test of fidelity for the newly formed Republican party was nonextension of slavery into the territories, founded on their faith in natural rights and their interpretation of the Constitution as only tolerating slavery temporarily and locally. For the Democratic party the test was extension of slavery into the territories, property rights in the slaves' labor, states' rights, and their interpretation of the Constitution as permitting slavery in any territory or state where it was not forbidden by law. Into the Republican demand for nonextension of slavery, it should be noted, entered the hypocritical ambiguity that while for some Republicans nonextension meant granting to all men the same natural rights in federally-controlled territory, for others evidently it meant the nonextension of black persons into the territories and consequently into the projected new states. Moreover, it should be noted also that neither political party went to the logical extreme of its own interpretation. The full spectrum of opinion would include at the one extreme the abolitionist demand for the total eradication of slavery, the granting of all political rights to the African-American, and the alteration of the Constitution to forbid slavery anywhere in the nation; while at the other extreme would be the fire-eating secessionists' demand that slavery be nationalized and the Constitution altered to allow the institution everywhere.

The language of the respective party platforms bears out the existence of the radically differing interpretations about the meaning of the founding faith which I contend furnish the question that provides the structure of the arguments in *The Confidence-Man*. The Democratic platform that was drawn up at Cincinnati in June of 1856 called for strict adherence to the "principles" of the Kansas-Nebraska Act—*i.e.* "Non-interference by Congress with slavery in the territories or in the District of Columbia," which was taken to mean clearly the affirmation of the right to hold property in slaves as a national right, when not prohibited by state law. Implicit in this particular "test" was the inherent assumption that not all men are naturally good nor equally entitled to liberty, as well as the corollary view that the rights expressed in the Constitutional Bill of Rights did not apply to all persons living in the United States. Upon this issue the Democracy relied, as they stated, "to test the fidelity of the people, North and South, to the Constitution and the Union." For its part, the Republican party demanded at Philadelphia in June of 1856 the "non-extension of slavery" into the territories, making as its test of fidelity the philanthropic creed of humanitarianism and the natural rights of the Declaration and an interpretation of the Constitution as limiting the right of property in slaves to a local or state law.[4] As Henry Wilson wrote, looking back upon the Republican movement, in which he was deeply involved:

> As never before it was a conflict of principles, not of political economy and commercial greed alone, but in the higher range of morals and religious obligation. For questions of tariffs, banks, internal improvements, and the like, were substituted those of philanthropy, true patriotism, and a wise statesmanship; of human rights and the higher law.[5]

This was how the Republicans felt about the issue; this was the test of "fidelity" to the Constitution and their view, in relationship to which a nonbelieving response was to be characterized as "heresy" or "infidelity." For example, Melville's friend, Richard Lathers, who was both a New York businessman and a South Carolina slave owner, wrote in his *Reminiscences* (1907) that "Abolitionism" was "a dominant political faith of people in the North" during the 1850s.[6] And Emory Washburne, conservative Whig and ex-governor of Massachusetts, said in response to the public pressures of the Republicans after the Brooks assault that "It is not enough that you agree with them . . . you must say your creed in their words with their intonation and just when they bid you or they hang or burn you as a heretic."[7]

Melville's analysis of the current political situation penetrated, I believe, through the specific issue of the extension of slavery into the Territory of Nebraska to the question of the underlying faiths of the two parties in question, and he discerned a fundamental difference between them. By their differing points of view on the question of the nature of mankind (whether benevolent or self-interested) one can distinguish the two conflicting political faiths of the period—faiths to one or the other of which each historical person alluded to in the satire can be assigned.

The whole question of "confidence" or "trust" or "faith" is the question upon which every significant action and argument in *The Confidence-Man* turns. Melville has translated the major political choice of his time into a series of rhetorical explorations of the question of the nature of mankind, each one illustrating some aspect of the question by alluding to a specific individual or political or ethnic group involved in the political action of the time.

Earlier it has been argued that the literary structure of *The Confidence-Man* is similar to the conventional dramatic structure of Pantomime: a series of episodes in which Harlequin-Confidence Man tries to deceive various types of men, who resemble the Pantalones, Dottores, Pulcinellas, and Capitanos, of the commedia dell'arte comic tradition. It may be observed, furthermore, that in each episode the Confidence Man calls for a judgment on the part of his interlocutor. That is, he functions as a rhetorician, seeking to persuade. Traditionally, the rhetorician, whether a lawyer, orator, or statesman, sought to persuade his audience to acquiesce in the view that he took of the case in question, whereas the philosopher sought to investigate impartially the truth in the subject under examination. In *The Confidence-Man* the protagonist always seeks acquiescence in a favorable view of his "case," whether it be the "worthiness" of Black Guinea, of Ringman, of the charity fund of the Man in Gray, of the stock of Truman's company, of the medicines of the Herb-Doctor, of the PIO Man's claims, or of Frank Goodman. Moreover, he does not seek merely acquiescence—merely agreement as to the genuineness of the "case" as he sees it—but he solicits *action* founded upon the agreement with him. That is, the judgment sought is to be the foundation for the positive action of giving money. Rhetorical persuasion leads to judgment and consequent action. What, then, we must ask, are the issues upon which the judgment and the action turn in the dialogues?

The first specific question, which is the organizing one of the plot, is raised for analysis by Black Guinea's request for charity in chapter 3: Is this free "negro," Black Guinea, worthy of confidence? Out of this question springs the prior or more generic question which must be answered first: "Is the black man ("race") worthy of confidence?" Springing in turn from this is a still more generic question: "Is mankind worthy of confidence?" Then, returning back down again through more and more specific questions a synthesis of the questions can explore the question: "Is the white man ("race") worthy of confidence?" And, even more specifically: "Is this particular white man worthy of confidence?" Next, the question can be further specified by the "cases" of the six fictional individuals—the characters whom Black Guinea has claimed will "speak" for him. For example: "Is John Ringman worthy of confidence?" or, "Is Frank Goodman worthy of confidence." And so forth. Lastly, the question being asked, when expressed through the topical allusions to historical persons may become the most specific of all: "Is William Cullen Bryant worthy of confidence?" or "Is Henry Ward Beecher worthy of confidence?" And so forth.

If we return to the most generic question being raised in the rhetorical analysis above ("Whether mankind is worthy of confidence") it can be seen that it is through this question that the rhetorical analysis can be linked to the political context. For, one way to explore the question whether mankind is worthy of confidence is by dividing it into two antithetical generic questions: (1) Whether mankind is naturally good or benevolent. (For if mankind is naturally benevolent, then each man is worthy of confidence.) Or (2) Whether mankind is naturally self-interested. (For if mankind is naturally self-interested, then no man is worthy of confidence.) Generally speaking, the various Confidence Men argue from the former premise, as if it were a universal truth—their "faith"—, while their interlocutors generally argue from the antithetical premise. It is the former premise, always defended by the Confidence Men, that carries the reader back in his consideration of the book to the Deaf-Mute's "message" of "charity" (love, trust) written on his slate, while the latter premise, assumed by the skeptical interlocutors, carries the reader back to the Barber's "message" of "No Trust." So the two parties to the dialogues usually hold mutually contradictory premises about the nature of mankind. It is, apparently, these mutually contradictory premises about mankind that Melville sees as being at the foundation of the political conflict.

If we look at the sort of statement the Deaf-Mute's "charity" message is, it becomes evident that it is not an experiential observation with which all would agree, since it is treated with skepticism and immediately contradicted by the Barber's "No Trust" message. It appears rather to be a moral injunction or a statement of opinion. It is, in fact, a powerfully connotative imperative with the paraphrasable meaning: One should feel the emotion of love or charity for every man irrespective of one's knowledge or lack of knowledge of his essential nature. The direct sources of this doctrine are not to be found in the Christian theological interpretation of St. Paul's words, with its implicit assumption of original sin and of man's need for grace from God in order to love, but are rather in the sentimental Rousseauistic doctrine of romantic love—a doctrine of Christian sentimentalism founded upon the premise of man's natural goodness. However, in the wording which the Deaf-Mute borrows from the Pauline Epistle, the doctrine carries with it to its audience the aura of Christian Revelation—the aura of authority and of powerful feeling. Yet, it is presented by a character who has "no badge of authority," and it is ripped from its complex Christian doctrinal and theological context and hence can be made subject to the various ambiguous interpretations that the later Confidence Men impose upon it. They exploit it as moral doctrine, carrying connotations of Christian authority, even while disregarding the Christian assumption of original sin, and substituting instead the Enlightenment premise of man's natural benevolence. I believe that Melville saw this premise, with its strong religious overtones, as the foundation of the Republican "faith."

In each of his arguments the intention of the Confidence Man is to convince his interlocutor to accept his assumption, for, if he succeeds, he can draw, then, the logical conclusion, which the interlocutor must accept, that he, personally, is worthy of confidence. His rhetorical method, then, in each particular case takes the form of a syllogism: If one grants that all mankind are to be presumed to be benevolent (following the "Christian" injunction that "charity thinketh no evil"), and if one grants that the speaker is a man, then, one must grant that the speaker is benevolent and therefore worthy of trust. Within the syllogistic paradigm all of the explorations of collateral themes and opinions take place. For example: the themes of the existence and prevalence of the "Misanthrope" and the "Philanthropist." Charlie Noble, by taking up the specific question of the reality of a true "Misanthrope" and by demonstrating his existence by relating the story of the racist Indian-hater Colonel Moredock, gives a decidedly negative answer to the question whether mankind is naturally benevolent. He defends with historical evidence his assumption of the malevolence of at least two portions of mankind—the Indians and the frontier settler responding to the Indians. His "faith" is manifestly different and his premises, too, from the Confidence Man's. This is why the only response to Noble's story that Frank Goodman—the defender of natural goodness—can make is that he does not believe the story of Moredock to be true. For the sake of his "creed" he is obliged to deny historical evidence. Hence, Noble, having utterly denied Goodman's premise, is not caught in his syllogistic trap, when he is asked to loan him money, even though for the sake of conviviality he has pretended friendship.

257

It appears, then, that the opposite assumption about the nature of mankind is made by those interlocutors of the Confidence Man who are not taken in—the most pessimistic being the Wooden-Legged Man-Bennett, Invalid Titan-Calhoun, and Peddler-Wise. All share some belief in the Barber's injunction not to trust, which is based on the inherent assumption that men are by nature self-interested. The background of this injunction is represented as either classical (Aristotelean-Tacitean) or Christian (Augustinian-Calvinistic). I believe that Melville saw this premise as being at the root of the Southern insistence upon the maintenance and the extension of the enslavement of the black people, and of the Democratic party as it was taken over by the Southern interests.

The rhetorical analysis is connected to Melville's political analysis by way of the philosophical question as to the nature of man, for it is by their differing points of view on this question that one can distinguish the two conflicting political "faiths" of the period—faiths to one or the other of which each historical person alluded to in *The Confidence-Man* can be assigned. The Confidence Man is typically a Republican, who professes a political creed that is founded on faith in the goodness of mankind, while his antagonist is a Democrat, Nativist, or other opponent of the Republicans whose creed is implicitly based on the view that mankind is fundamentally self-interested. These creeds, in their opposition to one another, reflect a long-standing difference of opinion about the "Founding Faith" of the United States and differing interpretations of the meaning of the Declaration of Independence and of the Constitution.

The political analysis, in paralleling the rhetorical analysis, gives the scheme of the characters. Generally speaking, the formation and action of the Republican party is represented by the actions and persuasions of the various Confidence Men, while the fragmented Democratic party and the broken-up Whig party, the Nativists and the one Temperance party man are represented by the various interlocutors. Each of these in differing ways either places trust in the Confidence Man, revealing thus his espousal of the creed of benevolence—joins the new party—or he suspects and repulses him—remains Democratic or Whig or, at the extreme, remains secessionist. Of the antagonists, those who trust the Confidence Man (*e.g.* Country Merchant-Wilmot, Collegian-Raymond, Miser-Blair, Sick Man-Old Whig, Thomas Fry-Law, and Old Man-McLean) all represent various former Democrats, Whigs, or Nativists who went over to the Republican cause. Those who trust him only temporarily (*e.g.* Pitch-Benton and Barber-Douglas) represent Democrats who were sympathetic with Northern views but did not go for Republicanism. Of those who do not put their faith in the "confidence" creed of the Confidence Man certain figures (*e.g.* the Hard-Hearted Man-Cass) represent those who remained either Hunker Democrats or Whigs, while others (*e.g.* Titan-Cal-houn, Noble-Yancey, and Juvenile Peddler-Wise) represent the extreme pro-slavery Southern sectionalists. Though not all of the characters have been identified with equal probability and at least two not yet specifically, sufficient evidence has been adduced to indicate the existence of a pattern in the satire according to which important figures in the public political context of the 1850s take their places either as believers in the creed of confidence in man-kind or as disbelievers. And within the pattern some figures are delineated as hypocritical (professing the philanthropic creed even while exploiting it to their own advantage), while others are shown as inconsistent, these charac-teristics forming part of Melville's satirical commentary upon human nature.

The main impulse to the satire of the Republicans as confidence men seems to have been Melville's conviction that they were founding their appeal upon an inadequate and untrue view of the nature of man and society. In claiming that human nature was good and might be capable of perfection within the nineteenth century they were simply wrong and their motives had to be interpreted as either those of fools (*i.e.* they really believed what they said) or knaves (*i.e.* they said things they did not really believe). Because of this judgment of them he saw the formation of the Republican party—a sectional party—as a menace to the Union.

The concluding chapter of *The Confidence-Man* is important for under-standing Melville's overall criticism of both sides in the political crisis of 1856 and in showing that his view was probably not unique. The contrasting antithetical points of view, represented on the one side by the characters from the Deaf-Mute-Lundy through Goodman-Beecher, and on the other side by those of Barber-Douglas through Peddler-Wise, are depicted in the last chap-ter as being possibly in dangerous collusion with one another. In the Gentle-men's Cabin, Goodman-Beecher confronts Juvenile Peddler-Wise—the one representing Republicanism and the other secessionism—, yet the Peddler tips Beecher a "wink expressive of an indefinite degree of knowingness" and says that "those who give blacksmiths the most work" (*i.e.* thieves) seldom use locks to protect their money. The secret collusion of apparent rivals or enemies that is hinted at here between them suggests a criticism of the political situation in 1856 by Melville that has parallels in other observers, such as Benton and Bennett, and is clearly exemplified by three prints, two earlier and one later than Melville's book.

The first is the print entitled "The Hurly-Burly Pot" (1850), already referred to in earlier Chapters (plate 6). Expressing an indictment of extremist agitators of proslavery as well as antislavery views, it shows Wilmot, Garrison, and Greeley, on the one hand, as "stirring" up trouble by casting into a pot bags labelled "Free-Soil," "Abolition," "Fourierism," and "Blue Laws," while

Calhoun casts in "Treason." Wilmot says, "Bubble, bubble . . . Free Soil the Union spoil, / Come grief and moan, / Peace be none, / Til we divided be!" Calhoun says, "For success to the whole mixture, we invoke our great patron Saint Benedict Arnold." Underneath the pot Arnold says, "Well done . . ."[8] The second print, "A Pictorial Parody," which appears in the New York *Lantern* in 1852, shows Young Diogenes (the character who represents the periodical itself) in the role of the Infant Hercules in his cradle "strangling the serpents of Disunion and Abolitionism"—the snakes being labelled respectively "Secession" and "Abolitionism."[9] This artist, who is Frank Bellew, saw—and I suggest that Melville did also—the destructive effects of extremism on both political sides as similar in their danger to the nation and sought to use the power of satirical commentary as a corrective. A third print, later than *The Confidence-Man*, which makes its point by means of individual caricatures is the famous one in *Vanity Fair* in 1861 entitled "'Like Meets Like'" (plate 26). In this, the artist depicts Garrison, dressed as a Quaker, shaking hands with Lawrence Keitt, the South Carolina fire-eating representative (his trousers marked with the palmettos and crossed arrows of his state) saying "Well, friend, at last we meet in unity to destroy 'this accursed Union.' 'Twas only a misunderstanding this many years. We were always one at heart."[10] The two political extremes, differing in their ultimate premises, are seen as destructively alike in their aims and effects. The Garrisonian abolitionists' purely humanitarian cause, founded upon the theoretical premise of natural goodness, is depicted as similar to and in agreement with the proslavery fire-eating inhumanitarian extremism of the South—the theoretical institutionalization of depravity, which Melville himself called "the systematic degradation of man." In the end, the Republicans such as Beecher, innocently or not, represented to Melville the politically effective extension of the Garrisonian position, a position that he saw as potentially destructive of the nation and possibly, even, conducive to slavery's extension and continuation.[11]

It must constantly be remembered that *The Confidence-Man* was written before the military civil conflict, before the emergence of Lincoln, and before Emancipation. There is no way that Melville could have predicted—although he feared—the full tragedy of the war, or that the North would win, or that the slaves would be freed by executive action, ending the moral nightmare of slavery without the widely feared "servile insurrection." Nor could he have predicted that a politician might appear who would become truly a statesman. Rather, for him and for other intelligent men the strong possibility still existed in 1856, besides that of a civil war, that the South, influenced by extremists on both sides, might secede and form an independent nation which might extend and perpetuate slavery indefinitely immediately on the border of the free American nation, throughout the Caribbean area, and into Central and even South America. He mentions this possibility in his prose "Supplement" to *Battle-Pieces*. Another possibility to which extremism might lead would be a civil war in which the South would win and which would, then, result in making slavery *national* throughout the United States. We must use our historical imagination to see the contemporary situation in a time of great crisis as Melville saw it: as a choice among greater and lesser evils, some actual and some potential. The rise of the sectionalizing Republican party, threatening to evoke a sectional secessionist response from the South, might, then, seem to pose the eventual threat of one or another of these three evils: (1) the breakup of the Union in a civil war; (2) a powerful, independent nation totally committed to slavery bordering the United States and commanding the mouth of the Mississippi; or (3) a civil conflict in which the slave states might possibly win and might then be able to impose slavery nationally. To us with the hindsight of actual history, these two latter possibilities are difficult to recreate imaginatively, but they were real threats to antebellum Northern thinkers. It should not, then, be a matter of wonder to us that Melville might see as dangerous both the Republican extremists, such as Parker, Sumner and Greeley, and those Republicans, such as Bryant, Weed, and Beecher, who were not extreme in their expression but naïve about the possible consequences of the rise of the sectional party not just to the Union but to the perpetuation of slavery on the American continent. Unlike many of the abolitionists and Republicans Melville did not, I think, merely wish to rid himself or his section of the "sinful" guilt of slavery at any cost to the nation or to the enslaved African-Americans. Nor did he wish to run the risk of destroying the Union by precipitating a violent conflict that might well fail to achieve its intended benign end—like the mad ship in his poem "The Berg: A Dream." Rather, I think that he did not have any political solution to present other than mutual tolerance and patience (such as he counselled to both sides after the war in the "Supplement" to *Battle-Pieces*), but that he wished that his audience see that the issues involved were clouded over to the point of obscurity by bad reasoning, opportunistic political action, inadequate and unrealistic conceptions of human nature and history, and especially by human greed, ambition, hypocrisy, fear, pride, and ignorance. As literary satirist he delineated certain public men of his time as worse, probably, than they really were in order to shock them into seeing themselves as considerably less than they imagined themselves to be.

Melville wrote of Northern philanthropic intentions after the conclusion of the Civil War in the "Supplement" a statement that summarizes the single observation (if it can be reduced to a single observation) underlying *The Confidence-Man*: "Benevolent desires, after passing a certain point, can not undertake their own fulfillment without incurring the risk of evils beyond those sought to be remedied." The benevolent desire to abolish slavery in the immediate historical circumstances of the 1850s ran, in his view, I suggest, not only the risk of civil war but also that of extending and perpetuating slavery on the American continent. Of the Southerners, as influenced by the ultra secessionists he observed that they were "a people for years politically misled by designing men, and also by some honestly erring men, who [were] influential," and that they "sought to perpetuate the curse of slavery, and even extend it" though they were not authors of it, but the "fated inheritors" of it. Reflecting, I suggest, upon the persuasive rhetoric in the orations and writings of men such as Calhoun, Keitt, Yancey, Wise, Davis, Rhett, Ruffin, and others, he says that the people of the South were "cajoled into revolution" under the plea, plausibly urged, that certain inestimable rights guaranteed by the Constitution were directly menaced. The "arts of conspirators and the perversity of fortune" entrapped their love of liberty into support of a war "whose implied end was the erecting . . . of an Anglo-American empire based upon the systematic degradation of man."[12] It seems evident from these explicit reflections of Melville, made after the war was over, that he saw the origins of the conflict in retrospect—and with a more dispassionate eye— much as an understanding of the political analysis in *The Confidence-Man* and of its topical context of persons and issues reveals that he saw it ten years earlier.

Notes

1. *The Problem of* The Confidence Man: His Masquerade

1. Watson G. Branch, ed. *Melville: The Critical Heritage* (London and Boston, 1974), pp. 37–38, 369, 373.
2. For a study of the demonic imagery, John W. Shroeder, "Sources and Symbols for Melville's *Confidence-Man,*" *Publications of the Modern Language Association of America,* 66 (1951), 363–80; for general interpretation and historical notes, see Herman Melville, *The Confidence-Man: His Masquerade,* ed. Elizabeth Foster (New York, 1954), pp. xiii–xcv, 287–365 (hereafter cited as Foster, ed., *C-M*). Throughout my book page references to Melville's text are to Foster's edition. For the work's place in the Ship of Fools tradition, see Edward Rosenberry, "Melville's Ship of Fools," *PMLA,* 75 (1960), 604–08. For a history of the work's reception, Watson Branch, Hershel Parker, Harrison Hayford, and Alma A. MacDougall, "Historical Note," in Harrison Hayford, Hershel Parker, and G. Thomas Tanselle, ed., *The Confidence-Man: His Masquerade* (Evanston and Chicago, 1984).
3. Foster, ed., *C-M,* pp. xiv, xxxv, xlvii–xlix, lvi–lvii, lxviii–lxix.
4. Yvor Winters, *Maule's Curse* (Norfolk, Conn., 1938), p. 85 (rpt. in *In Defense of Reason* (New York, 1947); Egbert S. Oliver, "Melville's Picture of Emerson and Thoreau in *The Confidence-Man,*" *College English,* 8 (1946), 61–72 (rpt. in his *Studies in American Literature: Whitman, Emerson, Melville, and Others* [New Delhi, 1965], pp. 86–104); Foster, ed., *C-M,* lxxiii–lxxxii, 351–61.
5. Oliver, "Emerson and Thoreau in *C-M,*" pp. 68–72; Hershel Parker, "Melville's Satire of Emerson and Thoreau: An Evaluation of the Evidence," *American Transcendental Quarterly,* No. 7, pt. 2 (Summer 1970), pp. 61–67 (rpt. in Raymona E. Hull, ed., *Studies in the Minor and Later Works of Melville* [Hartford, 1970]); Foster, ed., *C-M,* pp. 351–52.
6. Harrison Hayford, "Poe in *The Confidence-Man,*" *Nineteenth-Century Fiction,* 14 (1959), 207–18.
7. William Norris, "Abbott Lawrence in *The Confidence-Man*: American Success or American Failure?" *American Studies,* 17 (Spring 1976), 25–38.
8. This discussion of commedia dell'arte and Pantomime in relationship to *The Confidence-Man* is based on Helen P. Trimpi, "Harlequin-Confidence Man: The Satirical Tradition of Commedia Dell'Arte and Pantomime in Melville's *The Confidence-Man,*" *Texas Studies in Literature and Language,* 16 (Spring 1974), 147–93. Cf. Tom Quirk, *Melville's Confidence Man: From Knave to Knight* (Columbia, Mo., 1982), pp. 19–30.

9. David Mayer, *Harlequin in His Element: The English Pantomime, 1806–1836* (Cambridge, Mass., 1969), pp. 1–5, 24. Trimpi, "Harlequin-Confidence Man," pp. 162–67.
10. Trimpi, "Harlequin-Confidence Man," pp. 156–58.
11. Johannes Dietrich Bergmann, "The Original Confidence Man," *American Quarterly*, 21 (Fall 1969), 560–77.
12. For further discussion of Lawrence as the Gentleman with Gold Sleeve-Buttons and of Theodore Parker as the Man in Grey, see Chapter 7.

2. Melville's Political World, 1819–1860, and His Early Satire On It

1. Sources for the historical summaries contained in this chapter will be found in the historical, biographical and other studies to be cited in later chapters. For the record of Melville's contacts with contemporaries see Jay Leyda, *The Melville Log: A Documentary Life of Herman Melville, 1819–1891* (New York, 1951; 1969), *passim*.
2. Quoted in Hershel Parker, "Melville and Politics: A Scrutiny of the Political Milieux of Herman Melville's Life and Works" (Ph.D. diss., Northwestern University, 1963), p. 21. I am indebted throughout this summary of Melville's immediate political milieu to Parker's dissertation and his article, "Gansevoort Melville's Role in the Campaign of 1844," *New York Historical Society Quarterly*, 49 (April 1965), 143–73.
3. William H. Gilman, *Melville's Early Life and "Redburn"* (New York, 1951), pp. 15–16.
4. Gilman, *Melville's Early Life*, p. 106; Parker, "Melville and Politics," p. 41.
5. Harrison Hayford and Merrell Davis, "Herman Melville as Office-Seeker," *Modern Language Quarterly*, 10 (June 1949), 168–83, and (September 1949), 377–88, *passim*.
6. Hayford and Davis, "Melville as Office-Seeker," p. 387.
7. *Collected Poems of Herman Melville*, ed. Howard P. Vincent (Chicago, 1947), p. 461.
8. Richard Lathers, *Reminiscences of Richard Lathers . . . ,* ed. Alvan F. Sanborn (New York, 1907), p. 328.
9. *The Letters of Herman Melville*, ed. Merrell R. Davis and William H. Gilman (New Haven, 1960), p. 29.
10. Leon Howard, *Herman Melville: A Biography* (Berkeley and Los Angeles, 1951), p. 124.
11. Emory Washburne quoted in David Donald, *Charles Sumner and the Coming of the Civil War* (New York, 1960), p. 303.
12. Parker, "Melville and Politics," p. 75.
13. Parker, "Melville and Politics," pp. 182–86.
14. Melville, *Letters,* eds. Davis and Gilman, p. 86.
15. *Yankee Doodle*, 2:152, 167, 172, 188, 199, 202, 229 (24, 31 July; 7, 14, 21, 28 August; 11 September 1847); repr. in *Herman Melville's Authentic Anecdotes of Old Zack*, ed. Kenneth Starosciak (New Brighton, Minn., 1973).

Cf. Perry Miller, *The Raven and the Whale: The War of Words and Wits in the Era of Poe and Melville* (New York, 1956), pp. 213–14.

16. On political caricature and cartoons as art see E. H. Gombrich and E. Kris, *Caricature* (Harmondsworth, England, 1940); E. H. Gombrich, "Imagery and Art in the Romantic Period" and "The Cartoonist's Armoury," in *Meditations on a Hobby Horse and Other Essays on the Theory of Art* (London and New York, 1963), pp. 120–26, 127–142. On European political caricature and for reproductions of prints see W. M. Thackeray, *The Paris Sketch Book of Mr. Titmarsh* (London, 1840), pp. 60–69; Werner Hofmann, *Caricature from Leonardo to Picasso* (New York, 1957); Enrico Gianeri, *Storia della caricatura* (Milano, 1959); M. Dorothy George, *English Political Caricature 1793–1832: A Study of Opinion and Propaganda* (Oxford, 1959); Bevis Hillier, *Cartoons and Caricatures* (London, 1970); Arthur B. Maurice and Frederic T. Cooper, *The History of the Nineteenth Century in Caricature* (New York, 1904; 1970); Ronald Searle, Claude Roy, and Bernd Bornemann, *La caricature: Art et manifeste du XVIe siècle à nos jours* (Geneva, 1974); and William Feaver, *Masters of Caricature* (New York, 1981).

17. On American political prints see Joseph B. Bishop, *Our Political Drama: Conventions, Campaigns, and Candidates* (New York, 1904); Frank Weitenkampf, *American Graphic Art* (New York, 1924); Frank Luther Mott, *A History of American Magazines: 1741–1850* (New York, 1930); William Murrell, *A History of American Graphic Humor* (New York, 1933–38); Frank Luther Mott, *A History of American Magazines: 1850–1865* (Cambridge, Mass., 1938); Harry T. Peters, *Currier & Ives: Printmakers to the American People* (Garden City, N.Y., 1942); Allan Nevins and Frank Weitenkampf, *A Century of Political Cartoons: Caricature in the United States from 1800 to 1900* (New York, 1944); Frederic A. Conningham, *Currier & Ives: An Illustrated Check List* (New York, 1949); Frank Weitenkampf, *Political Caricature in the United States in Separately Published Cartoons: An Annotated List* (New York, 1953; 1971); Stefan Lorant, *The Presidency: A Pictorial History of Presidential Elections from Washington to Truman* (New York, 1951); Stephen Hess and Milton Kaplan, *The Ungentlemanly Art: A History of American Political Cartoons*, rev. ed. (New York and London, 1975); and Ron Tyler, ed., *The Image of America in Caricature & Cartoon* (Fort Worth, Tex., 1976). Special studies will be cited in connection with individual prints.

18. Frank Weitenkampf, "New York State in National Politics: Notes for a Cartoon Record," *New York Historical Society Quarterly*, 30 (April 1946), 80.

19. Herman Melville, *Mardi: And a Voyage Thither,* ed. Harrison Hayford, Hershel Parker, and G. Thomas Tanselle (Evanston and Chicago, 1970), pp. 465–555; Merrell Davis, *Melville's "Mardi": A Chartless Voyage* (New Haven, 1952), pp. 81–99, 156–59.

20. See Davis, *Chartless Voyage,* pp. 88, 158. For additional details of Allen's career, appearance, and style, see Reginald Charles McGrane, *William Allen: A Study in Western Democracy* (Columbus, Ohio, 1925). McGrane notes Allen's

"insatiable love for talking" (p. 48), his "tall, erect figure, . . . deep and powerful voice, his impassioned and energetic gesticulation" (p. 76), and describes his famous speech on the Oregon Question as a "philippic against English diplomacy and methods" (p. 109). The New York *Herald* called his Oregon speech "mere Mark Anthony bombast" (pp. 114–15).

21. See Chapter 9 for the public image in the North of Calhoun.

22. For Dallas's appearance see prints in Albert Shaw, *Abraham Lincoln: His Path to the Presidency* (New York, 1929), I (of two vols., hereafter cited as Shaw, *AL,* I), pp. 99, 106, 107, 108, 110, and 113.

23. *Dictionary of American Biography,* ed. Allen Johnson and Dumas Malone (New York, 1928–36), "Gideon Pillow." Nicholas Trist called Pillow an "intriguer" and one who "gives himself out as the *maker* of the President . . . and as the President's *other self.*" Znobbi's act of theft may allude to one of several questionable incidents in Pillow's Mexican War career, where he had the reputation of being not only conceited, as Znobbi is, but as unprincipled, according to Trist, for his connections with bribery and alleged theft; Irving Eugene McCormac, *James K. Polk: A Political Biography* (Berkeley, 1922), pp. 340, 511, 526, 531. Pillow is caricatured blowing up "Polk's Patent Self-Inflating Pillow" in a Library of Congress print, repr. Charles A. McCoy, *Polk and the Presidency* (Austin, 1960), fig. 6. Znobbi's being "a runaway native of Porpheero" does not, however, have any parallel circumstance in Pillow's life.

24. Davis, *Chartless Voyage,* pp. 87–90.

25. Parker, "Melville and Politics," p. 176.

3. Melville's "Graphic" Methods

1. John Dixon Hunt, "Dickens and the Traditions of Graphic Satire," in John Dixon Hunt, ed., *Encounters: Essays on Literature and the Visual Arts* (New York, 1971), p. 126.

2. "The 'Mustang' Team" (1856), Department of Special Collections, University Research Library, University of California, Los Angeles (hereafter cited as UCLA); repr. Shaw, *AL,* I, 185 (plate 15); "Col. Fremont's Last Grand Exploring Expedition in 1856," Huntington Library, San Marino (hereafter cited as HL), repr. Shaw, *AL,* I, 187 (plate 14); poster, *"Black Republican,"* repr. Allan Nevins, *Frémont: The West's Greatest Adventurer* (New York, 1928), II, 516; "The 'Irrepressible Conflict' . . ." (1860), HL and American Antiquarian Society Print Collection (hereafter cited as AAS), repr. Albert Shaw, *Abraham Lincoln: The Year of His Election* (New York, 1929), II (of two vols., hereafter cited as Shaw, *AL,* II), 51 (plate 22).

3. "Political Jugglers Losing Their Balance" (1840), AAS, repr. Shaw, *AL,* I, 89; "The Captain & Corporal's Guard" (1841), AAS (plate 3). "Patent Balancing by an Amateur" (1848), AAS; "Experiments on the Tight Rope" (1852), AAS; "Presidential Trio," *Young America,* 1, n.s. (1856), 307, AAS copy (plate 20). In 1852 in the New York *Lantern,* "The Whig Organ;

Exhibiting a Specimen of the Feathered Tribe" shows Greeley performing as an organ-grinder in company with Winfield Scott, his monkey, while Raymond of the *Times* is drawn as his trick dog on a leash, *Lantern,* 2 (28 August 1852) n.p., New York Historical Society (hereafter cited as NYHS) copy. "The Political Heller; Or Second-Sight Cabinets" portrays Seward as Robert Heller, the conjurer, and Greeley as his small boy medium, *Lantern,* 3 (January–July 1853), n.p., NYHS copy. Combining the idea of an entertainment with a contest is "The Rival Babies: A Comedy in One Act, Now Performing . . . through All the States," in the *Lantern* in 1852, in which Greeley holds Scott as his baby, while James Gordon Bennett, editor of the *Herald,* holds Pierce, his candidate, *Lantern,* 2 (23 October 1852), n.p., NYHS copy. Likewise, "The Massachusetts Baby Show" (1852?) makes use of the baby-show situation, concentrating on politics in that state, NYHS and Massachusetts Historical Society (hereafter cited as MHS). Entertainment and begging appear in "The Great Exhibition of 1860" (1860), HL, and in "'Taking the Stump' or, Stephen in Search of His Mother" (1860), HL (plates 23 and 24).

4. "The Plumb-Pudding in Danger . . ." (1805), repr. Gombrich, *Meditations,* fig. 94 and Shaw, *AL,* I, 36; "The Old 'Un and the Young 'Un" (1855?), repr. Maurice and Cooper, *Nineteenth Century in Caricature,* p. 128. A good example from 1860, "Settling Vexation by Annexation," shows John Bull with his port wine at table with Jonathan with his mint julep and cigar, discussing "this plaguy French business," *Vanity Fair,* 2 (25 August 1860), 105, repr. Shaw, *AL,* I, 221 (plate 21).

5. Examples of cockfighting: "Political Cock Fighters" (1844), repr. Shaw, *AL,* I, 104: "Grand Fight for the Champion's Belt Between Granite Pierce and Old Chapultepec" (1852), NYHS; and "The Great Match at Baltimore Between the 'Illinois Bantam' and the 'Old Cock' of the White House" (1860), repr. Shaw, *AL,* II, 79. Examples of prizefights: "Set-To Between the Champion Old Tip and the Swell Dutchman of Kinderhook. 1836" (1836), AAS, repr. Shaw, *AL,* I, 52, and "The Undecided Political Prize Fight" (1858), repr. Shaw, *AL,* I, 218. Examples of card games: "A Political Game of Brag" (1831), AAS; "All Fours, or Old Sludge" (1840), AAS (plate 2); and "The Political Game of Bluff" (1860), repr. Shaw, *AL,* II, 33. Examples of hunting and fishing: "The Hunter of Kentucky" (1844), repr. Shaw, *AL,* I, 102; "The Great American Buck Hunt of 1856," AAS, repr. Shaw, *AL,* I, 189; and "The Presidential Fishing Party of 1848," Peters, *Currier & Ives,* p. 154.

6. "The Man Wot Drives the Constitution" (1844), AAS (plate 4); "The Great Presidential Race of 1856," AAS and the Harry T. Peters Collection of the Smithsonian Institution in the National Museum of History and Technology; "The Great American Buck Hunt of 1856," AAS, repr. Shaw, *AL,* I, 189. Prints of races include an untitled poster of a footrace among Jackson, William H. Crawford, John Quincy Adams, and Clay in 1824, repr. Shaw,

AL, I, 37; one among Scott, Webster, and Pierce in "Great Footrace for the Presidential Purse ($100,000 and Pickings) Over the Union Course 1852," repr. Shaw, *AL,* I, 164; "The Great American Steeplechase for 1844," AAS; "Handicap Race, Presidential Stakes. 1844," AAS; "The Great Presidential Sweepstakes of 1856," repr. Shaw, *AL,* I, 184; and the "Grand Sweepstakes for 1862," AAS, among the Republican contenders themselves.

7. For Marcy see "Liberty the Fair Maid of Kansas—in the Hands of the 'Border Ruffians'" (1856), Houghton Library and Stanford Museum Print Collection, repr. Shaw, *AL,* I, 169 (plate 12). For one of many of Jackson see "Great Presidential Steeple Chase of 1844," repr. Shaw, *AL,* I, 101. For one of many of Greeley, "The Great Exhibition of 1860," HL, repr. Shaw, *AL,* II, 99 (plate 23).

8. For Webster, "A Piercing Piece of Loco Foco Hocus Pocus" (1852), AAS. For Jackson's habit of using the expletive "By the Eternal" as a verbal tag, see "The Death of Locofocoism" (1840), AAS (plate 1), "Requesting Him to Resign" (1844), repr. Shaw, *AL,* I, 99, and "Matty Meeting the Texas Question" (1844), repr. Shaw, *AL,* I, 106.

9. On the Doyles see Bishop, *Our Political Drama,* pp. 112–17; Maurice and Cooper, *Nineteenth Century in Caricature,* p. 149; John Doyle, *The Seven Years of William IV: A Reign Cartooned by John Doyle,* ed. G. M. Trevelyan (London, 1952), *passim*; Feaver, *Masters of Caricature,* p. 69.

10. Greeley as a horse, "Col. Fremont's Last Grand Exploring Expedition in 1856," HL, repr. Shaw, *AL,* I, 187 (plate 14) and as a lamb, "The Lion and the Lamb" (1856), *Young America,* 1, n.s. (1856), 295 (plate 19); Scott as a turkey and Pierce as a cock, "Ornithology. Two Great Birds of the United States, Not Described by Audubon" (1852), repr. Shaw, *AL,* I, 167; Van Buren as a fox, "The Man Wot Drives the Constitution" (1844), AAS (plate 4); "The Democratic Funeral of 1848," repr. Shaw, *AL,* I, 154; Bennett as a lion, "The Lion and the Lamb," (plate 19) and as a terrier, "Badgering Him," *Vanity Fair,* 2 (29 December 1860), 321, repr. Shaw, *AL,* II, 207; members of Jackson's cabinet as rats in "The Rats Leaving a Falling House" (1831), repr. Murrell, *American Graphic Humor,* I, 109; Buchanan, Frémont, George Law and others as rats, "Fancied Security, or the Rats on a Bender" (1856), UCLA, repr. Nevins and Weitenkampf, *Century of Political Cartoons,* p. 75 (plate 16); Lincoln as a stick man, "A 'Rail' Old Western Gentleman," repr. Shaw, *AL,* II, 42.

11. Examples of this are prints of Napoleon as Harlequin in a French print (1814), repr. Feaver, *Masters of Caricature,* p. 19, and of King William IV as Harlequin, repr. George, *English Political Caricature,* II, pl. 94; President Tyler as Harlequin in "The Man Wot Drives the Constitution" (1844), AAS (plate 4); Fillmore as a monkey-Harlequin, "The Presidential Harlequin" (1851), HL (plate 7); of a German journalist as Harlequin in "Der journalistische Eiertanz" and of King Victor Emmanuel as Harlequin, repr. Searle, Roy, and Bornemann, *La caricature,* pp. 159, 169. For Melville's adaptation

of the other commedia dell'arte and Pantomime masks to his characters see Trimpi, "Harlequin-Confidence Man," pp. 170–90.

12. "The Hurly-Burly Pot" (1850), Library of Congress (hereafter referred to as LC), plate 6; "A Proslavery Incantation Scene . . . ." (1856), AAS. Other examples are "New Edition of Macbeth. Bank-Oh's! Ghost" (1837?), repr. Shaw, *AL*, I, 85 and "Dogberry's Last Charge," *Vanity Fair*, 2 (15 December 1860), 297, repr. Shaw, *AL*, II, 145.

13. "[Mad Tom in a Rage]" (1801?), Houghton, repr. Thomas A. Bailey, *The American Pageant: A History of the Republic*, 4th ed. (Lexington, Mass., 1971), I, 197 and Thomas C. Blaisdel, Jr., Peter Selz and Seminar, *The American Presidency in Political Cartoons, 1776–1976* (Berkeley, 1976), p. 45. For "A Late Student," see John Sullivan, "The Case of 'A Late Student': Pictorial Satire in Jacksonian America," *Proceedings of the American Antiquarian Society*, 83 (October 1973), 277–86; for "Nick" Biddle, "The Downfall of Mother Bank" (1832?), AAS; for Jackson as demonic, "Polk's Dream" (1846), repr. Shaw, *AL*, I, 124 and Blaisdel, *American Presidency*, p. 77; "The Death of Locofocoism" (1840), AAS (plate 1); "The Captain & Corporal's Guard" (1841), AAS (plate 3); "The Hurly Burly Pot" (1850), LC (plate 6); "The Position of the Democratic Party in 1852," repr. Blaisdel, *American Presidency*, p. 83; "Worship of the North," HL; "Worship of the North" and "Writing of the Emancipation Proclamation," repr. in *The Work of Adalbert Johann Volck 1828–1912, Who Chose for His Name the Anagram V. Blada*, ed. George McCullough Anderson (Baltimore, 1970), n.p. and "Worship of the North," repr. Shaw, *AL*, I, 62–63 (plate 28).

14. Foster, ed., *C-M*, pp. xlix–l; Shroeder, "Sources and Symbols," pp. 363–80; Hershel Parker, ed. *The Confidence-Man: His Masquerade* (New York, 1971), p. ix.

15. See Linda Kerber, *Federalists in Dissent: Imagery and Ideology in Jeffersonian America* (Ithaca, 1970).

16. Wilson Walker Cowen, "Melville's Marginalia" (Ph.D. diss., Harvard University, 1965), "Introduction."

4. The First Two Confidence Men (the Deaf-Mute and Black Guinea) and Two Antagonists (the Barber and the Drover)

1. For Woolman see John Greenleaf Whittier's Introduction to his edition of *The Journal of John Woolman* (Boston, 1871), pp. 1–49; his poem, "To — with a Copy of Woolman's Journal," which terms him "frail and weak . . . poor and lowly . . . / Yet may prove an angel holy / In a pilgrim's guise," *Complete Poetical Works of John Greenleaf Whittier* (Boston, 1894), pp. 171–73; Janet Whitney, *John Woolman: American Quaker* (Boston, 1942), pp. 276–77; David Brion Davis, *The Problem of Slavery in Western Culture* (Ithaca, N.Y., 1966), pp. 483–93; John Woolman, *The Journal and Major Essays*, ed. Phillips P. Moulton (New York, 1971), p. 13. Passages on his clothing are

in *Journal*, ed. Whittier, pp. 179–83 (Chap. VIII, 1761, 1762), 269–70 (Chap. XII, 1772).

2. Thomas Earle, *The Life, Travels and Opinions of Benjamin Lundy Including His Journeys to Texas and Mexico* . . . (Philadelphia, 1847; rpt. New York, 1969), frontispiece portrait, pp. 307–08. The account of Lundy in Henry Wilson, *History of the Rise and Fall of the Slave Power in America* (Boston, 1872), I, 167–74, seems to be based on Earle and on Garrison's statements.

3. Wendell P. Garrison and Francis J. Garrison, *William Lloyd Garrison: 1815–1879* . . . (New York, 1885), I, 87–99; Merton L. Dillon, *Benjamin Lundy and the Struggle for Negro Freedom* (Urbana, 1966), p. 132.

4. William Goodell, *Slavery and Anti-Slavery: A History of the Great Struggle in Both Hemispheres* . . . (New York, 1852), pp. 386, 436. Other accounts may be found in Horace Greeley, *The American Conflict* (Hartford, Conn., 1864), I, 111–15, and Francis Curtis, *The Republican Party: A History of Its Fifty Years Existence* . . . *1854–1904* (New York, 1904), I, 83–85. See also Mott, *American Magazines, 1741–1850*, pp. 162–64.

5. Earle, *Life*, p. 31; Dillon, *Lundy*, pp. 141, 180–81.

6. Earle, *Life*, p. 306. Davis notes that "ascetic travel had long been accepted by Quakers as a means of self-discipline and social purification," *Problem of Slavery*, p. 483.

7. Earle, *Life*, p. 306; Goodell, *Slavery*, pp. 385–86.

8. Gilbert Hobbes Barnes, *The Anti-Slavery Impulse: 1830–1844* (New York, 1933; rpt. Gloucester, Mass., 1957), p. 128; Samuel Flagg Bemis, *John Quincy Adams and the Union* (New York, 1956), pp. 355–57; Dillon, *Lundy*, pp. 228–35.

9. Barnes, *Anti-Slavery Impulse*, calls Lundy "pioneer abolitionist" and "persistent little Quaker," pp. 26, 128; Ulrich B. Phillips, *The Course of the South to Secession: An Interpretation*, ed. E. Merton Coulter (New York, 1939), p. 104, notes that Robert J. Turnbull, one of the first Fire-eaters, knew Lundy's *Genius* and reacted violently to it in his pamphlet, *The Crisis* (Charleston, 1827); Dwight L. Dumond, *Antislavery Origins of the Civil War in the United States* (Ann Arbor, 1939; rpt. 1959), in his chapter, "The Spirit of the Mississippi Valley: Northwest Versus Southwest," p. 100, traces a historical connection between Lundy's *Genius* and Lincoln's antislavery stance by way of Lundy's training of Zebina Eastman to continue his paper as the *Western Citizen*.

10. Earle, *Life*, p. 29; Goodell, *Slavery*, p. 436. Samuel J. May, *Some Recollections of Our Antislavery Conflict* (Boston, 1869), writes that, "Not unfrequently he met with angry rebuffs and violent threats of personal injury," and that he was "a man of the most quiet courage, as well as indomitable perseverance," p. 13; Dillon, *Lundy*, p. 119.

11. Dillon, *Lundy*, pp. 208–09.

12. Dillon, *Lundy*, pp. 129–30.

13. Goodell, *Slavery*, p. 386.

14. An atmosphere of ambiguity, similar to that of the Deaf-Mute's appearance (whether apostle or imposter, whether saint or devil), surrounded the public image of another famous antislavery agitator of the period, the English lecturer and journalist George Thompson. Thompson, an ally and friend of Garrison, made his second speaking tour of the United States in 1851, which was called his "second advent" by Frederick Douglass (*Liberator,* 28 March 1851). He was hailed by the *Liberator* as a great man with a holy message, even while the *Liberator,* in its characteristic fashion, reprinted editorials from an opponent, the Richmond *Republican,* that called Thompson ironically, "St. George Thompson," the "Apostle of Abolition," who speaks by the "authority of the Everlasting God," and that asked him to show his "commission" from God, unless he be one of the "imposters and humbugs" that have appeared lately—as the Southern editor obviously believes he is. This editor demands Thompson's biblical proof that slavery is the "crime of crimes," the absolute sin, and writes that Thompson is "as deaf as [he is] besotted," or he would hear the Mosaic commandment not to covet his neighbor's maid- or manservant. Like other Southern papers this editor calls him an "arrant imposter and cowardly caitiff." Thompson's antislavery lectures aroused possibly even more hostility (or so they were reported) from his audiences— because of American Anglophobia—than did those of Lundy and other American speakers (*Liberator,* 7 March 1851).
15. James Ford Rhodes, *History of the United States from the Compromise of 1850* (New York, 1902), I (1850–54), 493.
16. See, for example, "Political Hypocrisy," (1852), "Young America" (1854?), and "Liberty the Fair Maid of Kansas" (1856), in Shaw, *AL,* I, 162, 183, 169. Later than 1856 cartoons and posters showing him with Lincoln exaggerate their contrasting statures to extremes: Shaw, *AL,* I, 197, and *AL,* II, 69, 85, 93, 103.
17. John W. Forney, *Anecdotes of Public Men* (New York, 1873), p. 19.
18. Shaw, *AL,* II, 113; *AL,* I, 199; *AL,* II, 9.
19. Rhodes, *History,* I, 245.
20. Robert W. Johannsen, *Stephen A. Douglas* (New York, 1973), pp. 110, 137.
21. *Polk: The Diary of a President, 1845–1849,* ed. Allan Nevins (New York, 1968), p. 117.
22. Johannsen, *SAD,* pp. 111, 250, 264, 278, 332–33.
23. Johannsen, *SAD,* pp. 333, 661.
24. George W. Bungay, *Off-Hand Takings; Or, Crayon Sketches of the Noticeable Men of Our Age* (New York, 1854), p. 385.
25. Johannsen, *SAD,* pp. 79, 132.
26. Forest L. Whan, "Stephen A. Douglas," in William Norwood Brigance, ed., *A History and Criticism of American Public Address* (New York, 1943), II, 805 (hereafter cited as Brigance, ed. *APA*).
27. Johannsen, *SAD,* pp. 429, 588; "The Political Quadrille," in Boston Public Library Print Collection (hereafter cited as *BPL*), and Shaw, *AL,* I, 193.

28. Whan, "SAD," in Brigance, ed. *APA*, II, 797, 804; Rhodes, *History*, I, 492.

29. Murat Halstead, *Trimmers, Trucklers, & Temporizers: Notes of Murat Halstead from the Political Conventions of 1856*, ed. William B. Hesseltine and Rex G. Fisher (Madison, Wis., 1961), pp. 63–64. An allusion to Douglas's presidential hopes may lie in the elaborate description of the "throne-like" barber's chairs, in one of which Cream seats himself beside Goodman (pp. 255, 261). The presidency is represented in cartoons as an elaborately made chair, similar in appearance to Melville's "great stuffed chair, high-backed, and high-armed, crimson-covered, and raised on a sort of dais, and which seemed but to lack a canopy and quarterings, to make it in aspect quite a throne." An early print "Granny Harrison Delivering the Country of the Executive Federalist" (1840), shows Van Buren in ermine sitting in a chair that is high-backed, high-armed, and has a canopy over it. Two cartoons of President Tyler, "Requesting Him To Resign" (1844) and "Whig Appeal for an Excuse" (1844), show him seated in a high-backed, high-armed chair, raised on a dais in each print. Another shows the chair, without anyone in it, as the object of the efforts of several competitors, repr. Tyler, ed. *Image of America*, fig. 37 and Shaw, *AL*, I, 99, 111.

30. Whan, "SAD," in Brigance, ed. *APA*, II, 801; Johannsen, *SAD*, pp. 570–71.

31. George Fort Milton, *The Eve of Conflict: Stephen A. Douglas and the Needless War* (Boston and New York, 1934), p. 167. See also Johannsen, *SAD*, pp. 443–45.

32. Melville, *Collected Poems*, ed. Vincent, p. 235.

33. Other views on this textual problem may be consulted in Foster, ed., *C-M*, p. 300; H. Bruce Franklin, ed., *The Confidence-Man: His Masquerade* (Indianapolis and New York, 1967), pp. xx–xxiv; Parker, ed., *C-M*, p. 10; Watson G. Branch, "The Genesis, Composition, and Structure of *The Confidence-Man*," *Nineteenth-Century Fiction*, 27 (March 1973), 428–34.

34. Examples illustrating the use of the image of an African-American to represent the slave system are: "The Oregon & Texas Question" (1844), in which Texas as a slave state is represented by a black figure (Houghton); "Matty Meeting the Texas Question" (1844), in which Texas as a slave state appears as a wild-haired, dark-faced, half-naked female carrying whips, chains, and a knife, Shaw, *AL*, I, 106; "Handicap Race: Presidential Stakes 1844," a pro-Clay print that depicts Calhoun carrying as a burden two black youths, AAS; "Slavery as it Exists in America; Slavery as it Exists in England" (1850), depicting happy black slaves and unhappy English white "wage-slaves," (LC); "The Democratic Platform" (1856), showing a white Southerner with pistol, whip, and knife facing a black youth in tow cloth, both sitting on Buchanan, who is the "platform" with which he claimed to identify himself and who is supported in turn on the backs of Benton, Pierce, and John Van Buren. The meaning is that Buchanan supports slavery, AAS

(plate 13); "The Great Presidential Race of 1856," showing a chained black man on a platform laughing as Buchanan's buck crashes on the platform, AAS; "Forcing Slavery Down the Throat of A Freesoiler" (1856), showing a black man in simple clothing forced into the throat of a huge white man by Douglas, Pierce, Buchanan, and Lewis Cass, repr. Shaw, *AL*, I, 176.

35. Examples illustrating the use of the image of the African-American to represent the free members of that group are: "Immediate Emancipation Illustrated" (183?), an anti-abolitionist print that alludes to Garrison and to "Arthur" (Tappan?) and shows a freed slave naked, almost, and hungry, AAS; "Practical Amalgamation" (1839), showing a black man embracing a white woman and a white man wooing a black woman, in a room displaying portraits of Arthur Tappan, Daniel O'Connell, and John Quincy Adams, Houghton; "Dancing for Eels–1848–Catherine Mkt. N.Y.," showing a black youth dancing, Houghton; "Marriage of the Free Soil and Liberty Parties" (1848), showing two black couples, one fairly well-dressed, the other less so, as representatives of the Liberty party, repr. Shaw, *AL*, I, 153; "Practical Illustration of the Fugitive Slave Law" (1850?), showing Garrison defending free blacks in Massachusetts, AAS; "The Great Republican Reform Party" (1856), an anti-Republican print showing an overdressed black man as representative of the free African-Americans who would be supporters of the Republicans, repr. Shaw, *AL*, I, 174; "The Political Quadrille: Music by Dred Scott" (1860), showing Lincoln dancing with a well-dressed dark-skinned woman, repr. Shaw, *AL*, I, 193. (There is in the Boston Public Library Print Collection an interesting variant of this print, which is otherwise identical, showing the woman dancing with Lincoln as having a white face and wearing a Liberty Cap.)

36. Prints illustrating the use of the image of a black figure to represent the slavery issue are: "Pilgrims of the Rhine-O!" (1852), showing a black youth riding on the back of David Wilmot, depicted as an ass, alluding to Wilmot's introduction of the famous proviso of 1846 excluding slavery from newly acquired territories, which reintroduced slavery as a national issue in politics, LC; "A Dish of Black Turtle" (1852), showing the Whig candidate, Winfield Scott, obliged to swallow a black figure to please the North, LC; "'The Irrepressible Conflict' Or the Republican Barge in Danger" (1860), after Lincoln's nomination, shows various members of the Republican party—all identifiable as individuals—in a boat with a young black, who is wearing "Discords Patent Life-Preserver" and exultant that, even if the boat sinks, he will survive—clearly alluding to the party's use of the slavery issue, HL, BPL; repr. Shaw, *AL*, II, 51 (plate 22).

37. Prints of Frederick Douglass include: "A Distinguished Turn-out on Pennsylvania Avenue," by Frank Bellew, *Lantern*, (January–June 1852), 208; "Experiments on the Tight Rope" (1852), an anti-Whig print showing Douglass in association with Raymond, Garrison, Wilmot, and Seward pulling a rope down from the presidential chair to cause Scott's fall, LC; "Great Presidential

Sweepstakes Over the Washington Course" (1852), has Douglass riding the "Woolly Nag," who is identified as John P. Hale, the Free-Soil candidate of 1852, AAS; "Why Not Hang Them All?" (1859), a sketch of Douglass and other abolitionist leaders being dragged into Virginia by Governor Henry Wise after the Harper's Ferry insurrection, repr. Shaw, *AL*, I, 256. Of Henry Box Brown, an escaped slave, "The Resurrection of Henry Box Brown at Philadelphia" (n.d.) in David M. Potter, *The Impending Crisis, 1848–1861*, ill. 23. Of Dred Scott, though not, apparently, an attempt at realistic portraiture, "The Political Quadrille: Music by Dred Scott" (1860), BPL, repr. Shaw, *AL*, I, 193.

38. "'Taking the Stump' or Stephen in Search of his Mother" (1860), AAS; repr. Shaw, *AL*, II, 90 (plate 24).

39. Another pro-Lincoln Currier & Ives cartoon exemplifying that to be crippled represents the possession of a political liability is "The Political Gymnasium" (1860), where Seward is shown on crutches with both feet bandaged. He says to Lincoln, who is poised on the "Nomination Bar," "You'd better be careful my friend, that you don't tumble off as I did before I was fairly on, for if you do you'll be as badly crippled as I am." Evidently, Seward's crippled condition represents the political liability he suffered after losing the nomination at Chicago in 1860, Shaw, *AL*, II, 85.

40. An early literary example of lameness meaning a political liability is found in a squib in *John-Donkey* (26 February 1848), that alludes to Henry Clay's being "lame" and perhaps not able to "run races" any more, probably because of his two previous defeats as the Whig candidate. Bungay in his descriptive sketch of Stephen Douglas in *Off-Hand Takings* (1854), p. 383, uses the metaphor in the latter sense, when he writes of Douglas as a man whose "selfish ambition has overleaped itself, and his fall has rendered him a political cripple for life."

41. Mastheads for 28 May 1831, 17 May 1850, and 14 June 1850 are reproduced in Garrison and Garrison, *WLG*, III, facing p. 308; the earliest is also reproduced in Mott, *American Magazines: 1850–1865*, p. 277.

42. Donald, *Sumner*, p. 286.

43. Harvey Wish, *George Fitzhugh: Propagandist of the Old South* (Baton Rouge, La., 1943), pp. 78–80, 123–24, 160–73.

44. Calhoun anticipated this argument (Brigance, ed., *APA*, II, 658). Fitzhugh is echoing also Thomas Carlyle's views on the labor and slavery problems as he expressed them in *Latter-Day Pamphlets* (1850), where Carlyle, who popularized the phrase that Melville echoes, calls the unemployed "slaves without masters" and develops the idea that "slavery" means coercive labor in any form and is founded on the immutable diversities of human beings (Wish, *Fitzhugh*, pp. 71–76).

45. Repr. in Shaw, *AL*, I, 227.

46. Philip S. Foner, ed., *The Life and Writings of Frederick Douglass* (New York, 1950), II, 496. Earlier in his career Douglass used a theatrical metaphor to

say that he felt that he himself had been an "attraction in the road companies of the abolitionist show," Arna Bontemps, *Free at Last: The Life of Frederick Douglass* (New York, 1971), p. 143. Although I have searched for them, I do not currently find any specific traits of Douglass's public image, except his complexion and association with the slavery issue, that would link him as an individual to Black Guinea.

47. Bertram Wyatt-Brown, *Lewis Tappan and the Evangelical War against Slavery* (Cleveland, 1969), p. 334.

48. "The Captain & Corporal's Guard" (1841), AAS (plate 3); "The Blind Beggar & His Dog," *John-Donkey* (7 October 1848), seems to parody Théodore Géricault's lithograph, "Pity the Sorrows of a Poor Old Man" (1821) from *Various Subjects Drawn from Life and on Stone (The English Series),* repr. *The Stanford Museum,* X–XI (1980–81), 50. Mott, in his commentary on *John-Donkey,* writes that F. O. C. Darley (whom Melville knew) probably drew most of the large political cartoons for this comic periodical, *American Magazines, 1741–1850,* p. 782.

49. Nevins, *Frémont,* II, facing p. 516.

50. Other political prints in which the Woolly Horse, or "Abolition Nag," symbolizes the slavery issue are: "Great Presidental Sweepstakes over the Washington Course" (1852), a pro-Democratic print by E. W. Clay, which has Douglass riding on a woolly nag named "Hale"—John P. Hale, the Liberty party candidate, AAS; "Col. Fremont's Last Grand Exploring Expedition in 1856," in which Seward is shown leading the Abolition Nag, with Greeley's head, toward Salt River (defeat) bearing Frémont and accompanied by Henry Ward Beecher—laden with rifles—and watched by a frontiersman, who comments that Frémont would do better to eat dead horse on the prairie than "Abolition Soup or Wooly head stew in the White house," HL, repr. Nevins, *Frémont,* II, facing p. 488 (plate 14); "The Great Presidential Sweepstakes of 1856," a Currier & Ives print in which "Greely, Weed, Beecher & Co." enter a scrawny, woolly "Canuck Pony," who was engendered by "Wooly Head" out of "Wooly horse," repr. Nevins, *Frémont,* II, facing p. 510; and "The 'Mustang' Team" (1856), a Currier & Ives print, in which the same beast is ridden by Greeley, Bennett, and Raymond—the three major New York City editors who endorsed Frémont, UCLA, repr. Nevins, *Frémont,* II, facing p. 510 (plate 15). A pictorial variant of the "black wool" theme as a representation of the antislavery theme is found in "The Lion and the Lamb," in *Young America,* I, n.s. (1856), 295, AAS copy (plate 19). It shows Greeley as a black woolly lamb, identifiable by the *Tribune* tag, and Bennett as a lion. It may be noted, also, that the antislavery Whigs under Seward in New York State were called, especially by Bennett, the "Woolly-Heads."

51. "The Great Exhibition of 1860," HL, repr. Shaw, *AL,* II, 99 (plate 23). See Chapter 3 for similar cartoons involving Greeley, Scott, Raymond, Bennett, and Pierce, which use the metaphor of entertainment for political solicitation.

52. "National Minstrels" (1844?), AAS; "Presidential Trio," *Young America,* 1, n.s. (1856), 307, AAS copy (plate 20).

53. For Volck's prints see Anderson, ed. *Work of Volck, passim*. Reproductions of some of his prints are in Shaw, *AL*, I, 12, 62–63 and II, 236, 253. The AAS Library has a fine set of his *Confederate War Etchings*, including the well-known "Worship of the North," which contains images of Greeley, Sumner, Beecher, Lincoln, Harriet Beecher Stowe, and others, repr. Shaw, *AL*, I, 62–63 (plate 28).

Minor links of Dred Scott to Black Guinea worth noting are his personal association with St. Louis, where he lived during the time of his suit (1846–1857), his short stature, and his solicitation of help in bringing his case to the Supreme Court in a pamphlet containing wording similar to Guinea's plea for someone to "speak for him." Stating he has no money "to pay anybody at Washington to speak for" him, he asks: "My fellow-men, can any of you help me in my day of trial? Will nobody speak for me at Washington . . . ?" *The Case of Dred Scott in the Supreme Court of the United States, December Term 1854* (n.p., n.d., [preface dated, "St. Louis, July 4, 1854"]), Houghton copy. The case emerged on the national scene in February 1856. See Gamaliel Bailey's account, 1 February 1856, in *Facts for the People* (LC copy) and the *Berkshire County Eagle*, 29 February, where it is noted as "A Very Important Case." For a full account of the historic case and its suspected involvement in Republican and Democratic politics see Don E. Fehrenbacher, *The Dred Scott Case: Its Significance in American Law and Politics* (New York, 1978), pp. 270–76, 282–90, 684, and *passim*.

5. Several Antagonists (the Wooden-Legged Man, the Episcopal Clergyman, the Methodist Minister, and the Country Merchant)

1. *The Diary of Philip Hone: 1828–1851,* ed. Allan Nevins, new ed. (New York, 1936), p. 195.
2. Isaac C. Pray, *Memoirs of James Gordon Bennett and His Times* (New York, 1855), frontispiece and p. 87.
3. Oliver Carlson, *The Man Who Made News: James Gordon Bennett* (New York, 1942), pp. 262, 74.
4. *Diary,* ed. Nevins, p. 464.
5. Bennett appears in many political prints, usually showing the squint-, cross-, or gimlet-eye (usually the right eye), his thin, tall, wiry body, Scots clothing (*e.g.,* a Scots cap, plaid, or argyle socks) or speaking Scottish dialect. Prints showing the defective eye are: "The Death of Old Tammany and His Wife Loco Foco" (1837), AAS; "A Sawney in Ireland Trying to Pass for an American Gentleman" (1843), AAS; "The Editor's Vision" (n.d.), AAS; "The Lion and the Lamb," *Young America,* 1, n.s. (1856), 295, AAS copy (plate 19), in which Bennett is a lion, an image relevant to the Wooden-Legged Man's comparison of himself to a "lion" (p. 36); "The Morning After the Election—November 1856," BPL, repr. Shaw, *AL,* I, 191. Later prints: "Soaping Him," showing Bennett as a barber soaping Buchanan, *Vanity Fair,* 1 (3 March 1860), 152, repr. Shaw, *AL,* II, 2; "What Will He Do With

It?" *Vanity Fair,* 2, (20 October 1860), 201; "Wonderful Surgical Operation, Performed By Doct. Lincoln on the Political Chang & Eng," *Vanity Fair,* 2 (3 November 1860), 225, repr. Shaw, *AL,* II, 143; "Badgering Him," *Vanity Fair,* 2 (29 December 1860), 321, repr. Shaw, *AL,* II, 207; "The Editorial Jim Crow," *Vanity Fair,* 3 (27 April 1861), 198; "Blood Will Tell! The Great Race for the Presidential Sweepstakes" (1868), AAS.

6. Halstead, *Trimmers,* pp. 73–74.
7. Pray, *Memoirs,* p. 454. A "croaking" voice means in this period a pessimistic or skeptical view.
8. *Diary of Hone,* ed. Nevins, pp. 549, 585, 649.
9. Pray, *Memoirs,* p. 456.
10. Pray, *Memoirs,* pp. 484, 166–67, 111, 173–74, 192–93.
11. Carlson, *Man Who Made News,* p. 269.
12. Carlson, *Man Who Made News,* p. 173.
13. Frank Luther Mott, *American Journalism: A History, 1690–1960,* 3rd ed. (New York, 1962), pp. 236–37; Carlson, *Man Who Made News,* pp. 184–90.
14. Halstead, *Trimmers,* p. 74. For a later attack on abolitionists for their "fratricidal agitation," especially in Kansas, see *Herald* editorial, 20 August 1856.
15. Pray, *Memoirs,* p. 104.
16. Pray, *Memoirs,* p. 466; Mott, *American Journalism,* p. 232.
17. *Yankee Doodle; Or Young America,* 2 (26 July 1856), 43. An earlier squib in the New York *Lantern,* 1 (1852), 9, ridicules this reputed desire for a consular or ministerial office, which Bennett never received from any president.
18. An anti-Republican cartoon issued apparently after his endorsement of Frémont, "The 'Mustang' Team" (1856), shows Bennett in Scots costume, riding the "Wooly Horse," along with Greeley and Raymond, and pulling Frémont and Jessie Frémont (?) in a wagon to which Webb clings, repr. Shaw, *AL,* I, 185 (plate 15).
19. *Herald,* 6 May 1856, editorial, "Great Annual Conventicle of Blacks and Whites," calling for dissent; 7 May editorial calling Garrison a "Robespierre"; 8 May report of the Tabernacle meeting; see also account in Garrison and Garrison, *WLG,* III, 281–300.
20. For both father and son, see *Appleton's Cyclopaedia of American Biography,* ed. James Grant Wilson and John Fiske (New York, 1888), "Stephen H. Tyng" and "Dudley Atkins Tyng." For account of Stephen H. Tyng's fame, see *Dictionary of American Biography,* "Stephen H. Tyng." I have found no evidence of Dudley Tyng's height or eye color.
21. Dudley A. Tyng, *A Sermon Preached in the Church of the Epiphany, Philadelphia, June 29, 1856,* was published in 1856 as a pamphlet: in Boston by Jewett; in Cleveland by Jewell, Proctor and Worthington; and in New York by Sheldon Blakeman—pretty good distribution, NYHS copy.
22. "Right and Wrong," *Democratic Review,* 7, n.s. (October 1856), 177.
23. See clipping from the Philadelphia *Ledger,* 4 November "Rev. Dudley A.

Tyng of Philadelphia," in a scrapbook of "Clippings from Albany and New York City Newspapers on the 1856 Presidential Campaign, and also on the Kansas Question," p. 33, in the Stanford University Library.

24. Microfilm of *Berkshire County Eagle,* courtesy of Berkshire County Athenaeum. For editorship of the *Eagle,* see Merton M. Sealts, Jr., *The Early Lives of Melville: Nineteenth-Century Biographical Sketches and Their Authors* (Madison, Wis., 1974), pp. 32–33.

25. Davis, *Chartless Voyage,* pp. 79–99. For information about *The Confidence-Man'*s composition: the entry of 15 July 1856, in Leyda, *Log,* quoting a letter of Lemuel Shaw, Jr., only reports that Melville is "now preparing another book for the press—of which Augusta is making a fair copy for the printer and which will be published before long" (Leyda, *Log,* II, 517). Shaw does not write that the book is done, nor does his reference to Melville's sister's copying out the book for the printer exclude the possibility that at that time she may have been copying out only parts of the book well before the manuscript as a whole was finished.

26. Alexander K. McClure, *Recollections of Half a Century* (Salem, Mass., 1902), pp. 222–26; E. Merton Coulter, *William G. Brownlow: Fighting Parson of the Southern Highlands* (Chapel Hill, N.C., 1937), *passim.* For a later caricature see "Parson Brownlow: Our Fighting Minister from Tennessee," *Vanity Fair,* 5 (31 May 1862), cover, where he has both arms raised and fists doubled ready for fighting.

27. McClure, *Recollections,* pp. 225–26.

28. Coulter, *Brownlow,* p. 44.

29. McClure, *Recollections,* pp. 222–25; Coulter, *Brownlow,* pp. 208–10. It is interesting to note that McClure's journalistic altercation with Brownlow was occasioned by Brownlow's "vehement broadside against the hypocrisy of the Abolitionists of the North," elicited, irrelevantly enough, by the conviction for murder and execution of Professor John W. Webster of Harvard in 1850. The judge and pronouncer of sentence in this celebrated criminal case was Lemuel Shaw, and it is just possible that Melville's attention may have been drawn to Brownlow's irresponsible attack, among others of the time, if, as was common, it had been picked up from the *Jonesboro Whig* and reprinted in eastern newspapers. Evidently, Brownlow like most of the editors of the time merely sought out any excuse to indulge in vigorous invective—abusing the abolitionists in the same way as later, after his change of attitude, he abused the South. McClure responded in defence of the Northern people and was in his turn vilified by Brownlow. It is possible also that Melville's brother Gansevoort while "stumping" in Tennessee in the summer of 1844 may have come under fire from Brownlow, who wrote at that time malign editorials concerning all Democrats and especially those who might be associated with Jackson or with Polk, as Gansevoort was. See Coulter, *Brownlow,* pp. 113–15.

30. Coulter, *Brownlow,* pp. 122–25; Halstead, *Trimmers,* pp. 2–5.

31. Howard P. Nash, Jr., *Third Parties in American Politics* (Washington, D.C., 1959), p. 111.
32. About six months later a bill for three million dollars for a similar purpose was brought before the House of the Twenty-ninth Congress on 1 February 1847, to which Wilmot again asked that his amendment be read as a proviso. Consideration was delayed for a week, and then he offered it on 7 February and spoke on the question. During February Melville was visiting in Washington, D.C., seeking a government position in the Treasury Department through his family's political connections with the New York Barnburner Democratic senator, John A. Dix, and the Hunker Democratic secretary of war, William L. Marcy. See Hayford and Davis, "Melville as Office-Seeker," 170–72. Leyda's *Log* suggests, on the basis of the caricatures of Webster ("Saturnina"), Calhoun ("Nulli"), and other political figures in the political chapters in *Mardi,* that Melville went to hear some congressional debate during his visit (Leyda, *Log,* I, 235–36). If he attended the House on 8 February, he may have heard Wilmot's historic vindication of the proviso. In any case he could have read about both bills and the proviso in the numerous press accounts. Going writes that "During the two weeks through which the Three Million Bill remained before the House, to the exclusion of all but minor routine or incidental business, nearly thirty important speeches were delivered, about equally divided between the friends and the enemies of the proviso, which received almost more emphasis in the discussion than the bill itself" (Charles B. Going, *David Wilmot: Free-Soiler: A Biography of the Great Advocate of the Wilmot Proviso* [New York, 1924], p. 183). It passed the House on 15 February with the proviso, but without it in the Senate on 1 March.
33. In 1855–56 Wheeling was not in Pennsylvania but in Virginia. Either Melville was simply mistaken in his geographical knowledge, or there may be some special political allusion lurking in the placement of Wheeling in Pennsylvania. Wheeling, located on the Ohio River, was a slave-trading center, the one probably most often seen by Northerners, except for the market in Washington, yet it was located in a geographical area which was generally at odds with the slave-holding power of eastern Virginia and which succeeded in forming a separate constitution in 1861 and becoming the state of West Virginia in 1863.
34. Going, *Wilmot,* pp. 127–28, 146.
35. George W. Julian, *Political Recollections, 1840 to 1872* (Chicago, 1884), p. 73; *John-Donkey,* 1, (1848), 28–29; Going, *Wilmot,* p. 474; Halstead, *Trimmers,* p. 100.
36. Going, *Wilmot,* pp. 128, 503, 510.
37. Going, *Wilmot,* p. 30.
38. Going, *Wilmot,* p. 24.
39. Going, *Wilmot,* pp. 316–29. A political print, "Bagging the Game" (1848), depicts Wilmot as a farmer, whose chicken—"Proviso"—has been stolen by Martin Van Buren, AAS.

40. Going, *Wilmot,* pp. 30, 42, 43. Wilmot was a guest speaker at the meeting at Herkimer of the New York State Democracy, November 1847, which made the proviso its point of difference with the regular (Hunker) Democrats (Going, *Wilmot,* pp. 291–92). He attacked Edwin Croswell, Buchanan, James Forney, and the other Hunker Democrats (Oliver Cromwell Gardiner, *The Great Issue: Or, The Three Presidential Candidates . . .* [New York, 1848; repr. Westport, Conn., 1970], pp. 57–62).

41. Going, *Wilmot,* pp. 465–84.

42. Halstead, *Trimmers,* p. 100.

43. Going, *Wilmot,* pp. vii, 486–94, 490.

44. Going, *Wilmot,* p. 544.

45. For Wilmot's close relationship in the public eye with the slavery issue, as represented by the image of a black man, see the print "Pilgrims of the Rhine-O!" (1852), in which he is depicted as an ass carrying a black man and riding toward Salt River, while Seward, as a dog, leads General Winfield Scott—the Whig presidential candidate—blindfolded and scenting "saltiness" in the same direction. Other asses in the print represent Joshua Giddings and Greeley. Seward says, "Place the utmost confidence in me gentlemen asses, for when was I ever known to betray those with whom I was associated?" LC. Another print commenting on the same election, "Experiments on the Tight Rope" (1852), shows Wilmot in association with Raymond, Frederick Douglass, Garrison, and Seward, all pulling down a rope from the presidential chair, from which Scott falls, weighted down by "Free-Soil" and "Abolition" stones. Two well-dressed blacks observe the scene, LC.

46. That Wilmot was still associated with extremist views in 1852 is evident in a political print, "The Hurly-Burly Pot" (1850), satirizing extremists of proslavery as well as antislavery views, LC (plate 6). Wilmot, wearing a jester's or fool's cap and carrying a wand, is depicted with Garrison, Greeley and Calhoun—all "stirring" up trouble by putting into one pot bags that are labelled "Free Soil," "Anti-rent," "Treason," "Abolition," "Fourierism," and "Blue Laws." Wilmot says, "Bubble, bubble, . . . Free Soil, / The Union spoil; / Come grief and moan, / Peace be none / Til we divided be!" All are evidently regarded as different kinds of fanatics, contributing equally to the national troubles of 1850. Pictured underneath the pot on the fire is Benedict Arnold, symbolic of treachery, who says, "Well done." This print seems to be a double indictment of agitators both North and South and is, I shall suggest in Chapter 14, not unsimilar to Melville's own satirical stance.

47. Halstead, *Trimmers,* p. 102.

48. McClure, *Recollections,* pp. 237, 239; Going, *Wilmot,* pp. 509–10.

6. The Third Confidence Man (John Ringman the Man with the Weed) and His Antagonist (the Collegian)

1. "Masquerading Mendicants," notes the dodge of the man in mourning: "We have seen the same man with a piece of crape round his hat for the same

wife for six or seven successive years; and the female professors are quite as tenacious of the weeds of their widowhood. 'Once a widow or widower, always a widow or widower,' appears to be the motto of these," *Punch,* 16 (January–June 1849), 22.

2. For Bryant's life, see Parke Godwin, *A Biography of William Cullen Bryant with Extracts from His Private Correspondence* (New York, 1883); James Grant Wilson, *Bryant and His Friends: Some Reminiscences of the Knickerbocker Writers* (New York, 1886); John Bigelow, *William Cullen Bryant* (Boston, 1890); Allan Nevins, *The Evening Post: A Century of Journalism* (New York, 1922); Harry H. Peckham, *Gotham Yankee: A Biography of William Cullen Bryant* (New York, 1950; rpt. 1971); and Charles H. Brown, *William Cullen Bryant* (New York, 1971).

3. Godwin, *Biography,* II, 43, 80, 88–91; Nevins, *Evening Post,* pp. 242–53; Brown, *Bryant,* pp. 283–387; see also Allan Nevins, *Ordeal of the Union* (New York, 1947), II, 488. A print showing the power that Bryant wielded through the *Evening Post* is "The Blight-Spell" in *Vanity Fair,* 5 (29 March 1862), 155. He appears with full white beard in a wizard's costume, with Greeley in witch costume, casting spells of "detraction," "slander," and "hatred" in order to "worke a blyghte" on General MacClellan. Bryant is called "ye water-foule wizard of ye Evening Poste." Another print that shows both Bryant's and Greeley's continued and collusive interest in Frémont's political fortunes is "An Unfinished Work of Art," in *Vanity Fair,* 6 (6 September 1862), 120. This shows the two editors exhibiting an immense carved bust of Frémont, with a scroll reading "Original Design for President by H.G. & W.C.B."—the implication being that both journals were actively creating a Presidential "image"—as we would say today—for Frémont.

4. Brown, *Bryant,* p. 3.

5. Godwin, *Biography,* I, 334.

6. Brown, *Bryant,* pp. 262, 275–76.

7. Peckham, *Gotham Yankee,* p. 121.

8. Brown, *Bryant,* p. 277. There is reason to believe that Melville knew Godwin personally, for he was an associate editor of *Putnam's Magazine* during the period in which Melville contributed stories, articles, and his historical novel, *Israel Potter* (1855), which was serialized 1854–55; see Leyda, *Log,* I, 270; Miller, *Raven and Whale,* pp. 315–21; and Brown, *Bryant,* pp. 370, 374.

9. Brown, *Bryant,* pp. 321, 325, 401–02; see also p. 507. His friend, the painter and art critic William James Stillman, wrote, "The character of his poetry, little sympathetic with human passion, and given to the worship of nature, confirmed the general impression of coldness which his manner suggested," Brown, *Bryant,* pp. 374–75.

10. James Russell Lowell, "A Fable for Critics," *Complete Poetical Works* (Boston, 1896), pp. 131–32.

11. Brown, *Bryant,* p. 285; see also pp. 304, 394. Bryant's association with melancholy seems to be used in a comical way in a political print, "Barn-

Burners in a Fix" (1852), that shows him on the roof of a burning barn, crying, "Woe is me! I can't get off, and if I stay up here it's sure destruction!" while Franklin Pierce, stuck in the mud, says, "Alas, Bryant! There's more truth than poetry in what you say. We never needed your help more, for we are stuck in the mud and want your shoulder at the wheel!" AAS (plate 8). The mixed image of Bryant as melancholy poet and unhappy politician is a comment on the potentially disastrous effects of the split in New York state of the Democracy into the Barnburners (first, against borrowing money for public works and, later, against slavery extension) and the party regulars or Hunkers.

12. *Diary,* ed. Nevins, pp. 55, 686–87; Hone's perception is echoed by the Harvard classicist, C. C. Felton (Brown, *Bryant,* p. 282).

13. Brown, *Bryant,* p. 320; Godwin, *Biography,* I, 7. For early Barnburners see Joseph G. Rayback, *Free Soil: The Election of 1848* (Lexington, Ky., 1970), pp. 60–72.

14. Brown, *Bryant,* p. 281; Godwin, *Biography,* I, 255.

15. *Cyclopaedia of American Literature . . ,* ed. Evert A. Duyckinck and George L. Duyckinck (New York, 1856), I, 184.

16. Cf. Foster's discussion, *The Confidence-Man,* pp. liii, 303.

17. John Stafford, *The Literary Criticism of "Young America"* . . . (Berkeley, 1952), p. 10; Miller, *Raven and Whale,* pp. 110–11; Brown, *Bryant,* p. 289. See also Herbert W. Schneider, *A History of American Philosophy* (New York, 1946), pp. 133–44, and Merle E. Curti, "'Young America,'" *American Historical Review,* 32 (October 1926), 34–55.

18. Godwin, *Biography,* I, 254–55, 260–62; Brown, *Bryant,* p. 264.

19. Merton M. Sealts, Jr., *Melville as Lecturer* (Cambridge, Mass., 1957), p. 34.

20. For Raymond's life, see Augustus Maverick, *Henry J. Raymond and the New York Press for Thirty Years* . . . (Hartford, Conn., 1870); Ernest Francis Brown, *Raymond of the Times* (New York, 1951). He was New York State Assembly Speaker again in 1862 and U.S. congressman, 1865–67.

21. Maverick, *Raymond,* p. 139; Brown, *Raymond,* pp. 14, 161. At least four political prints portray Raymond as youthful or as a boy. "The Happy Family," in *The Old Soldier* (New York: J. L. Magee), I, No. 6 (1 June 1852), ·depicts him as a little boy in a velvet vest sitting on the lap of Bennett in Scots dress, HL, AAS (plate 9); he is small in "The 'Mustang' Team" (1856), UCLA (plate 15); "The Great Exhibition of 1860" shows Raymond as a boy in short trousers, HL, repr. Shaw, *AL,* II, 99 (plate 23); and "Henry J. Raymond, Trying to Go Ahead with the 'Times,'" *Vanity Fair,* 6 (2 August 1862), 49, a cover sketch, shows him as one of his own newsboys running to sell an extra.

22. Maverick, *Raymond,* pp. 83, 139–41; Henry Adams, *The Education of Henry Adams* (New York, 1931), p. 101; Henry B. Stanton, *Random Recollections,* 3rd ed. (New York, 1887), p. 261.

23. Brown, *Raymond,* pp. 134, 161.

24. Brown, *Raymond*, pp. 12–13, 29, 32–33, 85, 158–59.
25. Maverick, *Raymond*, pp. 462–69.
26. Maverick, *Raymond*, pp. 469–71.
27. Maverick, *Raymond*, pp. 480–81.
28. Maverick, *Raymond*, p. 75.
29. Brown, *Raymond*, pp. 79–80, 159, 320, 161.
30. Brown, *Raymond*, p. 79.
31. On Raymond's close political relationship to Weed see Thurlow Weed Barnes, *Life of Thurlow Weed Including His Autobiography and a Memoir* (Boston and New York, 1883–84), II, 191; Rhodes, *History*, II, 46, 63; Andrew W. Crandall, *The Early History of the Republican Party, 1854–1856* (Boston, 1930), pp. 32–33; Brown, *Raymond*, pp. 6, 68, 81–82, 132 (on his financial tie to Weed), 133, 137, 148–51.
32. David M. Potter, *Lincoln and His Party in the Secession Crisis* (New Haven, 1942), pp. 1–19, esp. pp. 12–15. It was only in November 1860 that Raymond and Weed began to editorialize about the seriousness of the Southern threats to secede (Potter, *Secession Crisis*, pp. 63–73).
33. Brown, *Raymond*, pp. 141–42, 146–47, 148–49. In 1860 Raymond preferred Seward again at the Chicago Republican convention, but he accepted Lincoln's nomination and spoke and editorialized for him as "eminently conservative" (Brown, *Raymond*, pp. 191–93). After the election, he addressed a series of open letters in the *Times* to William Lowndes Yancey, the Southern extremist orator, who had been campaigning in the North (for Yancey's caricature as Charles Arnold Noble, see Chapter 10). Raymond defended "the final authority of the Constitution over the dispute between the sections," and he rejected the Southern theory that the Union was only a compact between sovereign states. In his view the individual owed an allegiance to the federal Union which superseded that owed to the state (Maverick, *Raymond*, Appendix C, pp. 384–447). Unlike Greeley, he consistently supported the Union and Lincoln's policies, and he published a biography of him in 1864.

7. *The Fourth and Fifth Confidence Men (the Man in Gray and John Truman) and Several Antagonists (the Gentleman with Gold Sleeve-Buttons, the Charitable Lady, the Elderly Quaker, the Dried-Up Man, and Others)*

1. For example, "The Modern Colossus: Eighth Wonder of the World" (1848). One of the pious-faced men on the left may be intended to be Parker, but without other similar caricatures of him it is uncertain (Peters, *Currier & Ives*, plate 154).
2. For Parker's life see John Weiss, *Life and Correspondence of Theodore Parker*, 2 vols. (New York, 1864); Octavius B. Frothingham, *Theodore Parker: A Biography* (Boston, 1874); Henry Steele Commager, *Theodore Parker* (Boston, 1936); Roy C. McCall, "Theodore Parker," in Brigance, ed., *APA*, I, 238–64; Robert C. Albrecht, *Theodore Parker* (New York, 1971).

3. Thomas Wentworth Higginson, *Contemporaries* (Boston, 1899), p. 49.

4. Clergymen of this period customarily wore a white tie, cravat, or collar, although Parker in fact does not wear such in the portraits in the biographies I have examined. George Templeton Strong in his *Diary* laments being "brought up in an accursed feminine reverence for the White Cravat," *The Diary of George Templeton Strong,* ed. Allan Nevins and Milton H. Thomas (New York, 1952), II, 157. Melville seems to assume this symbolism in chapter 3, when the Methodist Minister shakes the Wooden-Legged Man by his coat collar, and a "voice" cries out, " 'The white cravat against the world!' " (*C-M,* p. 15). As for the gray coat I have not found that Parker wore such, but his friend and colleague in religion and politics, T. W. Higginson, made a specific point of wearing a gray coat to distinguish himself from less liberal clergymen who wore black. It is possible that Melville adapted the gray coat as symbolic of the radical cleric. See Lawrence Lader, *The Bold Brahmins: New England's War Against Slavery, 1831–1863* (New York, 1961), p. 184.

5. McCall, "Parker," I, 259–60. Wright quoted in Walter M. Merrill, *Against Wind and Tide: A Biography of Wm. Lloyd Garrison* (Cambridge, Mass., 1963), p. 244. Beman Brockway described Parker as rather "short" with a "benignant face," *Fifty Years in Journalism Embracing Recollections and Personal Experiences . . .* (Watertown, N.Y., 1891), p. 126.

6. Lowell, "A Fable for Critics," *Poetical Works,* pp. 130–31.

7. Ralph Waldo Emerson, "Theodore Parker: An Address at the Memorial Meeting, at the Music Hall, Boston, June 15, 1860," *Miscellanies* (Boston, 1884), p. 268.

8. McCall, "Parker," I, 259.

9. Weiss, *Life,* I, 50–52, 290.

10. Bungay, *Off-Hand Takings,* p. 257; McCall, "Parker," I, 261; Higginson, *Contemporaries,* p. 47; Emerson *Miscellanies,* p. 268; McCall, "Parker," I, 248, 250.

11. McCall, "Parker," I, 256.

12. See, for example, "The Present Crisis in American Affairs" (1856), in Theodore Parker, *The Rights of Man in America,* ed. F. B. Sanborn (Boston, 1911; rpt. New York, 1969), pp. 430–90.

13. McCall, "Parker," I, 244; John Edward Dirks, *The Critical Theology of Theodore Parker* (New York, 1948), p. 35; Higginson, *Contemporaries,* pp. 45–46.

14. See for example, "The Rights of Man in America," in Parker, *Rights of Man,* ed. Sanborn, pp. 333–96.

15. On the pin, cf. Foster, ed., *C-M,* p. 306. Higginson applies Parker's own description of Luther's style to Parker's style, which has "the homely force of Luther, who in the language of the farm, the shop, the boat, the street or the nursery, told . . . high truths," *Contemporaries,* p. 48; McCall, "Parker," I, 257.

16. Weiss, *Life,* II, 71–73; Frothingham, *Parker,* p. 339; Higginson, *Contempo-*

raries, p. 47; Commager, *Parker,* p. 192; Albrecht, *Parker,* p. 51; Parker, *Speeches, Addresses and Occasional Sermons* (Boston, 1852), I, 133–62; and Parker, *Rights of Man,* ed. Sanborn, 1–47, 92–131, 153–95, 196–279.

17. Commager, *Parker,* p. 153. For explicit evidence of Melville's attitude toward reformers, see Sealts, *Melville as Lecturer,* pp. 170–72, where reviewers of his lecture on "The South Seas" report his scornful references to reformers who hope "to find a fitting place for the good time coming" [Greeley's phrase], to the Fourierites, to the "Free Lovers," and to the Mormons. The Fourierites and Free Lovers were specifically caricatured in an anti-Republican cartoon in 1856: "The Great Republican Reform Party Calling on their Candidate," repr. Peters, *Currier & Ives,* plate 155; both groups plus the Mormons were associated with the Republicans in 1860 in "The Republican Party Going to the Right House," repr. Shaw, *AL,* I, 141.

18. Commager, *Parker,* p. 163.

19. Commager, *Parker,* p. 249.

20. In several articles in the scrapbook of "Clippings from Albany and New York City Newspapers on the 1856 Presidential Campaign and also on the Kansas Question," in the Stanford University Library, the introduction of politics into the pulpit was deemed particularly offensive (p. 33), and Democratic candidates inveighed against the "impious work" of the "misguided preacher" in carrying on Kansas "agitation" (p. 39).

21. Commager, *Parker,* pp. 255–57, 259–61.

22. Albrecht, *Parker,* pp. 9, 78, 86, 136; Frothingham, *Parker,* p. 432.

23. "Loco Foco Candidates . . . ," repr. Bishop. *Our Political Drama,* p. 102; "Liberty . . . ," Stanford Museum Print Collection, repr. Shaw, *AL,* I, 169 (plate 12). Cass's bulkiness is humorously played upon in "Presidential Candidates Sparring at the Washington Academy," in *The Old Soldier,* 1, No. 5 (1 May 1852), n.p., where he is called "Lou' Cass!! Old Fogy Champion of the Democratic Heavy 'Weights,'" AAS copy. A print of the Mexican War period which illustrates well the balloon-like stomach and also puns on "Cass:gas" is reprinted without a specific title but featuring the words, "A War President," in Shaw, *AL,* I, 133. It satirizes "Progressive Democracy" and Cass as full of warlike gasses both fore and aft. Two others from 1848 punning again on "Cass:gas" are: "The Democratic Funeral of 1848," in which he is depicted as a gasbag, repr. Shaw, *AL,* I, 154, and "Who Says Gas? Or the Democratic B-Hoy," a pro-Cass print which shows him as a New York tough defeating in a fistfight his opponents Van Buren and Taylor, LC. Cass appears as an "Old Hunker" in "The Strife between an Old Hunker, a Barnburner, and a No Party Man" (1848) with Van Buren and Taylor, AAS, and as a "B'Hoy" in "The Political Mose," *Young America,* n.s. (1856), 259, AAS copy (plate 18).

24. Samuel A. Johnson, *The Battle Cry of Freedom: The New England Emigrant Aid Company in the Kansas Crusade* (Lawrence, Kan., 1954), p. 224.

25. William Norris, "Abbott Lawrence in *The Confidence-Man*: American Success or American Failure?" *American Studies,* 17 (Spring 1976), 25–38.

26. My reading of the significance of the charitable actions of the Gentleman in Gold Sleeve-Buttons differs widely from Norris's, who does not connect the portrait of the Man in Gray with Theodore Parker.

27. Sarah M. Maury, *The Statesmen of America in 1846* (London, 1847), pp. 89–90.

28. *John-Donkey,* 4 March 1848, and 1 April 1848.

29. Johnson, *Battle Cry of Freedom,* pp. 14–15, 125, 129–33, 184. Amos A. Lawrence was reported by the New York *Times* (14 July 1856) as supporting Frémont although offered a chance to be a Know-Nothing elector. Contradicting this, the *Dictionary of American Biography* states that he was opposed to the Republican party in 1856. See also Hannah Josephson, *The Golden Threads: New England's Mill Girls and Magnates* (New York, 1949), p. 302.

30. Nevins, *Ordeal of the Union,* II, 126; Donald, *Sumner,* pp. 156–58.

31. Mott, *American Magazines: 1741–1850,* p. 388; Gordon S. Haight, *Mrs. Sigourney: The Sweet Singer of Hartford* (New Haven, 1930), pp. 165, 166; E. and G. Duyckinck, *Cyclopaedia,* II, 137; Haight, *Sigourney,* pp. 169, 191, 23–37, 123.

32. For length of mourning period see Julia Ward Howe, *Reminiscences: 1819–1899* (Boston and New York, 1899), p. 47.

33. Lydia Sigourney, *Past Meridian* (New York and Boston, 1854). Chapter XII, entitled "Westering Sunbeams," lists elderly virtuous notables such as Josiah Quincy.

34. Sigourney, *Poems* (Philadelphia, 1834), pp. 73–74.

35. Haight, *Sigourney,* p. 58.

36. Haight, *Sigourney,* pp. 99, 102, 44.

37. For an example of the power of feminine opinion see Glyndon G. Van Deusen, *William Henry Seward* (New York, 1967), pp. 126–27, for the influence of Frances Miller Seward upon her husband.

38. Glyndon G. Van Deusen, *Thurlow Weed: Wizard of the Lobby* (Boston, 1947), p. 31. The "whisker" that Truman displays (p. 51) raises a problem if it is taken to refer to either a moustache or a beard, for it does not match with Weed's usually clean-shaven appearance. However, it is possible that "whisker" here refers to a portion of the hair that grew close to the cheek. According to the *OED* "whisker (4)" was restricted by the mid-nineteenth century to the hair that grows "on the cheeks or sides of the face." Hence it is possible that Truman's "whisker" may be a portion or a curl of hair that reached forward into the face. The reason for mentioning the whisker at all may be that Melville wished to introduce an allusion to the notorious whisker-shaving or whisker-pulling incident of which Weed was accused in the Morgan episode and the memory of which clung to him the rest of his political career. See editorials from newspapers in 1828 in his autobiography which call him "this man of whisker-pulling memory," "of Morgan manufacturing and whisker pulling memory," and one who can "make and unmake whiskers," Barnes, *Life of Thurlow Weed,* I, 353. It does not seem presently possible to account entirely satisfactorily for the detail of Truman's "whisker."

39. Van Deusen, *Weed,* pp. 31, 83, 128, 138.
40. Leyda, *Log,* II, 635–36; see also Parker, "Melville and Politics," p. 89, for his personal acquaintance with both Weed and Greeley.
41. Van Deusen, *Weed,* p. 31.
42. See Barnes, *Life of Thurlow Weed,* I, 165, 448, for his "warm personal friend-ships," even with political enemies; Barnes, *Life of Thurlow Weed,* II, 34.
43. See for use of "confidence," Barnes, *Life of Thurlow Weed,* II, 171–72, 230; Van Deusen, *Weed,* p. 84; Barnes, *Life of Thurlow Weed,* II, 232.
44. Weed, *Letters from Europe and the West Indies: 1843–1852* (Albany, 1866), *passim,* NYHS copy.
45. Edward L. Pierce, *Memoir and Letters of Charles Sumner* (Boston, 1893), II, 279.
46. Hone, *Diary,* ed. Nevins, p. 659; Van Deusen, *Weed,* pp. 145–46; McClure, *Recollections,* p. 214.
47. Van Deusen, *Weed,* p. 280; Adams, *Education,* pp. 146–47.
48. Adams, *Education,* p. 147. For another sketch of Weed's "rare qualities as a manager," see Edward Cary, *George William Curtis* (Boston and New York, 1895), p. 133.
49. Van Deusen, *Weed,* pp. 77–78, 80–81.
50. In his autobiography Weed admits that when he began writing he had very little schooling and was "ignorant of the first principles of grammar" (Barnes, *Life of Thurlow Weed,* I, 62). His faulty grammar is still apparent, when he is writing at the end of his career, in the dangling participle at the opening of the following sentence concerning a visit to Lincoln: "Calling after break-fast upon President Lincoln he [Lincoln] remarked, in his peculiar way, that he understood I had had 'considerable experience in belling cats' and with this introduction proceeded to say that, in view especially of the influence the 'Herald' was exerting in Europe, he deemd it of the greatest importance that Mr. Bennett should be satisfied that the course of the 'Herald' was endangering the government and Union, adding his belief that if Mr. Bennett could be brought to see things in that light he would change his course" (Barnes, *Life of Thurlow Weed,* I, 616). This sentence also shows the same loose and tortured syntax, the use of "deem," and the locution of "seeing things in a certain" light that Truman exhibits in his conversation with Roberts.
51. Van Deusen, *Weed,* p. 80.
52. Van Deusen, *Weed,* pp. 74–75, 206–07.
53. The metaphor of the Devil's "stock-company" for a group of New York editors is used in a short good-natured satirical piece, "The Devil Taking Account of Stock," in *John-Donkey* 1 (29 January 1848), 75. The firm of "Old Splitfoot & Co." includes as members the following editors: "H———— G————," "J———— W———— W————," "Rev. D———— Hale" (who de-nounces "sin and iniquity with one hand and coolly pockets blackmail with the other"), the "Evening Slipslop," "Commercial Humdrum," "M————

Y——— B———," "J——— G——— B———" (a "magnificent chap" according to the Devil's inventory), and "N——— P——— W———." These journalists or papers are, respectively: Greeley, James Watson Webb of the *Courier & Enquirer,* David Hale of the *Journal of Commerce,* the *Evening Post* (Bryant's paper), the *Commercial Advertiser,* Moses Yale Beach (owner and editor of the *Sun*), Bennett of the *Herald,* and Nathaniel Parker Willis of the *Home Journal.* The conception of the Confidence Men as the different guises of a single devil-figure may have owed something to such a satirical prose piece, although one must also consider the general influence of humorous graphic prints in which political figures are depicted as demons as well as the conventions in Federalist literary satire of using Milton's image of Pandemonium. See Kerber, *Federalists in Dissent,* pp. 176–77, and George Sensabaugh, *Milton in Early America* (Princeton, N.J., 1964), pp. 243–64.

54. Van Deusen, *Weed,* p. 174.
55. Van Deusen, *Weed,* p. 230.
56. Barnes, *Life of Thurlow Weed,* II, 159.
57. Barnes, *Life of Thurlow Weed,* I, 319.
58. "The Political Drill of the State Officers" (183?), broadsheet with text by William L. Marcy, Regency Democratic leader, AAS; repr. as "The Jolly Drummer Beats Time for the Whig State Officers," in Van Deusen, *Weed,* opp. p. 113.
59. "The Inside Track," by H. L. Stephens, *Vanity Fair,* 3 (2 March 1861), 103, repr. Shaw, *AL,* II, 209 (plate 27). Two later prints of Weed that make use of verbal-visual puns on "weed" as a plant are "H. G. upon Weed," *Vanity Fair,* 3 (30 March 1861), 148, repr. Shaw, *AL,* II, 57, and "The Smelling Committee, or the Confusion of the Radicals" (1868), in Van Deusen, *Weed,* opp. p. 319.
60. Samuel T. Pickard, *Life and Letters of John Greenleaf Whittier* (Boston and New York, 1894), I, 358; Lewis Leary, *John Greenleaf Whittier* (New York, 1961), pp. 1–40, 53.
61. Bungay, *Off-Hand Takings,* p. 133; Leary, *Whittier,* p. 74; T. W. Higginson, *John Greenleaf Whittier* (New York, 1902), p. 104.
62. Leary, *Whittier,* p. 86; Wyatt-Brown, *Tappen,* p. 328; *The Complete Poetical Works of John Greenleaf Whittier,* pp. 315–16.
63. Wilson, *Slave Power,* I, 261; Leary, *Whittier,* p. 103.
64. *DAB,* "Myron Holley Clark"; Jeter Allen Isely, *Horace Greeley and the Republican Party, 1853–1861 . . .* (Princeton, 1947), p. 81; Charles H. Brown, *Bryant,* p. 378; Van Deusen, *Weed,* p. 200; Van Deusen, *Seward,* pp. 158–59; Barnes, *Life of Thurlow Weed,* II, 226; Nevins, *Ordeal,* II, 320. It is possible that Truman-Weed's comparison of the Dried-Up Man's "geniality" which has no expression in action to "a water-power in a land without mills" is a topical allusion to a quarrel that Weed had in the *Albany Evening Journal* with Greeley. Van Deusen notes that Greeley, who quarrelled with Weed most of 1854, during the period of the maneuvering for control of the Whigs

in that year, had criticized making Weed's newspaper the state paper—an action achieved by Weed through the aid of Clark—and that they also "rowed over prohibition," and they "disagreed with more or less incivility over a Rochester miller's rights to water from the Genesee" river (*Weed*, p. 203). The exact nature of this quarrel I have not determined.

65. "A Political Game of Brag, Or the Best Hand out of Four," AAS; "Political Game of Brag. Shew of Hands," repr. Shaw, *AL*, I, 152. Others are: "All Fours, or Old Sludge" (1840), which includes, among other things, Francis P. Blair, Sr., snuffing a candle, AAS (plate 2); and one later than *The Confidence-Man*, "The Political Game of Bluff" (1860), which shows one cardplayer, who represents the Democratic party, and another, the Republican, and comments upon the need for the Republicans to nominate before knowing who the Democratic candidate or candidates would be in the summer of 1860, Shaw, *AL*, II, 33.

8. *The Sixth Confidence Man (the Herb-Doctor) and Two Antagonists (the Miser and the Sick Man)*

1. Halstead, *Trimmers*, p. 92.
2. See: "Rats Quitting A Ship" (1832?), "Democratic Simplicity, Or the Arrival of our Favorite Sun" (1836?), "The Globe-Man After Hearing of the Vote on the Sub-Treasury Bill" (1838), "Bubble-Bursting (183?), all the preceding AAS; "The Secretary of War Presenting a Stand of Colours to the 1st Regiment of Bloodhounds" (183?), NYPL; "A Galvanized Corpse" (183?), "Expansion & Contraction, as Witnessed in the Senate March 5, 1840, during Mr. Buchanan's Remarks on the Currency" (1840), "Granny Harrison Delivering the Country of the Executive Federalist" (1840), "Political Jugglers Losing Their Balance" (1840?), "'Clar de Kitchen'" (1840), all the preceding AAS; "All Fours or Old Sludge" (1840), AAS (plate 2); "The North Bend Farmer and His Visitors" (1840), repr. Shaw, *AL*, I, 90; "The Death of Locofocoism" (1840), AAS (plate 1). Reproductions of "Granny Harrison . . ." may be seen in Tyler, ed., *Image of America*, p. 68, where Blair is misidentified as Jackson; of "Political Jugglers . . ." in Shaw, *AL*, I, 89; and of "'Clar de Kitchen,'" in Bishop, *Our Political Drama*, p. 97. Blair's head is well seen in a photograph in Burke Davis, *Old Hickory, A Life of Andrew Jackson* (New York, 1977) betw. pp. 246–47.
3. McClure, *Recollections*, pp. 44–45, Elbert B. Smith, *Francis Preston Blair* (rpt. New York, 1980), pp. 45, 4, xi, 73 (Rives quotation); William E. Smith, *The Francis Preston Blair Family in Politics* (New York, 1933), II, 428–29 (*Cincinnati Commercial* quotation). Brockway, *Fifty Years*, p. 33.
4. Brockway, *Fifty Years*, p. 33.
5. W. E. Smith, *Blair Family*, I, 20–21.
6. E. B. Smith, *Blair*, pp. 1, 91; W. E. Smith, *Blair Family*, I, 245, 182–84; Brockway, *Fifty Years*, pp. 33–35.
7. W. E. Smith, *Blair Family*, I, 95, 144–81, 331–35.

8. Brockway, *Fifty Years,* pp. 33–35; Richard H. Thornton, *An American Glossary* (New York, 1962): "guardeen," "herb," "nature."

9. W. E. Smith, *Blair Family,* I, 190; E. B. Smith, *Blair,* p. 173; W. E. Smith, *Blair Family,* I, 186. The personal or political context for the striking use of bird imagery ("oriole," "penguin," "pelican") is as yet unidentified.

10. W. E. Smith, *Blair Family,* I, 241, 267, 297, 315, 331, 352; Going, *Wilmot,* pp. 483, 486.

11. W. E. Smith, *Blair Family,* I, 315, 323–24, and Donald, *Sumner,* p. 276.

12. William N. Chambers, *Old Bullion Benton: Senator from the New West . . .* (Boston, 1956), p. 419.

13. W. E. Smith, *Blair Family,* I, 348–49; Donald, *Sumner,* p. 315.

14. Crandall, *Early History,* pp. 51–53; W. E. Smith, *Blair Family,* I, 319–21, 325–28.

15. Potter, *Impending Crisis,* pp. 231–32; Arthur C. Cole, *The Whig Party in the South* (Washington, 1913), pp. 222–23; Van Deusen, *Weed,* p. 207; Halstead, *Trimmers,* p. 110.

16. Crandall, *Early History,* pp. 150–51, 253; see also Cole, *Whig Party,* p. 326; Leonard W. Levy, *The Law of the Commonwealth and Chief Justice Shaw . . .* (New York, Evanston, and London, 1957), p. 91.

17. "The Old-Line Whigs for Buchanan! Letters of Rufus Choate and George T. Curtis" (Boston, 1856), Harvard College Library pamphlet.

18. Crandall, *Early History,* p. 253.

19. Nevins, *Ordeal,* II, 491; Crandall, *Early History,* p. 256.

20. Donald, *Sumner,* p. 214; Edward L. Pierce, *Memoir and Letters of Charles Sumner* (Boston, 1893), III, frontispiece.

21. R. Elaine Pagel and Carl Dallinger, "Charles Sumner," in Brigance, ed., *APA,* II, 765; Bungay, *Off-Hand Takings,* p. 276; D. A. Harsha, *The Life of Charles Sumner with Choice Specimens of His Eloquence . . .* (New York, 1856), p. 151; *Atlas,* quoted in Donald, *Sumner,* p. 320; Harsha, *Life,* p. 153; Julian, *Political Recollections: 1840 to 1872,* p. 100; Pagel and Dallinger, "Sumner," in Brigance, ed., *APA,* II, 765.

22. Harsha, *Life,* p. 158; Pierce, *Memoir,* II, 342; Whittier, *Poetical Works,* pp. 208–10; Bungay, *Off-Hand Takings,* p. 276; Henry Ward Beecher, "Charles Sumner," in *Lectures and Orations,* ed. Newell D. Hillis (New York, 1913), pp. 200, 197; Pierce, *Memoir,* III, 70–72. Edward Everett Hale, *Memories of a Hundred Years* (New York, 1904), writes that Sumner was "the most unpopular man who was ever in the United States Senate," because "without in the least meaning to do so, he would speak with this air of superiority, which was really droll." Hale adds that he did not think Sumner "arrogant" but that he "did sometimes think of himself more highly than he ought"—a "fault which most members of most Senates share with him" (II, 196–97).

23. Pierce, *Memoir,* II, 356–57; III, 302–03, 523–24; Rhodes, *History,* II, 137.

24. T. W. Higginson speaks of Sumner's lack of humor, *Contemporaries,* p. 290; Howe, *Reminiscences,* pp. 170–71; Donald, *Sumner,* pp. 173–75.

25. Donald, *Sumner,* pp. ix–x.
26. Adams, *Education,* p. 30; Donald, *Sumner,* pp. 120–29; *Yankee Doodle,* 2 (1847–48), 197.
27. Pagel and Dallinger, "Sumner," in Brigance, ed., *APA,* II, 763–65; Donald, *Sumner,* pp. 215–19; Harsha, *Sumner,* p. 157; Higginson, *Contemporaries,* p. 287; Adams, *Education,* p. 31; Howe, *Reminiscences,* p. 175.
28. Higginson, *Contemporaries,* p. 286; Donald, *Sumner,* pp. 217, 188. "The Massachusetts Baby Show," AAS, MHS, NYPL, and NYHS. This anti–Free-Soil, anti–Know-Nothing print also shows Henry Wilson, Theodore Parker, Henry Gardner, George Boutwell, Nathaniel Banks, and several other Massachusetts figures, who are difficult to identify. This print is listed in Weitenkampf, *Political Caricature in the United States,* p. 113.
29. For accounts of the assault see *Tribune,* 23, 24 May; *Daily Times,* 23, 24, 31 May 1856; *Herald,* 23 May 1856. Pierce, *Memoir,* III, 462–84; Rhodes, *History,* II, 139–40; Donald, *Sumner,* pp. 288–311; Potter, *Impending Crisis,* pp. 209–11.
30. Certain descriptive details of the Titan's appearance suggest the possibility that a famous graphic print of the assault by J. L. Magee (plate 11) may possibly have formed part of Melville's perception of the event. In "Southern Chivalry—Argument Versus Club's [sic]" (1856), AAS; repr. Shaw, *AL,* I, 179, the slanting posture of Brooks, who looms almost like a giant figure over the recumbent figure of Sumner, is strikingly like the posture of the Titan as described by Melville: "The stranger was bowed over, and might have seemed bowing for the purpose of picking up something, were it not that, as arrested in the imperfect posture, he for the moment so remained; slanting his tall stature like a mainmast yielding to the gale, or Adam to the thunder" (p. 98). The Titan, however, it should be noted, is not bowing thus at the precise moment of striking but earlier in the scene.
31. Donald, *Sumner,* pp. 293–94.
32. For example, as late as 1899 Higginson refers to it as of oak, and he even claims that it was made of the oak of the brig *Acorn,* that took Thomas Sims back into slavery, *Contemporaries,* p. 283.
33. Donald, *Sumner,* pp. 289–90; Garrison and Garrison, *WLG,* III, 434.
34. Pierce, *Memoir,* III, 470–71; Donald, *Sumner,* 294–95.
35. Lader, *Bold Brahmins,* p. 222; see also Donald, *Sumner,* p. 264.
36. Besides the widely distributed "Southern Chivalry—Argument Versus Club's" (plate 11) there is a sketch of Brooks striking Sumner that forms part of the print "Democratic Platform Illustrated: 1856," BPL. "Arguments of the Chivalry" (1856) is another of the assault, which shows Robert Toombs, Douglas, John Crittenden, and Laurence Keitt besides the two main figures. Keitt holds a gun behind his back and a cane to deter Crittenden from from aiding Sumner. Henry Ward Beecher is quoted as saying, "The symbol of the North is the pen; the symbol of the South is the bludgeon," LC. In this and in "Southern Chivalry . . ." Sumner is depicted holding a

pen. These three prints are discussed by David Tatham, "Pictorial Responses to the Caning of Senator Sumner," in *American Printmaking before 1876: Fact, Fiction, and Fantasy,* . . . (Washington, D.C., 1975), pp. 11–19.

37. Donald, *Sumner,* pp. 322–26.

38. Arthur Hobson Quinn, *A History of the American Drama from the Beginning to the Civil War* (New York, 1943), pp. 303–07; Robert C. Toll, *On With the Show: The First Century of Show Business in America* (New York, 1976), pp. 13–14. Thornton, *An American Glossary,* cites for "B'Hoy": Cornelius Mathews, "Money-penny" (1850): a town-rowdy, always "in his shirt sleeves."

39. "Dancing for EEls . . . in Catherine Mkt., N.Y." (1848), Houghton; "Dancing for Eels" (1848), LC; "Mose, Lize, and Little Mose Going to California" (1851), NYHS.

40. *Young America,* 1, n.s. (1856), 259; *Vanity Fair,* 1 (2 April 1860), 256, repr. Shaw, *AL,* II, 17; *Lantern,* I (1852), 14.

41. "The Democratic B'Hoy" (1848), AAS, of which there is an apparent variant entitled "Who Says Gas? Or the Democratic B'Hoy" (1848), LC; "Who's Dat Knockin' at De Door?" (1848), LC.

42. There is a relevant print of Sumner giving a coin to a black girl and refusing one to a ragged white girl, entitled "I'm not to Blame for Being White, Sir" (n.d.) in MHS, which seems to make a point somewhat similar to the one suggested here for the contrast of the B'Hoy and the "unhappy-looking woman" (plate 10).

9. *The Seventh Confidence Man (The PIO Man) and Three Formidable Antagonists (the Invalid Titan, the Soldier of Fortune Thomas Fry, and Pitch the Missouri Bachelor)*

1. "Virtuous Harry . . ." (1844) and "Matty Meeting . . ." (1844), repr. Shaw, *AL,* I, 107, 106. "Cleansing the Augean Stable" (1844) shows Texas as an elegant woman repulsed by the Whigs, repr. Shaw, *AL,* I, 103. Strong uses "Creole" several times for the people of Cuba, *Diary,* II, 65. Since Calhoun was dead by 1856 and since the Titan contains elements of Brooks, it is possible that Melville's Puny Girl alludes to further Southern agitation for expansion, into Cuba through annexation and into Central and South America.

2. Donald, *Sumner,* p. 272.

3. Harriet Martineau, *Retrospect of Western Travel* (London, 1838), I, 242; Charles M. Wiltse, *John C. Calhoun: Sectionalist, 1840–1850* (Indianapolis and New York, 1951), pp. 415–16; 418–22.

4. Margaret L. Coit, *John C. Calhoun: American Portrait* (Boston, 1950), p. 47; Oliver Dyer, a contemporary, notes that he was "tall and gaunt," as quoted in Herbert L. Curry, "John C. Calhoun," in Brigance, ed., *APA,* II, 646; George F. Milton calls the three senators "Titans," "aging giants," "dying gods," reflecting contemporary imagery, *Eve of Conflict,* pp. 48, 52, 63; Nathaniel P. Willis, *Hurry-Graphs; Or, Sketches of Scenery, Celebrities, and So-*

ciety, Taken from Life (New York, 1851), p. 180. Like Calhoun, Brooks, too, was tall—over six feet, Lader, *Bold Brahmins,* p. 222; Donald, *Sumner,* p. 289. Hone, *Diary,* p. 459; Curry, "Calhoun," in Brigance, ed., *APA,* II, 645–46; Martineau, *Retrospect,* I, 244; Elias Lyman Magoon, *Living Orators in America* (New York, 1854), p. 237; Coit, *Calhoun,* p. 52.

5. Magoon, *Living Orators,* pp. 190, 222–23, 228, 229, 237.

6. Wiltse, *Calhoun,* pp. 423, 304, 366, 460–61.

7. Thomas Hart Benton, *Thirty Years' View . . .* (New York, 1856), II, 740. Melville may have seen Calhoun in the Senate in early February 1847, when he visited Washington. Calhoun spoke 9 February in an important and well-attended speech on the Mexican War. See Wiltse, *Calhoun,* pp. 297–99.

8. "George Law," *Appleton's Cyclopaedia;* "George Law," *DAB;* Carleton Beals, *Brass-Knuckle Crusade: The Great Know-Nothing Conspiracy, 1820–1860* (New York, 1960), pp. 17–18. For Law's political involvement with the 1852 campaign and with filibustering, see Charles H. Brown, *Agents of Manifest Destiny: The Lives and Times of the Filibusters* (Chapel Hill, 1980), pp. 17, 96–98, 100–07, 365–67.

9. Halstead, *Trimmers,* pp. 5–11, 68–69; Fred H. Harrington, *Fighting Politician: Major General N. P. Banks* (Philadelphia, 1948), pp. 36–38; Isely, *Greeley,* p. 166.

10. Crandall, *Early History,* pp. 180–83, 246, 254–55. See also Louis Dow Scisco, *Political Nativism in New York State* (New York, 1901), pp. 147, 172–81; Philip S. Foner, *Business and Slavery: The New York Merchants and the Irrepressible Conflict* (Chapel Hill, 1941), p. 117. See "Fancied Security; Or, the Rats on a Bender" (1856), UCLA (plate 16)—a copy in which Law's name is printed by his figure. See also for Barker and Law, Mark L. Berger, *The Revolution in the New York Party Systems: 1840–1860* (Port Washington, N.Y., 1973), pp. 15, 75–76, 111–12, 130–32.

11. Halstead, *Trimmers,* p. 73; "The American Gulliver Bringing in Cuba," repr. Beals, *Brass-Knuckle Crusade,* p. 152. Undated prints later than 1856 are "Ye Mightie Live Oak Giant Indulgeth in a . . . Broil" and "Ye Mightie Live Oak Giant Devouring Ye Citie of New Yorke," NYPL.

12. Michael F. Holt, "The Politics of Impatience: The Origins of Know Nothingism," *Journal of American History,* 60 (June 1973), 309–29.

13. See prints of James H. Hackett as Nimrod Wildfire in *The Lion of the West,* a comedy based on the life and attributed writings of the Western politician David Crockett (1786–1836), which was rewritten as *The Kentuckian;* and of Dan Marble as Sampson Hardhead in *The Backwoodsman,* in Francis Hodge, *Yankee Theatre: The Image of America on the Stage 1825–1850* (Austin, 1964), plates 21 and 30. The "Backwoodsman type" also appears as a "Western lad," wearing fringed coat and coonskin cap and holding a rifle in the political print, "Set-To Between the Champion Old Tip & the Swell Dutchman of Kinderhook 1836," in which he is a second to William Henry Harrison in a fist fight with Van Buren, AAS.

14. "The Hunter of Kentucky" (1844), repr. Shaw, *AL,* I, 102; "The New Davy Crockett," *John-Donkey,* 1 (29 January 1848), 73. Harvard College Library copy. Benton wears no hat. Chambers, *Old Bullion,* pp. 309–12; *Yankee Doodle,* 1 (1846–47), 278; 2 (1847), 9. With regard to Pitch's "Spartan Manners," another print, "The Funeral of Loco Focoism" (1840) depicts Blair calling the mourners (Benton, Calhoun, Woodbury, Kendall, Jackson, and Van Buren) "The Spartan Band," as if "Spartan" were a popular term for certain Democrats, AAS.

15. E. B. Smith, *Blair,* p. 66; Magoon, *Living Orators,* pp. 336–37, 303, 339; *John-Donkey,* (22 April 1848); W. E. Smith, *Blair Family,* I, 265–66; Chambers, *Old Bullion,* pp. xiii, 61. Hone compares Benton to a hyena and a steer, *Diary,* pp. 150, 311.

16. Chambers, *Old Bullion,* pp. xiv, 61, 15–17.

17. *The Confessions of St. Augustine,* tr. E. B. Pusey (London, 1907), p. 26.

18. Magoon, *Living Orators,* pp. 337–38; Chambers, *Old Bullion,* p. xiii; Thomas Hart Benton, *Historical and Legal Examination of . . . the Dred Scott Case* (New York, 1857), p. 190; Strong, *Diary,* II, 167; Halstead, *Trimmers,* p. 22, and for other examples of his speech exhibiting similar characteristics, pp. 29–30, 87. For other imitations of Benton's speech style see W. E. Smith, *Blair Family,* I, 275: "Douglas never can be President, sir. His legs are too short, sir. His coat, like a cow's tail, hangs too near the ground, sir."

19. Chambers, *Old Bullion,* p. 20.

20. Chambers, *Old Bullion,* p. 419.

21. Benton, *Thirty Years' View,* II, 759.

22. Benton, *Thirty Years' View,* II, 695.

23. A chain and a brass plate were typical of dog collars in this period. See "Lost and Found" columns of the *Tribune* and *Herald,* for examples. For prints of editors as dogs see, for example: "Let Every one Take Care of Himself (As the Jack ass said when he was dancing among the Chickens)" (1832?), which caricatures five editors who supported Andrew Jackson, Houghton; "The People Putting Responsibility to the Test, Or the Downfall of the Kitchen Cabinet and Collar Presses" (1834), which is excellent for caricaturing newspapers controlled by politicians as collared dogs, AAS and NYPL; for politicians as dogs, "The South Carolina Stag at Bay," where Calhoun as a deer is attacked by dogs—among them Benton and Ritchie—and "The Home Branch of the Caudle Family," where Benton is a faithful bulldog wearing a collar, both in *Yankee Doodle,* 1 (1846–47), 241 and 266; "Conquering Prejudice to Save the Union" (1850), in which both Webster and Lewis Cass are depicted as collared dogs, the meaning being that they are controlled by the South in their attitudes toward the Fugitive Slave Bill, AAS; "The Whig Organ: Exhibiting a Specimen of the Feathered Tribe," *Lantern,* 28 August 1852, showing Raymond as a trick dog on a leash held by Greeley the organ-grinder, NYHS copy; and "Pilgrims of the Rhine-O!" (1852), which caricatures Seward as a dog leading a blindfolded Winfield Scott, LC.

24. For Greeley's life, see James Parton, *The Life of Horace Greeley* . . . (New York, 1855; revised and augmented, Boston, 1872); Horace Greeley, *Recollections of a Busy Life* (New York, 1868); Constance Rourke, *Trumpets of Jubilee* . . . (New York, 1927), pp. 241–365; Jeter Allen Isely, *Horace Greeley and the Republican Party, 1853–1861* (Princeton, 1947); William Harlan Hale, *Horace Greeley: Voice of the People* (New York, 1950); Glyndon G. Van Deusen, *Horace Greeley: Nineteenth-Century Crusader* (New York, 1953).

25. Isely, *Greeley*, pp. 53, 151.

26. Among the graphic prints prior to 1856 that fix the conventional image of shabby coat, rundown boots, disarrayed cravat and beaten hat: "Yankee Doodle's Statue Gallery, No. 1: The Head of the Tribunes," "The Grease Spot Man," and "Pictures of Progress," in *Yankee Doodle,* 1 (1846–47), 82, 125, 272; an untitled sketch of only his face and boots, and another, "The Modern Pandora," in *John-Donkey,* 1 (1848), 22 January and 24 June 1848; "The Modern Colossus: The Eighth Wonder of the World" (1848) in Peters, *Currier & Ives,* pl. 154; "Marriage of the Free Soil and Liberty Parties" (1848), repr. Shaw, *AL,* I, 153; "The Hurly Burly Pot" (1850), LC; an untitled sketch showing Greeley with a half-black and half-white face, in the *Lantern,* January 1852; "Pap, Soup and Chowder" (1852), repr. Shaw, *AL,* I, 165; "The Great Presidential Sweepstakes of 1856," "The Mustang Team" (1856), and "The Great American Buck Hunt of 1856," repr. Shaw, *AL,* I, 184, 185, 189 (see plates 6 and 15). Later political prints that reemphasize the shabby image are: "Political Blondins Crossing Salt River" (1860), "An Heir to the Throne" (1860), "The Rail Candidate" (1860), "The Irrepressible Conflict" (1860), "Et Tu, Greeley?" *Vanity Fair,* 2 June 1860, "'The Impending Crisis,' Or Caught in the Act" (1860), "The Great Exhibition of 1860," "Letting the Cat Out of the Bag," (1860), and "Horace is Sick!" (1861), repr. Shaw, *AL,* II, 31, 37, 49, 51, 55, 59, 99, 101, 213 (see plates 22 and 23). An interesting later print shows Greeley as Jeremy Diddler: "Raising the Wind," in *Vanity Fair,* 6 (11 October 1862), 175.

27. Maverick, *Raymond,* pp. 42–43. Melville's first published work that has been traced (a public exchange of acrimonious letters about the Philo-Logos Society) was in the *Albany Microscope* in 1838; he probably was acquainted with the public image of Greeley from his early manhood in Albany. See Leyda, *Log,* I, 69–79; and Gilman, *Melville's Early Life,* pp. 90–98.

28. Rourke, *Trumpets,* pp. 266, 313–14.

29. "The Untranslated Don Quixote," *John-Donkey,* 1 (1848), 8, 15, 22, 29 January; 5, 12, 19, 26 February; 4 March.

30. Whether Greeley was satirized on the stage I have not determined. That there was interchange between graphic caricature and stage types is evident from the many graphic prints of stage types and of actors and from remarks such as that in a New York *Herald* review, 15 April 1856, concerning a current play at Burton's Chambers Street Theatre, that the play was "based on *Punch* caricatures." Conversely, public figures were often caricatured as characters in well-known plays, especially Shakespeare's.

31. Parton, *Life* (1872), pp. 25, 94–95, 296–97; Hale, *Horace Greeley*, pp. 77–78; Rourke, *Trumpets*, p. 266. Prints show sometimes a wide-brimmed, low-crowned country hat and sometimes a crushed beaver hat. Prints that show especially well his clothing are: "Patent Balancing by an Amateur" (1848), which is good for showing the disarrayed cravat, AAS, repr. Isely, *Greeley*, opp. p. 18; "The Great Presidential Sweepstakes of 1856," and "The Mustang Team" (plate 15) for the shabby coattails, repr. Shaw, *AL*, I, 184 and 185; and "An Heir to the Throne" (1860), Shaw, *AL*, II, 37.

32. To be "baker-kneed" means to incline the right knee joint inward until it resembles the right side of the letter "K." See *OED* under "Baker." Parton, *Life* (1872), pp. 63, 73, 296; in the 1855 edition the sketch is opposite the frontispiece. A leg injured in 1829, when Greeley was about nineteen, may have accounted for his peculiar walk; see Parton, *Life* (1872), p. 69.

33. "A Member of the Press . . . ," Houghton; "The Rival Babies: A Comedy in one act, now performing with immense success through all the States," *Lantern*, 23 October 1852, NYHS copy.

34. Rourke, *Trumpets*, p. 265; Hale, *Horace Greeley*, pp. 77, 88; Rourke, *Trumpets*, p. 341; "Great Speech of Clay . . ." (1847) and "Managing a Candidate," (1852), AAS.

35. Parton, *Life*, pp. 50, 78, 297–98; Hale, *Horace Greeley*, pp. 78, 88, 202; Rourke, *Trumpets*, p. 342.

36. Letter to editor of the *Christian Ambassador*, in Parton, *Life*, pp. 523–24.

37. *Encyclopaedia Britannica*, 14th ed., "Universalist Church."

38. Greeley's more pessimistic later views as expressed in *Recollections* (1868) could not affect the early public image of his personality and principles as expressed in the *Tribune* and as revealed in Parton's *Life* (1855).

39. Horace Greeley, *Hints Toward Reforms, in Lectures, Addresses, and Other Writings* (New York, 1850), pp. 45, 73, 78–79. Melville or Allan Melville purchased this book in 1850; see Merton M. Sealts, Jr., *Melville's Reading: A Check-List of Books Owned and Borrowed* (Madison, Wis., 1966), no. 234.

40. Leyda, *Log*, II, 582.

41. Ralph Waldo Emerson, "Nature," in *Selected Writings*, ed. Brooks Atkinson (New York, 1940), pp. 14–16. Greeley acknowledged his debt to and admiration of Emerson and the transcendentalists in "The Formation of Character," *Hints*, pp. 86, 106; see also Van Deusen, *Horace Greeley*, p. 61.

42. Eric Voegelin, "Response to Professor Altizer's 'A New History and a New But Ancient God?'" *Journal of the American Academy of Religion*, 43 (December 1975), 771; and *The Ecumenic Age* (Baton Rouge, La., 1974), p. 264 (vol. 4, *Order and History* [Baton Rouge, La., 1956–74]).

43. Parker, ed., *C-M*, p. 98, n. 1.

44. Greeley was dubbed "The Philosopher" at least as early as 1847 in a squib in *Yankee Doodle*, 2, 19; he was consistently called "Philosopher Greeley"—ironically—in the 1850s by Bennett in the *Herald* and by William Herndon, Theodore Parker, and others; the nickname was retained when he campaigned

for president in 1872. See Rourke, *Trumpets,* p. 342; and the print, "A Philosopher in Ecstasy" (1872), Peters, *Currier & Ives,* pl. 153.

45. For a typical use of "confidence"in a political context, see *New York Times* editorial (possibly by Raymond), 20 June 1856, just after the Republican nominating convention in Philadelphia, which speaks of the candidates Frémont and Dayton as "every way worthy of the confidence of the people"— phrasing echoed by Black Guinea's plea that "dis poor ole darkie is werry well wordy of all you kind ge'mmen's kind confidence" (Foster, ed. *C-M,* p. 13).

46. Isely, *Horace Greeley,* pp. 47, 66, 159–60.

10. The Eighth and Last Confidence Man (Frank Goodman the Cosmopolitan) and His Antagonist (Charles Arnold Noble)

1. It has been argued that Melville intended to portray the poet, translator, lecturer and translator Bayard Taylor (1825–1878) in his portrait of the Cosmopolitan, Hans-Joachim Lang and Benjamin Lease, "Melville's Cosmopolitan: Bayard Taylor in *The Confidence-Man,*" *Amerikastudien/American Studies,* 22 (1977), 286–89. I feel that a better case can be made for Beecher as the object of his satire.

2. For Beecher's life see: Augusta Moore, ed. *Notes from Plymouth Pulpit: A Collection of Memorable Passages from the Discourses of Henry Ward Beecher with a Sketch of Mr. Beecher and the Lecture Room* (New York, 1859), pp. xxiii–xlviii; Lyman Abbott, *Henry Ward Beecher. A Sketch of His Career . . .* (New York, 1883); Joseph Howard, Jr., *Life of Henry Ward Beecher the Eminent Pulpit and Platform Orator . . .* (Philadelphia, 1887); Thomas W. Knox, *Life and Work of Henry Ward Beecher . . .* (Hartford, 1887); John Henry Barrows, *Henry Ward Beecher: The Shakespeare of the Pulpit* (New York, 1893); Paxton Hibben, *Henry Ward Beecher: An American Portrait* (New York, 1927); Constance Rourke, *Trumpets of Jubilee* (New York, 1927), pp. 149–237; Lionel Crocker, "Henry Ward Beecher," in Brigance, ed., *APA,* I, 265–93; William G. McLoughlin, *The Meaning of Henry Ward Beecher: An Essay on the Shifting Values of Mid–Victorian America, 1840–1870* (New York, 1970); Clifford E. Clark, Jr., *Henry Ward Beecher: Spokesman for a Middle-Class America* (Urbana, 1978).

3. *Young America,* 1, N.S. (28 March 1856), 149; Bellows quoted in Clark, *Beecher,* p. 122. Three anti-Republican prints that show Beecher: "The Great American Buck Hunt of 1856," in which he is stuck in "Abolition Bog," AAS and repr. Shaw, *AL,* I, 189; "The Great Presidential Sweepstakes of 1856," in which he offers to help draw Frémont's wagon, pulled by the "Wooly Nag" led by Greeley, out of the "Abolition Cess Pool," repr. Shaw, *AL,* I, 184; and "Col. Fremont's Last Grand Exploring Expedition in 1856," in which Beecher carries a supply of rifles and says, "Be heavenly minded, my bretheren all / But if you fall out at trifles, / Settle the matter with

powder and ball / And I will furnish the rifles." The Abolition Nag which Frémont is riding has the face of Greeley, while Seward leads the way to Salt River, HL, repr. Shaw, *AL,* I, 187 (plate 14). Beecher is associated with liquor in a full-page print in *Young America,* 1, NS, (19 April 1856), 187, where he is depicted, wearing a paper hat labelled "Independent," as a "Kansas Crusader," astride a "Sharps" rifle and carrying a bottle of "Scheid—m Schnapps"—a kind of German liquor, AAS copy (plate 17). Later than Melville's literary caricature is Adalbert Volck's series of Civil War etchings, "Comedians—Tragedians of the North" (1863?) with its magnificent study of Beecher in blackface as "Broder Beechar," as well as Volck's better-known print, "Worship of the North," in *Confederate War Etchings* (1863), which shows him in a Roman-style priestly robe offering up a young man as sacrifice at the altar of "Negro Worship," in association with Greeley, Sumner, Benjamin F. Butler, Lincoln, Seward and other Northern figures, AAS (plate 28); "Broder Beechar," repr. Anderson, *Work of Volck,* n.p., "Worship of the North," repr. Shaw, *AL,* I, 62–63.

4. Albert Bigelow Paine, *Th. Nast., His Period and His Pictures* (New York, 1904), p. 110; also John Chalmers Vinson, *Thomas Nast: Political Cartoonist* (Athens, Ga., 1967), pl. 20; *Vanity Fair,* 5 (22 March 1862), 140.
5. Quoted in W. H. Yeager, "Wendell Phillips," in Brigance, ed. *APA,* I, 335.
6. Rourke, *Trumpets,* p. 167; Hale, *Greeley,* p. 156; Hibben, *Portrait,* frontispiece; Rourke, *Trumpets,* p. 184; Knox, *Beecher,* pp. 449–50; *Vanity Fair,* 5 (19 April 1862), 187.
7. Rourke, *Trumpets,* p. 163; Howard, *Life,* pp. 159, 187; Abbott, *Beecher,* p. 186; Moore, ed. *Notes,* p. xxv; Abbott, *Beecher,* p. 186; Crocker, "Beecher," in Brigance, ed., *APA,* I, 280.
8. Moore, ed., *Notes,* p. xxix; Hibben, *Portrait,* pp. 47–49; Abbott, *Beecher,* pp. 135–36.
9. Stowe quoted in Barrows, *Shakespeare of the Pulpit,* p. 396; Moore, ed., *Notes,* pp. xxviii, xxx; Abbott, *Beecher,* pp. 73, 186; Knox, *Beecher,* pp. 457, 290; Howard, *Life,* pp. 229–30; Parker quoted in Rourke, *Trumpets,* p. 176; Whitman quoted in Crocker, "Beecher," in Brigance, ed., *APA,* I, 276.
10. Moore, ed., *Notes,* p. xxiv; Abbott, *Beecher,* p. 190; Howard, *Life,* p. 134.
11. Rourke, *Trumpets,* p. 165.
12. *Harper's Monthly Magazine,* 11 (June–November 1855), 405; Moore, ed., *Notes,* p. xxviii; Hibben, *Portrait,* pp. 145, 149; *Berkshire Eagle* microfilm courtesy of Berkshire County Athenaeum.
13. Barrows, *Shakespeare of the Pulpit,* p. 171; Bradford and Mallary in *Henry Ward Beecher as His Friends Saw Him* (New York, 1904), pp. 126, 91, and photograph of Beecher's tombstone on p. 124.
14. Knox, *Beecher,* pp. 481, 542–43.
15. Crocker, "Beecher," in Brigance, ed., *APA,* I, 267, 271; Holmes quoted in Howard, *Life,* pp. 291–92.
16. Moore, ed., *Notes,* pp. 189–90.

17. Crocker, "Beecher," in Brigance, ed., *APA*, I, 276; Abbott, *Beecher*, p. 89.
18. Hinrichs in *Beecher as His Friends Saw Him*, p. 127; Moore, ed., *Notes*, pp. xxvii–xxviii; E. and G. Duyckinck, ed., *Cyclopaedia*, I, 645; *Vanity Fair*, 3 (16 February, 1861), 75; Knox, *Beecher*, p. 289; Seward quoted in Hibben, *Portrait*, p. 158; Rourke, *Trumpets*, p. 178; Barrows, *Shakespeare of the Pulpit*, p. 118.
19. Barrows, *Shakespeare of the Pulpit*, p. 481.
20. Rhodes, *History*, II, 210.
21. Melville, *Poems*, ed. Vincent, pp. 235–36.
22. Nevins, *Frémont*, II, 516.
23. Melville, *Poems*, ed. Vincent, pp. 234, 465.
24. The bar setting in chapters 29–35 bears a resemblance to earlier literary treatments of confidence men; for example, James Kenney's comic dramatization of the "diddling" of Fainwould by Jeremy Diddler in the public room of an inn, in *Raising the Wind* (1803), and, more closely related, Joseph Rodman Drake's "Ode to Impudence" (1819), where, in this number of the *Croaker Papers*, he presents a New York type who by "looks of brass and words of honey" in Niblo's restaurant obtains meals and wine without paying for them—despite a sign that reads "Pay to-day and trust to-morrow," *New York Drama; A Choice Collection of Tragedies, Comedies, Farces, Etc.* (New York, 1876), III, 17–26; *The Life and Works of Joseph Rodman Drake 1795–1820. A Memoir and Complete Text of His Poems and Prose*, ed. Frank Lester Pleadwell (Boston, 1935), pp. 330–31.
25. Murat Halstead, *Three Against Lincoln. Murat Halstead Reports the Caucuses of 1860*, ed. William B. Hesseltine (Baton Rouge, 1960), p. 8; Emerson D. Fite, *The Presidential Campaigns of 1860* (New York, 1911), p. 214; Dumond, *Antislavery Origins of the Civil War*, p. 99; Malcolm C. McMillan, "William Lowndes Yancey and the Historians: One Hundred Years," *Alabama Review*, 20 (1967), 164. See also William Garrott Brown, *The Lower South in American History* (New York, 1903), pp. 118–19, and Chaplain W. Morrison, *Democratic Politics and Sectionalism: The Wilmot Proviso Controversy* (Chapel Hill, 1967), pp. 49–50.
26. Halstead, *Three Against Lincoln*, p. 8; Foote quoted in Joseph Hodgson, *The Cradle of the Confederacy, Or, The Times of Troup, Quitman and Yancey . . .* (Mobile, 1876; rpt. Spartanburg, S.C., 1975), p. 262; John W. DuBose, *The Life and Times of William Lowndes Yancey . . .* (Birmingham, 1892; rpt. New York, 1942), I, 189, 318; Clement Eaton, *The Mind of the Old South* (Baton Rouge, 1967), p. 277; Rhodes, *History of the U.S. 1850–1877*, II, 447; Shaw, *AL*, II, 10; Eaton, *Mind*, p. 273; Foote quoted in Hodgson, *Cradle*, p. 262; Rexford S. Mitchell, "William L. Yancey," in Brigance, ed., *APA*, II, 741.
27. Eaton, *Mind*, pp. 267, 277; DuBose, *Life*, I, 404, 75. "West" here means Alabama, from which the Indians had only recently been removed. I have found no evidence that Yancey traveled on the Indiana frontier as Noble claims to have done as a child.

28. The violent Southern type was frequently caricatured in prints not only carrying a whip, alluding to slave punishment, but wearing either a pistol or a bowie knife or both in his belt. See, for examples, two prints from *Punch* reproduced in Shaw, *AL*, II, 133 and 161. In Henry James, *The Bostonians* (1885), the hero Basil Ransom, a Mississippian, says ironically and angrily to his Bostonian hostess: "'Oh yes; when I dine out I usually carry a six-shooter and a bowie knife.'" See also William R. Taylor, *Cavalier and Yankee: The Old South and American National Character* (New York, 1961) for other aspects of this type.

29. Halstead, *Three Against Lincoln,* pp. 8, 52, 80, 267–68; Mitchell, in Brigance, ed., *APA,* II, 741; DuBose, *Life,* I, 190; Hodgson, *Cradle,* p. 262; Eaton, *Mind,* p. 269.

30. On this movement see Merle Curti, "'Young America,'" *American Historical Review,* 32 (October 1926), 34–44; Merle Curti, "George N. Sanders, American Patriot of the Fifties," *South Atlantic Quarterly,* 27 (1928), 79–87; Merle Curti, "George Nicholas Sanders," in *DAB*; Potter, *Impending Crisis,* p. 197. For Melville's connection with Young America see Miller, *Raven and Whale,* pp. 110–11. In Hershel Parker's "Melville and Politics" Gansevoort Melville is quoted using the sobriquet "Young Hickory" for James Polk during the campaign of 1844, when Young America supported him, so there seems little doubt that Melville was familiar with the rhetoric and symbols of this group. See Frederick Merk, *Manifest Destiny and Mission in American History: A Reinterpretation* (New York, 1963), pp. 54–55; Parker, "Melville and Politics," p. 96. For crowing of the rooster as symbolic of the Democrats' political optimism, see David L. Cohn, *The Fabulous Democrats: A History of the Democratic Party in Pictures* (New York, 1956), pp. 53–54.

31. Eaton, *Mind,* p. 278.

32. DuBose, *Life,* I, 189; Mitchell, in Brigance, ed., *APA,* II, 740–41; DuBose, *Life,* I, 404; Halstead, *Three Against Lincoln,* pp. 52, 276; Chesnut quoted in McMillan, "Yancey and the Historians," p. 171.

33. DuBose, *Life,* I, 341–42; Curti, "'Young America,'" does not trace the Young America movement beyond its role in the 1852 election, nor does he associate Yancey with them as Yancey himself does. Charles H. Brown, *Agents of Manifest Destiny: The Lives and Times of the Filibusters* (Chapel Hill, 1980), terms Young America a "catchword rather than party or faction" (p. 95) and carries Sanders' career further. DuBose, *Life,* I, 342.

34. DuBose, *Life,* I, 318, 189, 289.

35. Maverick, *Raymond,* pp. 384–447. Wiltse, *Calhoun,* III, 210.

36. "Scan. Mag. at Washington," *Vanity Fair,* 2 (29 September 1860), 165, and "Coming 'Round," *Vanity Fair,* 2 (17 November 1860), 249, repr. Shaw, *AL*, II, 110, 155 (plate 25). Yancey is also depicted with Robert Toombs and Lawrence Keitt in "The Rising of the Afrite," *Vanity Fair,* 3 (19 January 1861), 31, repr. Shaw, *AL,* II, 156.

11. Two Antagonists (Mark Winsome and Egbert the Disciple) and Their Antagonist (the Crazy Beggar)

1. Everett quoted in Rhodes, *History,* I, 458; Melville, *Poems,* ed. Vincent, p. 465.
2. Winters, *In Defence of Reason,* p. 229; Oliver, "Emerson and Thoreau in *C-M,*" pp. 61–72; Foster, ed., *C-M,* pp. lxxiii–lxxxiv, 351–61.
3. Oliver Wendell Holmes, *Ralph Waldo Emerson* (Boston, 1885), p. 359; Herbert A. Wichelns, "Ralph Waldo Emerson," in Brigance, ed., *APA,* II, 517; Holmes, *Emerson,* p. 360; Bungay, *Off-Hand Takings,* p. 122; Holmes, *Emerson,* p. 361; Charles J. Woodbury, *Talks with Ralph Waldo Emerson* (New York, 1890), p. 128.
4. Oliver, "Emerson and Thoreau in *C-M,*" pp. 62–63; Woodbury, *Talks,* p. 122; Edwin Percy Whipple, "Some Recollections of Ralph Waldo Emerson," in Carl Bode, ed., *Ralph Waldo Emerson: A Profile* (New York, 1968), p. 5; John Burroughs quoted in James Elliot Cabot, *A Memoir of Ralph Waldo Emerson* (Boston, 1888), II, 613.
5. Cabot, *Memoir,* I, 368–69; Holmes, *Emerson,* pp. 368–69; Franklin B. Sanborn, *Recollections of Seventy Years* (Boston, 1909), II, 436; Woodbury, *Talks,* pp. 76, 124; Hecker quoted in Edith Roelker Curtis, *A Season in Utopia: The Story of Brook Farm* (New York, 1961), p. 199.
6. Holmes, *Emerson,* p. 359; Whipple, "Recollections," in Bode, ed., *Profile,* p. 5; Holmes, *Emerson,* pp. 360, 379; Woodbury, *Talks,* pp. 130, 126.
7. John Albee, *Remembrances of Emerson* (New York, 1901), p. 21; Woodbury, *Talks,* p. 48; Wichelns, "Emerson," in Brigance, ed., *APA,* II, 516; Woodbury, *Talks,* p. 95; Sanborn, *Recollections,* II, 349; *De Bow's* quoted in Jay Hubbell, *The South in American Literature: 1607–1900* (Durham, N.C., 1954), p. 384.
8. Albee, *Remembrances,* pp. 120, 129.
9. Wichelns, "Emerson," in Brigance, ed., *APA,* II, 518, 502, 511.
10. Wichelns, "Emerson," in Brigance, ed., *APA,* II, 518.
11. *The Letters of Ralph Waldo Emerson,* ed. Ralph L. Rusk (New York, 1939), V, 3–15; *The Journals and Miscellaneous Notebooks of Ralph Waldo Emerson (1854–1861),* ed. Susan Sutton Smith and Harrison Hayford (Cambridge, Mass., 1978), XIV, 437; Foster, ed., *C-M,* p. 351; Emerson, *Journals,* XIV, 63.
12. Emerson, *Journals,* XIV, 63, 97; Emerson, *Journals and Miscellaneous Notebooks (1848–1851),* ed. A. W. Plumstead, William H. Gilman, and Ruth H. Bennett (Cambridge, Mass., 1975), XI, 385; Emerson, *Journals and Miscellaneous Notebooks (1852–1855),* ed. Ralph H. Orth and Alfred R. Ferguson (Cambridge, Mass., 1977), XIII, 198; Emerson, "The Fugitive Slave Law," *Miscellanies* (Boston, 1904), pp. 180–84; Emerson, *Journals,* XI, 361.
13. Emerson, *Journals,* XIV, x; Emerson, "The Fugitive Slave Law," *Miscellanies,* pp. 184, 214. I have been unable to locate the text of "American Slavery," but it is likely that its content would be similar to the other address on the

Fugitive Slave Law that was given in the New York Tabernacle 7 March 1854, on the fourth anniversary of Webster's speech in favor of the bill, which carries on the condemnation of Webster (dead by then) and describes two kinds of judges—the "liberal" judge who reads the law one way and the "servile" judge who reads it another, *Miscellanies,* p. 225.

14. Ralph L. Rusk, *The Life of Ralph Waldo Emerson* (New York, 1949), pp. 389–91; Emerson, *Miscellanies,* p. 257.

15. Emerson, *Letters,* IV, 497; Emerson, *Journals,* XIII, 49.

16. Harrison Hayford, "Poe in *The Confidence-Man,*" *Nineteenth-Century Fiction,* 14 (December 1959), 207–18.

17. Rufus W. Griswold article rpt. as "The 'Ludwig Article' " in James A. Harrison, ed., *The Complete Works of Edgar Allan Poe* (New York, 1902; rpt. New York, 1965), I, 352; Arthur Hobson Quinn, *Edgar Allan Poe: A Critical Biography* (New York, 1941), p. 646, and illustration of a crayon portrait from a daguerreotype, ca. 1849, opp. p. 622.

18. Hayford, "Poe in *C-M,*" p. 214; Woodbury, *Talks,* pp. 62–64.

19. Griswold in Harrison, ed., *Works of Poe,* I, 356; Emerson, *Letters,* IV, 160.

20. Hubbell, *South in American Literature,* p. 535; Griswold in Harrison, ed., *Works of Poe,* I, 355–56.

21. Harrison, ed., *Works of Poe,* XV, 260.

22. Hubbell, *South in American Literature,* pp. 378–79. Hubbell claims that Poe, on his part, had no sectional prejudice before coming to New York but came to see that the New England writers were sectionally prejudiced against the South and West. He scandalized the New England literati by his attacks on their sectionalism and earned the name of an "unprincipled man of genius" and the long-lasting dislike and disapproval of most of the New England writers (pp. 543–46). Howard R. Floan, also, finds "enmity" toward the South in the New England writers but "sympathy" and "goodwill" as the attitude of the New York writers, among whom he includes Melville and the editors of *Putnam's,* in which Melville was publishing in the early and middle 1850s, *The South in Northern Eyes: 1831 to 1861* (Austin, Tex., 1958), pp. viii, 122–30.

23. Oliver, "Melville's Picture of Emerson and Thoreau," pp. 68–72; Foster, ed., *C-M,* pp. lxxiii–lxxxii, 351–52; Parker, "Melville's Satire of Emerson and Thoreau," pp. 64–65.

24. George F. Hoar, *Autobiography of Seventy Years* (New York, 1906), I, 70; Rusk, *Life of Emerson,* p. 364; Joseph Wood Krutch, *Henry David Thoreau* (n.p., 1948), p. 45; Franklin B. Sanborn, *Henry D. Thoreau* (Boston, 1888), p. 199.

25. Sanborn, *Thoreau,* p. 198; Sanborn, *Recollections of Seventy Years,* II, 469; Woodbury, *Talks,* p. 75; Walter Harding, *The Days of Henry Thoreau* (New York, 1965), p. 65. See also for Thoreau's seeming "a notable instance of unconscious imitation" of Emerson in manner, tone, voice, and inflections, Henry Williams, "Henry David Thoreau," in Samuel Arthur Jones, *Pertain-*

ing to Thoreau: A Gathering of Ten Significant Nineteenth-Century Opinions (Detroit, 1901; rpt. Hartford, 1970), p. 50.

26. Woodbury, *Talks*, pp. 76–78, 80; John Weiss, "Thoreau," in Jones, *Pertaining to Thoreau*, pp. 40–41, 43; Walter Harding and Michael Meyer, *The New Thoreau Handbook* (New York and London, 1980), p. 121.

27. Emerson quoted in Krutch, *Thoreau*, p. 42; Sanborn, *Recollections*, II, 348; Sanborn, *Thoreau*, p. 280; Emerson quoted in Woodbury, *Talks*, pp. 90–91; the Hawthornes quoted in Harding, *Days*, pp. 243–44; James quoted in Leon Edel, *Henry D. Thoreau* (Minneapolis, 1970), p. 18; Emerson and Stevenson in *The Recognition of Henry D. Thoreau: Selected Criticism since 1848*, ed. Wendell Glick (Ann Arbor, 1969), pp. 20, 85; Henry Seidel Canby, *Thoreau* (Boston, 1939), p. 201.

28. Canby, *Thoreau*, p. 19.

29. Sanborn, *Thoreau*, p. 279; Howells quoted in Canby, *Thoreau*, pp. 165–66; Nathaniel Hawthorne, *The American Notebooks*, ed. Claude M. Simpson (Columbus, Ohio, 1972), pp. 353–54; Stevenson in Glick, ed., *Recognition*, p. 69; Hawthorne, *American Notebooks*, p. 354; Channing quoted in Sanborn, *Recollections*, II, 353.

30. Emerson in Glick, ed., *Recognition*, pp. 31–32.

31. Hawthorne, *American Notebooks*, p. 357.

32. Hans-Joachim Lang and Benjamin Lease have made an interesting case that Egbert caricatures George William Curtis (1824–1892), in "Melville and 'The Practical Disciple': George William Curtis, in *The Confidence-Man*," *Amerikastudien/American Studies*, 26 (1981), 181–91. However, neither their evidence nor my independent research on Curtis has made a better case for him than that for Thoreau. Other candidates researched for this book (some extensively, some minimally) are the following: Amos Bronson Alcott, Nathaniel Banks, John Bigelow, George Boutwell, Anson Burlingame, James Elliot Cabot, Moncure Conway, Christopher P. Cranch, Charles Anderson Dana, Parke Godwin, John P. Hale, Charles G. Loring, Horace Mann, Charles Newcomb, John Gorham Palfrey, Stephen C. Phillips, Wendell Phillips, George Ripley, Franklin Sanborn, and Jones Very. All these were men who lived in the ambiance of Emerson—some intimately (as Adams, Alcott, Bradford, Channing, Cabot, Forbes, Newcomb, and Ward), others very remotely (as Bigelow, Burlingame, Banks, Boutwell, and Godwin)—but all of them have had, for one reason or another (age, appearance, personality, style, or other) to be presently disqualified.

33. Krutch, *Thoreau*, p. 237.

12. *The Cosmopolitan and His Final Antagonists (the Barber, the Clean Comely Old Man, the Juvenile Peddler, and the Irish Voice)*

1. Foster, ed., *C-M*, p. 363.

2. His preaching helped to reduce the importance of the church and contributed

to the secularization of Christianity according to his intellectual biographer Clark, *Henry Ward Beecher,* p. 61.

3. For examples of presentation scenes see: Rembrandt, "The Presentation in the Temple" (painting ca. 1628, Hamburg, Kunsthalle), "The Presentation in the Temple" (painting, 1631, The Hague, Mauritshuis), and "The Presentation in the Temple" (etching, ca. 1654), in Jakob Rosenburg, *Rembrandt: Life & Work* (London and New York, 1968), pls. 154, 155, figs. 153, 271; Rogier van der Weyden, altarpiece for St. Columba Church (Munich Alte Pinakothek), in Dorothy C. Shorr, "The Iconographic Development of the Presentation in the Temple," *Art Bulletin* (1946), pp. 17–32 and fig. 31. All the foregoing show Simeon with a high baldish forehead, long hair on either side, and a beard, as does the "Presentation" by Andrea Schiavone (ca. 1510/15–1563) now in the Princeton University Art Gallery.

4. Francis P. Weisenburger, *The Life of John McLean, A Politician on the United States Supreme Court* (Columbus, Ohio, 1937), passim.

5. Shaw, *AL,* II, 45, 71; Maury, *Famous Statesmen: 1846,* pp. 166–67, 189; Weisenburger, *Life,* pp. 226–27.

6. Weisenburger, *Life,* p. 64 and passim; John Quincy Adams, *Memoirs . . . Comprising Portions of His Diary from 1795 to 1848,* ed. Charles Francis Adams (Philadelphia, 1876), VIII, 25; *Appleton's Cyclopaedia,* "John McLean." For 1848 campaign see Rayback, *Free Soil,* pp. 1–10, 45.

7. Crandall, *Early History,* pp. 168–74; Weisenburger, *Life,* pp. 146, 147, 148–49, 151, 152.

8. Weisenburger, *Life,* pp. 118, 7, 223, 226, 224, 227.

9. Robert M. Cover, *Justice Accused: Antislavery and the Judicial Process* (New Haven, 1975), pp. 247–48; Potter, *Impending Crisis,* p. 280 and n. 26.

10. Halstead, *Trimmers,* p. 89.

11. Halstead, *Trimmers,* pp. 89–90.

12. Halstead, *Trimmers,* pp. 96–98, 101–102.

13. Halstead, *Three Against Lincoln,* p. 157.

14. "The Oregon and Texas Question" (1844), Houghton; "The American Twins—North and South," *Punch* (27 September 1856), repr. Shaw, *AL,* II, 161.

15. Melville may possibly also have known and intended to evoke the meaning of the original Arabic word "kāfir," meaning "infidel" from which Kaffir the name of a South African Bantu tribe is taken (*OED,* "Caffre"). In Afrikaans it is a derogatory term for Africans.

16. Sources consulted on Wise are: Barton H. Wise, *The Life of Henry A. Wise of Virginia, 1806–1876* (New York, 1899); John S. Wise, *The End of an Era* (Boston, 1902); Robert Douthat Meade, "Henry A. Wise," *DAB*; Clement Eaton, "Henry A. Wise and the Virginia Fire Eaters of 1856," *Mississippi Valley Historical Review,* 21 (March 1935), 495–512; and Eaton, *Mind,* Chapter V, "A Progressive in an Old State," pp. 90–109.

17. "A Bull Chase, 'The Words of the Wise, are as Goads'" (1839) and "The

Captain & Corporal's Guard" (1841), AAS (plate 3); "'Taking the Stump' or Stephen in Search of his Mother" (1860), AAS (plate 24). Wise appears as a boy in a later print "School of the C.S.A.," in *Vanity Fair,* 4 (26 October 1861), cover.

18. Halstead, *Trimmers,* pp. xi, 105; Nevins, *Evening Post,* p. 265. Horace Greeley writes in his *Recollections* (1868) that Buchanan's conduct in office was "unaccountable on any hypothesis but that of secret pledges, made by him or for him, to the Southern leaders when he was an aspirant to the Presidency, that fettered and paralyzed him when they perverted the powers enjoyed by them as members of his Cabinet to the disruption of the Union" (p. 359).

19. A print of Buchanan as an old bachelor concerned with his unmended wardrobe is "A Serviceable Garment—Or Reverie of a Bachelor" (1856), repr. Shaw, *AL,* I, 222; as an old maid, "Scan. Mag. at Washington," *Vanity Fair,* 2 (29 September 1860), 165. Bungay, *Off-Hand Takings,* mentions contemptuously Douglas's attempt to purchase the "bauble" of the presidency from the South, alluding to Douglas's sponsorship of the Kansas-Nebraska bill in 1854 (p. 384); Forney, *Anecdotes,* terms the presidency a "bauble" (p. 68).

20. Roy F. Nichols, *The Disruption of American Democracy* (New York, 1948), p. 44; Potter, *Impending Crisis,* pp. 262–63.

21. B. H. Wise, *Life,* pp. 67, 417, 58; Meade, "Wise," *DAB;* B. H. Wise, *Life,* pp. 403–04; Hone, *Diary,* p. 305; Eaton, *Mind,* p. 93; Hone, *Diary,* pp. 547–48, 583.

22. Helen C. Boatfield, "Michael Walsh," *DAB;* Robert Ernst, "The One and Only Mike Walsh," *New York Historical Society Quarterly,* 36 (January 1952), 43–65.

23. Ernst, "Walsh," pp. 50–51, 55. Walsh claimed to have invented the term "Hunker" for office-seeking Democrats, who, he said, "hunkered" after government positions. Forney, *Anecdotes,* pp. 113–14.

24. Ivor Debenham Spencer, *The Victor and the Spoils: A Life of William L. Marcy* (Providence, 1959), p. 273; Jerome Mushkat, *Tammany: The Evolution of a Political Machine, 1789–1865* (Syracuse, 1971), pp. 250–52; Coit, *Calhoun,* pp. 303–04; William V. Shannon, *The American Irish* (New York, 1963), pp. 51–54. See also on Walsh, Arthur M. Schlesinger, Jr., *The Age of Jackson* (Boston, 1945), pp. 408–10.

25. Carl Wittke, *The Irish in America* (Baton Rouge, 1956), pp. 109–16; Forney, *Anecdotes,* p. 113; Ernst, "Walsh," pp. 56–57.

26. Leyda, *Log,* I, 187, 188; Herman Melville, *Journal of a Visit to Europe and the Levant: October 11, 1856–May 6, 1857,* ed. Howard C. Horsford (Princeton, 1955), pp. 167–68; Boatfield, "Walsh," *DAB.*

13. The Political Commedia

1. Trimpi, "Harlequin-Confidence Man," pp. 170–93.

14. The Political Argument

1. Melville, *Poems,* ed. Vincent, p. 57.
2. Samuel Gilman Brown, *The Life of Rufus Choate* (Boston, 1891), I, 274.
3. Herman Melville, *Clarel: A Poem and Pilgrimage in the Holy Land,* ed. Walter E. Bezanson (New York, 1960), p. 422.
4. Halstead, *Trimmers,* p. 38.
5. Wilson, *Rise and Fall of the Slave Power,* II, 517.
6. Richard Lathers, *Reminiscences,* p. 136.
7. Washburne quoted in Donald, *Sumner,* p. 303.
8. "The Hurly-Burly Pot" (1850), LC (plate 6), listed in Weitenkampf, *Political Caricature in the U.S.,* p. 101.
9. *Lantern,* 1 (January–June 1852), 56. The editor of the *Lantern* was John Brougham, the comic actor and playwright, who acted the role of the "brazen" Confidence Man in, and claimed to have written the stage farce called, "The Confidence Man" produced in 1849. On the *Lantern,* see Frank L. Mott, *American Magazines,* II, 181.
10. "'Like Meets Like,'" *Vanity Fair,* 3 (26 January 1861), 42, repr. Shaw, *AL,* I, 228 (plate 26).
11. David Brion Davis treats extensively this polarization in thought and political rhetoric in chapter 2 of *The Slave Power Conspiracy and the Paranoid Style* (Baton Rouge, 1969), pp. 32–61. He notes the reality in the minds of this period of the idea of conspiracy and treats it as "a symbolic means of accounting for the subtle truth that abolitionists and Southern secessionists often played mutually supporting roles and seemed to be staging a premeditated performance to a bewildered and powerless audience" (p. 23).
12. *Poems,* ed. Vincent, pp. 465, 464, 461–62.

Selected Bibliography

Abbott, Lyman. *Henry Ward Beecher: A Sketch of His Career with an Analysis of His Power as a Preacher, Lecturer, Orator, and Journalist, and Incidents and Reminiscences of His Life.* New York, 1883.

Adams, Henry. *The Education of Henry Adams.* New York, 1931.

Adams, John Quincy. *Memoirs of John Quincy Adams Comprising Portions of His Diary from 1795 to 1848.* Ed. Charles Francis Adams. 12 vols. Philadelphia, 1874–77.

Adler, Joyce Sparer. "Melville and the White Man's War Against the American Indian." *Science & Society,* 36 (Winter 1972), 417–42.

Albee, John. *Remembrances of Emerson.* New York, 1901.

Albrecht, Robert C. *Theodore Parker.* New York, 1971.

Anderson, George McCullough, ed. *The Work of Adalbert Johann Volck, 1828–1912, Who Chose for His Name the Anagram V. Blada.* Baltimore, 1970.

Arnaud-Marçais, Dominique. "*The Confidence-Man: His Masquerade* et le problème noir." In *Le Blanc et le Noir chez Melville et Faulkner.* Ed. Viola Sachs. Paris, 1974.

Augustine of Hippo. *The Confessions of Saint Augustine.* Trans. E. B. Pusey. London, 1907.

Bailey, Gamaliel. *Facts for the People.* Washington, D. C., 1856. Vol. 1.

Bailey, Thomas A. *The American Pageant: A History of the Republic.* 4th ed. 2 vols. Lexington, Mass., 1971.

Barnes, Gilbert Hobbes. *The Anti-Slavery Impulse: 1830–1844.* New York, 1933; rpt. Gloucester, Mass., 1957.

Barnes, Thurlow Weed, ed. *Life of Thurlow Weed Including His Autobiography and a Memoir.* 2 vols. Boston and New York, 1883–84.

Barrows, John Henry. *Henry Ward Beecher: The Shakespeare of the Pulpit.* New York, 1893.

Beals, Carleton. *Brass-Knuckle Crusade: The Great Know-Nothing Conspiracy, 1820–1860.* New York, 1960.

Henry Ward Beecher as His Friends Saw Him. New York, 1904.

Beecher, Henry Ward. "Charles Sumner." In *Lectures and Orations.* Ed. Newell D. Hillis. New York, 1913.

Bemis, Samuel Flagg. *John Quincy Adams and the Union.* New York, 1956.

Benton, Thomas Hart. *Historical and Legal Examination of that Part of the*

Decision of the Supreme Court of the United States in the Dred Scott Case. . . New York, 1857.

————. *Thirty Years' View; Or, A History of the Working of the American Government for Thirty Years, from 1820 to 1850.* 2 vols. New York, 1854–56.

Bergmann, Johannes Dietrich. "The Original Confidence Man." *American Quarterly,* 21 (Fall 1969), 560–77.

Berger, Mark L. *The Revolution in the New York Party Systems: 1840–1860.* Port Washington, N.Y., 1973.

Berlin, Ira. *Slaves Without Masters: The Free Negro in the Antebellum South.* New York, 1976.

Bigelow, John. *William Cullen Bryant.* Boston, 1890.

Bishop, Joseph B. *Our Political Drama: Conventions, Campaigns, and Candidates.* New York, 1904.

Blaisdel, Thomas C., Jr., Peter Selz, and Seminar. *The American Presidency in Political Cartoons, 1776–1976.* Berkeley, 1976.

Bontemps, Arna. *Free at Last: The Life of Frederick Douglass.* New York, 1971.

Branch, Watson G. "The Genesis, Composition, and Structure of *The Confidence-Man.*" *Nineteenth-Century Fiction,* 27 (March 1973), 424–48.

————, ed. *Melville: The Critical Heritage.* London and Boston, 1974.

Brigance, William Norwood, ed. *A History and Criticism of American Public Address.* 3 vols. New York, 1943–55.

Brockway, Beman. *Fifty Years in Journalism Embracing Recollections and Personal Experiences with an Autobiography.* Watertown, N.Y., 1891.

Brodhead, Richard H. *Hawthorne, Melville and the Novel.* Chicago, 1976.

Brown, Charles H. *Agents of Manifest Destiny: The Lives and Times of the Filibusters.* Chapel Hill, N.C., 1980.

————. *William Cullen Bryant.* New York, 1971.

Brown, Ernest Francis. *Raymond of the Times.* New York, 1951.

Brown, Samuel Gilman. *The Life of Rufus Choate.* 6th ed. Boston, 1891.

Brown, William Garrott. *The Lower South in American History.* New York, 1903.

Bungay, George W. *Off-Hand Takings; Or, Crayon Sketches of the Noticeable Men of Our Age.* New York, 1854.

Cabot, James Elliot. *A Memoir of Ralph Waldo Emerson.* 2 vols. Boston, 1888.

Canby, Henry Seidel. *Thoreau.* Boston, 1939.

Carlson, Oliver. *The Man Who Made News: James Gordon Bennett.* New York, 1942.

Cary, Edward. *George William Curtis.* Boston and New York, 1895.

Chambers, William N. *Old Bullion Benton; Senator from the New West: Thomas Hart Benton, 1782–1858.* Boston, 1956.

Choate, Rufus and George T. Curtis. *The Old-Line Whigs for Buchanan! Letters of Rufus Choate and George T. Curtis*. Pamphlet. Boston, 1856.

Clark, Jr., Clifford E. *Henry Ward Beecher: Spokesman for a Middle-Class America*. Urbana, Ill., 1978.

Clippings from Albany and New York City Newspapers on the 1856 Presidential Campaign, and also on the Kansas Question. Scrapbook in the Stanford University Library. n.p., 1856.

Cohn, David L. *The Fabulous Democrats: A History of the Democratic Party in Pictures*. New York, 1956.

Coit, Margaret L. *John C. Calhoun: American Portrait*. Boston, 1950.

Cole, Arthur C. *The Whig Party in the South*. Washington, D.C., 1913.

Commager, Henry Steele. *Theodore Parker*. Boston, 1936.

Conningham, Frederic A. *Currier & Ives: An Illustrated Check List*. New York, 1949.

Coulter, E. Merton. *William G. Brownlow: Fighting Parson of the Southern Highlands*. Chapel Hill, N.C., 1937.

Cover, Robert M. *Justice Accused: Antislavery and the Judicial Process*. New Haven, 1975.

Cowen, Wilson Walker. "Melville's Marginalia." 11 vols. Ph.D. diss. Harvard University, 1965.

Crandall, Andrew W. *The Early History of the Republican Party, 1854–1856*. Boston, 1930.

Crocker, Lionel. "Henry Ward Beecher." In *A History and Criticism of American Public Address,* ed. William N. Brigance. 3 vols. New York, 1943–55.

Curry, Herbert L. "John C. Calhoun." In *A History and Criticism of American Public Address,* ed. William N. Brigance. 3 vols. New York, 1943–55.

Curti, Merle. "George N. Sanders, American Patriot of the Fifties." *South Atlantic Quarterly,* 27 (1928), 79–87.

———. "'Young America.'" *American Historical Review,* 32 (October 1926), 34–55.

Curtis, Edith Roelker. *A Season in Utopia: The Story of Brook Farm*. New York, 1961.

Curtis, Francis. *The Republican Party: A History of Its Fifty Years Existence and a Record of Its Measures and Leaders, 1854–1904*. 2 vols. New York, 1904.

Davis, Burke. *Old Hickory: A Life of Andrew Jackson*. New York, 1977.

Davis, David Brion. *The Problem of Slavery in Western Culture*. Ithaca, N.Y., 1966.

———. *The Slave Power Conspiracy and the Paranoid Style*. Baton Rouge, 1969.

Davis, Merrell. *Melville's "Mardi": A Chartless Voyage*. New Haven, 1952.

Dillon, Merton L. *Benjamin Lundy and the Struggle for Negro Freedom*. Urbana, Ill., 1966.

Dirks, John Edward. *The Critical Theology of Theodore Parker.* New York, 1948.

Donald, David. *Charles Sumner and the Coming of the Civil War.* New York, 1960.

Douglass, Frederick. *The Life and Writings of Frederick Douglass*. 3 vols. Ed. Philip S. Foner. New York, 1950.

Doyle, John. *The Seven Years of William IV: A Reign Cartooned by John Doyle*. Ed. G. M. Trevelyan. London, 1952.

Drake, Joseph Rodman. *The Life and Works of Joseph Rodman Drake, 1795–1820: A Memoir and Complete Text of His Poems and Prose*. Ed. Frank Lester Pleadwell. Boston, 1935.

DuBose, John W. *The Life and Times of William Lowndes Yancey: A History of Political Parties in the United States from 1834 to 1863. . . .* 2 vols. Birmingham, Ala., 1892; rpt. New York, 1942.

Dumond, Dwight L. *Antislavery Origins of the Civil War in the United States*. Ann Arbor, 1939; rpt. 1959.

Duyckinck, Evert A., and George L. Duyckinck, eds. *Cyclopaedia of American Literature Embracing Personal and Critical Notices of Authors and Selections from Their Writings. . . .* 2 vols. New York, 1856.

Earle, Thomas. *The Life, Travels and Opinions of Benjamin Lundy, Including His Journeys to Texas and Mexico, with a Sketch of Contemporary Events, and a Notice of the Revolution in Haiti*. Philadelphia, 1847; rpt. New York, 1969.

Eaton, Clement. "Henry A. Wise and the Virginia Fire Eaters of 1856." *Mississippi Valley Historical Review,* 21 (March 1935), 495–512.

———. *The Mind of the Old South*. Rev. ed. Baton Rouge, 1967.

Edel, Leon. *Henry D. Thoreau*. Minneapolis, 1970.

Emerson, Ralph Waldo. "The Fugitive Slave Law." In *Miscellanies*. Boston, 1904.

———. *The Journals and Miscellaneous Notebooks of Ralph Waldo Emerson*. Ed. William H. Gilman et al. Vol. 11: *The Journals and Miscellaneous Notebooks (1848–1851)*, ed. A. W. Plumstead, William H. Gilman and Ruth H. Bennett. Cambridge, Mass., 1975.

———. *The Journals and Miscellaneous Notebooks of Ralph Waldo Emerson*. Ed. William H. Gilman et al. Vol. 13: *The Journals and Miscellaneous Notebooks (1852–1855)*, ed. Ralph H. Orth and Alfred R. Ferguson. Cambridge, Mass., 1977.

———. *The Journals and Miscellaneous Notebooks of Ralph Waldo Emerson*. Ed. William H. Gilman et al. Vol. 14: *The Journals and Miscellaneous Note-

books (1854–1861), ed. Susan Sutton Smith and Harrison Hayford. Cambridge, Mass., 1978.

———. *The Letters of Ralph Waldo Emerson.* Ed. Ralph L. Rusk. 6 vols. New York, 1939.

———. "Nature." In *Selected Writings of Ralph Waldo Emerson.* Ed. Brooks Atkinson. New York, 1940.

———. "Theodore Parker: An Address at the Memorial Meeting, at the Music Hall, Boston, June 15, 1860." In *Miscellanies.* Boston, 1884.

Ernst, Robert. "The One and Only Mike Walsh." *New York Historical Society Quarterly,* 36 (January 1952), 43–65.

Feaver, William. *Masters of Caricature from Hogarth and Gillray to Scarfe and Levine.* New York, 1981.

Fehrenbacher, Don E. *The Dred Scott Case: Its Significance in American Law and Politics.* New York, 1978.

Fite, Emerson D. *The Presidential Campaign of 1860.* New York, 1911.

Floan, Howard R. *The South in Northern Eyes: 1831 to 1861.* Austin, Tex., 1958.

Foner, Philip S. *Business and Slavery: The New York Merchants and the Irrepressible Conflict.* Chapel Hill, N.C., 1941.

———, ed. *The Life and Writings of Frederick Douglass.* 3 vols. New York, 1950.

Forney, John W. *Anecdotes of Public Men.* New York, 1873.

Frederickson, George M. *The Inner Civil War: Northern Intellectuals and the Crisis of the Union.* New York, 1965.

Frothingham, Octavius B. *Theodore Parker: A Biography.* Boston, 1874.

Gardiner, Oliver Cromwell. *The Great Issue; Or, the Three Presidential Candidates, Being a Brief Historical Sketch of the Free Soil Question. . . .* New York, 1848; rpt. Westport, Conn., 1970.

Garrison, Wendell P., and Francis J. Garrison. *William Lloyd Garrison: 1805–1879, The Story of His Life Told by His Children.* 4 vols. New York, 1885–89.

George, M. Dorothy. *English Political Caricature, 1793–1832: A Study of Opinion and Propaganda.* 2 vols. Oxford, 1959.

Gianeri, Enrico. *Storia della caricatura.* Milano, 1959.

Gilman, William H. *Melville's Early Life and "Redburn."* New York, 1951.

Glick, Wendell, ed. *The Recognition of Henry D. Thoreau: Selected Criticism since 1848.* Ann Arbor, 1969.

Godwin, Parke. *A Biography of William Cullen Bryant with Extracts from His Private Correspondence.* 2 vols. New York, 1883.

Going, Charles B. *David Wilmot; Free-Soiler: A Biography of the Great Advocate of the Wilmot Proviso.* New York, 1924.

Gombrich, E. H., and E. Kris. *Caricature*. Harmondsworth, England, 1940.

————. "Imagery and Art in the Romantic Period" and "The Cartoonist's Armoury." In *Meditations on a Hobby Horse and Other Essays on the Theory of Art*. London and New York, 1963.

Goodell, William. *Slavery and Anti-Slavery: A History of the Great Struggle in Both Hemispheres with a View of the Slavery Question in the United States*. New York, 1852.

Greeley, Horace. *The American Conflict*. 2 vols. Hartford, Conn., 1866–67.

————. *Hints Toward Reforms, in Lectures, Addresses, and Other Writings*. New York, 1850.

————. *Recollections of a Busy Life Including Reminiscences of American Politics and Politicians. . . .* New York, 1868.

Grejda, Edward S. *The Common Continent of Men: Racial Equality in the Writings of Herman Melville*. Port Washington, N.Y., 1974.

Haight, Gordon S. *Mrs. Sigourney: The Sweet Singer of Hartford*. New Haven, 1930.

Hale, Edward Everett. *Memories of a Hundred Years*. 2 vols. Rev. ed. New York, 1904.

Hale, William Harlan. *Horace Greeley: The Voice of the People*. New York, 1950.

Halstead, Murat. *Three Against Lincoln: Murat Halstead Reports the Caucuses of 1860*. Ed. William B. Hesseltine. Baton Rouge, 1960.

————. *Trimmers, Trucklers, & Temporizers: Notes of Murat Halstead from the Political Conventions of 1856*. Ed. William B. Hesseltine and Rex G. Fisher. Madison, Wis., 1961.

Harding, Walter. *The Days of Henry Thoreau*. New York, 1965.

———— and Michael Meyer. *The New Thoreau Handbook*. New York, 1980.

Harrington, Fred H. *Fighting Politician: Major General N. P. Banks*. Philadelphia, 1948.

Harsha, D. A. *The Life of Charles Sumner with Choice Specimens of His Eloquence, a Delineation of His Oratorical Character, and His Great Speech on Kansas*. New York, 1856.

Hawthorne, Nathaniel. *The American Notebooks*. Ed. Claude M. Simpson. Columbus, Ohio, 1972.

Hayford, Harrison, and Merrell Davis. "Herman Melville as Office-Seeker." *Modern Language Quarterly*, 10 (June 1949), 168–83 and (September 1949), 377–88.

————. "Poe in *The Confidence-Man*." *Nineteenth-Century Fiction*, 14 (1959), 207–18.

Hess, Stephen, and Milton Kaplan. *The Ungentlemanly Art: A History of American Political Cartoons*. Rev. ed. New York and London, 1975.

Hibben, Paxton. *Henry Ward Beecher: An American Portrait*. New York, 1927.

Higginson, Thomas Wentworth. *Contemporaries*. Boston, 1899.
——. *John Greenleaf Whittier.* New York, 1902.
Hillier, Bevis. *Cartoons and Caricatures*. London, 1970.
Hoar, George F. *Autobiography of Seventy Years*. 2 vols. New York, 1906.
Hodge, Francis. *Yankee Theatre: The Image of America on the Stage, 1825–1850*. Austin, Tex., 1964.
Hodgson, Joseph. *The Cradle of the Confederacy; Or, The Times of Troup, Quitman and Yancey*. . . . Mobile, 1876; rpt. Spartenburg, S.C., 1975.
Hofmann, Werner. *Caricature from Leonardo to Picasso*. New York, 1957.
Holmes, Oliver Wendell. *Ralph Waldo Emerson*. Boston, 1885.
Holt, Michael F. "The Politics of Impatience: The Origins of Know Nothingism." *Journal of American History*, 60 (June 1973), 309–29.
Hone, Philip. *The Diary of Philip Hone, 1828–1851*. Ed. Allan Nevins. New ed. New York, 1936.
Howard, Joseph, Jr. *Life of Henry Ward Beecher, the Eminent Pulpit and Platform Orator, Being a Graphic Sketch of His Early Life, His Career in the West and His Crowning Glory of a Forty Years' Pastorate in Brooklyn*. . . . Philadelphia, 1887.
Howard, Leon. *Herman Melville: A Biography*. Berkeley and Los Angeles, 1951.
Howe, Julia Ward. *Reminiscences, 1819–1899*. Boston, 1899.
Hubbell, Jay. *The South in American Literature, 1607–1900*. Durham, N.C., 1954.
Hull, Raymona E., ed. *Studies in the Minor and Later Works of Melville*. Hartford, Conn., 1970.
Hunt, John Dixon. "Dickens and the Traditions of Graphic Satire." In *Encounters: Essays on Literature and the Visual Arts*. Ed. John Dixon Hunt. New York, 1971.
Isely, Jeter Allen. *Horace Greeley and the Republican Party, 1853–1861: A Study of the New York Tribune*. Princeton, N.J., 1947.
Johannsen, Robert W. *Stephen A. Douglas*. New York, 1973.
John-Donkey (periodical). 1 vol. New York, 1848.
Johnson, Allen, and Dumas Malone, eds. *Dictionary of American Biography*. 26 vols. New York, 1928–36.
Johnson, Samuel A. *The Battle Cry of Freedom: The New England Emigrant Aid Company in the Kansas Crusade*. Lawrence, Kan., 1954.
Jones, Samuel Arthur, ed. *Pertaining to Thoreau: A Gathering of Ten Significant Nineteenth-Century Opinions*. Detroit, 1901; rpt. Hartford, Conn., 1970.
Josephson, Hannah. *The Golden Threads: New England's Mill Girls and Magnates*. New York, 1949.
Julian, George W. *Political Recollections, 1840 to 1872*. Chicago, 1884.
Kaplan, Sidney. "Herman Melville and the American National Sin: The Mean-

ing of 'Benito Cereno.'" *Journal of Negro History,* 41 (October 1956), 311–38 and 42 (January 1957), 11–37.

Karcher, Carolyn L. *Shadow over the Promised Land: Slavery, Race and Violence in Melville's America.* Baton Rouge, 1980.

Kenney, James. *Raising the Wind* (1803). In *The New York Drama: A Choice Collection of Tragedies, Comedies, Farces, etc.* 3 vols. New York, 1876.

Kerber, Linda. *Federalists in Dissent: Imagery and Ideology in Jeffersonian America.* Ithaca, 1970.

Knox, Thomas W. *Life and Work of Henry Ward Beecher: An Authentic, Impartial and Complete History of His Public Career and Private Life from the Cradle to the Grave.* Hartford, Conn., 1887.

Krutch, Joseph Wood. *Henry David Thoreau.* [New York], 1948.

Lader, Lawrence. *The Bold Brahmins: New England's War Against Slavery, 1831–1863.* New York, 1961.

Lang, Hans-Joachim, and Benjamin Lease. "Melville's Cosmopolitan: Bayard Taylor in *The Confidence-Man.*" *Amerikastudien/American Studies,* 22 (1977), 286–89.

————. "Melville's 'The Practical Disciple': George William Curtis in *The Confidence-Man.*" *Amerikastudien/American Studies,* 26 (1981), 181–91.

Lantern (*Diogenes Hys Lanterne*; periodical). 3 vols. New York, 1852–53.

Lathers, Richard. *Reminiscences of Richard Lathers: Sixty Years of a Busy Life in South Carolina, Massachusetts and New York.* Ed. Alvan F. Sanborn. New York, 1907.

Leary, Lewis. *John Greenleaf Whittier.* New York, 1961.

Levy, Leonard W. *The Law of the Commonwealth and Chief Justice Shaw: The Evolution of American Law, 1830–1860.* New York, Evanston and London, 1957.

Leyda, Jay. *The Melville Log: A Documentary Life of Herman Melville, 1819–1891.* 2 vols. New York, 1951; 1969.

Lorant, Stefan. *The Presidency: A Pictorial History of Presidential Elections from Washington to Truman.* New York, 1951.

Lowell, James Russell. *Complete Poetical Works.* Boston, 1896.

Magoon, Elias Lyman. *Living Orators in America.* New York, 1854.

Martineau, Harriet. *Retrospect of Western Travel.* 3 vols. London, 1838.

Maurice, Arthur B., and Frederic T. Cooper. *The History of the Nineteenth Century in Caricature.* New York, 1904; 1970.

Maury, Sarah H. *The Statesmen of America in 1846.* London, 1847.

Maverick, Augustus. *Henry J. Raymond and the New York Press for Thirty Years. . . .* Hartford, Conn., 1870.

May, Samuel J. *Some Recollections of Our Antislavery Conflict.* Boston, 1869.

Mayer, David. *Harlequin in His Element: The English Pantomime, 1806–1836.* Cambridge, Mass., 1969.

McCall, Roy C. "Theodore Parker." In *A History and Criticism of American Public Address.* Ed. William N. Brigance. 3 vols. New York, 1943–55.

McClure, Alexander K. *Recollections of Half a Century.* Salem, Mass., 1902.

McCormac, Irving Eugene. *James K. Polk: A Political Biography.* Berkeley, 1922.

McCoy, Charles A. *Polk and the Presidency.* Austin, Tex., 1960.

McGrane, Reginald Charles. *William Allen: A Study in Western Democracy.* Columbus, Ohio, 1925.

McLoughlin, William G. *The Meaning of Henry Ward Beecher: An Essay on the Shifting Values of Mid-Victorian America, 1840–1870.* New York, 1970.

McMillan, Malcolm C. "William Lowndes Yancey and the Historians: One Hundred Years." *Alabama Review,* 20 (1967), 163–86.

Melville, Herman. *Herman Melville's Authentic Anecdotes of Old Zack.* Ed. Kenneth Starosciak. New Brighton, Minn., 1973.

———. *Clarel: A Poem and a Pilgrimage in the Holy Land.* Ed. Walter E. Bezanson. New York, 1960.

———. *Collected Poems of Herman Melville.* Ed. Howard P. Vincent. Chicago, 1947.

———. *The Confidence-Man: His Masquerade.* Ed. Elizabeth Foster. New York, 1954.

———. *The Confidence-Man: His Masquerade.* Ed. Hennig Cohen. New York, 1964.

———. *The Confidence-Man: His Masquerade.* Ed. H. Bruce Franklin. Indianapolis and New York, 1967.

———. *The Confidence-Man: His Masquerade.* Ed. Hershel Parker. Norton Critical Ed. New York, 1971.

———. *The Confidence-Man: His Masquerade.* Ed. Harrison Hayford, Hershel Parker, and G. Thomas Tanselle. Northwestern-Newberry Ed. Evanston and Chicago, 1984.

———. *Journal of a Visit to Europe and the Levant: October 11, 1856–May 6, 1857.* Ed. Howard C. Horsford. Princeton, N.J., 1955.

———. *The Letters of Herman Melville.* Ed. Merrell R. Davis and William H. Gilman. New Haven, 1960.

———. *Mardi: And a Voyage Thither.* Ed. Harrison Hayford, Hershel Parker, and G. Thomas Tanselle. Northwestern-Newberry Ed. Evanston and Chicago, 1970.

Merk, Frederick. *Manifest Destiny and Mission in American History: A Reinterpretation.* New York, 1963.

Merrill, Walter M. *Against Wind and Tide: A Biography of Wm. Lloyd Garrison.* Cambridge, Mass., 1963.

Miller, Perry. *The Raven and the Whale: The War of Words and Wits in the Era of Poe and Melville.* New York, 1956.

Milne, Gordon. *George William Curtis and the Genteel Tradition.* Bloomington, Ind., 1956.

Milton, George Fort. *The Eve of Conflict: Stephen A. Douglas and the Needless War.* Boston and New York, 1934.

Mitchell, Rexford S. "William L. Yancey." In *A History and Criticism of American Public Address.* Ed. William N. Brigance. 3 vols. New York, 1943–55.

Moore, Augusta, ed. *Notes from Plymouth Pulpit: A Collection of Memorable Passages from the Discourses of Henry Ward Beecher with a Sketch of Mr. Beecher and the Lecture Room.* New York, 1859.

Morrison, Chaplain W. *Democratic Politics and Sectionalism: The Wilmot Proviso Controversy.* Chapel Hill, N.C., 1967.

Mott, Frank Luther. *American Journalism: A History, 1690–1960.* 3rd ed. New York, 1962.

———. *A History of American Magazines: 1741–1850.* New York, 1930.

———. *A History of American Magazines: 1850–1865.* Cambridge, Mass., 1938.

Murrell, William. *A History of American Graphic Humor.* 2 vols. New York, 1933–38.

Mushkat, Jerome. *Tammany: The Evolution of a Political Machine, 1789–1865.* Syracuse, 1971.

Nash, Howard P., Jr. *Third Parties in American Politics.* Washington, D.C., 1959.

Nevins, Allan. *The Evening Post: A Century of Journalism.* New York, 1922.

———. *Frémont: The West's Greatest Adventurer. . . .* 2 vols. New York, 1928.

———. *Ordeal of the Union.* 8 vols. New York, 1947–71.

———, ed. *Polk: The Diary of a President, 1845–1849.* New York, 1968.

Nevins, Allan, and Frank Weitenkampf. *A Century of Political Cartoons: Caricature in the United States from 1800 to 1900.* New York, 1944.

New York Drama; A Choice Collection of Tragedies, Comedies, Farces, Etc. 3 vols. New York, 1876.

Nichols, Roy F. *The Disruption of American Democracy.* New York, 1948.

———. *Franklin Pierce: Young Hickory of the Granite Hills.* 2nd ed. Philadelphia, 1958.

Norris, William. "Abbott Lawrence in *The Confidence-Man*: American Success or American Failure?" *American Studies,* 17 (Spring 1976), 25–38.

The Old Soldier Illustrated by His Son John (periodical). 1 vol. New York, 1852.

Oliver, Egbert S. "Melville's Picture of Emerson and Thoreau in *The Confidence-Man.*" *College English,* 8 (1946), 61–72.

————. *Studies in American Literature: Whitman, Emerson, Melville, and Others.* New Delhi, 1965.

Pagel, R. Elaine, and Carl Dallinger. "Charles Sumner." In *A History and Criticism of American Public Address.* Ed. William N. Brigance. 3 vols. New York, 1943–55.

Paine, Albert Bigelow. *Th. Nast, His Period and His Pictures.* New York, 1904.

Parker, Hershel. "Melville and Politics: A Scrutiny of the Political Milieux of Herman Melville's Life and Works." Ph.D. diss., Northwestern University, 1963.

————. "Gansevoort Melville's Role in the Campaign of 1844." *New York Historical Society Quarterly,* 49 (April 1965), 143–73.

————. "Melville's Satire of Emerson and Thoreau: An Evaluation of the Evidence." *American Transcendental Quarterly,* No. 7, pt. 2 (Summer 1970), 61–67.

Parker, Theodore. *The Rights of Man in America.* Ed. Franklin B. Sanborn. Boston, 1911; rpt. New York, 1969.

————. "A Sermon of the Perishing Classes in Boston." In *Speeches, Addresses, and Occasional Sermons.* 2 vols. Boston, 1852.

Parton, James. *The Life of Horace Greeley, Editor of the New York Tribune.* New York, 1855.

————. *The Life of Horace Greeley, Editor of the New York Tribune from His Birth to the Present Time.* Boston, 1872.

Peckham, Harry Houston. *Gotham Yankee: A Biography of William Cullen Bryant.* New York, 1950; rpt. 1971.

Peters, Harry T. *Currier & Ives: Printmakers to the American People.* Garden City, N.Y., 1942.

Phillips, Ulrich B. *The Course of the South to Secession: An Interpretation.* Ed. E. Merton Coulter. New York, 1939.

Pickard, Samuel T. *Life and Letters of John Greenleaf Whittier.* 2 vols. Boston and New York, 1895.

Pierce, Edward L. *Memoir and Letters of Charles Sumner.* 4 vols. Boston, 1893–94.

Poe, Edgar Allan. *The Complete Works of Edgar Allan Poe.* Ed. James A. Harrison. 17 vols. New York, 1902; New York, 1965.

Potter, David M. *The Impending Crisis, 1848–1861.* Ed. Don E. Fehrenbacher. New York, 1976.

————. *Lincoln and His Party in the Secession Crisis.* New Haven, 1942.

Pray, Isaac C. *Memoirs of James Gordon Bennett and His Times.* New York, 1855.

Quinn, Arthur Hobson. *A History of the American Drama from the Beginning to the Civil War.* 2nd ed. New York, 1943.

————. *Edgar Allan Poe: A Critical Biography.* New York, 1941.

317

Quirk, Tom. *Melville's Confidence Man: From Knave to Knight.* Columbia, Mo., 1982.

Rayback, Joseph G. *Free Soil: The Election of 1848.* Lexington, Ky., 1970.

Rhodes, James Ford. *History of the United States from the Compromise of 1850.* 8 vols. New York, 1896–1919.

Rogin, Michael Paul. *Subversive Genealogy: The Politics and Art of Herman Melville.* New York, 1983.

Rosenberry, Edward H. *Melville and the Comic Spirit.* Cambridge, Mass., 1955.

————. "Melville's Ship of Fools." *PMLA,* 75 (1960), 604–08.

Rosenburg, Jakob. *Rembrandt: Life & Work.* London and New York, 1968.

Rourke, Constance. *Trumpets of Jubilee: Henry Ward Beecher, Harriet Beecher Stowe, Lyman Beecher, Horace Greeley, P. T. Barnum.* New York, 1927.

Rusk, Ralph L. *The Life of Ralph Waldo Emerson.* New York, 1949.

Sanborn, Franklin B. *Recollections of Seventy Years.* 2 vols. Boston, 1909.

————. *Henry D. Thoreau.* Boston, 1888.

Schlesinger, Arthur M., Jr. *The Age of Jackson.* Boston, 1945.

Schneider, Herbert W. *A History of American Philosophy.* New York, 1946.

Scisco, Louis Dow. *Political Nativism in New York State.* New York, 1901.

Scorza, Thomas J. *In the Time Before Steamships: "Billy Budd," the Limits of Politics, and Modernity.* DeKalb, Ill., 1979.

[Scott, Dred]. *The Case of Dred Scott in the Supreme Court of the United States, December Term 1854.* n.p., n.d.

Sealts, Merton M., Jr. *The Early Lives of Melville: Nineteenth-Century Biographical Sketches and Their Authors.* Madison, Wis., 1974.

————. *Melville as Lecturer.* Cambridge, Mass., 1957.

————. *Melville's Reading: A Check-List of Books Owned and Borrowed.* Madison, Wis., 1966.

————. "Melville's Short Fiction." *ESQ: A Journal of the American Renaissance,* 25 (1979), 43–56.

Searle, Ronald, Claude Roy, and Bernd Bornemann. *La caricature: Art et manifeste du XVIᵉ siècle à nos jours.* Geneva, 1974.

Sensabaugh, George. *Milton in Early America.* Princeton, N.J., 1964.

Shannon, William V. *The American Irish.* New York, 1963.

Shaw, Albert. *Abraham Lincoln: His Path to the Presidency.* New York, 1929.

————. *Abraham Lincoln: The Year of His Election.* New York, 1929.

Shorr, Dorothy C. "The Iconographic Development of the Presentation in the Temple." *Art Bulletin* (1946), 17–32.

Shroeder, John W. "Sources and Symbols for Melville's *Confidence-Man.*" *PMLA,* 66 (1951), 363–80.

Sigourney, Lydia. *Past Meridian.* New York and Boston, 1854.

————. *Poems.* Philadelphia, 1834.

Simpson, Eleanor E. "Melville and the Negro: From *Typee* to 'Benito Cereno.'" *American Literature,* 41 (March 1969), 19–38.

Smith, Elbert B. *Francis Preston Blair.* Rpt. New York, 1980.

Smith, William E. *The Francis Preston Blair Family in Politics.* 2 vols. New York, 1933.

Spencer, Ivor Debenham. *The Victor and the Spoils: A Life of William L. Marcy.* Providence, R.I., 1959.

Stafford, John. *The Literary Criticism of "Young America": A Study in the Relationship of Politics and Literature, 1837–1850.* Berkeley, 1952.

Stanton, Henry B. *Random Recollections.* 3rd ed. New York, 1887.

Strong, George Templeton. *The Diary of George Templeton Strong.* Ed. Allan Nevins and Milton Halsey Thomas. 4 vols. New York, 1952.

Sullivan, John. "The Case of 'A Late Student': Pictorial Satire in Jacksonian America." *Proceedings of the American Antiquarian Society,* 83 (October 1973), 277–86.

Tatham, David. "Pictorial Responses to the Caning of Senator Sumner." In *American Printmaking Before 1876: Fact, Fiction, and Fantasy: Papers Presented at a Symposium at the Library of Congress, June 12 and 13, 1972.* Washington, D.C., 1975.

Taylor, William R. *Cavalier and Yankee: The Old South and American National Character.* New York, 1961.

Thackeray, William M. *The Paris Sketch Book. By Mr. Titmarsh.* London, 1840.

Thornton, Richard H. *An American Glossary.* 3 vols. New York, 1962.

Toll, Robert C. *On with the Show! The First Century of Show Business in America.* New York, 1976.

Trevelyan, G. M., ed. *The Seven Years of William IV: A Reign Cartooned by John Doyle.* London, 1952.

Trimpi, Helen P. "Harlequin-Confidence Man: The Satirical Tradition of Commedia Dell'Arte and Pantomime in Melville's *The Confidence-Man.*" *Texas Studies in Literature and Language,* 16 (Spring 1974), 147–93.

————. "Three of Melville's Confidence Men: William Cullen Bryant, Theodore Parker, and Horace Greeley." *Texas Studies in Literature and Language,* 21 (Fall 1979), 368–95.

Tuveson, Ernest Lee. *Redeemer Nation: The Idea of America's Millennial Role.* Chicago, 1968.

Tyler, Roy, ed. *The Image of America in Caricature & Cartoon.* Fort Worth, Tex., 1976.

Tyng, Dudley A. *A Sermon Preached in the Church of the Epiphany, Philadelphia, June 29, 1856.* Pamphlet. Boston, Cleveland, New York, 1856.

Van Deusen, Glyndon G. *Horace Greeley: Nineteenth-Century Crusader.* Philadelphia, 1953.

———. *William Henry Seward.* New York, 1967.

———. *Thurlow Weed: Wizard of the Lobby.* Boston, 1947.

Vanity Fair (periodical), 6 vols. New York, 1859–63.

Vinson, John Chalmers. *Thomas Nast: Political Cartoonist.* Athens, Ga., 1967.

Voegelin, Eric. "Response to Professor Altizer's 'A New History and a New But Ancient God?'" *Journal of the American Academy of Religion,* 43 (December 1975), 765–72.

———. *Order and History.* 4 vols. Baton Rouge, 1956–74.

Weed, Thurlow. *Letters from Europe and the West Indies, 1843–1852.* Albany, N.Y., 1866.

Weisenburger, Francis P. *The Life of John McLean, A Politician on the United States Supreme Court.* Columbus, Ohio, 1937.

Weiss, John. *Life and Correspondence of Theodore Parker.* 2 vols. New York, 1864.

———. "Thoreau." In *Pertaining to Thoreau: A Gathering of Ten Significant Nineteenth-Century Opinions.* Ed. Samuel Arthur Jones. Detroit, 1901; rpt. Hartford, Conn., 1970.

Weitenkampf, Frank. *American Graphic Art.* New York, 1924.

———. "New York State in National Politics: Notes for a Cartoon Record." *New York Historical Society Quarterly,* 30 (April 1946), 80–85.

———. *Political Caricature in the United States in Separately Published Cartoons: An Annotated List.* New York, 1953; rpt. 1971.

Whan, Forest L. "Stephen A. Douglas." In *A History and Criticism of American Public Address.* Ed. William N. Brigance. 3 vols. New York, 1943–55.

Whipple, Edwin Percy. "Some Recollections of Ralph Waldo Emerson." *Ralph Waldo Emerson: A Profile.* Ed. Carl Bode. New York, 1968.

Whitney, Janet. *John Woolman: American Quaker.* Boston, 1942.

Whittier, John Greenleaf. *Complete Poetical Works of John Greenleaf Whittier.* Cambridge ed. Boston, 1894.

Wichelns, Herbert A. "Ralph Waldo Emerson." In *A History and Criticism of American Public Address.* Ed. William N. Brigance. 3 vols. New York, 1943–55.

Widmer, Kingsley. *The Ways of Nihilism: A Study of Herman Melville's Short Novels.* Los Angeles, 1970.

Williams, Henry. "Henry David Thoreau." In *Pertaining to Thoreau: A Gathering of Ten Significant Nineteenth-Century Opinions.* Ed. Samuel Arthur Jones. Detroit, 1901; rpt. Hartford, Conn., 1970.

Willis, Nathaniel P. *Hurry-Graphs; Or, Sketches of Scenery, Celebrities, and Society, Taken from Life.* New York, 1851.

Wilson, Henry. *History of the Rise and Fall of the Slave Power in America.* 3 vols. Boston, 1872–77.

Wilson, James Grant. *Bryant and His Friends: Some Reminiscences of the Knickerbocker Writers.* New York, 1886.

———— and John Fiske, eds. *Appleton's Cyclopaedia of American Biography.* 6 vols. New York, 1888–89.

Wiltse, Charles M. *John C. Calhoun: Sectionalist, 1840–1850.* Indianapolis and New York, 1951.

Winters, Yvor. *Maule's Curse: Seven Studies in the History of American Obscurantism.* Norfolk, Conn., 1938.

————. *In Defense of Reason.* New York, 1947.

Wise, Barton H. *The Life of Henry A. Wise of Virginia, 1806–1876.* New York, 1899.

Wise, John S. *The End of an Era.* Boston, 1902.

Wish, Harvey. *George Fitzhugh: Propagandist of the Old South.* Baton Rouge, 1943.

Wittke, Carl F. *The Irish in America.* Baton Rouge, 1956.

Woodbury, Charles J. *.Talks with Ralph Waldo Emerson.* New York, 1890.

Woolman, John. *The Journal and Major Essays.* Ed. Phillips P. Moulton. New York, 1971.

————. *The Journal of John Woolman.* Ed. John Greenleaf Whittier. Boston, 1871.

Wyatt-Brown, Bertram. *Lewis Tappan and the Evangelical War Against Slavery.* Cleveland, 1969.

Yankee Doodle (periodical). 2 vols. New York, 1846–47.

Yankee Doodle; Or Young America (see *Young America*).

Yeager, S. H. "Wendell Phillips." In *A History and Criticism of American Public Address.* Ed. William N. Brigance. 3 vols. New York, 1943–55.

Yellin, Jean Fagan. *The Intricate Knot: Black Figures in American Literature, 1776–1863.* New York, 1972.

Young America (renamed *Yankee Doodle; or Young America*; periodical). N.S., 1 vol. New York, 1856.

Index of References to Prints

Index